The Giddens Reader

The Giddens Reader

Edited by

Philip Cassell

Stanford University Press
Stanford, California
1993

Stanford University Press
Stanford, California
Introduction, collection, and editorial matter
© 1993 Philip Cassell
Originating publisher: The Macmillan Press Ltd
First published in the U.S.A. by
    Stanford University Press, 1993
Printed in Hong Kong
Cloth ISBN 0-8047-2202-1
Paper ISBN 0-8047-2204-8
LC 93-83193
This book is printed on acid-free paper.

Contents

Acknowledgements

The author and publishers wish to thank the following who have kindly given permission for the use of copyright material.

Anthony Giddens for material from *New Rules of Sociological Method: A Positive Critique of Interpretive Sociologies*, 1976; *Studies in Social and Political Theory*, 1977; and *The Class Structure of the Advanced Societies*, 1973, rev. edn 1981.

Macmillan Publishers Ltd for material from *Politics and Sociology in the Thought of Max Weber*, 1972.

Macmillan Publishers Ltd and University of California Press for material from *A Contemporary Critique of Historical Materialism, Vol. 1: Power, Property and the State*. Copyright © 1981 Anthony Giddens; *Profiles and Critiques in Social Theory*. Copyright © 1982 Anthony Giddens; and *Central Problems in Social Theory: Action, Structure, and Contradiction in Social Analysis*. Copyright © 1979 Anthony Giddens.

Polity Press and University of California Press for material from *The Constitution of Society: Outline of the Theory of Structuration*. Copyright © 1984 Anthony Giddens; and *A Contemporary Critique of Historical Materialism, Vol. 2: The Nation-State and Violence*. Copyright © 1985 Anthony Giddens.

Polity Press and Stanford University Press for material from *Social Theory and Modern Sociology*, 1987; *The Consequences of Modernity*, 1990; *Modernity and Self-Identity: Self and Society in the Late Modern Age*, 1991; and *The Transformation of Intimacy*, 1992.

Wadsworth Publishing Co. for two diagrams from Ronald Duxbury *et al.*, *Human Geography in a Shrinking World*, 1975.

Every effort has been made to trace all the copyright-holders, but if any have been inadvertently overlooked the publishers will be pleased to make the necessary arangement at the first opportunity.

I wish to express my gratitude to Anthony Giddens for his suggestions and encouragement; his knowledgeability in regard to the subject matter of this volume has, of course, proven invaluable. Frances Arnold of the publishers has been especially adept at offering long-distance assistance, while Steven Kennedy deserves praise for his role in initiating the project. Finally, I must thank Fiona Colin and Ira J. Cohen for the part they have played in my involvement.

PHILIP CASSELL

Introduction

(i) *The Giddens Reader*

In 1985 Anthony Giddens wrote an essay, introducing the writings of the German social theorist Jürgen Habermas, which appeared in Skinner's *The Return of Grand Theory in the Human Sciences*. The book identified nine of the most significant social theorists and schools of the time, and a chapter, written by an 'authority', was devoted to each one. If such a work were to be assembled today however, the editor would have to take account of decisive shifts that have taken effect in the world of social science. There would still be an essay on Habermas, but a chapter about the work of Giddens himself would need to be included. He is presently at the very forefront of contemporary social theory, and is certainly the pre-eminent figure in the English-speaking world. It is impossible not to be impressed by the extraordinary range of his work, its inventiveness, and its ability to illuminate what is otherwise obscure. His writings are the subject of widespread critical attention – three compendiums of criticism have been produced since 1989 – and his influence on the social sciences is considerable and growing.

Nevertheless, Giddens' role in *The Return of Grand Theory* points to something resembling a problem in the reception of his work, in that he has come to possess a sort of dual identity. Although such a distinction should not be pressed too far, I think it is fair to say that there is a 'first' and a 'second' Giddens. The former is recognised by a comparatively wide audience as a virtuoso of critical interpretation and commentary. His introduction to Marx, Weber and Durkheim, *Capitalism and Modern Social Theory*, is more than a durable and authoritative text, it has recast the very scholarly terrain it seeks to describe. He is lauded for his ability to clarify and criticise the work of significant and difficult continental thinkers, such as Habermas. He has written a superior introductory text, *Sociology*,

1

which is about as close as it is possible to get to a masterwork in that genre. Yet the 'second' Giddens, creator of 'structuration theory' and analyst of modernity *par excellence*, is appreciated and understood by a significantly smaller (though influential) audience, made up largely of specialist students and professionals in the social sciences.

The major aim of *The Giddens Reader* is to demonstrate the importance of this 'second Giddens' to a broader public, but there is also a secondary aim: to show that the two aspects of Giddens' intellectual identity constitute, to some degree, two dimensions of a unified project. What then is the nature of Giddens' project? And how do the 'two sides' of his enterprise fit together? To begin with it is helpful to return to the rather strong statements made in the opening paragraph, in which I asserted Giddens' pre-eminence in relation to other social theorists. At this point the reader might wonder at the need for such claims, especially at a time when radically relativistic and pluralistic conceptions are experiencing a boom. Why not settle for the more modest contention that Giddens is a writer who presents us with another interesting and challenging perspective? To do so, however, is to misrepresent the ambitions, and hence the character, of his work.

Two points can be made in regard to this matter. The first relates to social theory as a relatively autonomous practice and can be stated quite simply: Giddens thinks that some social theoretical formulations are *demonstrably* inadequate and must be improved upon by more adequate formulations. The second is that social theory is a highly consequential undertaking, one which addresses itself, very generally, to the many layers of the question 'what is going on in the social world?'. But the answers that theorists give to this question do not merely hover above and beyond the social world that is the object of their attention. Instead those theories, and the concepts that are interwoven with them, enter into the very constitution of that world; they become part of the world they are seeking to describe. If prominent theories are incapable of apprehending important aspects of social reality there are highly practical repercussions for general processes of understanding the world, for empirical social research, and for more 'concrete' social practices. Giddens' starting point is the idea that previous and competing theoretical endeavours are, in fact, both mistaken and inadequate to the task of posing, confronting and answering the major social theoretical questions. The work of the 'first Giddens' could be seen partly as a critical engagement with the schools and traditions he is seeking to surpass; the 'second Giddens' can be pictured as emerging from this encounter with the aim of creating a more adequate conceptual framework, and a more illuminating set of insights into the nature of the contemporary world.

It should be made clear at the outset, however, that Giddens sees no exact correspondence between knowledge of the social world and its control – the Enlightenment dream; yet in a world where rapid change, extreme complexity and high order risks are permanent features of the landscape, actors and collectivities have no alternative but to reflect upon the best possible knowledge of what is going on, no matter how fallible, how revisable, that knowledge might be. The success of Giddens' project then must be judged in terms of the question of transcendence, his ability to go beyond competing theories. This idea can be focused more sharply if we examine his determination to learn from, but surpass, successive 'generations' of social theorists; in the process some of the principal themes of his work will be introduced.

(a) Giddens and the classical traditions

The enduring theoretical traditions initiated by Marx, Durkheim and Max Weber can be characterised as the 'classical traditions'. This 'first generation' of social theorists was largely concerned with the problems created by the transition to the modern world. By the end of 1920, however, all three members of this 'first generation' were dead, Marx having died as long ago as 1883. The classical theorists had grown up and lived the greater part of their lives in the nineteenth century; their concepts and theories had been forged in a world that has been completely transformed. Giddens has observed that the profound insights of these traditions do not stretch to the developments that have altered the world in the last seventy years; yet social theory has, in so many respects, remained in their thrall. This has produced manifest distortions and neglect, evidenced, for example, by sociology's comparative lack of interest in the issues surrounding the growth of the nation-state and the industrialisation of war; a development of extraordinary and fateful significance.

Chapter I of this volume highlights Giddens' response to the writings of Weber, Durkheim and Marx respectively. The extracts on Weber and Durkheim, I (ii) and I (iii), represent Giddens' intervention in the scholarly debate over the relationship between the political and sociological writings of these two theorists, Giddens taking the view that the two spheres of interest (politics and sociology) should not be read as though they were sealed off from one another. But there is more to it than an important scholarly point: by showing the way in which sociological interests are refracted through specific political concerns (and domestic intellectual traditions), Giddens is implicitly demonstrating the profound contextuality of social thought. To acknowledge the impact of underlying political goals is not to invalidate the sociological positions taken by Weber and Durkheim; however, such an acknowledgement must cause the contemporary reader to wonder whether we should *necessarily* share their preoccupations, and the particular framework they developed to prosecute their interests. In other words, claims to universality must be relativised against an appreciation of the particularity of temporal and spatial location.

A similar line of reasoning can be applied to Marx, whose historical significance rests partly on the way crucial elements of his theory are linked to a revolutionary programme; a programme which has now taken on the aspect of a relic from a past age. But Giddens' critique of Marx goes deeper than this. The extract from *A Contemporary Critique of Historical Materialism*, I (i), highlights how fanciful it is to imagine that the abolition of class differences would be accompanied by an end to all forms of illegitimate domination. Marx's error lies in his adherence to an evolutionary schema in which class conflict plays a privileged role. Imagining that he has uncovered a master-key for unlocking the secrets of history, Marx tends to reduce social phenomena to the terms of his class paradigm; thus gender and ethnic divisions are read as merely derivative forms of the primary determinant, class, not forms of domination with their own logic.

Giddens has proclaimed as one of his aims the goal of 'deconstructing'[1] those theoretical formulations which claim to reveal some overarching historical law operating behind the backs of historically situated actors. This aim can be usefully contrasted with Habermas' project, which includes the goal of 'reconstructing' some of the great themes of the 'classical tradition'; in particular Weber's 'rationalisation', and Marx's 'historical materialism'. A good case could be made out to the effect that Habermas is the (usually) unstated antagonist in some of Giddens' later writings, and several authors have sought to compare them. Interestingly, however, in a move showing Giddens' 'debt to the classics', and the positive dimension to Marx's work, the former uses a phrase of the latter as a launching point for his deconstructive endeavours: 'Men [let us immediately say human beings] make history, but not in circumstances of their own choosing.'[2] If this aphorism encapsulates the core of his 'structuration theory', a sentiment derived from Weber exhibits something of the 'spirit' of Giddens' work; i.e. 'the necessity of facing up "without illusions" to the realities of the modern world'.[3] Such an orientation is bound to disappoint those expecting 'grand theory' in the old style. There is no 'grand narrative' here to give the reader a short cut to universal understanding; on the contrary, a conception which repudiates the presence of historical 'prime movers' causes us to reflect upon the vicissitudes we might expect in a world racked by contingency.

(b)   The orthodox consensus

The second 'generation' of social theorists inherited the legacy of the 'classical' tradition (minus Marx) and interpreted it according to its own needs. This resulted in what Giddens has called the 'orthodox consensus',[4] which predominated for a period after the Second World War. In this era social theory was characterised by the existence of a 'broad consensus' about the 'nature and tasks' of the 'social sciences as a whole'.[5] The 'orthodox consensus' was very much bound up with the dominance of American sociology, and the writings of Talcott Parsons in particular. Giddens' wish to discredit functionalist modes of thought is based on a perception of its chronic and pronounced limitations. The association with evolutionism, reduction of the action of individuals to the demands of internalised normative imperatives, leaning to naturalism, and 'functionalist explanation' in general, are singled out for scathing critical attention.

    In his earlier writings Giddens identifies the theoretical potency of functionalism with a period in the safely distant past. There is an essay in *Studies in Social and Political Theory* entitled 'Functionalism: *après la lutte'* (1976); but as Giddens himself acknowledges, the post-mortem turns out to be premature. Hans Joas[6] describes how functionalism and the critique of functionalism underwent a 're-naissance' in the decade following Giddens' essay: on the one hand there was Jon Elster's attack on the 'clandestine functionalism' of authors such as Marx and Engels; on the other hand there was the emergence of post-Parsonian functionalism, with Niklas Luhmann and Jeffrey Alexander being the most prominent exponents. Even Habermas, initially a trenchant critic of Luhmann, has incorporated elements of the latter's work in his own 'mature' theory.

In Giddens' writings after 1976 there is a clear appreciation that the 'struggle' against functionalism must go on: the label 'non-functionalist manifesto' is given to *Central Problems in Social Theory*, the first extended account of his 'structuration theory', and there is an extensive critique in his definitive *The Constitution of Society*. It should be stressed however that, despite trenchant opposition to its shortcomings, Giddens maintains a guarded respect for various aspects of Parsons' thought. This can be seen in the extract 'Parsons on Power', A (i), where Parsons is praised for his identification of the positive and generative features of power. The problem, however, is that in opposing 'zero-sum' conceptions of power – the idea that interaction is a conflict between those who have power and those who have none – Parsons goes too far. So much so that his functionalism is incapable of coping with conflicts between those with entrenched and competing sectional interests. When conflicts of this kind moved to centre stage in the western nations, Parsons' theoretical ascendancy began to wane.

(c)   Giddens and the pluralisation of social theory

According to Giddens the 'orthodox consensus' terminated in the late 1960s and early 1970s, as the middle ground shared by other-wise competing perspectives[7] gave way and was replaced by a baffling variety of competing perspectives.[8] This third 'generation' of social theory includes phenomenologically inspired approaches, critical theory, ethnomethodology, symbolic interactionism, struc-turalism, post-structuralism, and theories written in the tradition of hermeneutics and ordinary language philosophy. Giddens has appropriated a good many of the insights of these 'schools of thought', at the same time as he has engaged them in a critical dialogue.

But, like the 'classical traditions' and the 'orthodox consensus' which preceded them, the theories that comprise the 'third generation' of social theory are defective in many important respects. Despite their differences, these divergent approaches share a set of weaknesses that renders them incapable of satisfactorily addressing three questions that are fundamental to contemporary theoretical inquiry:

(1) How is the patterned or recursive character of social practices to be explained?
(2) How are the 'limitations of individual presence overcome in the "stretching" of social relations across time and space?'[9]
(3) What is 'the nature of that novel world which, in the late twentieth century, we now find ourselves?'[10]

The distinctive character of Giddens' project can be seen in the innovative and informative manner in which he answers these three questions. Chapter II of *The Giddens Reader* presents a series of extracts that can usefully be taken as responses to question (1); Chapter III deals with issues relevant to question (2); Chapter V deals directly with question (3); Chapter IV covers matters which connect all three questions; while Chapter VI takes up considerations which underlie and emerge from Giddens' approach to question (3). In what follows I will try to explain the importance of these questions; at the same time I will engage some of the more substantive elements of Giddens' writings. Again, it is important to note how Giddens' method differs from conventional 'grand theory'; there is no attempt to provide a systematic guide to the totality of the social system and history, such as one might find in Marx or Parsons. Instead Giddens sees social theory as a means of clearing up particular queries that arise in relation to the generic problems of the social sciences.

(ii) The problem of order

Those who inquire into the question of how it is that society is ordered, rather than in a state of disorder, are driven, whether explicitly or implicitly, to reflect upon the very nature of social life, of its various ingredients and modes of operation. In the nineteenth century, when serious students of society were dazzled by the accomplishments of the natural sciences, the orderliness of the social world was attributed to the fact that individuals are subject to binding inner and outer forces, over which they have no meaningful control; i.e. forces of an impersonal kind, which are on a par with those that press themselves on the elements of the natural world, the flowers, germs, clouds and so on. If the sphere of the social is continuous with that of the natural, made of the same 'stuff' as it were, then the scientific methods used in the study of the latter could be used in the study of the former. The sweeping 'derogation of the lay actor' that this viewpoint implies is untenable, but it also turned out to be highly consequential: it allowed someone like Marx to flirt with the idea that he had 'discovered' the ineluctable laws of history, so that some followers were led to feel that they need simply sit back and wait for the inevitable and desired events to unfold. Or, more perniciously, the more actively minded could feel that they were the living instruments of History, entrusted with the weighty responsibility of ushering in the new order by crushing those who stood in its way.

On the other hand, there is a much older view of things that sees the autonomous individual as the basic unit of social life. Adherents of this position imagine social order to arise (i) spontaneously, through the self-seeking activities of free-willed individuals, or (ii) deliberately, via action that secures order through some sort of contractual arrangement: either as a result of an agreement amongst equals, or as a 'pact' between a sovereign and his or her subjects. In this conception it is the individual who is 'real', and the social which is 'unreal'. Unhappily, the consequences of this view were neither neutral nor necessarily positive. In relation to (i) for example, a plausible case was advanced by Parsons who argued that the individualistic philosophies of the inter-war years were implicated in the social Darwinism and chaos of that period. Parsons' work can be read, in part, as a corrective to those 'utilitarian' theories that neglect the role of supra-individual factors in the achievement of a stable and humane social order.

However, Parsons' own strategy for solving the problem of order is far from satisfactory. The reason, in Giddens' view, is that the very terms in which the problem is posed – as a primordial conflict between the individual subject and the social object – prevents a satisfactory resolution. In the end, and despite his good intentions to the contrary, Parsons resorts to an equation which grants a primary status to the social object; this is at the expense of the subject, who is merely 'programmed' through socialisation to act in accord with the normative order. While the views of Parsons' subjectively inclined opponents (especially those writing in the phenomenological tradition) act as a vital corrective to his objectivism – by stressing the knowledgeability of skilled and reflexive character actors – they tend to an equally unsatisfactory 'imperialism' of the subject, or simply leave 'structural' matters to others, out of some misguided notion of the 'division of labour' in the social sciences. Recent sociology can be seen, then, to repeat the dualism of the earlier modes of thought, with theories tending to coalesce around the poles of objectivism or subjectivism.

If previous ways of posing 'the problem of order' are fatally flawed, and entangled with indefensible dualisms, we are led to wonder whether there is a solution at all. Giddens starts by rejecting 'centrifugal' images of the workings of the social world: our central concern should not be to explore the mystery of how it is that the human animal – an anti-social creature – comes to accept the burden of living in an ordered society. Instead, Giddens begins with the assumption that there is a generalised attachment on the part of actors to the routinised character of social life. The basic unit of analysis, for Giddens, is the recursive social practice: the daily trip to work on the train, the general election, the weekly seminar, the perfunctory chat, the football fixture and so on. The next step is to ponder the question: How is the recurrent nature of social practices to be explained? This is intertwined with the question of what 'action' and the sphere of the 'social' must be like and how they how should they be conceptualised. I will outline three levels of Giddens' response to these questions: the first (a) is the analysis of how a social practice, considered abstractly, is 'brought off'; the second (b) is to look into the matter of the recurrence of practices; and the third is the examination of the 'ontological' implications of (a) and (b). My coverage of the third level will be incorporated in my discussion of the first two.

(a) Meaning, power, action and structure

The preliminary answer to (a), see extract II (ii), is that there are three 'ingredients' involved in the enactment of a social practice: the production of 'meaningful' communication; power; and morality (though I shall consider here only the first two in any detail). Social practices are organised through the medium of language, and language is possible because of the ability of the human species to abstract, with the aid of an interpretative scheme, from the profusion of undifferentiated phenomena that are 'presented' to us via our senses. I am able to say 'Please put on your shoe William', and be understood because of a mutual recognition that a particular sequence and conglomeration of sounds refer to another conglomeration of phenomena that is called a shoe. And this is not a private agreement between William and me: we are able to communicate, to engage in this practice, because we have understood and followed rules of language that long predate us. But following these rules is not a simple matter. William will probably understand that by 'your shoe' I mean the one in front of him, not the one in his cupboard; as well it is unlikely that he will need to enter into a legal debate about the meaning of 'your' in my sentence; he will know that he should put his foot 'in' the shoe, not on top of it, and so on. For language to work, speakers must be able to fill in the gaps, and deal with the ambiguities that are associated with language use; to do this they must skilfully and creatively mobilise the 'stocks of knowledge' they hold in common with other language users.

Of singular importance for Giddens however, is the insight that in order to enact a social practice, participants must necessarily draw on a set of rules; these rules can be seen to *structure*, to give shape to, the practices that they help to organise. A simple example: the laying of house bricks requires knowledge of how to lay them; without this knowledge, which can be rendered as a set of rules, the action cannot be 'brought off'. This is not to say that action is rule-dominated, that in every situation there is a ready made rule that we are bound to follow; indeed this could not be so, given the extreme diversity of situations. Rather actors must engage in the sometimes tricky business of 'trying on' particular formulae to see if they fit. Another example: I am delivering a lecture during the course of which all the members of my audience unexpectedly begin to laugh. Have I inadvertently said something witty? or something incredibly stupid? or are they laughing at an event quite separate from me? There is no rule that I could draw on that would immediately define the situation, and allow me to continue my lecture, but I would have no choice but to make best use of the rule-based knowledge I do possess so that I might respond appropriately: ignoring the laughter knowing that it will recede, or repairing the situation so that it might continue intact. Keeping social practices afloat requires the active involvement of skilled actors, but these actors are in turn dependent on the structuring properties of 'rules'. A duality that incorporates 'action' and what Giddens calls 'structure' – those 'rules' which *structure* action – is thus a necessary postulate for the explanation of the enactment of a social practice.

This does not exhaust the meaning that Giddens gives to the concept of 'structure'. His definition includes the idea of 'resources': 'resources' that make the exercise of power possible. Power is arguably the axial concept in Giddens' entire repertoire. It is at the centre of his 'structuration theory' and his analysis of modernity. When social practices are enacted, more is involved than the communication of meaning and the following of moral norms. Social practices involve actions which 'make a difference' to the world in some way, no matter how small. But agents, those who are able to effect change, must possess appropriate resources in order to do so. If I am to 'make a difference to the world' by purchasing a product, it is necessary for me to possess the requisite money; if I am to sanction a wrong-doer, I must possess the necessary authority, or possess a resource whose mobilisation will have the same effect. The transformations of nature, and the deployment of persons that accompanies it, are inconceivable without human access to power and the resources that must facilitate it.

But how do 'resources' participate in the patterning of social life? The structuring properties of 'resources' can be grasped by analysing the relationship between owners of corporations and their employees. The relationship has a certain enduring form because the asymmetry of the 'resources' available to each remains relatively constant. The employees possess little or no capital and must therefore sell their labour power, week in and week out, in order to subsist. So long as their enterprise remains a going concern, owners will possess sufficient capital to allow them to purchase the workers' labour power and dictate the manner of its deployment. As this example implies, the structuring properties of resources 'work' only so long as actors draw on rules that are suitable for their use: if money is to serve as capital the owner must know how use that money to generate profit through investing in labour, capital equipment and so forth.

Giddens' novel concept of 'structure' is founded on the idea that
it is 'rules' and 'resources' which structure social practices. Note
that 'structure' is both enabling and constraining: the rules of
language, for example, enable the transmission of messages; but if
we wish to communicate we are constrained to abide by those same
rules. Note also that by 'rules' Giddens does not usually refer to
'formal' rules, which might be encoded in some publicly visible
way, such as obtains with the criminal law. In addition, an actor
may be incapable of offering an account of the rules that are drawn
upon, even though they are known in the sense that he or she
knows 'how to go on'. The example of the rules of language is an
obvious case: I might be able to speak a grammatically correct
sentence but be incapable of rendering the rules that I have followed in so speaking.

The difficulty for readers is that Giddens' 'structure' is quite
distinct from conventional social scientific usage, which leans towards objectivism. 'Structure' is usually connected with geological
or architectural metaphors, as in structural-functionalism; or it is
sometimes associated with quasi-natural phenomena outside the
control of agency in general, as in Lévi-Strauss' structuralism. In
its objectivist form 'structure' is depicted as having an existence
which is 'external' to the activities of knowledgeable and purposive
agents. The chronic deficiencies of such a conception can be
brought out by posing the question: if structure is 'external to
actors, how did it get there? how does it remain? Giddens' 'structure' has no reality except in so far as it is 'internal' to agents in the
form of memory traces; it is agents who bring 'structure' into being,
and it is 'structure' which produces the possibility of agency.

(b)   The duality of structure

The question of the 'patterning' of social practices, however, has yet
to be fully confronted. In the preceding paragraphs I have outlined
some of the factors that are implicated in the constitution of a given
social practice, but the question of the reproduction of such practices remains to be explained. There are two steps in Giddens'
answer: the first is to grasp the manner in which 'structure' is
reproduced; the second is to account for the use of that 'structure' in practices that are of a routine type.

(i) If 'structure' and 'action' are conjoined, then the patterning of practices across time and space must presume that the structuring properties themselves are trans-situational. The reproduction of 'structure' is explained by what Giddens calls 'the duality of structure'; it can be illustrated once again via the example of language use. Giddens says that 'When I utter a sentence, or make sense of an utterance of somebody else, I draw on an "absent corpus" of syntactic and semantic rules in order to do so'.[11] Giddens goes on to say that 'these structural features of the language are the medium whereby I generate an utterance'.[12] And here is the crucial point: 'in producing a syntactically correct utterance I simultaneously contribute to the reproduction of the language as a whole.'[13] Spoken English, for example, survives as a language only because actors say things in English which are understood by their listeners. The actor draws on the rules that govern the speaking of English in order to be understood, but the utterance has the unintended effect of contributing to the perpetuation of the language, i.e. to the vast network of rules that constitute English as a language. Because the language is thereby reproduced others will be able to make themselves similarly understood. The 'duality of structure' consists in structure's two-sided existence – as both the medium and unintended outcome of social practices.

The reader may object that the changing of rules is conceptually 'locked out' by this theoretical strategy. Giddens responds to such an objection by reaffirming the connection between rules and agents. Because agents draw on rules in the enactment of social practices the capacity to modify the 'rule' that is drawn on in any action is an ever-present possibility. Men and women may, for example, transform the traditional 'rules' which have structured their past interaction by eschewing sexist norms. At each point of structural reproduction there is also the potential for change.

(ii) The second step in the argument is necessary because the reproduction of 'structure' is only the precondition of the phenomenon that is to be explained; i.e. the existence of 'structure' only makes it *possible* for actors to engage in routine and recurrent practices. The central formulation here is that the 'patterning' of social practices is linked to highly generalised forms of motivation. This is based upon an idea that Giddens has derived from R.D. Laing, *viz* that the self has a need to maintain an 'ontological security': this is a psychological state that is equivalent to feeling 'at home' with oneself and the world, and is associated with the experience of low or manageable levels of anxiety. The threat to 'ontological security' is particularly pronounced when the subject's bodily autonomy is violated, or when the routine character of daily life is severely disrupted, as was the case for inmates of concentration camps in Nazi Germany. Giddens makes an explicit linkage between the integrity of the self and routine in *The Constitution of Society*: 'Ordinary day-to-day life – in greater or less degree according to context and the vagaries of individual personality – involves *an ontological security expressing an autonomy of bodily control within predictable routines.*'[14]

Greater specificity however needs to be given to the claim concerning the linkage between routine and the need for 'ontological security'. Two sorts of phenomena can be distinguished. Firstly, actors will draw on rules and mobilise resources to re-enact practices that are found comforting: waking at the same time each day; putting on clothes in a particular order; eating a familiar breakfast; catching the train at the same time each day and so on. Disruptions to the routine will typically be experienced as unsettling and care will be taken to ensure that events unfold predictably. This goes some way towards explaining the conservative nature of daily life. We become attached to the familiar, even to the point of reproducing aspects of life that are otherwise unpleasant. Thus a person may retain a boring job and a brutal marriage even though more rewarding options are available.

Secondly, there are those routines which are adopted by actors when they are in each other's presence. Giddens draws heavily on the work of Goffman in discussing this matter, for it is the latter author who reminds us of the potential riskiness of face-to-face encounters, and the steps actors take to make social interaction safe. What are the perils that the self must confront in face to face meetings? There is the possibility of the violation of bodily autonomy, or personal space, embarrassment or loss of 'face'; and there is also the possibility of boredom. All are in some sense a threat to the self or the self's sense of reality. Goffman shows how individuals cooperate, by using tact, to ensure that risks to the self are minimised in the course of an encounter. Actors have a responsibility to protect other participants from blows to their self-esteem; they also have a right to expect that others will refrain from such 'assaults' on their own self. It is the routine, taken-for-granted nature of tactful procedures that enables actors to enter into encounters with a degree of confidence.

Giddens attributes great significance to the means by which trust in others, and the world more generally, is sustained (see especially extract V (iii)). A basic experience of trust, and the containment of anxiety that this presumes, is indispensable for the actor's ability to negotiate the routine interpersonal engagements that are integral to the reproduction of social practices.

If the above seems to align Giddens with an image of an overly consensual and static social universe it is as well, in concluding this section, to examine: firstly, a 'concrete' case of the enactment of social practices from the perspective of structuration theory; and secondly, Giddens' analysis of the factors that contribute to social change.

(c) Conflict and social change

If we take the example of the school portrayed in Willis' study *Learning to Labour*, which Giddens comments on in *The Constitution of Society* (see II(vi)), it is apparent that the myriad of practices that go on in the classroom, and elsewhere in the school, are marked by dissent. The 'lads' – rebellious working-class students – operate within interpretative and normative frameworks that are quite different in many respects from those of the staff; conflict is chronic as each party mobilises their respective 'resources' to prosecute their particular purposes. The school authorities are incapable of achieving anything more than an 'effort bargain', a sort of uneasy truce, with the 'lads', whose 'resources' are, nevertheless, far more limited than those available to the staff. One might expect this scenario to produce chaos, but Willis' study reveals the manner in which the practices, the conflicts, actually form a pattern, to the extent that events are in some sense predictable; horribly so, one suspects for the participants. Although all parties are striving to achieve a routine which will guarantee their 'ontological security', the presence of the opposing party – who must 'eat into' the security of the other to stabilise their own position – makes its achievement highly elusive and unstable. Willis' school is an evocative illustration of the way that the 'system' – conceived as the reciprocal relationships between the diverse actors in the situation – is structured by 'rules' and 'resources'.

Giddens' analysis of social change can also be elaborated with reference to the school example. Let us imagine that over time a gradual process of 'gentrification' takes hold of the working-class areas that surround the school. After a few years the children of the professional classes become more numerous; the *milieu* that boys such as the 'lads' move in is progressively worn away; and those 'lads' who remain to continue the 'tradition' of resistance, are more easily marginalised. The balance of power moves strongly in favour of the school authorities and conventional educational values.

This incremental process of change can be contrasted with the 'reflexive monitoring' initiated by organisations; this refers to the ability of institutions to bring about change by employing knowledge of how the social world operates. Responding to educational research a reformist government might seek immediately to improve the life chances of 'the lads' by actively intervening in their education, transporting them to middle-class schools that will – the government hopes – break down the boys' aversion to scholarship. Of course the change might not work out as planned; the unintended consequences of action can never be neglected by social scientists. The resentment of middle-class parents to the reformist policy could conceivably provoke a backlash, resulting ultimately in the unseating of the ruling party and the election of a conservative government. Policy might then be changed so that resources are funnelled away from poorer schools. In practice, of course, social change will flow from an amalgam of incremental change, reflexive monitoring and unintended consequences.

If we return to Marx's aphorism, it is possible to see the school as a locale where agents 'make history', but apparently not in circumstances of their own choosing. To theorise adequately institutions like the school, and the practices with which it is associated, one must look to the broader social system and thus to the theme of the 'stretching of practices' over time and space. This is the theme I will now move on to consider.

(iii) Time, space and social theory

With the publication of *Central Problems in Social Theory* in 1979, Giddens announced his intention to place time and space at the very core of his social theory. The successful realisation of this theoretical aim stands as one of his most significant intellectual achievements. Giddens' subsequent major works, especially *A Contemporary Critique of Historical Materialism* (1981), *The Constitution of Society* (1984), *The Nation-State and Violence* (1985), *The Consequences of Modernity* (1990), and *Modernity and Self-Identity* (1991) have re-focused and broadened the insights first provided by *Central Problems*, so that it is no longer possible to recapitulate the basic concepts of structuration theory, and the major themes of Giddens' more substantive works, without reference to spatial and temporal conceptions.

Already, in the discussion of the 'patterned or recursive character of social practices', it has been apparent that time is an ineradicable factor in the actions and institutions that constitute the 'social'. The routines that comprise, and attach themselves to, social practices gain their 'routineness' only in so far as they persist in time. Social practices have beginnings and ends that must be managed by the participants. The communication of meaning through language is achieved partly through the interplay of what has been said and what might be said in the future. And institutions, the most deeply ingrained practices, gain their identity and structuring potential only through their endurance in the *longue durée*, the 'long haul' of time. It is interesting too that in *The Class Structure of the Advanced Societies* (1973), written before time–space takes up its core status, class structuration is depicted in terms of physical proximity and long periods of time; i.e. classes form only where actors, sharing a common market capacity, live and work together for generations, thereby producing and reproducing a common culture. (For a detailed discussion of Giddens' conception of class see extract IV (iii).)

Giddens' insight is that time and space are not just topics worthy of consideration by those interested in the social sciences. What he is arguing is much more radical: that excluding time and space from social analysis, or privileging a *priori* one above the other, seriously distorts our understanding of the way social reality is constituted.

(a)   Time–space paths and the constitution of the social world

Before turning directly to the second of the fundamental questions – 'How are the "limitations of individual presence" overcome in the "stretching" of social relations across time and space?' – it is necessary to be more specific about why time and space should be at the 'core' of social theory, and what such a claim might mean. Though Giddens' inspiration in these matters is Heidegger, a set of images suggested by the work of the time-geographer Hagerstrand provides a somewhat more concrete *entrée* to these questions. Hagerstrand is interested in the idea that an actor will trace out a specifiable time–space path on any given day: we wake at a particular time and place, later on we might leave the house, mingle with others at various locales for given lengths of time before returning home, where we prepare for the repetition of the day's cycle. Generalising this idea we can observe that every day, the world's entire population participates in a mass movement through time–space – though it is apparent that some actors will travel further than others, in time as well as space! This travelling through time and space is inseparable from, and consubstantial with, the very being of individual agents, institutions, organisations and indeed nations, and must therefore be of great interest to social theory.

The example of a factory illustrates this point in regard to the workings of an organisation. The factory's institutional properties, and status as a going concern, are reproduced only to the extent that its operatives continue to retrace specifiable time–space paths. Not only must workers wend their way to work at the right time; once in the factory the following of very precisely planned and coordinated time–space paths is of the utmost importance for the execution of successful production. This precision will often involve extremely subtle variations in the timing of bodily movement in relationship to other workers, machines and raw materials. The difficulty of achieving the necessary exactitude has sent many factory owners broke; on the other hand it is innovations in coordinating time and space that have played a major part in the extraordinary leaps in productivity and quality that have been witnessed this century: 'mass' and so called 'lean' production (including the 'just in time' method) are cases in point.

In addition, we can see that having the resources to traverse specific time–space paths is of the highest consequence, not only for the structuration of organisations, but also for the individual actor. Giddens cites the case of single women who live with their young children in working-class outer suburbs. They may be so separated from crucial services (child-care, transport), places of employment and centres of conviviality, that their chance of leading fulfilling lives is drastically (though not terminally) reduced; the poverty of their choices often condemns them to spending large tracts of time in miserable places.

(b) Locales and power

The example in the paragraph above may be construed as evidence in favour of a type of geographical determinism; but the physical aspects of locales, while limiting and facilitating certain forms of action, are not themselves responsible for 'causing' what ensues in any given setting. Study of the structuration of locales, and the time–space paths with which they are associated, must be undertaken under the theoretical auspices of the 'duality of structure'. Researchers should appreciate that actors work at the reproduction of the setting of their interaction (and the 'filling up' of the time they spend there[15]). A prison building operates as a prison only if the actors involved draw on the explicit and implicit rules that structure prison life. This entails the active cooperation, albeit grudging, of prisoners and warders in their collective journey through the daily prison time-table. This is not to ignore the continuous or. intermittent conflict that is sometimes associated with locales: in Willis' study, the school setting is the site of a form of struggle, with the staff's attempt to establish a more or less scholarly space in the classroom being met by the concerted resistance of the 'lads'[16].

   As the previous example should make clear, the setting of interaction is not some neutral backdrop to events that are unfolding independently in the foreground. 'Locales' enter into the very fabric of interaction in a multiplicity of ways. They figure in the normative basis of action – implicit rules cover what one might do and not do in a given place; and they serve as sources of meaning – aspects of the setting are routinely incorporated, usually implicitly, in conversation.

Of special interest to Giddens, however, is the way locales provide resources for the exercise of various forms of domination: of persons and of nature. Some locales – cities and nation-states to name but two prime cases – are locales where power is generated and concentrated. These 'power-containers' permit an organisation, such as a state administrative apparatus, to maintain the capacity to control subordinates who are far away in space, and therefore in time (i.e. if someone is distant in space it will take a finite amount of time to traverse that distance to reach them). At the same time, this establishment of reciprocal relations between actors, or achievement of 'systemness', will ensure that subordinates are in a position to affect the actions of the state, and thus the operations of the power-container. It is difficult to overstate the importance of these processes. From this perspective action can be seen to be structured not only by that which is present, but also by that which is absent, in time–space.

(c)   Time–space distanciation and resources

The ' "stretching" of social relations across time and space', or time–space distanciation, can best be understood by taking note of a distinction Giddens makes between 'social integration' and 'system integration'. The former refers to relations of reciprocity between persons who are in each other's presence; the latter refers to reciprocal relations between persons and collectivities who are not in circumstances of co-presence. Tribal and traditional small scale agricultural societies are characterised by what Giddens terms 'high presence-availability'; systemness is guaranteed or achieved through social integration – there is very limited 'stretching' of systemness in time–space. There are two modes of time–space distanciation in these social types: 'the grounding of legitimation in tradition, and the role played by kinship in the structuration of social relations'.[17] In contrast, civilizations of the class-divided type[18] (traditional societies), owing to the existence of the city, the pre-eminent power-container of pre-capitalist societies, are able through administrative means to stretch well beyond the immediacy of co-presence to take in regions outside of the city itself.

In societies characterised by the existence of a state, the administrative authority is able to store resources that make it possible to transcend the limitations of presence and human memory; the ruler is able to record what is owned and therefore owed by those who are ruled. This ability is dependent in the first instance on the invention of writing (or its analogue): 'Writing seems everywhere to have originated as a direct mode of storage: as a means of recording information relevant to the administration of societies of an increasing scale.' The *'retention and control of information or knowledge'*[19] is identified as providing the basis of surveillance, a concept that Giddens takes over (in modified form) from Foucault. 'Surveillance' encompasses the idea that coded information can be used as a resource in the supervision of subordinates and collectivities, even when the superordinate authority is distant in time–space.

Recognition of the significance of resources (such as list keeping), which facilitate the control of persons who are distant in time–space, forms the basis for Giddens' sustained attack on historical materialism and other forms of evolutionism. For Giddens, system integration in the class-divided episode of world history is achieved primarily via 'authoritative resources', people's capabilities of controlling the humanly created world of *society itself*.[20] In contrast, the episode of class or capitalist society is substantially dependent on the control of things, or what Giddens calls 'allocative resources', i.e. 'capabilities of controlling not just "objects" but the *object-world*'.[21] Historical materialism and evolutionism are based upon the erroneous assumption that the universal priority of 'allocative resources' can be taken for granted in all descriptions of social change. In *The Constitution of Society*, Giddens states that: 'Any co-ordination of social systems across time and space necessarily involves a definite combination of these two types of resources',[22] and repudiates the notion that any theory should prejudge the question of which resource type has pre-eminence in any historical episode. Giddens' own conclusions in relation to the importance of authoritative resources in traditional societies are reached in the context of a study of that social type; a report of which provides much of the substance of *The Nation-State and Violence*.

The theoretical issue here is the problem of how social systems are able to extend themselves in both time and space; and Giddens' view is that different social types extend themselves in different ways. The concept of 'structural principles' – see extract II (iv) – denotes the means by which 'social systems "bind" time and space';

that is, those 'principles of organization which allow recognizably consistent forms of time–space distanciation on the basis of definite mechanisms of social integration'.[23] (It is important to note this last clause: even in societies where relations between the local and the distant are of outstanding significance, social integration remains a vital means of social reproduction.) Modernity is characterised by the prominence of structural principles of a highly novel and dynamic kind, a consideration of which will structure the next section of this Introduction.

(iv) The modernity question

Early on in *The Nation-State and Violence* Giddens proclaims that: 'It is the task of sociology, as I would formulate the role of that discipline at any rate, to seek to analyze the nature of that novel world which, in the late twentieth century, we now find ourselves'.[24] This statement signals a move away from his specific focus upon the details of structuration theory to a more substantive concern with the nature of modernity. Though all Giddens' works shed light in some way upon the 'modernity question', the books prior to 1985 generally do so as part of another programme: in the case of *A Contemporary Critique* the rudiments of a theory of modernity are presented in the context of a direct encounter with historical materialism; in *The Class Structure of the Advanced Societies* the emphasis is placed on the 'class question'; while *Central Problems* and *The Constitution of Society* are principally vehicles for the elaboration of 'structuration theory'. It is only with the last four books, *The Nation-State and Violence*, *The Consequences of Modernity*, *Modernity and Self-Identity* and *The Transformation of Intimacy* that Giddens fully immerses himself in an examination of the present epoch, and its historical novelty.

Though Giddens' analysis of modernity is already extremely wide-ranging his project remains incomplete. *The Nation-State and Violence*, and the writing that precedes it, are primarily preoccupied with the institutional features of the modern constellation. It is only in quite recent publications that his attention has extended to the 'personal' and cultural dimensions of modernity; a planned book on religion will presumably provide readers with a more comprehensive analysis of modern culture.

(a)   The theory of industrial society; the theory of capitalist society

Giddens touches on the problem of capturing the essence of the 'advanced societies' as far back as *The Class Structure* (1973), in which he compares two conflicting approaches that have dominated sociological thinking: what he calls 'the theory of industrial society', and its rival 'the theory of capitalist society'. The former theory, advocated by Dahrendorf and Aron in Europe, and Bell, Lipset and Parsons in the USA, views modernity as substantially defined by the progressive effects of industrialisation. In contrast to the theory of capitalist society, the theory of industrial society explains class conflict as resulting from the 'strains involved in the transition from an agrarian order to an industrial society'.[25] These transitional strains have been eased through industrial bargaining and the granting of citizenship rights by the liberal democratic state. The 'theory of capitalist society', on the other hand, takes its line from Marx, and aligns modernity with the most basic features of capitalism: class conflict is intrinsic, the state is 'an expression of class power',[26] and the development of bourgeois ideology is largely responsible for tempering the revolutionary potential of the working class.

Though he sees merit in both approaches, and comes down on the side of the theory of capitalist society in one major respect – modern society is regarded essentially as a 'class society' – Giddens is highly critical of the dualistic and reductionist terms of the debate: modernity is depicted either as an industrial or a capitalist order. Furthermore, both approaches fail fully to appreciate the radical novelty of modernity; they are devoted to unfolding or endogenous models of social change that portray the present era as an outgrowth of tendencies of the preceding social order. Giddens repudiates these standpoints by taking up his own anti-evolutionist stance; he argues persuasively for a dialectic of the endogenous and the exogenous, and the essentially contingent nature of the modern world, two positions that will be outlined later in this Introduction

(b)   Discontinuism and a differentiated conception of modernity

Extracts V (i) and V take up two central themes of Giddens' work that have already been alluded to. The first is Giddens' historical 'discontinuism'. Here he appropriates an alternative strand of Marx's writings that runs counter to the conventional 'continuist' or evolutionary interpretations of his work. Giddens is indebted to Lefort's[27] reading of the 'Forms of Society that Precede Capitalist Production'[28] (the *Formen*) which points to an image of Marx as a 'discontinuist': capitalism is seen to be radically different from the preceding social forms, and the transition to capitalism is characterised by a major disjunction. The problem with Marx's discontinuism however is its attachment to the theory of capitalist society; i.e. the key to the profound *difference* of modernity from preceding social forms is attributed overwhelmingly to the arrival of mature capitalism.

Giddens' efforts to correct the perceived reductionism of rival approaches is the subject of the second theme. It entails an insistence upon the plurality of 'institutional dimensions' that constitute the modern order. In extract V (ii) four such dimensions are identified: in addition to capitalism and industrialism, there is the phenomenon of surveillance, and the 'industrialisation of war'. Though capitalism is granted a highly qualified primacy in the modern scheme of things, each of the four dimensions is seen to possess a 'logic' of its own that cannot be reduced to the 'logic' of the other three. Each represents a radical discontinuity with non-modern forms of life – even modern capitalism is composed of practices that bear only a distant 'family resemblance' to its ancient forms. And all four are made possible by, and contribute to, the proliferation of novel conceptions of time and space, such as 'clock' time and 'empty' space. As I have tried to show in the factory example, these cultural innovations permit the precise coordination of time–space paths that underpin the operation of modern organisations.

(c) 'Biting into' time and space; the case of industrialism

To understand more fully the globalising dynamic of the four institutional dimensions one must appreciate what these modern practices *do* to time and space. I will deal here only with industrialism at any length, though the analysis of the three other dimensions are to be found in *The Nation-State and Violence* and elsewhere. The spread of industrialism across space, and its persistence through time, can be seen to inhere in its ability to overcome the temporal constraints that limited the productivity of traditional forms of labour. A craft worker's output is largely determined by how much working time can be expended; doubling the number of items produced will entail a doubling of work time. Industrial techniques, such as those developed by Henry Ford, altered this equation entirely. Due to innovations at every level of the production process, his workers were able radically to decrease the amount of time needed to manufacture a motor car. Competitors were forced to adopt Ford's methods or go out of business. An industrial worker might, in an eight hour day, create more goods than could be produced by hundreds of traditional workers in the same time. It is the advanced societies' victories over time that have underwritten their global supremacy and caused the virtual demise of traditional life.

Industrialism is equally effective in its ability to conquer the constraints of space: innovations in communications and transportation radically undermine traditional equations of 'long' time with great distance. The extract taken from *The Nation-State, and Violence*, IV(v), demonstrates the extraordinary significance of these changes in time–space distanciation, especially for the consolidation of the nation-state. The industrialisation of war is the rawest exemplar of what technology and industrial organisation can do to the constraints of time and space. The destructive capabilities of traditional armies were limited by the enormous difficulties posed by shifting large numbers of men, and by the relative puniness of non-modern weaponry. Nowadays, of course, intercontinental ballistic missiles with nuclear warheads are able to travel internationally, in extremely quick time, to wreak havoc of an almost unimaginable kind.

(d) Synergies of modernisation; the nation-state and capitalism

It needs to be emphasised that, for Giddens, there are extremely significant interconnections between the four institutional dimensions. The dynamism of modernity is partly explicable in terms of the power that is generated when capitalism combines with industrialism, when industrial technology and practices are applied to surveillance, and so on. Indeed one of the major claims of *The Nation-State and Violence* is that capitalism in its modern incarnation comes about only because of its position of mutual interdependence with the emerging nation-state. The defining characteristics of modern capitalism, the generalisation of commodity and labour markets, and the 'insulation of the polity from the economy' are possible only because of the activities of a particular kind of centralising state. A 'modernising' state administration has the power to provide services to the private economy that are indispensable to its reproduction. The state through its monopolisation of violence and surveillance operations is able to: construct a legal order which ensures contractual arrangements; guarantee private property; facilitate a comparatively predictable investment climate; and underwrite a monetary system which is the *sine qua non* of widespread commodification.[29] Despite the power of the emerging state apparatus a 'space' is left for the growth of the private economy. This is in contrast to non-Western traditional states where the political rulers maintain a stranglehold on the control of economic resources; thus preventing the dynamic potential created by the insulation of the economy from the polity.

(e)   Reflexivity, contingency and the system of nation-states

This highly specialised involvement of the state administration in the capitalist economy must include reference to the state's profound reflexivity. However, the monitoring of trends, collection and analysis of data, and engagement in a variety of discourses about its actions is a distinctive feature not only of the modern state administration but of modern life more generally. Information and theories of how things work are chronically brought to bear on the enactment of social practices of all kinds. Of course the state in a capitalist society is itself dependent, to a marked degree, on the reflexively ordered practices of the private economy – the state is not the sole 'brain' of a modern society, though Giddens is careful to emphasise that the state cannot be seen to be determined 'by its reliance upon the accumulation of capital'.[30]

The distinctiveness of Giddens' understanding of all these matters resides not merely in its insistence upon the inclusion of conceptions of time–space and power. The emphasis upon the degree of contingency ascribed to the development of the institutional dimensions and their mutuality must also be recognised. Giddens opposes the view that the 'needs' of capitalism somehow conjured up the type of state that it 'required' in order to fulfil its historical destiny. Moreover, he connects the genesis of particular nation-states to the growth of the system of nation-states, which is itself a contingent phenomenon. In *The Nation-State and Violence* Giddens notes that it is only with the First World War and the Treaty of Versailles that the principle of state sovereignty becomes entrenched and institutionalised. Similarly, it was the contingency of 'total' war, and the rise of the nationalist sentiments that were associated with it, that dashed pre-war hopes of internationalism.

(f)   Globalisation and its consequences

The impact of treaties on Germany and Japan after the Second World War also shows the inadequacy of endogenous accounts of social change and the make-up of the contemporary world. The conditions imposed by the victorious powers had a determinate effect on both of the defeated nations. The socio–political profiles of post-war Japan and Germany could hardly be explained entirely by 'domestic' events alone; the social scientist would be forced, in this instance, to acknowledge the limitations of an unfolding model of development and take a more global perspective. This penetration of local contexts by the contingencies of the distant is a generic feature of the contemporary world. However the local must not be viewed as if it were simply dominated or overrun by distant events. Endogenous and exogenous factors enter into a dialectical relationship: local agencies react to the impact of distant forces, transforming the 'outside' agency in the process. Post-war Japan, for example, has been transformed by developments associated with the intrusion of the USA into its affairs, yet the Japanese response has had significant repercussions not only for Japan itself but for the USA and the world more generally, particularly in regard to economic matters.

In *The Consequences of Modernity* Giddens extends his analysis of the globalising process, showing how it radically alters the fundamental character of the 'local' itself. Particular locales are affected by more than the mere 'contingencies' of far off events, if by 'contingency' we mean occurrences that are largely unpredictable or unintended, such as war, drought and so forth. Globalisation has had the effect of linking the local to the distant in a routine manner, so that local institutions are chronically connected to external agencies. One's neighbourhood bank, supermarket, department store and other major commercial outlets will generally exist as branches of much wider networks. A chain store, for example, has a curious reality: it is present in the physical sense of course, but it subsists as an entity in a web of relations that are not present; a substantive part of the store's being is absent.

(g)   Disembedding mechanisms and abstract systems

Such intertwining of the local and the global is thoroughly typical of institutions in the present phase of modernity. This contrasts with the situation in non-modern, and early modern societies, where the vast majority of institutions were rooted or *embedded* in the confines of their own locality. The peasant's holding has a high degree of self-sufficiency; its connection with distant and more encompassing agencies is extremely limited compared to the modern case. How are we then to account for the way that social relations become *disembedded*, i.e. 'lifted out' of local contexts of interaction and restructured 'across indefinite spans of time–space'?[31]

Take the case of a modern bank. To increase its profits and market share the bank may develop, and then expand, a network of branches; the branches are able to proliferate because of the deployment of what Giddens terms 'disembedding mechanisms'. Starting a new branch of a bank relies on the portability of professional expertise; a banking network can be expanded globally by organising the transfer of systematically formulated banking expertise to agents who are employed in local contexts. This allows new branches to be 'placed into' any number of new contexts. The 'expert system' acts as a disembedding mechanism in that it supplies an operational prototype, a knowledge of 'how to do banking' that can be codified and therefore reliably applied to an indefinite number of cases; this permits the 'stretching' of bank practices across vast reaches of time and space.[32]

Giddens shows how modern life is in fact influenced in a '*continuous*' way by 'systems in which the knowledge of experts is integrated'.[33] He cites driving a car and travelling by plane as instances where automotive and aeronautical expertise underpin taken-for-granted activities; but the list of ways in which expert systems affect our lives can be extended almost indefinitely. This generalisation and globalisation of expert systems has placed daily life under the auspices of technical and professional knowledge. The modern person's faith in the reliability of their everyday world is based on a (usually implicit) trust in the efficacy of expert systems. Giddens does, however, take account of an opposing tendency, where actors experience a degree of unease in their dealings with expert systems. Often this unease is a result of the obvious fallibility of expert systems – planes do crash on occasion, for instance – but it also stems from an awareness that expert knowledge and practice is revisable and contested.

What is of particular interest to Giddens here is that the trust we place in expertise is not just a by-product of the success of modern systems; rather the smooth operation of those systems presumes the active involvement of trusting agents. The medical system can operate only on the basis that patients willingly submit themselves to the doctor's 'baroque arsenal' of surgery, diagnostic tests and drugs, all of which can involve experiences of the most harrowing kind; and in circumstances where actors will ordinarily possess only the most limited understanding of the practices to which they are submitting. The same principle applies to the workings of another system of crucial importance for the modern world, the money economy; it can function only when agents trust in the value of the symbolic tokens of which a currency is composed. Money also serves as a disembedding mechanism because of its ability to remove the owner from the necessity of being present at the point of exchange. (Expert systems and symbolic tokens are categorised by Giddens as 'abstract systems' because both operate on the basis of impersonal principles; the particularities of the system's 'players' being irrelevant to its operation.)

(h) The extensional and the intentional

The disembedding mechanisms that are intrinsic to the dynamics of globalisation are sources of trust, so long as they make good their claim successfully to organise determinate areas of the social and natural world; but, as I have tried to show in the previous paragraph, this success is itself dependent on the continued presence of trust in relations between actors and systems. Giddens' more recent writings revolve around this complex connection between extensionality (i.e. globalisation) and intentionality (i.e. matters centring on the self).

Such a focus allows Giddens to explore some extremely consequential processes, such as the connection between trust and high consequence risks. Take the example of threats to the environment. Despite the significant misgivings of environmentalists and a good number of experts, industrial systems are generally invested with a significant degree of trust, if only of an implicit kind. This trust can be explained by two factors: (i) industry's prime role in reducing the risks that make life insecure in non-industrialised societies; and (ii) the ubiquity of the effects of industrial production. A radical undermining of the trust normally placed in industry would have potentially damaging consequences for the actor's ontological security. This is because the globalising of industry and its far reaching impact on the world's ecology make it impossible to escape negative side-effects. If one were to become seriously and continuously worried by the unknown (and presently unknowable) effects of polluted air and toxic substances on one's bodily system, daily life would become very difficult indeed; anxiety would spill into, and skew, all one's activities. The problem is exacerbated by the fact that the individual is virtually powerless to deal with problems emanating from sources as distant as other continents. With the prospect of not only pollution, but also global warming, ozone depletion, etc. it is little wonder that profound doubts about the security of the industrial system will usually be 'bracketed out'. But at a collective level such bracketing will tend to forestall a confrontation with the risk environment; putting it off to a point in the future, when the dangers will most certainly have intensified.

(i)   Intimacy, self-identity and abstract systems

Giddens also devotes considerable attention to the relationship between extensionality and intentionality in so far as it affects personal relationships and the nature of self-identity. The rise of abstract systems has coincided with the decline of kinship relations (see extract V (iii)) 'as a device for stabilising social ties across time–

space').[34] Abstract systems do not themselves guarantee satisfying personal relationships; the impersonality they engender has given rise to a whole genre of sociological writings that take up, in one form or another, Tönnies' distinction between *Gemeinschaft* and *Gesellschaft*. The rise of the latter as the dominant form of association, and the decline of the former, are taken to be responsible for the attenuation of social solidarity. Habermas, for example, describes the tendency for the money economy and the bureaucracy to 'colonise the lifeworld', setting off a series of pathological processes that threaten daily life. Giddens however takes a different tack and, while acknowledging that important structural changes have taken place (such as the influence that distant happenings have on the individual), suggests that human relations in this era of high modernity are subject to *transformation* not disintegration.

Giddens' view is that relationships are increasingly set free from ties that are 'external' to the relationship itself; e.g. as the capitalist economy, media, formal educational institutions and other abstract systems increasingly attract the commitment of individuals, there is a weakening of the 'compulsory' nature of the rights and obligations that served to bind members of the traditional family. We can no longer count on the presence of a network of kin to provide us with trustworthy companions; at the same time we are freed from the necessity to provide such companionship to relatives whose company we find unrewarding. As no abstract system has evolved to take the place of the family or close-knit village community, the onus is on the individual to seek out and cultivate those trusting relations with others that remain essential for the integrity of the self. (Giddens should not, of course, be read as though he were advocating the weakening of ties between parents and dependent children.)

In a 'pure relationship' (Giddens' term for the form of affiliation most characteristic of the present epoch), the ties that bind persons are solely the product of the rewards the relationship brings to its participants. Because the 'pure relationship' is not fully 'anchored' in the manner of its traditional predecessor, partners to such an association must exert a significant degree of reflexive control over its direction. Both developments – the increasing prominence of the pure relationship, and the necessity for its reflexive control – are historically novel and represent a marked discontinuity with the past. As with the other discontinuities that Giddens analyses, something like a 'cultural lag' is evident; i.e. participants in relationships have not always fully grasped the nature of the transition that is taking place. For example, despite the very telling divorce statistics, many actors still expect their wedding vows to guarantee the continuation of their marriage, regardless of the horrors that transpire in their daily marital lives. Men, apparently, are especially resistant to the idea that relationships might have to be monitored and reflexively managed.

Giddens makes reference to a large body of literature that aims to inform spouses, lovers and friends about matters relevant to the reflexive conduct of their relationship. Even persons who actively spurn this literature may make implicit use of its 'findings', because of the tendency for useful information to find a place in the 'knowledge stocks' held in common by lay actors. Expert knowledge thus becomes a powerful constitutive factor in the 'pure relationship', and is not merely a description of what transpires. It is worthwhile noting here the double-edged character of expert systems: on the one hand the actor is 'deskilled' by the globalisation of abstract systems – expertise needed for the production of goods and many services is now held by specialised agencies and not by individuals; on the other hand, those expert systems have the potential to 'reskill' – by providing an information base that can be selectively drawn on to control important aspects of daily life.

The logic of abstract systems feeds into intimate relationships in another important way, and this is the theme of extract V (v). The principles of democracy are an integral element in the operation of modern political systems; they are involved in the extension of power beyond the 'administrative centre' to a multiplicity of local settings. Citizens at the local level broadly accept the legitimacy of the surveillance activities of the administrative state because of the state's democratic constitution. As such, democratic principles play a part in the disembedding process: legitimacy allows for the placement of distant forces into local contexts for given lengths of time. But the era of high modernity also sees the emergence of democratic principles as a powerful ethical imperative in the conduct of 'pure relationships'. The feminist movement has been at the forefront of this development, demanding an end to sexist practices on the grounds that traditional gender relations violate principles of equality and the rights of the individual. Giddens shows how the 'democratisation of intimacy' lends a degree of 'legitimacy' to relations between persons; a legitimacy which has the effect of generating and maintaining mutual trust. Because of the presence of powerful counter-trends, the achievement of interpersonal democracy is an ideal that must be continually 'worked at', and then constantly reproduced, even to the extent of using methods once considered appropriate for the conduct of 'public life', such as writing down rules and entering into negotiations with others in a more or less deliberate manner.

The sorts of considerations that Giddens brings to bear on the analysis of intimate relationships also apply, in many respects, to his views on self-identity: in high modernity personal identity is no longer ascribed by membership of an encompassing collectivity, instead 'it becomes a reflexively organised endeavour', and 'this reflexive project of the self, which consists in the sustaining of coherent, yet continuously revised, biographical narratives, takes place in the context of multiple choices as filtered through abstract systems'.[35] Thus far I have dealt with ways in which 'extensionality' enters into 'intentionality'; however Giddens' conception of the self opens up the possibility of grasping the other side of this process. The needs and demands of the high modern self can be fed back into the abstract systems to which they are connected.

(j) Emancipatory politics; life politics

The reflexively constituted self must construct a viable life and sense of identity by acting on, and in, the world. This inevitably entails that actors will make demands of some sort on the institutions that affect them. Two sorts of 'politics' are implicated in this process according to Giddens (see extract VI (iv)). The first type, 'emancipatory politics', concerns individual and collective demands for freedom and justice, and the struggle against barriers that prevent the possibility of leading an autonomous life. Such autonomy is gained by (i) constructing new abstract systems that guarantee a degree of freedom and equality – thus the creation of the modern democratic polity; and by (ii) altering the rules by which 'old' systems operate – the pre-modern legal system is 'adjusted' so that equality before the law is institutionalised.

The second type is 'life politics' which centres 'on questions of how we should live our lives in emancipated social circumstances'.[36] The problem of life politics is how power can be used to arrange the world in a way which permits self-actualisation. This cannot be achieved solely through abstract systems and 'emancipatory politics'; indeed life political goals will often necessitate that expert systems be used to roll back the 'boundaries' of abstract systems. An example: health care, and control of the body more generally, has increasingly been given over to the medical system, which happens to be closely integrated with another abstract system, the capitalist economy. It is difficult to deny that this has many positive benefits for individual health; at the same time it is associated with an alienation from the body – the individual gives over their body to be 'worked over' by experts. Health crises are also usually endured in situations that are cut off from the flow of daily life; this 'sequestration of experience' has the effect of limiting those experiences which raise important existential questions, so that we can live most of our lives with only sporadic contact with the profound issues of human being. Life politics might entail finding ways to organise health care so that these forms of alienation are diminished: actors could reskill themselves by making use of expert know-how, enabling them to work on themselves and be in more continuous and constructive contact with intimates when they face 'critical situations'.

The stakes in both forms of politics are extremely high. The enormous power generated by abstract systems has the potential to produce a modern apocalypse, and to drain life of any meaning; yet this energy also offers opportunities for resistance and reconstruction. The situation is greatly complicated, and yet facilitated, by the withering away of 'ultimate' forms of authority. The hopes of Habermas' attempts to 'ground' critical theory notwithstanding, there is no way of securely anchoring one's beliefs in infallible theories, ideologies and ethical systems; and no unproblematic expectation of a benign 'post-modern' order which will have solved the problems of the present. The extracts in Chapter VI deal with the issues facing critical theory in this era of 'radical doubt'; in a world where there can be no guarantees.

Giddens dramatises his prognosis for modernity, and the intensity of its barely controlled powers, by evoking the metaphor of the juggernaut which Giddens describes as

> a runaway engine of enormous power which, collectively as
> human beings, we can drive to some extent but which also

threatens to rush out of our control and could rend itself asunder . . . The ride is by no means wholly unpleasant or unrewarding; it can often be exhilarating and charged with hopeful anticipation. But so long as the institutions of modernity endure, we shall never be able to control completely either the path or the pace of the journey. We can ride the juggernaut, with its enormous destructive capacity, and we can steer it, but there are no guarantees of a benign outcome. The world is full of grave dangers, but the powers that are available to inhabitants of high modern societies ensure that there is also opportunity and hope.[37]

Finally, it seems appropriate to ponder, very briefly, the place of Giddens' own work in the world he is seeking to comprehend. The concept that is most strongly identified with his name – the 'double hermeneutic' – offers an appropriate starting point. The term refers to two processes: the necessity for social scientists to understand the 'world' of those lay actors whom they are seeking to understand; and the way in which the social theories that flow from this understanding are interpreted and appropriated by those same lay actors. The work of the influential social theorist is thus a highly productive and creative activity – his or her concepts, arguments, theories and definitions of 'what is going on' come to play a significant role in the constitution of social life; though how their work is interpreted and to what effect it will be put is largely beyond the control of the author. The writings of a social scientist such as Giddens present an interesting comparison with the work of the natural scientist. The latter advances frameworks and hypotheses for understanding the natural world, and although the natural scientist's knowledge may be used to intervene in the 'objective' world, his or her theories do not themselves alter the way that nature behaves. Atoms do not read scientific papers and change their behaviour accordingly. On the other hand, a social scientist's theories about the world can make a difference to the very nature of social life itself; unlike the elements of the natural world, actors do perform social practices on the basis of their theories about how society works. Thus Giddens' reflections upon social reality may not only become a component of that reality, but may serve to change it.

PHILIP CASSELL

Notes

1. Anthony Giddens, *The Constitution of Society*, p.227.
2. Giddens, *The Constitution of Society*, p.xxi
3. Anthony Giddens, *Politics and Sociology in the Thought of Max Weber*, p.46.
4. Giddens, *The Constitution of Society*, p.xv.
5. Giddens, *The Constitution of Society*, p.xiii.
6. Hans Joas 'Giddens' Critique of Functionalism', in Jon Clark, Celia Modgil and Sohan Modgil (eds), *Anthony Giddens: Consensus and Controversy* (Brighton: Falmer Press, 1990) p.91.
7. Giddens, *The Constitution of Society*, p.xiii.
8. Giddens, *The Constitution of Society*, p.xv.
9. Giddens, *The Constitution of Society*, p.xvi.
10. Anthony Giddens, *The Nation-State and Violence: Volume Two of A Contemporary Critique of Historical Materialism*, p.33.
11. Anthony Giddens, 'Action, Structure, Power', in A. Giddens, *Profiles and Critiques in Social Theory*, p.33.
12. Giddens, 'Action, Structure, Power', p.37.
13. Giddens, 'Action, Structure, Power'.
14. Giddens, *The Constitution of Society*, p.50.
15. The embarrassing silences that can arise in conversations are evidence that participants in interaction cannot take a passive approach to the passage of time. The conversation doesn't go on by itself: if silence provokes anxiety, participants must work to fill the time that elapses during their encounter.
16. Such struggles often result in compromises where an amount of 'territory' is virtually ceded by the competing parties. Giddens mentions the case of 'no-go' areas in large cities. This is a special case of a more general phenomenon; i.e. the zoning or regionalisation of social systems.
17. Anthony Giddens, *A Contemporary Critique of Historical Materialism*, vol.1, *Power, Property and the state*, p.5.
18. The distance, 'physical, social and cultural' between the classes, is the basis for Giddens' distinction between class-divided and class societies. The class divisions in traditional society do not produce chronic class warfare; conflict is sporadic and force is deployed by the rulers only for the purpose of maintaining the bare bases of rule, i.e. taxation and territorial defence. The history of traditional societies is certainly not the history of class struggle. This is clearly contrasted with the modern example, where the prevalence of surveillance at the workplace means that class conflict is both chronic and historically important; in class societies the dialectic of control takes on a significance that has major economic, political and cultural implications.
19. *A Contemporary Critique of Historical Materialism*, p.94.
20. *A Contemporary Critique of Historical Materialism*, p.51.
21. *A Contemporary Critique of Historical Materialism*.

22. Giddens, *The Constitution of Society*, p.258.
23. Giddens, *The Constitution of Society*, p.181.
24. Giddens, *The Nation-State and Violence*, p.33.
25. Anthony Giddens, *Sociology: A Brief but Critical Introduction*, p.34.
26. *Sociology: A Brief but Critical Introduction*, p.46.
27. Giddens, *A Contemporary Critique of Historical Materialism*, p.77–9.
28. From the *Grundrisse der kritik der Politischen Ökohomie*, a work comprised of notes made by Marx in the winter of 1857–8.
29. Contracts and financial agreements in traditional societies were not routinely backed by the power of the state, which lacked both the will and means for such enforcement. On the other hand the traditional sovereign was able, arbitrarily, to intervene in the course of economic arrangements as part of the royal prerogative, granting remissions to favoured parties, thereby undermining the predictability required for widespread entrepreneurial activity.
30. Giddens, *The Nation-State and Violence*, p.136.
31. Anthony Giddens, *The Consequences of Modernity*, p.21.
32. It is important to note that disembedding, in cases such as these, works only because of the possibility of reflexively managing the network; an activity that is made possible by codified knowledge but which also produces revisions to that 'know-how'. Furthermore, the articulation of headquarters and the branches is possible only because of communications systems that rely on global acceptance of 'clock' time and mensurable space. Disembedding mechanisms, reflexivity and the generalisation of artificial conceptions of time and space interact to produce the dynamism of modern institutions.
33. Giddens, *The Consequences of Modernity*, p.27.
34. Giddens, *The Consequences of Modernity*, p.102.
35. Anthony Giddens, *Modernity and Self-Identity: Self and Society in the Late Modern Age*, p.5.
36. Giddens, *Modernity and Self-Identity*, p.224.
37. Giddens, *The Consequences of Modernity*, p.139.

Chapter I

Encounters with the Classical Traditions

(i) Critical interpretations of Marx*

The problem of exploitation

The problem of how exploitation should be conceptualised in social theory is of equivalent importance to that of how we should seek to analyse domination and power. Easily the most influential theory of exploitation in sociology is that of Marx, and this has to form the initial point of reference for any appraisal of the notion. In Marx, the question of exploitation (*exploitieren, ausbeuten*) is inevitably bound up with his over-all characterisation of the nature and development of class systems. In tribal societies, according to Marx, production and distribution are communal. In such societies the productive forces are relatively undeveloped; there is little or no surplus production. Classes only come into being with the expansion of the productive forces, such that a surplus is generated, appropriated by an emergent dominant class of non-producers. Class relations are hence inherently exploitative, since the ruling class lives off the surplus production of the subordinate class or classes. There is a major difference, according to Marx, between the exploitative relation involved between the two main capitalist classes and the class relations found in the prior types of class society, the Ancient world and feudalism. In the latter two types of society exploitation takes the form of the appropriation of the

---

* A *Contemporary Critique of Historical Materialism*, pp. 55–61, 239–47.

surplus labour by the dominant class. In the feudal *levée*, for example, the exploitative element is direct and open; a proportion of the production of the serf is taken by the *seigneur*. In capitalism exploitation is organised quite differently, and is concealed from view. The main task of *Capital* was precisely to solve the 'hidden riddle' of capitalist production: to show how an exploitative class relation is to be discovered at the very heart of the capitalistic production process. Capitalism, which for the first time in history severs the mass of the working population from immediate control of their means of production, turning them into 'formally free' wage-workers, is based upon the appropriation of surplus *value* by the dominant class. The 'hidden riddle' of capitalist production – that labour-power sells at its value and yet is still caught in an exploitative relation with capital – is deciphered through the identification of surplus labour-time as the source of profit accruing to capital.

[T]he Marxian conception that, in capitalism, class relations intrude into the very centre of the production process is an extremely significant one. But I shall want to widen Marx's standpoint in so far as it involves the views that exploitation is (1) exclusively a feature of class relations, and (2) applicable only, within these confines, to human relationships. So far as (2) goes, I want to claim that the exploitation of nature cannot be treated as simply 'instrumental' or 'neutral' in regard of human interests. In Marx, nature appears above all as the medium of the realisation of human social development. The universal history of man is traced through the progressive elaboration of the productive forces, maximised in capitalism. It would not be true to say that from this standpoint nature is treated as merely inert or passive, since Marx emphasises that social development must be examined in terms of an active interplay between human beings and their material environment: 'By acting on the external world or changing it, [man] at the same time changes his own nature.'[1] But Marx's concern with transforming the exploitative human social relations expressed in class systems does not extend to the exploitation of nature. Certainly, in Marx's early writings, most notably in the *1844 Manuscripts*, one can find passages that suggest that nature is more than just the medium through which human history unfolds:

> Nature is the inorganic body of man; that is to say nature, excluding the human body itself. To say that man *lives* from

nature means that nature is his *body* with which he must remain in a continuous interchange in order not to die. The statement that the physical and mental life of man, and nature, are interdependent means simply that nature is interdependent with itself, for man is a part of nature.[2]

But the 'Promethean attitude' is always pre-eminent in Marx's writings, an attitude as unsurprising in the nineteenth century as it is indefensible in the twentieth century, when it has become apparent that the expansion of the productive forces can no longer be treated unproblematically as conducive to social progress.

Marx's linkage of exploitation to class domination is of course one aspect of the overriding importance he attributed to class and to class conflict . . . I shall simply assert that Marx tended to load the notions of class and class conflict with more conceptual burdens than they could possibly support. There are two aspects of this problem. One is the role Marx attributed to class in history, and the other, concomitant, issue is the question of what the 'classless' or socialist society will look like. If the exploitation of human beings by others begins with the first formation of class systems, then such exploitation will thereby disappear with the abolition of classes. But if, as I want to hold, exploitation exists before the emergence of class systems, and if within class systems not all forms of exploitation can be explained in terms of class domination, then the question of how exploitation can be transcended becomes correspondingly more complex.

I shall not deny that class relations are intrinsically exploitative, but shall suggest a more encompassing formulation of the notion of exploitation than that available in Marx. Exploitation, I want to propose, is most aptly conceptualised in relation to domination or *power*. In defining exploitation itself, we need not depart far from conventional English usage. According to the *Oxford English Dictionary*, 'to exploit' is 'to turn to account or utilise for one's own ends'. This is essentially the usage I shall suggest here. Exploitation may be regarded as domination *which is harnessed to sectional interests* (domination over nature or domination over human beings) (see Figure I.1).

This viewpoint links to the framework for the analysis of ideology which I have developed elsewhere.[3] The analysis and critique of ideology are concerned with showing how structures of significa-

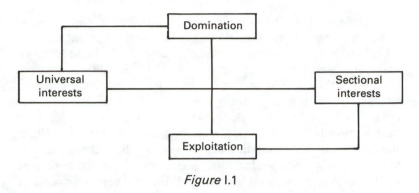

Figure I.1

tion are mobilised to legitimate the sectional interests of dominant groups, i.e. to legitimate *exploitative domination*. All forms of domination can be adjudged in terms of how far they are harnessed to the sectional interests of particular social categories, collectivities – or classes – and how far they serve the universal (generalisable) interests of broader communities or societies of which they are a part. The concept of interests raises numerous difficulties, which I shall not attempt to confront in this context. But it can be taken as axiomatic that sectional and universal interests are never wholly exclusive.

Exploitation, labour, surplus production

Marx's conception of exploitation is distinctively different from concepts of 'inequality', etc., as worked out in non-Marxist schools of social theory and politics. There are at least four respects in which this is so. First, Marx's treatment of exploitation is closely associated with his themes that production distinguishes man from the animals, and that the elaboration of the forces of production is the propelling impetus of societal advance.[4] In Marx, 'exploitation' is understood as the appropriation of the surplus product of subordinate classes by reference to production relations. Second, exploitation is therefore necessarily associated with classes, and is to be explicated in terms of the mechanisms of class domination. Third, the transcendence of exploitation is hence predicated upon the achievement of a society in which there are no longer any classes. Fourth, no ethical defence is offered, or thought neces-

sary, by Marx as to the identification of exploitation and its transcendence. This is again because of the involvement of the concept
with Marx's evolutionary scheme: the progressive ascendancy of
humanity from the classlessness of tribal communities, via class
conflict, to the classless society of the future finds no place for an
ethics justifying practical action. To further the cause of the proletariat is to be on the 'progressive' side of history, since the working
class represents the universal interests of human beings in creating a
classless order. The reasoning behind this can be reconstructed as
follows. Capitalism is the last form of class society; at the same time
as it maximises the self-alienation of human beings in a class
system, it prepares the way for the abolition of all class divisions
because the proletariat is the 'universal class'. The proletariat bears
within itself, as it were, the concentration of the evils inherent in the
oppression of some human beings by others. In struggling to throw
off its own chains, the proletariat thus fights for the universal
interest of humankind as a whole.

There seems no point in beating about the bush. Much of this has
today to be scrapped, and in any case loses its potency once Marx's
evolutionary scheme is discarded. There are quite fundamental
difficulties with Marx's writings on the transition from capitalism
to a (fully matured) socialist society. We know that he was reluctant
to say much about the projected society of the future, save for the
'transitional' stage of early socialist consolidation. The traditional
defence of this reserved attitude is that Marx had no wish to
produce just another version of utopian socialism, in which detailed blue-prints of the 'desirable' society would be drawn up; his
distaste for such schemes sprang from the same sources as his
distrust of ethics. But this paradoxically has the effect of leaving
a strong *potential* utopianism in his own work, especially when one
considers that, if he abandoned the more visionary statements of his
youth, he never returned to correct them. It is not enough to say, I
think, as proponents of Marxist orthodoxy have been prone to do,
that Marx's early writings are the philosophical ramblings of an
author who had not yet reached a mature view, and hence can be
largely ignored. There is a real tension here, expressed in the distance between Marx's earlier and later writings when considered in
the context of his intellectual career, and posed more concretely by
the problem of what else can be expected to disappear in socialism
when classes disappear.

Classes, the division of labour, the state, these are supposed to go – although no one thus far has managed to formulate particularly convincing versions of how such massive transformations are to be achieved while still preserving the fruits of industrial production. But what of political power, or, as Marx sometimes says, 'power' *tout court*? In linking these, as Marx does, to the state, one might presume that they will disappear in socialism. What of conflicts of interests, and struggles organised to further sectional interests? Marx connects division of interest in society so closely with class that once more it might appear that the dissolution of classes brings about the ending of all divisions of interest between different segments or collectivities in a society. Certainly one can find quotations that seem to imply this, if one cares to go quotation-mongering. What of ideology? Since again ideology seems to be intrinsically linked to class division, it might be presumed that it, too, will disappear in socialism – although Althusser has recently suggested to the contrary, at the cost of making ideology more or less convergent with the over-all symbol system of a society, and thus 'neutralising' it in respect of class domination.[5]

I shall concentrate for the moment upon the problem of exploitation . . . I [do not] pretend to do any more than indicate some of the threads that might be tied together into a critical theory based on the analyses developed [elsewhere]. I attempt here . . . to list a few considerations which link that conceptualisation to Marx's analysis:

(1) If capitalism is not the 'high point' of a universal history of humankind (in a condition that maximises the exploitation of the 'universal class' of the proletariat), then the transformation of capitalism will not bring about the disappearance of exploitation. To suppose anything else is to fall for a dialectical conjuring trick, in which there is a leap from 'necessity into freedom'. As far as Marx's own beliefs are concerned, I do not think it would be fair to criticise him as a utopian thinker, nor on the contrary to suppose him to be a hard-nosed realist. In the mature part of his career, I should say, the latter trait predominated over the former. But equally there can be no doubt that Marx continued to accept some of his earlier ideas throughout his intellectual career. I have tried to show that there are certain major inconsistencies and ambiguities that

appear in Marx's attitude towards evolution and the emergence of capitalism. One must accept that the same is true of large sectors of Marx's writings, with the exception of the only area upon which he worked in great detail: the critique of political economy. In his critical dismemberment of political economy Marx identified the sources of surplus value, and was able to make a far-reaching contrast between the exploitation of labour-power in capitalism and the exploitation of labour in prior types of society. (I have argued that this contrast bites deeper than even Marx tended to acknowledge, because he wished to interpolate it within his evolutionary scheme.) But the exploitation of labour, analysed as surplus value, either in capitalism or in other types of society, however important it may be, cannot provide an exhaustive theory of exploitation in human society as a whole. In particular, it is inadequate as a basis for the critique of exploitation in socialist society, where surplus value supposedly disappears (although not surplus production).

(2)   There are three axes of exploitative relationships – observable in societies at widely different times and places – which are not explained, though they may be significantly illuminated, either by the theory of the exploitation of labour in general or by the theory of surplus value in particular. These are: (a) exploitative relations between states, where these are strongly influenced by military domination; (b) exploitative relations between ethnic groups, which may or may not converge with the first; and (c) exploitative relations between the sexes, sexual exploitation. None of these can be reduced exhaustively to class exploitation, nor more particularly can they be derived from the theory of surplus value. None of them came into existence with capitalism, though they have taken particular forms with the development of capitalist society, and hence there can be no presumption that they will inevitably disappear if and when capitalism does. These are major 'absences' in Marxist theory, and notwithstanding a diversity of efforts to accommodate them to Marxism in a 'class-reductive' way they remain among its most obvious limitations. To say this is not, of course, to deny that Marx's analyses, especially his theory of the mechanics of capitalist production, do not illuminate each of these areas. Of course they do, or can be elaborated so

as to do so. I have tried to show how Marx's analysis of capitalism, linked into the commodification of time and space, and the prevalence of 'created space', connects closely to the theory of the nation-state as holding a monopoly of the means of violence. One could also offer analyses of the intersection of capitalistic mechanisms with the other two axes of exploitation. For example, on the level of international relations, the associations between capitalism, the nation-state and nationalism help to explain some of the most virulent forms of racism witnessed in our times. (Do not make the mistake of supposing that racism is an artefact of capitalism, however. There are clear evidences of its pervasiveness in ancient Sumer.) 'Internally', one can show how ethnic discrimination serves to create minority ethnic 'underclasses', whose economic circumstances are markedly inferior to those of the majority of the population.[6] The creation of 'everyday life' in capitalist time-space, with its characteristic separation of home and work-place, together with other aspects of the commodification of social relations, have decisively influenced the relations between the sexes, and at least in certain respects served to intensify the exploitation of women.[7] Feminism is, in my judgement, potentially more radical in its implications for a critical theory of contemporary society (capitalist and state-socialist) than Marxism is, however much each may help feed in to the other.

(3) 'Exploitation' is above all a concept that bears on the relations between power and *freedom*. This is an absolutely fundamental point, and hits at some of the most entrenched weaknesses of Marx's writings and those of subsequent Marxism. One way of grasping it within the nexus of Marx's own writings is by returning to the problem of the production of a surplus, and its part in Marx's interpretation of history. The origins of surplus production and the definition of 'surplus', although nowhere discussed with precision by Marx, are assumed by him to be economic – an assumption that conforms to the primacy which he accords to the expansion of the forces of production in stimulating social change. But I have sought to show that, until the arrival of capitalism and the transition from appropriation of surplus labour to the appropriation of surplus value, what is 'surplus' can only be specified in terms

of asymmetrical distributions of power. What is 'surplus' is
that which can be extracted, by whatever means, by the exploiting class. Now it might seem that surplus value in capitalism diverges from this, since it is calculated in units of
exchange-value (commodified time), and is therefore 'economic'. Indeed, I have constantly stressed the importance of this
contrast. But the 'surplus' is still formed by power relations,
even in this instance – for its extraction is only possible given
the framework of class domination that can be traced out
through the labour contract. In capitalism, control of allocative resources (capital) yields far more power than allocative
control in any previous society.

(4)   If the concept of exploitation is to do with the relations
between power and freedom, no theory concerned only with
the distribution of material wealth can suffice to explore more
than certain aspects of the patterns of exploitation formed in a
society. These assume particular importance in the context of
capitalism, for the reason just noted: that control of allocative
resources becomes of focal importance for the distribution of
power. Criticising Marx's formulation of surplus production
does not, I should hasten to add (although it should be clear
enough already), mean dismissing the relevance of his work to
the elucidation of power relations. For instance, in showing
capital to presuppose wage-labour, the two being connected
via the production of surplus value, Marx shows – *vis-à-vis*
political economy – that the 'freedom' of wage-labour dis-
guises coercive sanctions that employers are able to use to
enhance their power. However, the lack of a satisfactory
treatment of power, including the use of violence by individuals, collectivities and states, runs like a red thread (or
perhaps one should say here, a blue thread) through the
writings of Marx and of Marxists subsequently. The importance of this points both backwards and forwards: backwards
in the direction of the inadequacies of historical materialism
as an account of societal development; forwards to the anticipation of socialism. The influence of the Saint-Simonian
strain of socialist thought on Marx is one reason, although
only one, why Marx's thought supplies precious few clues
indeed about the continuing significance of power in socialist
society. But this is the century of Stalin and the Gulag. No

socialist can afford to ignore this very basic 'absence' in Marxist thought.

Although the concept of totalitarianism has a fraught history, being part of the liberal apparatus of political thought of the Cold War period (and, on the left, being greatly overextended by Marcuse), I think it to be an essential notion for examining exploitative aspects of state power. Certainly it cannot be applied as a concept *en bloc*; in the Cold War period liberal writers applied it to more or less all the industrialised societies that did not conform to their models of liberal democracy, to fascism and to the Eastern European societies. Instead of such a usage, I should want to distinguish between *right totalitarianism* (fascism), and *left totalitarianism* (Stalinism). I agree with Arendt that totalitarianism is a modern phenomenon, not to be equated with 'despotism' or its synonyms though I would not accept all the elements of her standpoint. I think an approach to the theory of totalitarianism can be worked out via the concept of surveillance, against the backdrop of . . . time–space transformations . . . The expansion of the surveillance activities of the state, which is contradictory (not simply a one-way movement towards the 'steel-hard cage' of Weber's fears), has to be recognised as one of the basic issues to be tackled in social and political theory. The extension of surveillance, plus the secret co-ordination of information in the hands of dominant elites, used to further policies formed mainly by those elites, can together be taken to represent a provisional definition of totalitarian power. But this is not to say that right and left totalitarianism can be explained in identical ways, or that there are not major variations within these two types of totalitarian control.

(5) The concept of exploitation has to include the power of human beings over nature as well as over other human beings. Such a notion is evidently in some part elliptical, since it depends, like the direct exploitation of human beings by others, ultimately upon how relations with nature affect human interests. But it touches upon a very important theme in respect of Marx's writings and those of most subsequent Marxists. I have already pointed out that Marx adopted an instrumental attitude to nature, common enough in the nineteenth century to be sure, and assumed by virtually all of those who felt them-

selves in opposition to Romanticism. Nature is to be mastered and subordinated to human purposes. This makes it difficult, within the compass of Marx's thought, to cope with two sets of phenomena whose potential significance has emerged more and more sharply in the twentieth century. One is that nature does not contain an inexhaustible reservoir of resources available to be transmuted to human ends. Nature is not merely the medium whereby human beings 'make their history, and thereby make themselves'; nature should rather be treated as an ally of humanity, in which human beings exist 'ecologically', depending upon natural phenomena which in principle or in practice they can destroy. There is more than a small theoretical hiatus between Marxism and 'ecological movements' of contemporary times, though it seems a matter of urgency that attempts at *rapprochement* should be set under way. This involves, in my opinion, drawing direct connections between modes in which capitalistic class exploitation intersects with the exploitation of nature. Some of these appear obvious: for example, the pressure towards accumulation may create a drive to the valorisation of capital in the short term regardless of the long-term consequences in respect of the exploitation of nature. But, in the contemporary world at least, it seems clear that the economic advantages of the exploitation of natural resources may equally well be sought after by those in the socialist societies. Scarcity of material resources is something else that does not disappear *ipso facto* with the dissolution of capitalism, if and when it should occur.

There are more subtle matters involved in human relations with nature than relatively straightforward questions of the damaging or exhaustion of resources which are of value to human beings. These bear in some part upon issues I have briefly touched upon in discussing contradiction. Nature, as the apparent infinity of time–space, is a 'mystery' to human beings; but nature as the intimate, aesthetically satisfying interchange between human beings and their immediate surrounds is a potential part of a 'meaningful' human existence. Certainly neither of these relations between human beings and nature can be grasped via the notion of labour, however broadly it is interpreted.[8] But some of the main ideas I have discussed in this book, especially those bearing upon the commodification of time and space, the dissolution of the differentiation between the city and the countryside, and the prevalence of 'created space', are relevant to these questions. And they have been addressed interestingly by various Marxist thinkers – although always those who have been strongly 'revisionist' in orientation, and critical of orthodox Marxism.

(6) The elaboration of a theory of exploitation in contemporary capitalism, as well as in contemporary socialism, seems likely to presuppose counterfactual conceptions of a normative kind. As I have pointed out previously, many difficulties are created for Marxism by the paucity of Marx's comments on what socialism can be expected to be like, at least in its 'higher phase'. Since Marxism is predicated so strongly on the critique of capitalism, and more specifically upon the critique of class domination as the focus of exploitation, it is open to the utopian readings I have referred to above. When classes are transcended, then division of interest in general, and therefore exploitation in general, might be presumed to be superseded also. It needs no great perspicacity to see that Marxism then becomes highly vulnerable to itself being translated into ideology: 'in the workers' state there can be no division of interests between different sections of the community', etc., etc. As I have argued elsewhere, any theory which might be taken to imply that there can be an 'end of ideology' in an empirical society displays a vulnerability to itself becoming ideological[9] – in virtue of the fact that a regime guided by that theory may choose to declare that the time has arrived, that henceforth ideology exists no longer.

A counterfactual theory of exploitation would recognise that, notwithstanding revolutions and reforms that might take place, there is always room for further advancement. In the contemporary literature of social theory and philosophy, there are various normative counterfactual theories which command attention. One, might instance especially, outside Marxism, Rawls' theory of justice and, more closely connected to Marxism, Habermas's conception of the 'ideal speech situation' as the basis for a critique of asymmetries of power. These have each been subject to considerable discussion, and each appears to have major weaknesses; but I do not intend to comment upon these debates here.[10]

(ii)   The political context of Max Weber's sociology*

It is often said that Weber's work represents a response to 'late' capitalism. Thus expressed, this is a misleading statement. What is specifically important as the political and economic background to Weber's sociological writings is, in fact, the *retardation* of German development.[11] Judged in terms of the British model, the concluding decades of the nineteenth century were indeed a period of 'mature' capitalist evolution: by 1900, Britain could be adjudged to have been 'industrialised' for more than half a century. Most sociologists in fact, when they speak generically of 'nineteenth-century capitalism', have in mind the case of Britain, which is treated as the exemplar of capitalist development. But the point is that the transition to capitalist industrialism took place in Germany only towards the latter part of the nineteenth century; it proceeded without the occurrence of a 'successful' bourgeois revolution, and in the framework of a process of political centralisation secured by Prussian military imperialism.

Weber's concern with 'capitalism', its presuppositions and consequences, in his sociological writings, thus has to be understood as an outcome, in large degree, of a preoccupation with the characteristics of the specific problems facing German society in the early phases of its industrial development. Such a concern underlies his study of the estates to the east of the Elbe. On its initial publication, the work received some considerable praise from conservative circles, because of its stance on the 'Polish question'. But his more general observations in the study actually contain an appraisal of the declining economic position of the large landowners; and this formed one main strand of his later political thinking. The 'feudal' agrarian structure in the east, which is the economic foundation of Prussia, will necessarily have to cede place to commercial capitalism.

Weber's analysis leads him to the conclusion, however, that neither the pre-existing hegemony of the *Junkers*, nor their declining position, can be explained in strictly economic terms. The *Junker* estates are not simply founded upon the economic 'exploitation' of the peasantry, but are spheres of political domination, rooted in strongly defined and traditional relationships of super-

---

* *Politics and Sociology in the Thought of Max Weber*, pp. 28–39.

ordination and subordination. The military successes of Prussia, and her political accomplishments in Germany, Weber asserts, were attained on the basis of this traditionalistic power of the *Junkers*. But precisely because of their accomplishments in securing the unity of the German state, the *Junkers* have 'dug their own grave': the political unification of the country which made Germany for the first time a major power-state in Central Europe, can henceforth be maintained only by the promotion of industrialisation. Only an industrialised state can hope to match the strength of the other Western countries – and will have the resources to meet what Weber, throughout his life, saw as the major threat in the east: Russia. In fact, Weber says, while they maintain 'aristocratic' pretensions, the *Junkers* have already, effectively become commercialised land proprietors. Capitalism has

> gnawed at the social character of the *Junker* and his labourers. In the first half of the last century [i.e. the nineteenth century] the *Junker* was a rural patriarch. His farm hands, the farmers whose land he had appropriated, were by no means proletarians . . . they were, on a small scale, agriculturalists with a direct interest in their lord's husbandry. But they were expropriated by the rising valuation of the land; their lord withheld pasture and land, kept his grain, and paid them wages instead. Thus, the old community of interest was dissolved, and the farm hands became proletarians.

The result of the increasing undermining of the position of the *Instleute*, the bonded labourers, produced an emigration of workers from the east to the expanding industries of the western part of Germany. 'For Germany, all fateful questions of economic and social policy and of national interest are closely connected with this contrast between the rural society of the east and that of the west, and with its further development.'[12]

Weber's analysis of these issues differs considerably from that advanced in orthodox SPD circles at the turn of the century. Whereas Marxist authors sought to interpret the changing character of the agrarian east almost wholly in economic terms, Weber distinguished a complicated interplay of economic, political and ideological relationships. Thus, in explaining the emigration of labourers from the landed estates, Weber rejects the notion that this can be explained by reference to purely economic considerations: rather, the immediate driving force is a generalised notion of attaining 'freedom', from the restrictive ties of bonded labour. The '"bread and butter question"', Weber asserted, 'is of secondary importance'.[13]

The Protestant Ethic combines together, and projects on to a general level, several of the implications which Weber drew from his interpretation of the agrarian question and its relationship to German politics. It is misleading to regard the work, as many have, as a frontal attack upon historical materialism. Rather, the emergent line of Weber's reasoning, both in relation to the social structure of Germany, and on the more general intellectual plane, led him towards a standpoint which cut across the typical conceptions embodied in Marxism. His rejection of affiliations with the Social Democrats in the political sphere, while based upon his interpretation of the trends of development in German society, received an intellectual underpinning from acceptance of certain elements of the neo-Kantianism of the Heidelberg school. Weber's methodological position, as elaborated during the course of 1904–5, leans heavily upon Rickert, and upon the dichotomy between fact and value which is basic to the latter's philosophy. Weber used this to formulate a methodological critique both of idealism and Marxism, as overall schemes applied to history; on the level of political action, this underlay his rejection of Social Democracy, as representing an illegitimate fusion of ethical and political claims. As he once remarked of socialism, 'I *shall not* join *such* Churches'.[14]

To these methodological objections to Marxism, Weber conjoined his appraisal of the specific characteristics of the economic and political development of Germany. He agreed with certain elements of the conventional Marxist analysis of religious ideology, but none the less rejected that 'one-sided' historical materialism which allowed no positive influence to the symbolic content of specific forms of religious belief-system. Thus he accepted that 'The Church belongs to the conservative forces in European countries: first, the Roman Catholic Church . . . but also the Lutheran Church'. In Calvinism, however, he found a religious impulse which was not conservative, but revolutionary. While, as is shown in *The Protestant Ethic*, Lutheranism marked an important 'advance' over Catholicism in promoting the penetration of religious ethics into the sanctioning of rational labour in a 'calling', the

Reformation did not, in itself, mark a radical break with traditionalism. On the whole, Lutheranism, like Catholicism, has acted to 'support the peasant, with his conservative way of life, against the domination of urban rationalist culture'. Both Churches consider that the personal ties pertaining between lord and serf can be more easily ethically controlled than the commercial relations of the market. 'Deep, historically conditioned contrasts, which have always separated Catholicism and Lutheranism from Calvinism, strengthen this anti-capitalistic attitude of the European Churches.'[15]

Thus, in seeking to identify the historical linkage between Calvinism and modern rational capitalism, Weber at the same time cast light upon the specific circumstances of the German case. Calvinism, by sanctioning 'this-worldly asceticism', served to cut through the traditionalism which had characterised previous economic formations. Germany experienced the first 'religious revolution' of modern times, but Lutheranism was not the break with traditionalism which generated the ethical impulse which underlies modern capitalism. Instead, the Lutheran Church became the bulwark of a system of political domination which lasted into the twentieth century. In his political writings, Weber makes this point explicitly, pointing out a direct connection between Lutheranism and the growth of the Prussian state: 'Protestantism legitimated the state as a means of violence, as an absolute divine institution, and as the legitimate power-state in particular. Luther took from the individual the ethical responsibility for war and transferred it to the state authority; to obey this authority in all matters other than religious belief could never entail guilt.'[16]

Since it brought Weber into a confrontation with Marxist analyses of 'ideology' and 'superstructure', it was inevitable that much of the controversy about *The Protestant Ethic* should centre upon the 'role of ideas' in historical development. Weber himself scathingly dismissed the claims of historical materialism in this respect: the notion that systems of ideas can be in any sense 'ultimately' reduced to economic factors is 'utterly finished'; the truth is that there is no unilateral line of relationship between 'material' and 'ideal' factors. But standing behind the work is a more deeply rooted divergence from Marxism, concerning the essential structure of capitalism and bourgeois rationality; and in working out the implications of this standpoint, as elaborated in his studies of the non-European civilisations, Weber again took his point of departure from his interpretation of the German situation and 'Bismarck's legacy'.

A key theme in Weber's writings is his emphasis upon the independent influence of the 'political' as opposed to the 'economic'. Now it is important to recognise that each of the most significant forms of social–political theory originating in the earlier part of the nineteenth century – liberalism and Marxism – are in accord in minimising the influence of the state. The 'political' is seen as secondary and derived. Marxism does admit the importance of the state in capitalism, but regards it as expressing the asymmetry of class interests, and therefore as a social form which will 'disappear' when class society is transcended by socialism. Weber readily perceived the disjunction between this conception, as advanced by the spokesmen for the Social Democrats, and the realities of the social circumstances in which the Marxist party found itself. The SPD was certainly, especially during the period of the anti-socialist laws, 'outside' the state; but the only chance, as Weber saw it, which the party had of acquiring power was through the electoral system. However, the more it became successful in this way, according to his analysis, the more it was forced to become a bureaucratised, 'mass' party, which would become integrated with the existing state mechanism, and would no longer offer any 'alternative' to it. He rejected the standpoint of the Left-Liberals for similar reasons. The 1848 style of liberalism, in Weber's eyes, was obsolete in the context of the post-unification period in Germany. The assumptions underlying their standpoint of the 'minimising' of political power through the full extension of rights of political franchise – was to Weber irreconcilable with the trend of development of German politics. Inside Germany, the main residue of Bismarck's domination was the existence of a bureaucratic state officialdom: a 'leaderless democracy' would be no advance over the present situation of the political hegemony of a doomed and declining class. Externally, Germany found itself surrounded by powerful states: the unification of Germany had been achieved through the assertion of Prussian military power in the face of the other major European nations. Thus, in becoming a 'bourgeois' society, Germany could not follow the same pattern as was shown by the political development of either Britain or the United States. On more than one occasion, Weber drew an explicit contrast between the historical circumstances of Germany and those of the United States. Germany had been placed in circumstances which 'have forced us to maintain the splendour of our old culture, so to speak, in an armed camp within a world bristling with arms'. The United States, on the other hand, 'does not yet know such problems', and 'will probably never encounter some of them'. The territorial isolation of the subcontinent which the United States occupies is 'the real historical seal imprinted upon its democratic institutions; without this acquisition, with powerful and warlike neighbours at its side, it would be forced to wear the coat of mail like ourselves, who constantly keep in the drawer of our desks the march order in case of war'.[17]

This assessment guided Weber in his general conceptualisation of the state and political power, as formulated in *Economy and Society*. In contrast to those contemporary thinkers (such as Durkheim) who regarded the modern nation-state primarily as a *moral* institution, Weber emphasises above all the capacity of the state to claim, through the use of force, a defined territorial area. The modern state is 'a compulsory association with a territorial basis', and monopolises, within its borders, legitimate control of the use of force. It is impossible, he held, to define a 'political' group (*Verband*) in terms of any definite category of ends which it serves: 'there is no conceivable end which *some* political association has not at some time pursued. And from the protection of personal security to the administration of justice, there is none which *all* have recognised.[18] Thus the 'political' character of a group can only be defined in terms of its monopoly of the disposal of a force – which is a 'means' rather than an 'end'.

The organisation of the legal-rational state, in Weber's sociology, is applied to derive a general paradigm of the progression of the division of labour in modern capitalism. His application of this scheme, which is mediated by the conception of bureaucratisation, again expresses, in a definite sense, the independent character of the 'political' as compared to the 'economic'. For Marx, and for most nineteenth-century social thought generally, the problem of bureaucracy is given little prominence – a fact which is to be traced directly to the treatment of political organisation as heavily dependent upon economic power (class domination). Weber does not deny, of course, that modern capitalism involves the emergence of a class system based upon capital and wage-labour. But this is not for him, as it was for Marx, the main structural axis of the increasing differentiation of the division of labour which accompanies the advance of capitalism. Rather than generalising from the economic to the political, Weber generalises from the political to the economic: bureaucratic specialisation of tasks (which is, first and foremost, the characteristic of the legal-rational state) is treated as the most integral feature of capitalism. Thus Weber rejects the conception that the expropriation of the worker from his means of production has been confined to the economic sphere alone; any form of organisation having a hierarchy of authority can become subject to a process of 'expropriation'. In the modern state, 'expert officialdom, based on the division of labour' is wholly expropriated from possession of its means of administration. 'In the contemporary "state" – and this is essential for the concept of state – the "separation" of the administrative staff, of the administrative officials, and of the workers from the material means of administrative organisation is completed.'[19]

At this point, Weber's analysis of the political development of Germany rejoins his general conception of the growth of Western capitalism and the likely consequences of the emergence of socialist societies in Europe. The specific 'problem' of German political development is that of the 'legacy' of Bismarck, which has left Germany with a strongly centralised bureaucracy that is not complemented by an institutional order which can generate an independent political leadership, as is demanded by the 'tasks of the nation'. Such a political leadership, provided in the past by the Prussian aristocracy, can no longer be derived from this source in a capitalist society. This leaves the working class and the bourgeoisie. Both Weber's analysis of the specific characteristics of the SPD, and his generalised formulation of the growth of the bureaucratised division of labour in capitalism, reinforce his conviction that a bourgeois constitution is the only feasible option for Germany. The ideological impetus of the Social Democrats, fostering the notion that the bureaucratic apparatus of the state could be overthrown and destroyed by revolutionary means, he considered simply as fantasy. Not only is it the case that a capitalist economy necessitates bureaucratic organisation, but the socialisation of the economy would inevitably entail the further spread of bureaucracy, in order to co-ordinate production according to central 'planning'. On the more general level, this conclusion is reached via the analysis of the process of 'expropriation' in the division of labour. The Marxist anticipation of socialism is grounded in the belief that capitalist society can be transcended by a new social order; but in Weber's conception, the possibility of the transcendence of capitalism is completely eliminated. The essential character of capitalism is not given in the class relationship between wage-labour and capital, but in the rational orientation of productive activity. The process of the 'separation' of the worker from his means of production is only one instance of a process of the rationalisation of conduct which advances in all spheres of modern society. This process, giving rise to bureaucratic specialisation, is irreversible. Since socialism is predicated upon the further imposition of rational control of economic conduct (the centralisation of the economy), and upon the 'disappearance' of the 'political' through its merging with the 'economic' (state control of economic enterprises), the result could only be an enormous expansion in bureaucratisation. This would not be the 'dictatorship of the proletariat', but the 'dictatorship of the official'.[20]

Weber's analysis of the political structure of Germany is concerned with the interplay of three main elements: the position of the traditionally established 'feudal' *Junker* landowners; the tendency towards 'uncontrolled bureaucratic domination' by the state officialdom; and the dearth of political leadership bound up with each of these factors. These three components reappear on the more general level in Weber's political sociology, in his typology of domination: traditional, legal and charismatic. The domination of the *Junkers* undoubtedly served him as the proximate model (together with the case of Rome, which he used as offering certain comparisons with Germany in his early writings) in drawing out the general implications of the contrast between the 'pure types' of traditional and legal domination, and the relationship between both and economic activity. 'The domination of a feudal stratum tends', Weber made clear, 'because the structure of feudalised powers of government is normally predominantly patrimonial, to set rigid limits to the freedom of acquisitive activity and the development of markets.[21] But in common with his general emphasis, he stressed that it is the administrative practices of traditional domination, rather than their purely economic policy, which inhibits the growth of rational capitalistic activity. Of particular significance here is the 'arbitrary' character of traditional administration, which militates against the emergence of formal rationality or 'calculability' in social action. The historical circumstances of Western Europe, according to Weber, are unique in having fostered the development of the rational state, with its expert officialdom. This has been one major condition (among others) which has facilitated the rise of modern capitalism in the West.

The case of Germany, however, shows that the growth of the rational state is in no sense a sufficient condition for the emergence of modern capitalism. In the countries in which capitalism came into being at an early date, England and Holland, the bureaucratic state has been less developed than in Germany. It is the existence of a bureaucratic state in Germany, and the specific direction in which it was channelled under Bismarck, which has left the country in the hands of politicians 'without a calling'. 'Professional politicians', as Weber demonstrates in his studies of the Eastern civilisations, have emerged in all developed patrimonial states. These are individuals who have come to prominence in the service of a king: 'men who, unlike the charismatic leader, have not wished to be lords themselves, but who have entered the *service* of political lords'. 'But only in the West have there been professional politicians whose lives have been devoted to 'the service of powers other than the princes'; who live 'off' politics, and who recognise only the legitimacy of impersonal legal principles. The development of this process occurred in Europe in different ways in different places, but has always involved the eventual development of a struggle for power between the king and the administrative staff which had grown up around him. In Germany, this took a particular form:

> Wherever the dynasties retained actual power in their hands – as was especially the case in Germany – the interests of the prince were joined with those of officialdom *against* parliament and its claims for power. The officials were also interested in having leading positions, that is, ministerial positions, occupied by their own ranks, thus making these positions an object of the official career. The monarch, on his part, was interested in being able to appoint the ministers from the ranks of devoted officials according to his own discretion. Both parties, however, were interested in seeing the political leadership confront parliament in a unified and solidary fashion.[22]

All modern states, of course, involve these two forms of officials: 'administrative' and 'political' officials. Weber's discussion of the relationship between these two forms of modern officialdom in Germany is based upon analysis of the qualities of political leadership which is directly connected with his formulation of charismatic domination in general. The bureaucratic official must carry out his duties in an impartial fashion: as Weber frequently said, *sine ira et studio*. The political leader, by contrast, must 'take a stand' and 'be passionate'. The 'routinisation' of politics – that is to say, the transformation of political decisions into decisions of administrative routine, through domination by bureaucratic officialdom – is specifically foreign to the demands which are most basic to political action. This phenomenon, which occupied much of Weber's attention in his analysis of the lack of political leadership in Germany, forms a major component of his generalised comparison of charisma with both traditional and rational-legal domination. Charisma is, as a 'pure type', wholly opposed to the routine, the *alltäglich*. Traditional and legal domination, on the other hand, are both forms of everyday administration, the one being tied to precedents transmitted from previous generations, the other being bound by abstractly formulated universal principles. The charismatic leader, 'like . . . every true leader in this sense, preaches, creates, or demands *new* obligations'.[23] It is for this reason that the 'charismatic element' is of vital significance in a modern democratic order; without it, no consistent policy-making is possible, and the state relapses into leaderless democracy, the rule of professional politicians without a calling.

(iii) Durkheim's political sociology*

It is undoubtedly the case that Durkheim's thought did undergo significant modification and elaboration over the course of his intellectual career. But this now apparently 'orthodox' view, which sees a pronounced discrepancy between Durkheim's earlier and later works, is highly misleading. The substance of this paper, indeed, is founded upon the premise that the truth of the matter is almost completely the reverse of the view suggested by Nisbet:

---

* *Studies in Social and Political Theory*, pp.236–40, 263–72.

that Durkheim continued in his later thinking to base his works upon the distinction between 'mechanical' and 'organic' solidarity; that the existence of solidarity deriving from the division of labour was always conceived by Durkheim to be the most distinctive feature of contemporary as opposed to traditional societies; that Durkheim's treatment of 'conflict and anomie' in his later writings cannot be understood apart from his analysis of the 'pathological' forms of the division of labour; and that 'the kinds of society, constraint, and solidarity dealt with in all his later works' have everything to do with the attributes of contemporary society as formulated in *The Division of Labour*. The overall continuity between Durkheim's early and later works does not become fully apparent, however, unless considerable attention is given to his political theory. Far from being of peripheral significance to his sociology, Durkheim's political thought has an important role in his ideas; and . . . an appreciation of this fact allows the correction of a prevalent, but mistaken, interpretation of the main sociological problem with which Durkheim was concerned in all of his major works: the theory of moral authority.

The social and political background of Durkheim's thought

It has often been remarked that Durkheim's sociology has to be understood as a response to the shattering effects upon French society of the German victory of 1870–1.[24] But this says too much, and too little. Too much, because Durkheim's writing also has to be seen as rooted in the traditions of French positivist philosophy which stretch back to Comte, Saint-Simon, and beyond; too little because – by this very token – the social and political background to Durkheim's thought embodies important elements which were the legacy of the Revolution in the eighteenth century, and of which the events of 1870–1 were in part a direct outcome.[25] If the Revolution successfully disposed of the *ancien régime*, it also prepared the ground for certain generic social and political problems which were to haunt France for more than a century afterwards. Rather than introducing the liberal, bourgeois society which was proclaimed in its slogans, the Revolution opened up social cleavages of a chronic nature. If it was a 'successful' revolution, it was not successful enough, and produced that cycle of revolution and restoration which has dominated French history to the present day. The 1789 Revolution did not create a 'bourgeois society', if this be taken to mean one which conjoined political democracy and the hegemony of a capitalist class; throughout the nineteenth century, heavily conservative elements, centred particularly in the church, rentiers and peasantry, retained a deep-seated influence in government and society. The writings of Saint-Simon and Comte, in their somewhat variant ways, embodied and gave expression to this precarious balance of liberal and conservative influences. Both perceived this as a transitory situation, and both looked forward to a new and more 'stable' order in the future. Their divergent conceptions of this future order are among the major problematic issues which Durkheim sought to resolve in his sociology. Is the emergent form of society to be one in which there is a single 'class' of *industriels*, where equality of opportunity will prevail, and in which government is reduced to the 'administration of things', not of persons; or is it to be the hierocratic, corporate state of Comte's *Positive Polity*?

As in the writings of Max Weber, the problem, not of 'order' in a generic sense,[26] but of the form of *authority* appropriate to a modern industrial state, is the leading theme in Durkheim's work. But whereas in Germany a different combination of political and economic circumstances helped to establish a tradition of *Nationalökonomie* which led liberal scholars of Weber's generation to an overwhelming concern with 'capitalism',[27] in France the problem was posed within the context of the long-standing confrontation between the 'individualism' embodied in the ideals of the Revolution, and the moral claims of the Catholic hierocracy. Thus the Third Republic certainly came into being amid an atmosphere of crisis – and of class conflict as manifest in the Paris Commune and its repression – but, so it seemed to Durkheim and his liberal contemporaries, the disasters of 1870–1 also provided both the possibility and the necessity of at last completing the process of social and political change which had been initiated in the Revolution almost a century earlier. In his sociological works, Durkheim was not, as is often stated, concerned above all with the nature of 'anomie', but rather with exploring the complex interrelationships between the *three* dimensions of 'anomie', 'egoism' and 'individualism'. *The Division of Labour* states Durkheim's thinking on this matter, and he did not afterwards deviate from the position set out therein, although he did not fully elaborate certain of its implications until later. The most important substantive conclusion which Durkheim reached in *The Division of Labour* is that organic solidarity presupposes *moral* individualism: in other words, that 'it is wrong to contrast a society which comes from a community of beliefs (mechanical solidarity) to one which has a cooperative basis (organic solidarity), according only to the first a moral character, and seeing in the latter simply an economic grouping'.[28] The immediate source of this moral individualism, as Durkheim made clear in his contribution to the public discussion of the Dreyfus affair,[29] is in the ideals generated by the 1789 Revolution. Moral individualism is by no means the same as egoism (i.e. the pursuit of self-interest), as is posited in classical economic theory and utilitarian philosophy. The growth of individualism, deriving from the expansion of organic solidarity, is not to be necessarily equated with anomie (the anomic condition of the division of labour is a *transitory* phenomenon, which stems precisely from the fact that the formation of contracts is insufficiently governed by moral regulation). Thus the social order which is coming into being demands the realization or *concrete implementation* of the ideals of the French Revolution.

This theory, therefore, provided a resolution of the issues separating Saint-Simon's and Comte's otherwise closely comparable views.[30] The emergent social order is certainly to be one founded in the complex division of labour entailed by modern industry – as specified by Saint-Simon; Comte was mistaken in supposing that the condition of unity in traditional societies, the existence of a strongly formed *conscience collective*, is necessary to the modern type of society.[31] But it is not to be a society in which authority will be confined to the 'administration of things', as Saint-Simon envisaged:[32] on the contrary, the division of labour in industry must be infused with *moral* controls, and these must be under the general moral guidance of the state.

Durkheim's assessment of the underlying factors in the Dreyfus affair, as well as his own active participation in it, focus these issues with great clarity. The immediate stimulus to Durkheim's discussion of the questions raised by the Dreyfus controversy was the publication of an article by Brunetière, the Catholic apologist, who accused the *dreyfusards* of fostering moral anarchy by rejecting traditional values in favour of an egoistic rationalism.[33] Durkheim replied by asserting the existence of a radical distinction between 'egoism' and 'rationalist individualism'. It is true that no society can be built upon the pursuit of self-interest; but the latter is not at all the same thing as 'individualism'. Individualism must not be identified with 'the utilitarian egoism of Spencer and of the economists'.[34] Indeed, Durkheim continued, there would be no need to attack individualism if it possessed no other representatives, for utilitarian theory is in the process of dying a natural death. Individualism is in fact quite distinct from this: it is not merely a 'philosophical construction', but is a living part of the social organization of contemporary society. It is 'that which the Declaration of the Rights of Man sought, more or less successfully, to give a formula to; that which is currently taught in our schools, and which has become the basis of our moral catechism'.[35] This is, in an important respect, the very opposite of egoism. It involves, not the glorification of self-interest but of the welfare of others: it is the morality of cooperation. Individualism, or the 'cult of the individual', is founded upon sentiments of sympathy for human suffering, a desire for equality and for justice. It in no sense derives from egoism, but is social in origin. The growth of individualism does not, therefore, intrinsically promote anomie, *the decay* of moral authority.

The critical evaluation of Durkheim's political thought

In this paper I have stressed the central role of Durkheim's political thought in his sociology as a whole. Consequently any attempt at a critical assessment of his political ideas must be placed within a broader evaluation of his writings in sociology and social philosophy. The 'orthodox' interpretation of Durkheim readily delivers him up to a number of apparently conclusive criticisms, such as that he emphasized the importance of cohesion or *consensus* in society to the almost total exclusion of conflict; that he failed to develop a theory of institutions, because he concentrated above all upon the relationship between society and the individual, neglecting intermediate structures; that he displayed a lack of concern with the role of political power, since he was overwhelmingly interested in the nature of moral ideals; and that 'he did not duly appreciate the import of social innovation and social change because he was preoccupied with social order and equilibrium'.[36] While each of these accusations contains an element of truth, none of them can be sustained in the sweeping fashion in which they are frequently made. Those who interpret Durkheim's work as being essentially concerned with a 'conservative' 'inclination to maintain the existing order of things'[37] – and such a view, although implicit, is as much contained in Parsons's basically sympathetic account of Durkheim's writings as it is in those of other authors, such as Coser or Zeitlin, who are heavily critical of Durkheim – have inevitably tended to present a misleading picture of Durkheim's position on each of these dimensions.

Both in political temper and in sociological conviction, Durkheim was an opponent of revolutionary thought. Evolution, not revolution, provided the framework for his conception of social change: he frequently emphasized that significant change only takes place through the cumulation of long-term processes of social development. His refusal to see in class conflict the mechanism which would generate a radical social transformation separated him conclusively from Marxism and from any other type of revolutionary activism. But to say this is not at all to say that he neglected the phenomenon of social conflict, or of class conflict, or that he sought to accommodate them to his theoretical position by denying the reality of the aspirations of the working class. His constantly echoed assertion that 'the social problem' (i.e., the problem of class conflict) cannot be solved through purely economic measures, because of the 'instability' of human appetites, has to be read against his equally emphatic stress upon the basic changes in the economic order which have to be made to complete the institutionalization of moral individualism. The reality behind the occurrence of class conflict is the new desire for self-realization and equality of opportunity of those in the lower socio-economic strata: this cannot be repressed but demands ultimately the abolition of all economic and social barriers to 'external equality', to 'everything that can even indirectly shackle the free unfolding of the social force that each carries in himself'.[38] Like Marx, Durkheim anticipated the emergence of a society in which class conflict would be eliminated, and where the element of coercion in the division of labour would be eradicated. But it is wholly mistaken to regard this as a scheme which absolved Durkheim from a concern with conflict. Indeed, the reverse is nearer to the truth: that the starting-point of his sociology was an attempt to analyse the sources of the conflicts which have characterized the expansion of industrialism.

Since the publication of *Leçons de sociologie*, it has become impossible to maintain that Durkheim gave no attention to intermediate institutions in society. He once defined sociology as the 'science of social institutions',[39] and it is evident that this was in fact central to his thought. *Leçons de sociologie* makes it particularly clear, however, that a profound transformation of the institutional organization of traditional forms of society is a necessary concomitant of the transition from mechanical to organic solidarity; the relationship between the state and the *corporations* is seen to be fundamental to the modern social order. It is in these terms that Durkheim sought to tackle the question of political power. Although it can hardly be granted that he dealt satisfactorily with the nature and sources of political power, it is quite clearly not the case that he merely ignored the issues posed by it. Finally, . . . not only is it fallacious to hold that 'he did not duly appreciate the import of social innovation and social change', but it is not possible to understand the main themes in his work without locating it within the scheme of social development, set out in *The Division of Labour*, which underlay all of his major writings. In one of his earliest works, a dissertation on Montesquieu, Durkheim established his position on this point. Montesquieu, he showed, 'fails to see that every society embodies conflicting factors, simply because it has gradually emerged from a past form and is tending towards a future one'.[40]

Durkheim frequently asserted that sociology should, at some point, find its justification in practice: that a sociology which had no relevance to practical problems would be a worthless endeavour. It is one of the major tasks of sociology to determine the nascent directions of change which a society at any given time is experiencing, and to show which trends 'should' be fostered as the coming pattern of the future. This closure between the 'is' and the 'ought' Durkheim sought to achieve in terms of his distinction between the 'normal' and 'pathological', conceived on analogy with health and disease in the organism. The theory set out in *The Division of Labour* is founded upon this conception: the work was conceived by Durkheim to show that the ideals of moral individualism correspond to the 'social needs' engendered by the growth of mechanical solidarity – that these ideals are 'normal' to the modern type of society, and hence are to be protected and promoted. No aspect of Durkheim's writings has been more universally rejected than his notion of normality and pathology, and rightly so: even if it were possible to determine 'scientifically' whether or not a given moral norm were a 'necessary' element in the functioning of a particular society, it is altogether another thing to hold this *ipso facto* to be 'desirable'. The questions at issue here are not to be resolved by any sort of appeal to the criteria of health and disease in biology: medicine, in this respect, is a technology to be applied in pursuit of given values. In spite of – or perhaps because of – the fact that the conception of normality was integral to Durkheim's work, he never fully clarified his position in this respect. In his most systematic formulation of the principle, in *The Rules of Sociological Method*, he definitely attempted to establish scientific criteria for the verification of ethical ideals, rejecting the view that 'science can teach us nothing about what we ought to desire'.[41] But, in replying later to critics of these views, he appeared to retract his earlier formulation, indicating that ethics and sociology are concerned with two 'different spheres', and claiming that 'we ask simply that ethical constructions should be preceded by a science of morality which is more methodical than the ordinary speculations of so-called theoretical ethics'.[42]

Durkheim's ambiguity on this matter is reflected in his failure to deal in an explicit manner with the relationship between sociological analysis and political intervention in the interests of securing practical social change. As Marx realized,[43] this demands a dialectical conception of the dual character of knowledge as a means of knowing the world, and at the same time as a mode of changing it. When pursued to its logical consequence, this leads to a stress upon the directly *political* role of sociology. But, although Durkheim wished to relate sociology to practical concerns, he also sought to advance a conception of the 'neutral' character of sociological analysis as a 'natural science of society'. Although this was no doubt reinforced by his personal characteristics and his disdain for the squabbles of party politics, his general aloofness from politics was certainly supported by this position. The result was that, in practice, the relevance of sociology to the achievement of real social change remained obscure. Durkheim attempted to escape from this difficulty by placing stress upon the 'partial' character of sociological knowledge: the emphasis that the advance of sociology is slow and painstaking, because it must conform to the rigorous criteria of scientific validation. Since the needs of life in an everyday social and political context require immediate decisions and policies, the relevance of the 'scientific' knowledge of the sociologist has definite limitations. But his own writing, often dealing with the broadest issues of social organization and social change, belies this sort of modest prescription – as, indeed, does the more abstract analysis of the 'therapeutic' role of sociology in diagnosing what is 'normal' and what is 'pathological' at given stages of societal evolution.

In Durkheim's writings this uneasy tension between theory and practice finds expression in a constant tendency, as Bendix has noted,[44] to shift from the analytical to the optative. Durkheim's discussions of extant reality frequently slide into a portrayal of what he expects to be the case in the future, because of what is supposedly entailed by the 'normal' conditions of functioning of a society or social institution. Thus the development and strengthening of the occupational associations is due to occur because this is demanded by the 'normal' operation of the division of labour. This analysis is not based upon an empirical demonstration that there is a discernible trend towards the emergence of such *corporations*: it derives from the attempt to implement the notion that the functionally necessary supplies the criterion of what is desirable – in this case, that 'the absence of all corporative institution creates . . . a void whose importance it is difficult to exaggerate'. As with all of Durkheim's attempts to diagnose 'normality', this barely avoids degenerating into crude teleology: the 'evil', the 'malady *totius substantia*' of the anomic division of labour, calls into being the 'remedy' of the development of the *corporations*.[45]

The shortcomings of Durkheim's writings in these very general respects are undoubtedly related to inadequacies in his conceptual treatment of the state and political power. While it is not the case that he 'ignored' the problem of power, or more specifically the role of force, in society, it is true that he established the basic framework of his thought, in *The Division of Labour*, before he developed a systematic analysis of the state and politics. His subsequent exposition of the partial 'independence' of state power only effected a restricted modification of the theory of the division of labour. While this enabled him to deal more adequately with the existence of coercive power it failed to deal with a really consequential point:

what are the *conditions* which generate the development of an absolute state? The analyses given in *Leçons de sociologie* and *Deux lois de l'évolution pénale* leave this as a residual factor: Durkheim nowhere undertook to show what *determines* the degree to which the state is able to 'separate itself', from society. He continually underlined the point that every form of state, weak or strong, is rooted in civil society, and nourished from it; but he failed to analyse in any detail at all the nature of these connections. Consequently there is in Durkheim's writings no systematic treatment of the mechanisms of legitimation in politics.[46] Political power is implicitly assumed to be an outcome of a pre-established moral ascendancy of the state: the more transcendent or 'religious' the moral basis of the state, the more absolute its power. But this conception allows no means of dealing with the tension between legitimation and power which is of crucial importance in all political systems: power, and force, in other words, are frequently *means* for the creation of values by dominant strata.

In this Durkheim certainly remained a prisoner of the main intellectual sources in which his thought is steeped. The concept of the state which he employed is a clear indication of this, and while he used it to attempt to break away from Comte's treatment of the state, his own conceptual formulation actually here resembles that of Comte.[47] The state is defined as the 'organ of social thought', the 'ego' of the *conscience collective*. Durkheim specifically rejected the notion that the state is primarily an executive agency. The main task of the state is to be 'a special organ whose responsibility it is to work out certain representations which hold good for the collectivity'; the 'true meaning' of the state 'consists not in exterior action, in making changes, but in deliberation'.[48] His treatment of democracy, of course, is intimately tied in with this conceptualization. In analysing the role of the occupational associations, he certainly saw them as 'balancing' the power of the state. But the view that an integral element in democratic government is the sharing of power, as he made fully explicit, is to him not a viable one. He rejected not only the classical conception of 'direct democracy', but also what has today come to be called the 'theory of democratic élitism'. A minority must govern, in any developed society, and it makes little odds how this minority comes to power: the activities of an aristocracy might often conform more closely to the will of the people than that of an elected élite. The difference between a system in which 'the governing minority are established once and for all', and one in which 'the minority that carries the day may be beaten tomorrow and replaced by another' is only 'slight'.[49] Democracy, for Durkheim, thus becomes a matter of the interplay of sentiments and ideas between government and mass; his discussion of democratic government contains no developed examination of the functioning of political parties, or of parliament, or of the franchise, and indeed these considerations are regarded as of purely minor significance.

The weaknesses inherent in this viewpoint are nowhere more clearly exposed than in Durkheim's discussion of the German state in *L'Allemagne au-dessus de tout*. As has been indicated previously, the weight of Durkheim's theoretical perspective directed his thinking towards asserting the basic compatibility, in the modern world, between national ideals, patriotism, and the growth of a pan-national European community. Characteristically, his response to the growth of German militarism – since the latter fell outside the expectations generated by his standpoint – was to treat it as a 'pathological' phenomenon. This 'pathology' is explained by Durkheim as a 'moral disorder' which is manifest in a grandiosity of national ambition such as is revealed in the ideological writings of Treitschke. The effect of Durkheim's analysis, however, is to consider power *itself* only from the moral aspect, in terms of the immoderate emphasis which Treitschke places upon the supremacy of the state. In point of fact, German militarism can only be properly interpreted in terms of the structural properties of the nineteenth-century German state – of the leading part played by Prussian military strength in securing the political unification of the country, and the continued domination of the landowning élite in government. These made Germany into a 'power-state', as Max Weber well understood, and it is, of course, no accident that Weber's conceptualization of the state, which eschews any possibility of defining the state in moral terms, places primacy upon just those aspects which Durkheim underplayed: the successful claim to monopoly of the legitimate deployment of force, and the existence of fixed territorial boundaries.[50]

Unlike Weber, Durkheim undeniably belongs to those traditions of nineteenth-century social thought which subordinate the state to society.[51] While he rejected the notion of the 'disappearance' of the state, and held instead that an expansion of the purview of the state is inevitable in modern society, he did not substantially break with the assumption that it is the movement of the 'infrastructure' which is of decisive significance in analysing social change. 'Infrastructure' here, of course, refers to the division of labour. In assessing Durkheim's theory of the division of labour in relation to his political sociology, it is important to evaluate what he shared in common with socialism (as he defined it).

Although Parsons has claimed that, according to his own definition of these terms, Durkheim's political sociology marks him out as being closer to 'communism' rather than 'socialism',[52] it is surely evident that the reverse is true. Communism, for Durkheim, expresses the constantly reappearing, but ultimately futile, hope that human egoism can be eradicated: it is thus essentially both a-historical and unrealizable. Socialism, on the other hand, according to Durkheim, is an expression of the consciousness that radical changes have and are occurring in contemporary societies, and that these changes have brought about a condition of crisis which presses for resolution. This consciousness is filtered by the social circumstances of which it is an expression. That is to say, it reflects a condition of society in which economic relationships have come to dominate social life; hence it assumes that the remedy for the modern crisis must be purely economic. The flaw in all socialist doctrines is that they fail to see that the resolution of the crisis must entail moral reorganization, whereby the primacy of the 'economic' over the 'social' will be readjusted in favour of the latter.[53] But they are correct in holding that regulation of the capitalist market is necessary. Although Durkheim repudiated the possibility of reorganizing capitalism by revolutionary means, it is an integral part of his ideas that the forced division of labour, the exploitative relationship of capital and wage-labour, must be eliminated. This is to be accomplished by the disappearance of the inheritance of property:

> Now inheritance as an institution results in men being born rich or poor; that is to say, there are two main classes of society, linked by all sorts of intermediate classes: the one which in order to live has to make its services acceptable to the other at whatever the cost; the other class which can do without these services, because it can call upon certain resources . . . as long as such sharp class differences exist in

society, fairly effective palliatives may lessen the injustices of contracts; but in principle, the system operates in conditions which do not allow of justice.[54]

The abolition of inherited property is a process which is to take place through the action of the state. Although Durkheim was not entirely unambiguous on this point, it seems that he did not envisage the abolition of private property as such,[55] but rather that differentials in possession of property should be entirely determined by differences in the services which men render to society. Functional importance in the division of labour is to govern property rights. This is a 'work of justice' which has to be accomplished if the morality of individualism is to have regulative force in modern society: the advance of moral individualism is incompatible with a social order in which class situation determines from birth an individual's position in the occupational structure. Thus there is an intrinsic connection between the elimination of the 'forced' division of labour and the amelioration of the 'anomic' division of labour. What is required in order to reduce anomie is not simply the imposition of regulation upon the existing market system: this would only lead to an intensification of class conflict. 'It is not sufficient that there be rules . . . for sometimes the rules themselves are the cause of evil.' The morality of organic solidarity demands major economic changes, which create a system in which there is a free or 'spontaneous' ordering of individuals in the division of labour, such that no 'obstacle, of whatever nature, prevents them from occupying the place in the social framework which is compatible with their faculties'.[56]

Seen in this light, it is hardly justified to argue that Durkheim's theory of the division of labour neglects the existence of interest conflict in modern societies. While it envisages the future development of an order in which such conflict will be, if not eliminated altogether, radically reduced, it is no different in this respect to that stream of thought which is generally taken to be the main source of 'conflict theory': Marxism. The real weaknesses in Durkheim's theory at this point derive from his failure, as noted previously, to work out the conditions under which the division of labour is linked to definite types of political formation. Thus, according to him, the elimination of the 'forced' division of labour is to be accomplished under the general patronage of the state. That basic changes of this sort might not be possible without a radical *transformation* of the existing system of political power is not seriously considered. It is just this premise, by contrast, which is built into Marx's conception: the class relations of the market are focused and stabilized by the capitalist state. No basic change in the class structure, in property relations, is capable of being achieved through the existing political apparatus: that is to say, apart from political change of a profound nature.

Conclusion

Durkheim's sociology was rooted in an attempt to re-interpret the claims of political liberalism in the face of a twin challenge: from an anti-rationalist conservatism on the one hand, and from socialism on the other. Each of these constituted major traditions in French social thought, and each of them, in the early part of the nineteenth century, represented a response to the legacy of the French Revolution. Durkheim borrowed elements from both in an attempt to transcend them through a revitalized liberal republicanism which would fully realize the structural changes in society which had been promised, but not achieved, by the Revolution. What has been remarked of Jaurès is an apt and exact description of Durkheim's viewpoint: he was concerned with, 'not the negation but the completion of the bourgeois Republic, the extension of the Rights of Man from the political to the economic and social spheres'.[57]

(iv)   Marx, Weber and capitalism*

Weber and Marx: the analytic problem

Weber's critique of Marx was sophisticated, and was not simply an abstract analysis of the 'logic' of Marx's theories, but embodied the very substance of Weber's studies of history and society. This very fact, however, means that Weber's own explicit evaluations of Marx's views cannot be regarded as the sole source of evidence on the matter. That Weber's own remarks on *The Protestant*

---

* *Studies in Social and Political Theory*, pp.195–203.

Ethic, for instance, are not completely unambiguous is indicated by the confusion over the objectives of the work in the large literature which has surrounded the subject since the first publication of Weber's essay.[58] Obviously, moreover, the evaluation of the differences between Marx and Weber must depend upon an accurate evaluation of the characteristic views of the former. In order to make clear the substance of Marx's basic theoretical position, it is necessary to touch briefly upon some themes in Marx's writings which, thanks to the enormous body of secondary works written on Marx since the Second World War, have by now become very familiar.

Much of the post-war literature on Marx has centred upon the writings of the 'young Marx': that is, prior to the completion of *The German Ideology* (1846). The debate over the relevance of these early writings to Marx's mature works will certainly continue; but it cannot be doubted that, firstly, there are, at the very least, certain definite threads of continuity which run through the whole of Marx's work, and that, secondly, some of the early writings allow us to clarify what these continuities are.[59] Marx did not ever write a systematic exposition of his 'materialism'. But certain of his early writings make it absolutely clear that his conception of his materialistic approach to history is quite different from what he called 'perceptual materialism'.[60] Marx, in common with the other 'Young Hegelians', began his intellectual development from the standpoint of the critique of religion, derived from a radicalization of Hegel, and based largely upon the thought of David Strauss and Feuerbach. Feuerbach's philosophy was founded upon a reversal of the major premise of Hegel's system. In place of Hegel's idealism, Feuerbach substituted his own version of materialism, stating bluntly that the starting-point of the study of man must be 'real man' living in the 'real material world'.[61] Feuerbach's writing remained mainly confined to the examination of religion: by 'standing Hegel on his feet',[62] he tried to show that the divine is an illusory product of the real. God is an idealized projection of man himself; God is the mythical projection of man's most cherished values, man alienated from his own (potential) self-perfection.

The consequence of Feuerbach's position is that religion is a symbolic 'representation' of human aspirations, and that to eliminate human self-alienation all that needs to be done is for religion to be de-mystified, and placed on a rational level. Marx rapidly perceived what appeared to him as fundamental defects in this view. Feuerbach's errors were, first, to speak of 'man' in the abstract, and thus to fail to perceive that men only exist within the context of particular societies which change their structure in the course of historical development; and, second, to treat ideas or 'consciousness' as simply the 'consequence' of human activities in the 'material' world. In Marx's words: 'The chief defect of all previous materialism (including Feuerbach's) is that the object, actuality, sensuousness, is conceived only in the form of the *object of perception*, but not as *sensuous human activity, practice*, not subjectively.'[63]

Marx referred to his materialism only as 'the guiding thread' in his studies: ideologies are 'rooted in the material conditions of life', but this does not entail that there is a universal or unilateral relationship between the 'real foundation' of society (the relations of production) and 'legal and political superstructures'.[64] On the contrary, the specific conclusion which Marx reached in criticizing Feuerbach was that ideas are social products, which cannot be explained by the philosopher who stands outside of history, but only by the analysis of particular forms of society.[65] We must, reject, Marx insisted, any kind of 'recipe or scheme . . . for neatly trimming the epochs of history', and must 'set about the observation and arrangement – the real depiction – of our historical material.'[66]

Where Marx did generalize about the relationship between ideology and material 'substructure', this was in terms of the specification that the class system is the main mediating link between the two. The class structure of society exerts a determinate effect upon which ideas *assume prominence* in that society. This is the sense of Marx's proposition that the ruling ideas in any epoch are the ideas of the ruling class.[67] It should be pointed out that, even in Feuerbach's theory, religion is something more than merely a complete reflection of material reality: it also provides values and ideals towards which men should strive. God is man as he ought to be, and therefore the image of the deity holds out the hope of what man could *become*. Marx took over this notion from Feuerbach, but mated it with the dialectical conception that it is the reciprocal interaction of such religious ideas with the social actions of 'earthly men' which must be examined. This reciprocity can be understood in terms of analysing the historical development of societies;

we cannot understand the relationship between ideology and society if we 'abstract from the historical process'.[68] There is no question, then, but that Marx recognized both that ideologies may have
a partially 'internal' autonomous development, and that the degree
to which this is so depends upon factors particular to specific
societies, which in every case have to be studied in empirical detail. This is both consistent with his general conception of materialism, and is evidenced in his more detailed studies.[69] Marx's
position, in other words, is not incompatible with recognition of
the unique characteristics and influence of ascetic Protestantism in
Europe.

All this is, by now, quite well known; what has not been so
generally appreciated is that even in matters of detail, Marx's
discussion of the course of historical development in Europe is in
several ways strikingly close to Weber's analysis: this is a fact which
has only become fully apparent with the publication of the draft-
notes (*Grundrisse*) which Marx wrote for *Capital* in 1857–8. Marx
acknowledged the importance of the early forms of capitalism
which developed in Rome, and his explanation of why these led
to a 'dead-end' is quite similar to that subsequently set out by
Weber.[70] Marx pointed out that certain of the conditions – including the existence of a nascent capitalist class – which played an
essential part in the development of capitalism in Western Europe
at a later period, were already present in Rome. Among the factors
he isolated as significant in inhibiting the emergence of full-scale
capitalism in Rome is that there was strong ideological pressure
against the accumulation of wealth for its own sake: 'Wealth does
not appear as the aim of production . . . The inquiry is always
about what kind of property creates the best citizens. Wealth as
an end in itself appears only among a few trading peoples.'[71]
Wealth was valued, not intrinsically, but for the 'private enjoy-
ment' it could bring; moreover, labour in general was regarded
with contempt, and as not worthy of free men.

Marx recognized that there existed numerous prior forms of
capitalism before the emergence of bourgeois society in post-medieval Europe. Thus mercantile capital has often existed – as in Rome
– in societies in which the dominant mode of production is not
capitalist. Mercantile operations have usually been carried on by
marginal groups, such as the Jews. Mercantile capital has existed 'in
the most diverse forms of society, at the most diverse stages of the

development of the productive forces'.[72] There are cases of societies, other than Rome, where certain segments of the social structure have been quite highly evolved, but where the lack of
development of other sectors has limited the ultimate level of
economic advancement. Marx quoted the instance of ancient
Peru, which in certain respects had a developed economy, but
which was kept to a low level of development by the geographical
isolation of the society, and by the lack of a monetary system.[73]

Marx's views on the emergence and significance of Christianity in
the development of the European societies have to be inferred from
various oblique statements in his critiques of Hegel and the 'Young
Hegelians'. As a close student of Hegel, Marx was obviously aware
of the overriding importance which historians and philosophers
attributed to Christianity in the West. Marx did not question the
validity of this. What he did attack was the idealistic standpoint
within which the influence of Christianity was analysed. Thus he
objected to Stirner's treatment of the rise of early Christianity in
that it is conducted wholly upon the level of ideas.[74] Christianity
arose, Marx stated, as a religion of wandering, uprooted vagrants,
and the causes of its expansion have to be related to the internal
decay of the Roman Empire: 'the Hellenic and Roman world
perished, spiritually in Christianity and materially in the migration
of the peoples'.[75] The Christian ethical outlook formed a vital new
moral current, contrasting with the moral decadence of Rome.
Christianity substituted for Roman pantheism the conception of a
single universal God, whose authority is founded upon uniquely
Christian notions of sin and salvation. In the later evolution of
Christianity in Europe, the Reformation provided a similar moral
regeneration in relation to an internally disintegrating feudal society. 'Luther . . . overcame bondage out of devotion by replacing it
by bondage out of conviction. He shattered faith in authority
because he restored the authority of faith . . . He freed man from
outer religiosity because he made religiosity the inner man.'[76]

To suppose that Marx was unaware of the 'ascetic' and 'rational'
character of modern European capitalism is to miss some of the
most basic premises upon which his analysis and critique of bourgeois society is founded. The 'rationalizing' character of capitalism
is manifest most directly, for Marx, in the utter dominance of
money in human social relationships, and in the pursuit of money
as an end in itself. Money is the epitome of human self-alienation

under capitalism, since it reduces all human qualities to quantitative values of exchange[77] Capitalism thus has a 'universalizing' character, which breaks down the particularities of traditional cultures: 'capital develops irresistibly beyond national barriers and prejudices . . . it destroys the self-satisfaction confined within narrow limits and based upon a traditional mode of life and reproduction.'[78] Capitalism is 'ascetic' in that the actions of capitalists are based upon self-renunciation and the continual re-investment of profits. This is manifest, Marx pointed out, in the theory of political economy: 'Political economy, the science of wealth, is, therefore, at the same time, the science of renunciation, of privation and saving . . . Its true ideal is the ascetic usurious miser and the ascetic but productive slave.'[79] The pursuit of wealth for its own sake is a phenomenon which is, as a general moral ethos, found only within modern capitalism. Marx was as specific on this matter as Weber: 'The passion for wealth as such is a distinctive development; that is to say, it is something other than the instinctive thirst for particular goods such as clothes, arms, jewellery, women, wine . . . The taste for possessions can exist without money; the thirst for self-enrichment is the product of a definite social development, it is not natural, but historical.'[80]

The point to be stressed, however, is that in broad terms Marx's conception of, and empirical treatment of, the role of ideology in society is quite compatible with the more detailed studies undertaken by Weber of the sociology of religion. Marx did not study religion in any detail because, in breaking with the 'Young Hegelians' and with Feuerbach, and in perceiving the need to begin to analyse sociologically the relationships between economy, politics and ideology, Marx effectively overcame – in terms of his own objectives – the need to subject religion to detailed analysis. The 'Young Hegelians', as Marx made clear in *The Holy Family*, continued to devote most of their efforts to the critique of religion, and thus always remained imprisoned within a world-view which was, even if only negatively, a religious one.[81]

To emphasize the general theoretical congruity of much of what Marx and Weber wrote on the history and origins of capitalism is *obviously not* to argue that their views are wholly identical, either in relation to particular problems or in respect of more general issues of social and political theory. It is evident that Marx, while disavowing 'the *passe-partout* of a general historical – philosophical

theory whose main quality is that of being superhistorical',[82] sought
to impose a pattern on historical development which Weber treated
as quite impermissible. The concept of charisma, and the basic role
which it plays in Weber's sociology, expresses Weber's conviction
that human history is not (as Marx believed it to be) rational. The
attribution of a discoverable rationality to history is an essential
element in the whole of Marx's thought, and is the main tie by
which he always remained bound to Hegel. But charisma is specifically irrational; thus the revolutionary dynamic in history, which for
Weber is constituted by the periodic emergence of charismatic
movements, cannot be connected to any overall rational pattern
in the historical development of man. Moreover, by stressing the
importance of class, and thus of economic interests, in social development, Marx tended to assimilate economic and political power
much more than Weber.'[83] This is very definitely a difference of
fundamental significance between the two authors. Nevertheless,
the divergence here must not be over-exaggerated.[84] Marx anticipated Weber, for example, in recognizing a parallel between the
organization of professional armies and the separation of the
labourer from his product under modern capitalism. Thus Marx
noted: 'In Rome there existed in the army a mass already quite
distinct from the people, disciplined to labour . . . it sold to the
State the whole of its labour-time for wages . . . as the worker
does with the capitalist.'[85]

Conclusion

My objective in this paper has been to separate out several basic
strands in the relationship between the writings of Marx and Weber. I have tried to make it clear that the tendency to assimilate
these together as forming a blanket 'critique of Marx has led many
commentators to oversimplify Weber's assessment of 'historical
materialism'. It has become something of a truism to say that the
'founders' of modern sociology – Weber, Pareto, and Mosca in
particular – developed their theories, at least in part, as 'refuta-
tions' of Marx. Each of these authors has at some time been called
'the bourgeois Marx'. This label, however, is inapt in the sense that
it implies that their work represents nothing more than a bourgeois
response to Marxism. It was this, but it was also much more. Thus

Weber's relationship to Marx and to Marxist thought cannot be assessed along a single dimension of 'confirmation' or 'refutation'; Weber's historical studies both destroy some of the cruder Marxist interpretations of historical development, and at the same time, *partly* vindicate Marx against his own professed disciples.

Weber wrote at a period when the character of the leading Western European countries generally, and that of Germany more specifically, had changed considerably from the time at which Marx formed his main views. All of the economically advanced societies of the West, by the turn of the twentieth century, had reached a high degree of economic maturity without experiencing the revolutionary reorganization which Marx expected. In Weber's time Marx's thought was carried, in Germany, by the Social Democratic Party. 'Historical materialism' came to be largely identified, in the eyes of Weber and other liberal critics of Marxism, as well as by Marxists themselves, with the systematic exposition of Engels in *Anti-Dühring* and later, *The Dialectics of Nature*.[86] While some commentators have exaggerated the difference between the thought of Marx and Engels,[87] the implications of the position which Engels took in these works are quite definitely at variance with the conception central to most of Marx's writing. By transferring the dialectic to nature, Engels obscured the most essential element of Marx's work, which was 'the dialectical relationship of subject and object in the historical process'.[88] In doing so, Engels helped to stimulate the notion that ideas simply 'reflect' material reality.[89] The political quietism of the Social Democratic Party – which Weber accurately perceived behind its revolutionary phraseology – was bound up with the general adoption of such an outlook, which made possible the preservation of a revolutionary posture in a set of social circumstances which had diverged substantially from the pattern of development anticipated by Marx. The wheel thus in a way came almost full circle. At the risk of oversimplifying what is actually a complicated question, it could be said that Weber's critique of Marxism, as regards the role of ideas in history, in fact came close to restating, in vast detail, certain elements of the original Marxian conception.

This went hand in hand, ironically, with a rejection of certain key aspects of Marx's analysis of contemporary capitalism, and of the latter's hopes for a future form of radically new society. Marx, writing a generation before Weber, believed that capitalism could,

and would, be transcended by a new form of society. Weber wrote
with the hindsight of having witnessed the formation of industrial
capitalism in Germany in quite different circumstances from Britain
or France. Weber's appreciation of this fact was one element in his
thought allowing him, while drawing heavily from Marx, to escape
from the strait-jacket which the followers of Marx in the Social
Democratic Party sought to impose upon history in the name of
historical materialism.

But it might be held that, in his analysis of the imminent trend of
development of capitalism, Weber himself fell prey to a sort of
materialistic determinism of his own. Weber perceived a primary
irrationality within capitalism: the 'formal' rationality of bureaucracy, while it makes possible the technical implementation of large-
scale administrative tasks, is 'substantively' irrational in that it
contravenes some of the most distinctive values of Western civilization. But he foresaw no way of breaking through this irrationality: the future holds out only the likelihood of the increasing
submergence of human autonomy and individuality within an
ever-expanding bureaucratization of modern life.[90] For Marx, on
the other hand, the essential irrationality of capitalism – the contradiction between the alienative impoverishment of the individual
and the immense potential, opportunities for self-fulfilment offered
by modern industry – creates the very conditions for the movement
to a form of society in which this irrationality will be overcome.
Undoubtedly there are problems of major significance for modern
social philosophy which stem from the question of how far the
alienative characteristic which Marx attributed to capitalism as a
specific form of class society, in fact derive from a bureaucratic
rationality which is a necessary concomitant of industrial society,
whether it be 'capitalist' or 'socialist'. Does the future promise only
the progressive expansion of an order in which, as Weber wrote,
'the technical and economic conditions of machine production
determine the lives of all the individuals who are born into this
mechanism . . . with irresistible force',[91] or is there a realistic
possiblity that, as Marcuse has expressed it 'not "pure", formal,
technical reason but the reason of domination erects the "shell of
bondage", and that the consummation of technical reason can well
become the instrument for the *liberation* of man'?[92]

Notes

1. Karl Marx, *Capital*, vol.1 (London: Lawrence & Wishart, 1970) p.185.
2. T.B. Bottomore, *Karl Marx: Early Writings* (New York: McGraw-Hill, 1964) pp.126–7).
3. Anthony Giddens, *Central Problems in Social Theory*, pp.188ff.
4. Habermas has accentuated this very strongly in many of his publications. I have a strong sympathy with the over-all trend both of his critique of Marx and with some of his conceptions of what the 'good society' could and should look like. But I think he was led up a wrong alley in basing his criticism of Marx on the distinction between 'labour' and 'interaction', accusing Marx of reducing the latter to the former. I have argued the case for this in my 'Labour' and 'interaction' in John B. Thompson and David Held (eds), *Habermas: Critical Debates* (London: Macmillan, 1982).
5. Louis Althusser, *Lenin and Philosophy* (London: New Left Books, 1971), and other works.
6. Anthony Giddens, *The Class Structure of the Advanced Societies*, pp.216–19.
7. Cf. Roberta Hamilton, *The Liberation of Women* (London: Allen & Unwin, 1975).
8. Giddens, *Central Problems in Social Theory*, Chapter 5.
9. Cf. Jean Baudrillard, *Le miroir de la production* (Tournai: Casterman, 1973).
10. On Habermas, see especially John Thompson, *Critical Hermeneutics* (Cambridge: Cambridge University Press, 1981), and various of the contributions in Thompson and Held (eds), *Habermas: Critical Debates*.
11. For an analysis of the problem of German 'backwardness' as related to the intellectual relationship between Marx and Weber, see Anthony Giddens, 'Marx, Weber, and the Development of Capitalism', *Sociology*, vol.iv, 1970. A Marxist treatment of the development of German philosophy and sociology in this context is given in Georg Lukács, *Die Zerstörung der Vernunft* (Berlin; Aufbau-Verlag, 1955).
12. See H.H. Gerth and C. Wright Mills (eds), *From Max Weber: Essays in Sociology* (New York: Galaxy, 1958) pp.382, 384. I have slightly amended the translation.
13. Max Weber, *Die Verhältnisse der Landarbeiter im ostelbischen Deutschland* (Leipzig; Dunover V. Humblot, 1982) p.798. It is quite misleading to say as Eugene Fleischmann does, 'De Weber à Nietzsche', *Archives européennes de sociologie*, vol.v, 1964, p.194, that 'Weber conceived most of his major works with the aim of "verifying" the correctness of the Marxian theory of the relations between infrastructure and superstructure'.
14. Quoted in Eduard Baumgarten (ed.), *Max Weber, Werk und Person* (Tübingen: Mohr-Siebeck, 1964) p.607.
15. Quotations all from Gerth J.C.B. Mohr, and Wright Mills (eds), *From Max Weber*.

16. Max Weber, *Gesammelte politische Schriften* (Tübingen: Mohr-Siebeck, 1958) pp.543–4. My translation [of the standard collected edition of Weber's political writings – Ed.]. A different version appears in Gerth and Wright Mills (eds), *From Max Weber*, p.124.

17. Gerth and Wright Mills (eds), *From Max Weber*, pp.384–5.

18. Max Weber, *Economy and Society*, 3 vols (New York Bedminster Press, 1968) vol.I pp.55–6.

19. Gerth and Wright Mills (eds), *From Max Weber*, p.82.

20. Max Weber, *Gesammelte Aufsätze zur Soziologie und Sozialpolitik* (Tübingen: Mohr-Siebeck, 1924) p.508.

21. J.C.B. Mohr, Weber, *Economy and Society*, vol.I, p.239, amended translation.

22. Gerth and Wright Mills (eds), *From Max Weber*, pp.83, 89–90. Weber contrasts this, as he often does, with the development of politics in England, 'where parliament gained supremacy over the monarch'.

23. Weber, *Economy and Society*, vol.I, p.243.

24. Melvin Richter, 'Durkheim's politics and political theory', in Kurt H. Wolff, *Emile Durkheim et al., Essays on Sociology and Philosophy* (New York: Harper's Row, 1964).

25. See Anthony Giddens, *Capitalism and Modern Social Theory*, Chapter 14. Cobban remarks: 'A revolution had laid the foundations of an intensely conservative society, nor is this difficult to understand. The classes which consolidated their victory in the Revolution were the peasant proprietors in the country and the men of property in the towns, neither with any vision beyond the preservation of their own economic interest, conceived in the narrowest and most restrictive sense'. Alfred Cobban, *A History of Modern France* (Harmondsworth: Penguin [New York: Braziller], 1968) vol.2, p.219.

26. Talcott Parsons, *The Structure of Social Action*, 2nd edn (New York: Free Press, 1949) p.307 and *passim*.

27. See the important analysis given in Chapter 14 of Dieter Lindenlaub: *Richtungskämpfe im Verein für Sozialpolitik* (Wiesbaden: Steiner, 1967) pp.272–384; also Anthony Giddens, *Politics and Sociology in the Thought of Max Weber*. As Friedrich Neumann remarked in 1911: '*Ungefähr so wie der Französe sein Thema hat: was ist die grosse Revolution, so haben wir durch unser Nationalschicksal für lange Zeit unser thema bekommen: was ist der Kapitalismus.*' Quoted in Lindenlaub, *Richtungskämpte*, p.280.

28. E. Durkheim, *The Division of Labour in Society* (Glencoe: Free Press, 1964) p.228. (I have modified the translation in this and certain other quotations.)

29. E. Durkheim, L'individualisme et les intellectuels', *Revue bleue*, vol.10, 1898, pp.7–13. A translation appears in Steven Lukes, 'Durkheim's "Individualism and the Intellectuals"', *Political Studies*, vol.17, 1969, pp.14–30.

30. In saying this, of course, I do not wish to hold that Saint-Simon and Comte were the only important influences exerting an important positive influence over Durkheim: other, more immediate influences

were Renouvier, Fustel de Coulanges, and Boutroux.

31. Cf. Alvin W. Gouldner: 'Introduction' to Durkheim's *Socialism and Saint-Simon* (London: Routledge & Negan Paul, 1952 [Kent, Ohio: Antioch Press, 1958]) pp.13–18.

32. Cf., on this point, Durkheim's interpretation of the final phase of Saint-Simon's career, as manifest in the latter's *Nouveau christianisme*, in *Socialism and Saint-Simon*, pp.229 ff.

33. See Lukes, 'Durkheim's "Individualism and the Intellectuals"', pp.15–19.

34. Durkheim, 'L'individualisme et les intellectuels', p.7.

35. Durkheim, 'L'individualisme et les intellectuels', p.8.

36. Lewis A. Coser, 'Durkheim's Conservatism and its Implications for his Sociological Theory', in Kurt H. Wolff, *Emile Durkheim et al., Essays on Sociology and Philosophy*, pp.211–12. Cf. Parsons, '[Durkheim] was almost wholly concerned with what Comte would have called "social statics"', Parsons, *The Structure of Social Action*, p.307.

37. Coser, 'Durkheim's Conservatism and its Implications for his Sociological Theory', p.212.

38. Durkheim, *The Division of Labour in Society* ([Glencoe: Free Press, 1947] London: Macmillan, 1964) p.377.

39. E. Durkheim, *The Rules of Sociological Method* ([Glencoe: Free Press, 1950] London: Macmillan, 1964) pp.lvi.

40. E. Durkheim, *Montesquieu and Rousseau* (Ann Arbor: University of, 1960) p.59.

41. Durkheim, *The Rules of Sociological Method*, p.47.

42. Durkheim's review of Simon Deploige, *Le Conflit de la morale et de la sociologie* (Paris: Institut Supérieur de Philosophie, 1911) in E. Durkheim, *Année sociologique*, vol.12, 1909–12, p.327.

43. See particularly the brief but deservedly famous 'Theses on Feuerbach', in Lloyd D. Easton and Kurt H. Guddat, *Writings of the Young Marx on Philosophy and Society* (New York: Doubleday, 1967) pp.400–402.

44. Reinhard Bendix, 'Social Stratification and the Political Community', *Archives européenes de sociologie*, vol.1, 1960, pp.184ff.

45. Durkheim, *The Division of Labour in Society*, p.29.

46. Cf. Anthony Giddens, '"Power" in the Recent Writings of Talcott Parsons', in Anthony Giddens, *Studies in Social and Political Theory* pp.333–46.

47. Cf. Raymond Aron, *Main Currents in Sociological Thought* (London: Penguin [New York: Basic Books], 1968) p.82ff.

48. E. Durkheim, *Professional Ethics and Civic Morals* (London: Routledge & Kegan Paul, 1957) pp.50–1.

49. Durkheim, *Professional Ethics*, p.78.

50. For background material on Weber's conception of the state, see Anthony Giddens, *Politics and Sociology in the Thought of Max Weber*.

51. See Sheldon S. Wolin, *Politics and Vision* ([Boston: Little, Brown & Co., 1960] London: Allen & Unwin, 1961).

52. Parsons, *The Structure of Social Action*, p.341; but cf. Melvin Richter, 'Durkheim's politics and political theory', p.208.

53. The publication of Marx's early writings has, however, made it apparent that this thesis of Durkheim's is erroneous, at least as applied to Marx. Marx was primarily concerned with the alienative dominance of economic relationships under capitalism: the regulation of the market was to Marx a means, not an end. See Giddens, *Capitalism and Modern Social Theory*, Chapter 15.

54. Durkheim, *Professional Ethics and Civic Morals*, p.213.

55. 'A limitation to the right of disposal is in no way an attack on the individual concept of property – on the contrary. For individual property is property that begins and ends with the individual', Durkheim, *Professional Ethics and Civic Morals*, pp.216–17.

56. E. Durkheim, *The Division of Labour in Society*, pp.374 and 377.

57. Robert Wohl, *French Communism in the Making*, 1914–1924 (Stanford: Stanford University Press, 1966) p.9.

58. Much of the dispute over Weber's objectives in the book stems from neglect of Weber's published replies to his early critics. Cf. his 'Antikritisches zum Geist des Kapitalismus', *Archiv für Sozialwissenschaft und Sozialpolitik*, vol.20, (1910); and his 'Antikritisches Schlusswort', *Archiv für Sozialwissenschaft und Sozialpolitik*, vol.31.

59. The most definite evidence for the continuity of Marx's thought is the draft version of *Capital*. This was published in 1939, but did not become generally available until 1953 as *Grundrisse der Kritik der politischen ökonomie* (Berlin, 1953). For an analysis of some of the phases in the development of differing 'interpretations' of Marx since the turn of the century, see Erich Thier, 'Etappen der Marxinterpretation', *Marxismusstudien*, 1954, pp.1–38.

60. 'Theses on Feuerbach', in Easton and Guddat, *Writings of the Young Marx on Philosophy and Society*, p.402 (Thesis 9).

61. Ludwig Feuerbach, *The Essence of Christianity* (London: Chapman's Quarterly Series: 1853).

62. This phrase was, of course, originally used by Engels to refer to Marx's relation to Hegel. Cf. Engels, 'Ludwig Feuerbach and the end of classical German philosophy', K. Marx and F. Engels, *Selected Works* (London: Lawrence & Wishart, 1950) vol.2, p.350.

63. 'Theses on Feuerbach', p.400 (Thesis 1).

64. 'Preface to *A Contribution to the Critique of Political Economy*', in Marx and Engels, *Selected Works*, vol.1, pp.328–9.

65. Cf. '*Theses on Feuerbach*', p.402 (Thesis 7).

66. Karl Marx and Frederick Engels, *The German Ideology* (Moscow: Progress Publish, 1968) pp.38–9.

67. Marx and Engels, *The German Ideology*. p.61.

68. 'Theses on Feuerbach', p.402 (Thesis 6).

69. Cf. for example, The Civil War in France', in Marx and Engels, *Selected Works*, vol.1, pp.429–40.

70. Marx, *Grundrisse*, pp.375–413; the relevant sections are mostly included in an English translation of a small section from the work, E.J.

Hobsbawm, *Pre-capitalist Economic Formations* (London: Lawrence & Wishart, 1964); Weber's discussion of Rome is to be found in 'Die sozialen Gründe des Untergangs der antiken Kultur', in *Gesammelte Aufsätze zur Sozial- und Wirtschaftsgeschichte* (Tübingen: Mohr-Siebeck, 1924) pp.289–311. In the subsequent part of this paper I do not deal with the discrepancies between Marx's discussion of 'the Asiatic mode of production', and Weber's analysis of China and India. It has often been stated that Weber's views upon the emergence of rational capitalism in the West can only be fully understood in the light of his writings on the various 'world religions'. This is undeniably true. It is, however, quite misleading to regard these writings, as many have, as a form of *ex post facto* experiment which 'tests' the 'independent' influence of ideology upon social development. What Weber shows is that *both* the content of the religious ethics he discusses *and* the specific combination of 'material' circumstances found in Europe, China and India differ. (Thus, for example, Weber laid stress upon the ease of communications in Europe, the peculiar economic and political independence of the European city, plus various other 'material' conditions in terms of which Europe differed from China and India.) These material and ideological factors form a definite, interrelated 'cluster' in each case: the material conditions cannot therefore simply be treated as a 'constant' against which the 'inhibiting' or 'facilitating' influence of religious ideology as a 'variable' can be determined.

71. Hobsbawm, *Pre-capitalist Economic Formations*, p.84.
72. Marx, *Grundrisse*, p.740.
73. Marx pointed out also that while the use of money was widespread in antiquity, only in certain trading nations did it become essential to the economy; in Rome, the monetary system came to be fully developed only during the period of the disintegration of the economy. *Grundrisse*, pp.23–4. Compare Engels' discussion of Rome, in his 'The origin of the family, private property and the state', in Marx and Engels, *Selected Works*, vol.2, pp.270–8.
74. See the discussion of Stirner's *Der Einzige und sein Eigentum* in Marx and Engels, *The German Ideology*, pp.143ff.
75. Marx and Engels, *The German Ideology*, p.151. Weber, on the other hand, stressed that Christianity has always been primarily a religion of the urban artisanate. See *Economy and Society*, vol.2 pp.481ff.
76. Karl Marx, 'Contribution to the critique of Hegel's Philosophy of Right' in *On Religion* (Moscow: Progress Publishers, 1957), p.50. Marx only briefly alluded to the significance of the ideological content of Calvinism. (See, for example, *Capital*, vol.1, p.79.) Engels, on various occasions, discussed Calvinism at greater length.
77. Karl Marx, 'Economic and Philosophical Manuscripts', in T.B. Bottomore, *Karl Marx: Early Writings* (New York: McGraw-Hill, 1964) pp.168 ff; see also Karl Löwith, 'Max Weber und Karl Marx', *Archiv für Sozialwissenschaft und Sozialpolitik*, vol.67, 1932, part 1, pp.77ff.
78. Marx, *Grundrisse*, pp.313. Cf., on the 'universalizing' character of money, George Simmel, *Philosophie des Geldes* (Leipzig: Frankfurt

am Main, 1900). Weber remarked of Simmel's book, that 'money economy and capitalism are too closely identified, to the detriment of his concrete analysis' (*The Protestant Ethic and the Spirit of Capitalism*. New York: Senbher 1958, p.185). Marx also noted the significance of a phenomenon which Weber later discussed at great length – the fact that Roman law played an important role in the formation of bourgeois society. Cf. *Grundrisse*, p.30; and p.916.

79.   Marx, 'Economic and Philosophical Manuscripts', p.171; cf. Shlomo Avineri, *The Social and Political Thought of Karl Marx* (Cambridge: Cambridge University Press, 1970) pp.110–11.
80.   Marx, *Grundrisse*, pp.133–4.
81.   Karl Marx and Frederick Engels, *The Holy Family* (Moscow: Foreign Languages Publishing House, 1956).
82.   Letter to the Editor of *Otyecestvenniye Zapisky*, 1877, Marx and Engels, *Selected Correspondence* (London: Lawrence & Wishart, 1934) p.355. (I have modified the translation.)
83.   Marx, of course realized that political structures could vary to a considerable degree independently of class interests. (See, for example, his letter in *Letters to Dr. Kugelmann*, London: Martin Lawrence, n.d., p.23.) Marx saw that the most developed society in economic terms, England, had a less complex state than Germany or France. The English state, Marx wrote in 1885, was 'an archaic, time-worn and antiquated compromise between the bourgeoisie, which rules over all the various spheres of civil society in reality, but not *officially*, and the landed aristocracy which rules *officially*'. 'Die britische Konstitution', *Werke*, 11 (Berlin: Dietz-Verlag, 1956) p.95.
84.   Gerth and Wright Mills (eds) *From Max Weber*, p.47.
85.   Marx, *Grundrisse*, p.428. Marx, however, noted that the case of the army and that of the capitalist organization differed in that the professional soldier was not hired in order to produce surplus value.
86.   Frederick Engels, *Anti-Dühring* (Moscow: Foreign Languages Publishing House, 1962); *Dialectics of Nature* (Moscow: Foreign Languages Publishing House, 1954).
87.   It would perhaps be nearest to the truth to say, in Laski's words, 'That the two men had, as it were, evolved in common a joint stock of ideas which they regarded as a kind of intellectual bank account upon which either could draw freely'. Harold J. Laski. 'Introduction to *The Communist Manifesto*' (New York: Washington Square Press, 1967) p.20.
88.   The phrase is Lukács': Georg Lukács, *Histoire et conscience de classe* (Paris: Editions de Minuit, 1960) p.20. Cf. MacIntyre's remarks on Kautsky, Bernstein and Lukács, in Alasdair MacIntyre, *Marxism and Christianity* (London: Penguin, 1969) pp.95 ff.
89.   Engels, in fact, disclaimed the writings of some of his intellectual disciples who were actually only drawing the logical implications of the main themes of *Anti-Dühring*. His attempt to escape the theoretical impasse to which his views led is given in his statement, 'According to the materialist conception of history, the determining element in his-

tory is *ultimately* the production and reproduction in real life. More than this neither Marx nor I have asserted' (Engels to Bloch, 21 September 1890, in *Selected Correspondence*, p.475). Marx had earlier, of course, also felt compelled to comment ironically that he 'was not a Marxist'.

90. On Marx's theory of bureaucracy, see Avineri, *The Social and Political Thought of Karl Marx*, pp.48ff.
91. Max Weber, *The Spirit Of Capitalism and the Protestant Ethic*, p.181.
92. Herbert Marcuse, 'Industrialization and capitalism in the work of Max Weber', in Herbert Marcuse, *Negations, Essays in Critical Theory* (London: Allen Lane, 1968 [Boston: Beacon Press, 1969]) p.223.

Chapter II

Problems of Action and Structure

(i) Social theory and the question of action*

Elements of the theory of structuration

In offering a preliminary exposition of the main concepts of structuration theory[1] it will be useful to begin from the divisions which have separated functionalism (including systems theory) and structuralism on the one hand from hermeneutics and the various forms of 'interpretative sociology' on the other. Functionalism and structuralism have some notable similarities, in spite of the otherwise marked contrasts that exist between them. Both tend to express a naturalistic standpoint, and both are inclined towards objectivism. Functionalist thought, from Comte onwards, has looked particularly towards biology as the science providing the closest and most compatible model for social science. Biology has been taken to provide a guide to conceptualizing the structure and the functioning of social systems and to analysing processes of evolution via mechanisms of adaptation. Structuralist thought, especially in the writings of Lévi-Strauss, has been hostile to evolutionism and free from biological analogies. Here the homology between social and natural science is primarily a cognitive one in so far as each is supposed to express similar features of the overall constitution of mind. Both structuralism and functionalism strongly emphasize the pre-eminence of the social whole over its individual parts (i.e., its constituent actors, human subjects).

---

* *The Constitution of Society*, pp. 1–14.

In hermeneutic traditions of thought, of course, the social and natural sciences are regarded as radically discrepant. Hermeneutics has been the home of that 'humanism' to which structuralists have been so strongly and persistently opposed. In hermeneutic thought, such as presented by Dilthey, the gulf between subject and social object is at its widest. Subjectivity is the preconstituted centre of the experience of culture and history and as such provides the basic foundation of the social or human sciences. Outside the realm of subjective experience, and alien to it, lies the material world, governed by impersonal relations of cause and effect. Whereas for those schools of thought which tend towards naturalism subjectivity has been regarded as something of a mystery, or almost a residual phenomenon, for hermeneutics it is the world of nature which is opaque – which, unlike human activity, can be grasped only from the outside. In interpretative sociologies, action and meaning are accorded primacy in the explication of human conduct; structural concepts are not notably prominent, and there is not much talk of constraint. For functionalism and structuralism, however, structure (in the divergent senses attributed to that concept) has primacy over action, and the constraining qualities of structure are strongly accentuated.

The differences between these perspectives on social science have often been taken to be epistemological, whereas they are in fact also ontological. What is at issue is how the concepts of action, meaning and subjectivity should be specified and how they might relate to notions of structure and constraint. If interpretative sociologies are founded, as it were, upon an imperialism of the subject, functionalism and structuralism propose an imperialism of the social object. One of my principal ambitions in the formulation of structuration theory is to put an end to each of these empire-building endeavours. The basic domain of study of the social sciences, according to the theory of structuration, is neither the experience of the individual actor, nor the existence of any form of societal totality, but social practices ordered across space and time. Human social activities, like some self-reproducing items in nature, are recursive. That is to say, they are not brought into being by social actors but continually recreated by them via the very means whereby they express themselves *as* actors. In and through their activities agents reproduce the conditions that make these activities possible. However, the sort of 'knowledgeability' displayed in nature, in the form of coded programmes, is distant from the cognitive skills displayed by human agents. It is in the conceptualizing of human knowledgeability and its involvement in action that I seek to appropriate some of the major contributions of interpretative sociologies. In structuration theory a hermeneutic starting-point is accepted in so far as it is acknowledged that the description of human activities demands a familiarity with the forms of life expressed in those activities.

It is the specifically reflexive form of the knowledgeability of human agents that is most deeply involved in the recursive ordering of social practices. Continuity of practices presumes reflexivity, but reflexivity in turn is possible only because of the continuity of practices that makes them distinctively 'the same' across space and time. 'Reflexivity' hence should be understood not merely as 'self-consciousness' but as the monitored character of the ongoing flow of social life. To be a human being is to be a purposive agent, who both has reasons for his or her activities and is able, if asked, to elaborate discursively upon those reasons (including lying about them). But terms such as 'purpose' or 'intention', 'reason', 'motive' and so on have to be treated with caution, since their usage in the philosophical literature has very often been associated with a hermeneutical voluntarism, and because they extricate human action from the contextuality of time–space. Human action occurs as a *durée*, a continuous flow of conduct, as does cognition. Purposive action is not composed of an aggregate or series of separate intentions, reasons and motives. Thus it is useful to speak of reflexivity as grounded in the continuous monitoring of action which human beings display and expect others to display. The reflexive monitoring of action depends upon rationalization, understood here as a process rather than a state and as inherently involved in the competence of agents. An ontology of time–space as constitutive of social practices is basic to the conception of structuration, which *begins* from temporality and thus, in one sense, 'history'.

This approach can draw only sparingly upon the analytical philosophy of action, as 'action' is ordinarily portrayed by most contemporary Anglo–American writers. 'Action' is not a combination of 'acts': 'acts' are constituted only by a discursive moment of attention to the *durée* of lived-through experience. Nor can 'action' be discussed in separation from the body, its mediations with the surrounding world and the coherence of an acting self. What I call a *stratification model* of the acting self involves treating the reflexive monitoring, rationalization and motivation of action as embedded sets of processes.[2] The rationalization of action, referring to 'intentionality' as process, is, like the other two dimensions, a routine characteristic of human conduct, carried on in a taken-for-granted fashion. In circumstances of interaction – encounters and episodes – the reflexive monitoring of action typically, and again routinely, incorporates the monitoring of the setting of such interaction. . . . This phenomenon is basic to the interpolation of action within the time–space relations of what I shall call co-presence. The rationalization of action, within the diversity of circumstances of interaction, is the principal basis upon which the generalized 'competence' of actors is evaluated by others. It should be clear, however, that the tendency of some philosophers to equate reasons with 'normative commitments' should be resisted: such commitments comprise only one sector of the rationalization of action. If this is not understood, we fail to understand that norms figure as 'factual' boundaries of social life, to which a variety of manipulative attitudes are possible. One aspect of such attitudes, although a relatively superficial one, is to be found in the commonplace observation that the reasons actors offer discursively for what they do may diverge from the rationalization of action as actually involved in the stream of conduct of those actors.

This circumstance has been a frequent source of worry to philosophers and observers of the social scene – for how can we be sure that people do not dissimulate concerning the reasons for their activities? But it is of relatively little interest compared with the wide 'grey areas' that exist between two strata of processes not accessible to the discursive consciousness of actors. The vast bulk of the 'stocks of knowledge', in Schutz's phrase, or what I prefer to call the *mutual knowledge* incorporated in encounters, is not directly accessible to the consciousness of actors. Most such knowledge is practical in character: it is inherent in the capability to 'go on' within the routines of social life. The line between discursive and practical consciousness is fluctuating and permeable, both in the experience of the individual agent and as regards comparisons between actors in different contexts of social activity. There is no bar between these, however, as there is between the unconscious and discursive consciousness. The unconscious includes those forms of cognition and impulsion which are either wholly repressed from consciousness or appear in consciousness only in distorted form.

Unconscious motivational components of action, as psychoanalytic theory suggests, have an internal hierarchy of their own, a hierarchy which expresses the 'depth' of the life history of the individual actor. In saying this I do not imply an uncritical acceptance of the key theorems of Freud's writings. We should guard against two forms of reductionism which those writings suggest or foster. One is a reductive conception of institutions which, in seeking to show the foundation of institutions in the unconscious, fails to leave sufficient play for the operation of autonomous social forces. The second is a reductive theory of consciousness which, wanting to show how much of social life is governed by dark currents outside the scope of actors' awareness, cannot adequately grasp the level of control which agents are characteristically able to sustain reflexively over their conduct.

The agent, agency

The stratification model of the agent can be represented as in Figure II.1. The reflexive monitoring of activity is a chronic feature of everyday action and involves the conduct not just of the individual but also of others. That is to say, actors not only monitor continuously the flow of their activities and expect others to do the same

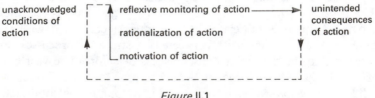

unacknowledged conditions of action — reflexive monitoring of action — unintended consequences of action

rationalization of action

motivation of action

Figure II.1

for their own; they also routinely monitor aspects, social and physical, of the contexts in which they move. By the rationalization of action, I mean that actors – also routinely and for the most part without fuss – maintain a continuing 'theoretical understanding' of the grounds of their activity. As I have mentioned, having such an understanding should not be equated with the discursive giving of reasons for particular items of conduct, nor even with the capability of specifying such reasons discursively. However, it is expected by competent agents of others – and is the main criterion of competence applied in day-to-day conduct – that actors will usually be able to explain most of what they do, if asked. Questions often posed about intentions and reasons by philosophers are normally only put by lay actors either when some piece of conduct is specifically puzzling or when there is a 'lapse' or fracture in competency which might in fact be an intended one. Thus we will not ordinarily ask another person why he or she engages in an activity which is conventional for the group or culture of which that individual is a member. Neither will we ordinarily ask for an explanation if there occurs a lapse for which it seems unlikely the agent can be held responsible, such as slips in bodily management . . . or slips of the tongue. If Freud is correct, however, such phenomena might have a rationale to them, although this is only rarely realized either by the perpetrators of such slips or by others who witness them . . .

I distinguish the reflexive monitoring and rationalization of action from its motivation. If reasons refer to the grounds of action, motives refer to the wants which prompt it. However, motivation is not as directly bound up with the continuity of action as are its reflexive monitoring or rationalization. Motivation refers to potential for action rather than to the mode in which action is chronically carried on by the agent. Motives tend to have a direct purchase on action only in relatively unusual circumstances, situations which in some way break with the routine. For the most part motives supply overall plans or programmes – 'projects', in Schutz's term – within which a range of conduct is enacted. Much of our day-to-day conduct is not directly motivated.

While competent actors can nearly always report discursively about their intentions in, and reasons for, acting as they do, they cannot necessarily do so of their motives. Unconscious motivation is a significant feature of human conduct, although I have some reservations about Freud's interpretation of the nature of the unconscious. The notion of practical consciousness is fundamental to structuration theory. It is that characteristic of the human agent or subject to which structuralism has been particularly blind.[3] But so have other types of objectivist thought. Only in phenomenology and ethnomethodology, within sociological traditions, do we find detailed and subtle treatments of the nature of practical consciousness. Indeed, it is these schools of thought, together with ordinary language philosophy, which have been responsible for making clear the shortcomings of orthodox social scientific theories in this respect. I do not intend the distinction between discursive and practical consciousness to be a rigid and impermeable one. On the contrary, the division between the two can be altered by many aspects of the agent's socialization and learning experiences. Between discursive and practical consciousness there is no bar; there are only the differences between what can be said and what is characteristically simply done. However, there are barriers, centred principally upon repression, between discursive consciousness and the unconscious.

discursive consciousness

practical consciousness

unconscious motives/cognition

. . . I offer these concepts, in place of the traditional psychoanalytic triad of ego, super-ego and id. The Freudian distinction of ego and id cannot easily cope with the analysis of practical consciousness, which lacks a theoretical home in psychoanalytic theory as in the other types of social thought previously indicated. The concept of 'pre-conscious' is perhaps the closest notion to practical consciousness in the conceptual repertoire of psychoanalysis but, as ordinarily used, clearly means something different. In place of the 'ego', it is preferable to speak of the 'I' (as, of course, Freud did in the original German). This usage does not prevent anthropomorphism, in which the ego is pictured as a sort of mini-agent; but it does at least help to begin to remedy it. The use of 'I' develops out of, and is thereafter associated with, the positioning of the agent in social encounters. As a term of a predicative sort, it is 'empty' of content, as compared with the richness of the actor's self-descriptions involved with 'me'. Mastery of 'I', 'me', 'you' relations, as applied reflexively in discourse, is of key importance to the emerging competence of agents learning language. Since I do not use the term 'ego', it is evidently best to dispense with 'super-ego' also – a clumsy term in any case. The term 'moral conscience' will do perfectly well as a replacement.

These concepts all refer to the agent. What of the nature of agency? This can be connected with a further issue. The *durée* of day-to-day life occurs as a flow of intentional action. However, acts have unintended consequences; and, as indicated in Figure II.1, unintended consequences may systematically feed back to be the unacknowledged conditions of further acts. Thus one of the regular consequences of my speaking or writing English in a correct way is to contribute to the reproduction of the English language as a whole. My speaking English correctly is intentional; the contribution I make to the reproduction of the language is not. But how should we formulate what unintended consequences are?

It has frequently been supposed that human agency can be defined only in terms of intentions. That is to say, for an item of behaviour to count as action, whoever perpetrates it must intend to do so, or else the behaviour in question is just a reactive response. The view derives some plausibility, perhaps, from the fact that there are some acts which cannot occur unless the agent intends them. Suicide is a case in point. Durkheim's conceptual efforts to the contrary, 'suicide' cannot be said to occur unless there is some kind of intent to precipitate self-destruction. A person who steps off the curb and is knocked down by an oncoming car cannot be said to be a 'suicide' if the event is accidental; it is something that happens to the individual, rather than something the individual does. However, suicide is not typical of most human acts, in respect of intentions, in so far as it can be said to have occurred only when its perpetrator intended it to occur. Most acts do not have this characteristic.

Some philosophers have argued, however, that for an event in which a human being is involved to count as an example of agency, it is necessary at least that what the person does be intentional under some description, even if the agent is mistaken about that description. An officer on a submarine pulls a lever intending to change course but instead, having pulled the wrong lever, sinks the *Bismarck*. He has done something intentionally, albeit not what he imagined, but thus the *Bismarck* has been sunk through his agency. Again, if someone intentionally spills some coffee, thinking mistakenly that it is tea, spilling the coffee is an act of that person, even though it has not been done intentionally; under another description, as 'spilling the tea', it is intentional.[4] (In most instances, 'spilling' something tends to have the implication that the act is unintentional. It is a slip intervening in a course of action in which the person is intending to do something different altogether, namely pass the cup to another person. Freud claims that nearly all such behavioural slips, like slips of the tongue, are actually unconsciously motivated. This, of course, brings them under intentional descriptions from another angle.)

But even the view that for an event to count as an instance of agency, it must be intentional only under *some* description or another is wrong. It confuses the designation of agency with the giving of act-descriptions;[5] and it mistakes the continued monitoring of an action which individuals carry out with the defining properties of that action as such. Agency refers not to the intentions people have in doing things but to their capability of doing those things in the first place (which is why agency implies power: cf. the *Oxford English Dictionary* definition of an agent, as 'one who exerts power or produces an effect'). Agency concerns events of which an individual is the perpetrator, in the sense that the individual could, at any phase in a given sequence of conduct, have acted differently. Whatever happened would not have happened if that individual had not intervened. Action is a continuous process, a flow, in which the reflexive monitoring which the individual maintains is fundamental to the control of the body that actors ordinarily sustain throughout their day-to-day lives. I am the author of many things I do not intend to do, and may not want to bring about, but none the less *do*. Conversely, there may be circumstances in which I intend to achieve something, and do achieve it, although not directly through my agency. Take the example of the spilled coffee. Supposing an individual, A, were a malicious spirit and played a practical joke by placing the cup on a saucer at such an angle that, when picked up, it would be very likely to spill. Individual B picks up the coffee, and it duly spills over. It would be right to say that what A did brought the incident about, or at least contributed to its coming about. But A did not spill the coffee; B did. Individual B, who did not intend to spill the coffee, spilled the coffee; individual A, who did intend that the coffee should be spilled, did not spill it.

But what is it to do something unintentionally? Is it different from bringing about consequences unintentionally? Consider the so-called 'accordion effect' of action.[6] An individual flicks a switch to illuminate a room. Although this is intentional, the fact that the turning on of the switch alerts a prowler is not. Supposing the prowler flees down the road, is caught by a policeman, and after due process spends a year in gaol on the basis of being convicted of the burglary. Are all these unintended consequences of the act of flicking the switch? Which are things the individual has 'done'? Let me mention an additional example, taken from a theory of ethnic segregation.[7] A pattern of ethnic segregation might develop, without any of those involved intending this to happen, in the following way, which can be illustrated by analogy. Imagine a chessboard which has a set of 5-pence pieces and a set of 10-pence pieces. These are distributed randomly on the board, as individuals might be in an urban area. It is presumed that, while they feel no hostility towards the other group, the members of each group do not want to live in a neighbourhood where they are ethnically in a minority. On the chessboard each piece is moved around until it is in such a position that at least 50 per cent of the adjoining pieces are of the same type. The result is a pattern of extreme segregation. The 10-cent pieces end up as a sort of ghetto in the midst of the 5-cent ones The 'composition effect' is an outcome of an aggregate of acts – whether those of moving pieces on the board or those of agents in a housing market – each of which is intentionally carried out. But the eventual outcome is neither intended nor desired by anyone. It is, as it were, everyone's doing and no one's.

To understand what it is to do something unintentionally, we have first of all to be clear how 'intentional' should be understood. This concept I define as characterizing an act which its perpetrator knows, or believes, will have a particular quality or outcome and where such knowledge is utilized by the author of the act to achieve this quality or outcome.[8] If the characterization of agency given above is correct, we have to separate out the question of what an agent 'does' from what is 'intended' or the intentional aspects of what is done. Agency refers to doing. Switching on the light was something that agent did, and alerting the prowler was also something that agent did. It was unintended if the actor did not know the prowler was there and if for some reason, while knowing the prowler was there, the agent did not seek to use this knowledge to alert the intruder. Unintentional doings can be separated conceptually from unintended consequences of doings, although the distinction will not matter whenever the focus of concern is the relation between the intentional and unintentional. The consequences of what actors do, intentionally or unintentionally, are events which would not have happened if that actor had behaved differently, but which are not within the scope of the agent's power to have brought about (regardless of what the agent's intentions were).

I think we can say that all the things that happened to the

prowler following the flicking of the switch were unintended consequences of the act, given that the individual in question did not
know the prowler was there and therefore initiated the sequence
unintentionally. If there are complexities in this, they are to do with
how it comes about that a seemingly trivial act may trigger events
far removed from it in time and space, not whether or not those
consequences were intended by the perpetrator of the original act.
In general it is true that the further removed the consequences of an
act are in time and space from the original context of the act, the
less likely those consequences are to be intentional – but this is, of
course, influenced both by the scope of the knowledgeability that
actors have . . . and the power they are able to mobilize. We would
ordinarily think of what the agent 'does' – as contrasted with the
consequences ensuing from what has been done – in terms of
phenomena the agent has more or less within his or her control.
In most spheres of life, and in most forms of activity, the scope of
control is limited to the immediate contexts of action or interaction.
Thus we would say that turning on the light was something the
agent did, and probably also alerting the prowler, but not causing
the prowler to get caught by the policeman or to end up spending a
year in gaol. Although it might be the case that these events would
not have happened when and where they did without the act of
flicking the switch, their occurrence depended on too many other
contingent outcomes for them to be something the original actor
'did'.

Philosophers have used up a great deal of ink attempting to
analyse the nature of intentional activity. But from the point of
view of the social sciences, it is hard to exaggerate the importance
of the unintended consequences of intentional conduct. Merton has
provided perhaps the classical discussion of the issue.[9] He points
out, entirely correctly, that the study of unintended consequences is
fundamental to the sociological enterprise. A given item of activity
may have either (a) non-significant or (b) significant consequences;
and either (c) singly significant consequences or (d) multiply significant consequences. What is judged 'significant' will depend upon
the nature of the study being undertaken or the theory being
developed.[10] However, Merton then goes on to couple unintended
consequences with functional analysis, a conceptual move which,
although conventionally made in the sociological literature, I wish
to reject. In particular, it is important to see that the analysis of

unintended consequences does not (as Merton claims it does) make sense of seemingly irrational forms or patterns of social conduct. Merton contrasts intentional activity (manifest functions) with its unintended consequences (latent functions). One of the aims of identifying latent functions is to show that apparently irrational social activities may not be so irrational after all. This is particularly likely to be the case, according to Merton, with enduring activities or practices. These may often be dismissed as '"superstitions", "irrationalities", "mere inertia of tradition", etc.'. However, in Merton's view, if we discover that they have a latent function – an unintended consequence, or set of consequences, which help to secure the continued reproduction of the practice in question – then we demonstrate that it is not so irrational at all.

Thus a ceremonial, for example, 'may fulfil the latent function of reinforcing the group identity by providing a periodic occasion on which the scattered members of a group assemble to engage in a common activity'.[11] But to suppose that such a demonstration of a functional relation provides a reason for the existence of a practice is mistaken. What is being more or less surreptitiously smuggled in here is a conception of 'society's reasons' on the basis of imputed social needs. Thus if we understand that the group 'needs' the ceremonial to enable it to survive, we see its continuation as no longer irrational. But to say that the existence of a social state A needs a social practice B to help it to survive in recognizably similar form is to pose a question that then has to be answered; it does not itself answer it. The relation between A and B is not analogous to the relation that obtains between wants or needs and intentions in the individual actor. In the individual, wants that are constitutive of the motivational impulses of the actor generate a dynamic relation between motivation and intentionality. This is not the case with social systems, except where actors behave in cognizance of what they take to be social needs.[12]

This point having been made, there can be no quarrel with Merton's emphasis upon the significance of connecting unintended consequences of action with institutionalized practices, those deeply embedded in time and space. This represents the most important of three main research contexts – separable from one another only analytically – in which the influence of unintended consequences can be analysed. One is the turning on the light/alerting the prowler/causing the prowler to flee/etc. type of example. The interest of the researcher here is in the cumulation of events deriving from an initiating circumstance without which that cumulation would not have been found. Max Weber's analysis of the effects of the Battle of Marathon on the subsequent development of Greek culture, and thence of the formation of European culture in general, is a case in point, as is his discussion of the consequences of the firing of the bullet that killed Archduke Ferdinand at Sarajevo.[13] The concern is with a singular set of events, traced through and analysed counter-factually. The researcher asks, 'What would have happened to events B, C, D, E . . . if A had not occurred?' – thereby seeking to identify the role of A in the chain or sequence.

A second type of circumstance upon which the social analyst might focus is one in which, instead of a pattern of unintended consequences initiated by a single event, there is a pattern resulting from a complex of individual activities. The discussion of ethnic segregation mentioned above is an example of this. Here a definite 'end result' is taken as the phenomenon to be explained, and that end result is shown to derive as an unintended consequence from an aggregate of courses of intentional conduct. The theme of rationality tends to surface again here, although this time there is no logical objection to be made to it. As game theorists have convincingly pointed out, the outcome of a series of rational actions, undertaken separately by individual actors, may be irrational for all of them.[14] 'Perverse effects' are only one type of unintended consequences, although it is no doubt true that situations where they occur are of particular interest.[15]

The third type of context in which unintended consequences may be traced out is that pointed to by Merton: where the interest of the analyst is in the mechanisms of reproduction of institutionalized practices. Here the unintended consequences of action form the acknowledged conditions of further action in a non-reflexive feedback cycle (causal loops). I have pointed out that it is not enough to isolate functional relations in order to explain why such feedback occurs. How, then, does it happen that cycles of unintended consequences feed back to promote social reproduction across long periods of time? In a general way, this is not difficult to analyse. Repetitive activities, located in one context of time and space, have regularized consequences, unintended by those who engage in those activities, in more or less 'distant' time–space contexts. What happens in this second series of contexts then, directly or indirectly, influences the further conditions of action in the original context. To understand what is going on no explanatory variables are needed other than those which explain why individuals are motivated to engage in regularized social practices across time and space, and what consequences ensue. The unintended consequences are regularly 'distributed' as a by-product of regularized behaviour reflexively sustained as such by its participants.

(ii)   The production and reproduction of social life*

The production or constitution of society is a skilled accomplishment of its members, but one that does not take place under conditions that are either wholly intended or wholly comprehended by them. The key to understanding social order – in the most general sense of that term . . . – is not the 'internalization of values', but the shifting relations between the production and *reproduction* of social life by its constituent actors. *All reproduction is necessarily production*, however: and the seed of change is there in *every act* which contributes towards the reproduction of any 'ordered' form of social life. The process of reproduction begins with and depends upon the reproduction of the material circumstances of human existence: i.e. the re-procreation of the species and the transformation of nature. Human beings, as Marx says, produce 'freely' in interchange with nature, in the paradoxical sense that they are *forced* actively to transform the material world in order to survive in it, since they lack an apparatus of instincts which would provide for a more mechanical adaptation to their material environment. But what above all distinguishes humans from the animals is that the former are able reflexively to 'programme' their environment, thereby monitoring their own place in it; this is made possible only by language, which is first and foremost the *medium of human practical activities*.

What are, analytically, the main conditions relevant to the reproduction of structures of interaction? These can be discussed as being of the following kinds: The constituting skills of social actors; the rationalization of these skills as forms of agency; the unexplicated features of settings of interaction that promote and permit the exer-

---

* *New Rules of Sociological Method*, pp. 102–13.

cise of such capacities, which can be analysed in terms of *elements of motivation*, and what I shall call the *'duality of structure'*.

I shall develop the argument . . . with reference to language, not because it is helpful to regard social life as some sort of language, information system or, whatever, but because language, as a social form itself, exemplifies some aspects – and only some aspects – of social life as a whole. Language may be studied from at least three aspects of its production and reproduction, each of which is characteristic of the production and reproduction of society more generally. Language is 'mastered' and 'spoken' by actors; it is employed as a medium of communication between them; and it forms a 'structure' which is in some sense constituted by the speech of a 'language community' or collectivity. From the aspect of its production as a series of speech acts by an individual speaker, language is (a) a skill, or very complex set of skills, that is possessed by each person who 'knows' the language; (b) used to 'make sense', literally, as a creative art of an active subject; (c) something which is *done*, accomplished, by the speaker, but not in full cognizance of how he does it. That is to say, he is likely to be able to offer only a fragmentary account of what the skills are that he exercises, or of how he exercises them.

From its aspect as a *medium of communication in interaction*, language involves the use of 'interpretative schemes' to make sense not only of what others say, but of what they *mean*: the constitution of 'sense' as an *intersubjective* accomplishment of mutual understanding in an ongoing exchange; and the use of contextual cues, as properties of the setting, as an integral part of the constitution and comprehension of meaning. Considered as a *structure*, language is not 'possessed' by any particular speaker, but can be conceptualized only as characteristic of a community of speakers; it can be conceived of as an abstract set of rules which are not mechanically applied, but are employed in a generative mode by speakers who are members of the language community. Social life, I shall wish to say, then, may be treated as a set of *reproduced practices*. Following the threefold approach distinguished above, social practices may be studied, first, from the point of view of their constitution as a series of *acts*, 'brought off' by actors; second, as constituting forms of *interaction*, involving the communication of meaning; and third, as constituting *structures* which pertain to 'collectivities' or 'social communities'.

The production of communication as 'meaningful'

The production of interaction has three fundamental elements: its constitution as 'meaningful'; its constitution as a moral order; and its constitution as the operation of relations of power. I shall still for the moment defer consideration of the latter two, but only because they are so important as to warrant detailed treatment, and in the end these elements have to be reunited, since though they may be separated analytically, in social life itself they are subtly yet tightly interwoven.

The production of interaction as meaningful depends first of all upon mutuality of 'uptake' (Austin) in communicative intent, in which language is the primary but certainly not the only medium. In all interaction there is a constant interest in, and ability to disclose, modes of understanding of the conduct of the other apart from uptake of communicative intent – for example, in the understanding of motives. The subtleties of the everyday production of interaction can easily appear as merely peripheral nuisances if idealized models of dialogue as 'perfect mutual understandings' are treated as anything more than a possible world of philosophy only. Merleau-Ponty says: 'The will to speak is one and the same as the will to be understood.'[16] But whereas this presumably applies to itself as a statement of the philosopher, in everyday situations of interaction the will to speak is also sometimes the will to baffle, puzzle, deceive, to be misunderstood.

It is essential to any adequate analysis of interaction as a product of the constituting skills of actors to recognize that its 'meaningfulness' is actively and continually negotiated, not merely the programmed communication of already established meanings: this, I take it, is the substance of Habermas' differentiation of 'linguistic' from 'communicative competence'. Interaction, as I have already emphasized, is temporally and spatially situated. But this is no more than an uninteresting truism if we do not see that it is typically used or *drawn upon* by actors in the production of interaction: anticipations of the responses of others mediate the activity of each actor at any one moment in time, and what has gone before is subject to revision in the light of subsequent experience. In this way, as Gadamer emphasizes, practical social life displays ontologically the characteristics of the 'hermeneutic circle'. 'Context-dependence', in the various ways in which this term can be interpreted, is aptly regarded as integral to the production of meaning in inter-action, not as just an embarrassment to formal analysis.

In relation to theories of definite descriptions, philosophers have frequently discussed the ambiguity of such sentences as 'A wants to marry someone of whom his parents disapprove'.[17] But it is impor-tant to see that such discussions can become wholly misleading if set up as attempts to isolate an abstract logical structure from the communication of meaning in interaction. Here 'ambiguity' is am-biguity-in-context, and must definitely not be confused with the existence of a range of senses which a given word or sentence may have in circumstances other than those in which it is uttered by a particular speaker at a particular time. The sentence mentioned above is probably not ambiguous, for example, if uttered in the course of a conversation in which the individual figuring in the marriage plans of A has already been referred to; or alternatively if the course of such a conversation has made it clear to the participants that A was set on choosing a spouse who would prove objectionable to his parents, although having no one in particular in mind as yet. On the other hand, a statement which out of context might appear quite unambiguous, such as 'A is looking forward to getting married tomorrow', may in fact be ambiguous if, for exam-ple, uttered with a sufficient hint of sarcasm for a listener to be unsure whether or not the speaker 'means what he says'. Hu-mour, irony and sarcasm all in some part depend upon such open possibilities of discourse, as recognized elements of the skills where-by interaction is constituted as meaningful.[18]

While such skills obviously involve 'knowledge' that is in princi-ple capable of being expressed in propositional form, their satura-tion by temporal and spatial aspects of the context of communication is evidently not to be dealt with solely in these terms. Take an example discussed by Ziff. It is sometimes held by linguists that the meaning of a sentence such as 'The pen on the desk is made of gold', when used in an everyday context of com-munication, could be expressed in a formal language as a series of statements, known implicitly by the participants, describing 'rele-vant' contextual characteristics.[19] Thus the exact referent could be indicated by substituting for 'the pen on the desk', 'the only pen on the desk in the front room of number 10 Hertford Street, Cam-bridge, at 9.00 a.m. in the morning of June 29th 1975'. But as Ziff points out, this sentence does not make explicit what was known to the participants in the encounter within which the utterance was made and understood, or used by them to produce the mutual understanding of the sentence. A hearer may be quite able to understand what was said, and the referent of the phrase, without being aware of any of the additional elements brought into the longer sentence at all. Moreover, it would be mistaken to suppose that, were everyday communication to be phrased in terms of sentences such as the longer one, there would be an increase in precision or a loss of ambiguity. The first sentence, uttered in a specific context, is neither imprecise nor ambiguous, whereas the use of the longer might bring about more vagueness and uncertainty, since it would extend the range of what has to be 'known' in common to accomplish the communication of meaning.

The use of reference to physical aspects of context is no doubt fundamental to the sustenance of an intersubjectively 'agreed upon' world within which most forms of day-to-day interaction occur. But 'awareness of an immediate sensory environment', as an element drawn upon in the production of interaction, cannot be radically severed from a backdrop of, largely implicit, mutual knowledge which is drawn upon to create and sustain encounters, since the former is categorized and 'interpreted' in the light of the latter. I use the term 'mutual knowledge' to refer generically to taken-for-granted 'knowledge' which actors assume others possess, if they are 'competent' members of society, and which is drawn upon to sustain communication in interaction. This includes 'tacit knowledge', in Polanyi's sense; mutual knowledge is 'configurative' in character.[20] Even the most cursory verbal interchange presupposes, and draws upon, a diffuse stock of knowledge in the uptake of communicative intent. One person says to another: 'Do you want a game of tennis?', to which a second replies, 'I have work to do'. What is the connection between question and answer?[21] To grasp what has been said, 'by implication', it is necessary to know not merely what 'game' and 'work' mean as lexical items, but other much less easily formulated elements of knowledge of social practices which make the second utterance a (potentially) *appropriate* answer to the first. If the reply is not a particularly quizzical response, it is because it is mutually 'known' that work generally takes precedence over play when they conflict in the allocation of a person's time, or something of the sort. How far the questioner would 'let the response pass' as 'adequate' would of course depend upon a variety of circumstances particular to the situation in which he made his enquiry.[22]

Mutual knowledge is applied in the form of *interpretative schemes* whereby contexts of communication are created and sustained in interaction. Such interpretative schemes ('typifications') can be regarded analytically as a series of generative rules for the uptake of the illocutionary force of utterances.[23] Mutual knowledge is 'background knowledge' in the sense that it is taken for granted, and mostly remains unarticulated; on the other hand, it is not part of the 'background' in the sense that it is constantly actualized, displayed, and modified by members of society in the course of their interaction. Taken-for-granted knowledge, in other words, is never fully taken for granted, and the relevance of some particular element to an encounter may have to be 'demonstrated', and sometimes fought for, by the actor; it is not appropriated ready-made by actors, but is produced and reproduced anew by them as part of the continuity of their lives.

Moral orders of interaction

The moral elements of interaction connect in an integral way with its constitution both as meaningful and as a set of relations of power. Each of these connections must be regarded as equally basic. Norms figure in an important way in the writings both of those who have taken a strongly naturalistic stance in social theory (especially Durkheim) and those who have been their most fervent critics. Although Durkheim came to elaborate his original views in his later works, he nevertheless always tended to stress the significance of norms as *constraining* or obligating: to be approached through the notion of *sanctions*. Schutz, Winch and others, on the other hand, have been more preoccupied with the 'conferring' or 'enabling' qualities of norms. I wish to argue that all norms are both *constraining* and *enabling*. I propose also to distinguish between 'norms' and 'rules', which are casually used as synonymous by most post-Wittgensteinian philosophers; normative or moral rules I shall treat as a sub-category of the more all-inclusive notion of 'rule', which I shall wish to connect with that of 'structure'.

The constitution of interaction as a moral order may be understood as the actualization of *rights* and the enactment of *obligations*.

There is a logical symmetry between these which, however, can be factually broken. That is to say, what is a right of one participant in an encounter appears as an obligation of another to respond in an 'appropriate' fashion, and vice versa; but this tie can be severed if an obligation is not acknowledged or honoured, and no sanction can effectively be brought to bear. Thus, in the production of interaction, all normative elements have to be treated as a series of *claims* whose realization is contingent upon the successful actualization of obligations through the medium of the responses of other participants. Normative sanctions are thus essentially different (as Durkheim recognized) from those connected with the transgression of technical or utilitarian prescriptions, which involve what von Wright calls 'anankastic propositions'.[24] In prescriptions such as 'avoid drinking contaminated water', the sanction that is involved (the risk of being poisoned) follows 'mechanically' from the execution of the act: it depends upon causal relations that have the form of natural events.

In making this distinction, however, Durkheim also obliterated a quite vital sense in which norms may be approached in a 'utilitarian' fashion by participants in the production of interaction, and which must be conceptually related to the contingent character of the realization of normative claims. This is that a normative claim may be acknowledged as binding, not because an actor to whom it applies as an obligation accepts that obligation as a moral commitment, but because he anticipates, and wants to avoid, the sanctions which will be applied in the case of his non-compliance. In relation to the pursuance of his interests, therefore, an actor may approach moral claims in exactly the same way as he does technical prescriptions; in each case he may also 'calculate the risks' involved in a particular act in terms of the probability of escaping sanction. It is an elementary mistake to suppose that the enactment of a moral obligation necessarily implies a moral commitment to it. Elementary though it may be, it is important to insist upon this point, because it is systematically ignored in that tradition of social thought linking Durkheim and Parsons. Since the sanctions which follow the transgression of moral claims do not operate with the mechanical inevitability of events in nature, but involve the reactions of others, there is typically some 'free space' for the transgressor, if identified as such, to *negotiate* the character of the sanction which is to follow. This is *one* way in which the production of a normative order exists in close relation to the production of meaning: what the transgression *is* is potentially negotiable, and the manner in which it is characterized or identified affects the sanctions to which it may be subject. This is familiar, and formalized, in courts of law, but also pervades the whole arena of moral constitution as it operates in day-to-day life.

Sanctions are easily classified, on an abstract level, in terms of whether the resources which are mobilized to produce the sanction are 'internal': i.e. involve elements of the actor's personality, or 'external': i.e. draw upon features of the context of action. Each of these may be further categorized in terms of whether the resources which the sanctioning agent is able to mobilize are 'positive' or 'negative' with regard to the wants of the actor who is the target of sanction. Thus the actualization of 'internal' sanctions may draw upon a positive moral commitment of the actor, or negatively upon anxiety, fear or guilt; the actualization of 'external' sanctions may draw upon offers of reward or on the other hand may hold out the threat of force. Obviously, in actual situations of interaction several of these may operate simultaneously; and no 'external' sanction can be effective unless it brings into play an 'internal' one: a reward is only such if it impinges upon a person's wants.

The 'interpretation' of norms, and their capability to make an 'interpretation' *count*, by participants in interaction is tied in subtle ways to their compliance to moral claims. Failure to see this, or at any rate to spell out its implications, is bound up with some characteristic defects of both Durkheimian–Parsonian functionalism and post-Wittgensteinian philosophy. The moral co-ordination of interaction is asymmetrically interdependent with its production as meaningful and with its expression of relations of power. This has two aspects, themselves closely associated with one another: (a) the possibility of clashes of different 'world-views' or, less macroscopically, definitions of what *is*; (b) the possibility of clashes between diverging understandings of 'common' norms.

Relations of power in interaction

The notion of 'action', I wish to claim, is *logically tied to that of power*. This is in a certain sense recognized by philosophers, who talk of 'can', 'is able to', or 'powers', in relation to the theory of action. But such discussions are rarely if ever related by their authors to analyses of the concept of power in sociology, and are thus not connected to the analysis of *relations of power* among actors or in collectivities. The connection of 'action' to 'power' can be simply stated. Action intrinsically involves the application of 'means' to achieve outcomes, brought about through the direct intervention of an actor in a course of events, 'intended action' being a sub-class of the actor's doings, or his refraining from doing; power represents the capacity of the agent to mobilize resources to constitute those 'means'. In this most general sense, 'power' refers to the *transformative capacity* of human action, and I shall henceforth for the sake of clarity employ this second term, reserving the former one for a more restricted, relational, use of 'power', to be further explicated below.

The transformative capacity of human action is placed in the forefront in Marx, and is the key element in the notion of *Praxis*. All systems of social theory have had to deal, in some way, with this, with man's transformation of nature and with the restlessly self-modifying character of human society. But in many schools of social thought, the transformative capacity of action has been conceived of in terms of a dualism, as an abstract contrast between the neutral world of nature on the one hand, and the 'value-laden' world of human society on the other. In such schools of thought, particularly those associated with functionalism, with its emphasis upon social 'adaptation' to an 'environment', the grasp of man's historicity is easily relinquished. Only in the linked traditions of Hegelian philosophy and (certain versions of) Marxism has the transformative capacity of action, as the self-mediating process of labour, been made the centre-point of social analysis. Labour is, as Löwith says, 'a movement of mediation . . . a fashioning or "forming" and therefore positive destruction of the world which is present in nature'.[25] There seems little doubt that this broad emphasis remained basic to Marx's mature thought, although not significantly elaborated in it; in the *Grundrisse* we find affirmed, in language that closely echoes his early immersion in the 'brook of fire', that 'labour is the living, shaping fire; it represents the impermanence of things, their temporality, in other words their formation in the course of living time'.[26] However, Marx became increasingly preoccupied, not with labour as the transformative capacity of agency, but with its deformation as 'occupation' within the capitalist–industrial division of labour; and power as involved in social intercourse between men, as I have indicated in a preliminary way earlier, is analysed as a specific property of class relations rather than as a feature of social interaction in general.

'Power' in the sense of the transformative capacity of human agency is the capability of the actor to intervene in a series of events so as to alter their course; as such it is the 'can' which mediates between intentions or wants and the actual realization of the outcomes sought after. 'Power' in the narrower, relational sense is a property of interaction, and may be defined as the capability to secure outcomes where the realization of these outcomes depends upon the agency of *others*. It is in this sense that men have power 'over' others: this is power as *domination*. Several basic points have to be made here. (a) Power, in either the broad or restricted sense, refers to *capabilities*. Unlike the communication of meaning, power does not come into being only when being 'exercised', even if ultimately there is no other criterion whereby one can demonstrate what power actors possess. This is important, because we can talk of power being 'stored up' for future occasions of use. (b) The relation between power and conflict is a contingent one: as I have formulated it, the concept of power, in either sense, does not logically imply the existence of conflict. This stands against *some* uses, or misuses, of what is perhaps the most famous formulation of 'power' in the sociological literature, that of Max Weber, according to whom power is 'the capacity of an individual to realize his will, even against the opposition of others'.[27] The omission of the 'even' in some renderings of this definition is significant: then it becomes the case that power presupposes conflict, since power only exists when the resistance of others has to be overcome, their will subdued.[28] (c) It is the concept of 'interest', rather than that of power as such, which relates directly to conflict and solidarity. If power and conflict frequently go together, it is not because the one logically implies the other, but because power is linked to the pursuance of interests, and men's interests may fail to coincide. All I mean to say by this is that, while power is a feature of every form of human interaction, division of interest is not. (d) This does not imply that divisions of interest can be transcended in any empirical society; and it is certainly necessary to resist the linkage of 'interest' to hypothetical 'states of nature'.

The use of power in interaction can be understood in terms of resources or facilities which participants bring to and mobilize as elements of its production, thereby directing its course. These thus include the skills whereby the interaction is constituted as 'meaningful', but also – and these need only to be stated abstractly here – any other resources which a participant is capable of bringing to bear so as to influence or control the conduct of others who are parties to that interaction, including the possession of 'authority' and the threat or use of 'force'. It would be quite out of place to attempt to set out an elaborate typology of power resources in this study. My only concern at this point is to offer a generalized conceptual scheme which integrates the notion of power into the theoretical account developed in the present extract. What it is necessary to do, however, is to relate this analysis of power back to the production of meaning in interaction.

This can best be accomplished by reverting briefly to Parsons' 'action frame of reference', or more specifically to criticism voiced about it by some of those influenced by ethnomethodology. Such criticism has taken roughly the following form. In Parsons' theory, it is argued, the actor is programmed to do what he does as a result of values 'internalized' as need-dispositions of personality (in conjunction with non-normative 'conditions' of action): he is portrayed as an unthinking dupe of his culture and his interaction with others as the enactment of such need-dispositions rather than as, as it truly is, a series of skilled performances. I think this is right; but those who have expressed this sort of view have failed to pursue its consequences far enough. That is to say, following Garfinkel, they have been interested only in 'accountability', in the cognitive management of communication and communication settings. This is treated as the result of mutual 'labour' on the part of actors, but as if it were always the collaborative endeavour of *peers*, each contributing equally to the production of interaction, whose only interests are in sustaining an appearance of 'ontological security' whereby meaningfulness is constituted. In this one can trace the strong residual influence of Parsons' problem of order, but denuded of its volitional content, and reduced to a disembodied dialogue.

As against this, we must emphasize that the creation of frames of meaning occurs *as the mediation of practical activities*, and in terms of differentials of power which actors are able to bring to bear. The significance of this is crucial in social theory, which must find as one of its chief tasks the mutual accommodation of power and norms in social interaction. *The reflexive elaboration of frames of meaning is characteristically imbalanced in relation to the possession of power*, whether this be a result of the superior linguistic or dialectical skills of one person in conversation with another; the possession of relevant types of 'technical knowledge'; the mobilization of authority or 'force', etc. 'What passes for social reality' stands in immediate relation to the distribution of power; not only on the most mundane levels of everyday interaction, but also on the level of global cultures and ideologies, whose influence indeed may be felt in every corner of everyday social life itself.[29]

(iii)   The concept of structure*

Time, structure, system

In social science, the term 'structure' appears in two main bodies of literature: that of functionalism, which is often in contemporary versions called 'structural–functionalism'; and the tradition of thought that has embraced it most completely, structuralism. So far as the first of these is concerned, 'structure' normally appears in conjunction with 'function'. Spencer and other nineteenth-century authors who employed these terms did so often in the context of fairly bluntly-expressed schemes of biological analogies. To study the structure of society is like studying the anatomy of the organism; to study its functions is like studying the physiology of the organism. It is to show how the structure 'works'. Although more recent functionalist authors have become wary of employing direct or detailed biological parallels, the same sort of presumed relation between structure and function is readily apparent in their works. Structure is understood as referring to a 'pattern' of social relationships; function, to how such patterns actually operate as systems. Structure here is primarily a descriptive term, the main burden of explanation being carried by function. This is perhaps why the literature of structural–functionalism, both sympathetic and critical, has been overwhelmingly concerned with the concept

---

* *Central Problems in Social Theory*, pp. 59–73.

of function, barely treating the notion of structure at all. It is in any case indicative of the degree to which the critics of functionalism have taken over the parameters of their opponent.

In structuralism, by contrast, 'structure' appears in a more explanatory role, as linked to the notion of transformations. Structural analysis, whether applied to language, to myth, literature or art, or more generally to social relationships, is considered to penetrate below the level of surface appearances. The division between structure and function is replaced by one between code and message. At first sight, structure in this usage, and other concepts associated with it, seem to have little or nothing in common with the notions employed by functionalist authors. But . . . although internally diverse traditions of thought, structuralism and functionalism do share certain overall themes and characteristics, a fact which in some part reflects the influence of Durkheim over each. Two common features are worth reiterating here: one is the initial commitment of each to a distinction between synchrony and diachrony, or statics and dynamics; the other is their mutual concern not only with 'structures' but with 'systems'. These are obviously in each case connected perspectives, because the methodological isolation of a synchronic dimension is the basis for the identification of the characteristics of structure/systems. The differentiation of synchrony and diachrony is a basic element of structuralism and functionalism alike; but both have generated attempts to transcend it. So far as the latter is concerned, the most interesting and important of such attempts involves complementing the notion of function with a conception of dysfunction, thus treating social processes in terms of a tension between integration and disintegration. I have commented on the deficiencies of this view elsewhere.[30] Within structuralist thought, the attempt to overcome the synchronic/diachronic distinction has produced an emphasis upon structuration, or as Derrida puts it, 'the structuring of structure'. . . . Such notions of structuration tend to remain 'internal' to designated components of structural relations.

I shall elaborate below a conception of structuration that is directly linked to the account of human agency mentioned previously [extract II (i) p. 88)]. But first it is necessary to consider briefly the relation between structure and system. While both terms appear in the respective literatures of structuralism and functionalism, the distinction between them in each is an unstable one, so that the one tends to collapse into the other. Saussure used the term 'system' rather than 'structure', meaning by the former the set of dependencies between the elements of *langue*. The introduction of 'structure' by Hjelmslev and the Prague group did not so much create a complementary concept to that of system, as substitute the former for the latter. The subsequent history of structuralism suggests that one or other of the terms is redundant, since their usage overlaps so much: system often appears as a defining characteristic of structure.[31] In functionalism there seems at first sight to be a basis for distinguishing between structure and system, following the structure/function contrast. Structure could be taken to refer to 'patterns' of social relationships, system to the actual 'functioning' of such relationships. This is indeed a distinction that often is made in functionalist writings. But it is not surprising that it is not one which is clearly sustained, resting as it does upon a supposed parallel with a differentiation between anatomy and physiology in the study of the organism. The 'structure' of an organism exists 'independently' of its functioning in a certain specific sense: the parts of the body can be studied when the organism dies, that is, when it has stopped 'functioning'. But such is not the case with social systems, *which cease to be when they cease to function*: 'patterns' of social relationships only exist in so far as the latter are organised as systems, reproduced over the course of time. Hence in functionalism also, the notions of structure and system tend to dissolve into one another.

The concept of structuration I wish to develop depends upon making distinctions between structure and system (without questioning that these have to be closely connected); but it also involves understanding each of the terms differently from the characteristic usages of both structuralism and functionalism.

I want to suggest that *structure, system* and *structuration*, appropriately conceptualised, are all necessary terms in social theory. To understand why a use can be found for each of these notions, we have to turn to the theme of temporality . . . In functionalism and structuralism alike, an attempt is made to exclude time (or more accurately, time–space intersections) from social theory, by the application of the synchrony/diachrony distinction. However, social systems are 'taken out of time' in differing fashion in the two types of theoretical tradition. In functionalism, and more generally in Anglo–Saxon sociology and anthropology, the attempt to bracket time is made in terms of 'taking a snapshot' of society, or 'freezing' it at an instant. The logical defects of such a view should be obvious, and it only retains whatever plausibility it has because of the implicit comparison that lies behind it. The anatomy of a body, or the girders of a building, the sort of imagery that is involved with this conception of structure, are perceptually 'present' in a sense which 'social structure' is not. Consequently, in this mode of thinking the synchrony/diachrony distinction is unstable. Time refuses to be eliminated . . . The term 'social structure' thus tends to include two elements, not clearly distinguished from one another: the *patterning of interaction*, as implying relations between actors or groups: and the *continuity of interaction* in time. Thus Firth writes in *Elements of Social Organisation* that 'The idea of the structure of society . . . must be concerned with the ordered relations of parts to a whole, with the arrangement in which the elements of social life are linked together.' But then later he adds, talking of structural elements running through the whole of human behaviour', that these consist 'really in the *persistence or repetition* of behaviour', in the '*continuity* in social life'[32] (emphasis added).

What this comes down to is an implicit recognition of syntagmatic dimension (patterning in time–space) and a paradigmatic dimension (continuity-producing, virtual order of elements) in social analysis – although no account is provided of how these interconnect. Now this differentiation (although with certain confusions . . . is just that employed by Lévi-Strauss, and one might therefore suppose that Lévi-Strauss's conception of structure might be simply adopted in place of the idea of 'social structure' typically employed in functionalist versions of social science. And I do want to suggest a usage of 'structure' that is closer to that of Lévi-Strauss than to functionalism. But there are at least five limitations that compromise the usefulness of Lévi-Strauss's notion.

1. Lévi-Strauss holds that structure connotes a model constructed by the observer, and in his words 'has nothing to do with empirical reality'.[33] I do not want to accept this curious mixture of nominalism and rationalism that Lévi-Strauss appears to advocate. I shall argue that structure has a 'virtual existence', as instantiations or moments; but this is not the same as identifying structure merely with models invented by socio-

logical or anthropological observers. Although I shall not defend the claim, I regard the concepts I formulate below as compatible with a realist epistemology.

2.   Lévi-Strauss's structuralism lacks a concept of structure-as-structuration. Processes of structuration, in other words, are treated by Lévi-Strauss, in the mode suggested by his persistent allusion to musical scores, as combinatory forms produced by an external player (the unconscious, in Lévi-Strauss's sense). But a theory of structuration that is concerned with all types of social processes and modes of reproduction, while not disavowing unconscious mental operations, must allocate a central place to discursive and practical consciousness in the reproduction of social practices.

3.   Lévi-Strauss's approach appears ambiguous in regarding structure as relations between a set of inferred elements or oppositions, and as rules of transformation that produce equivalences across sets. The same sort of ambiguity tends to appear in mathematical concepts of structure, which usually treat structure as a matrix of admissible transformations of a set 'Structure' can be understood either as the matrix, or the laws of transformation, but usually tends to merge the two together. I shall not regard structure as referring in its most basic sense to the form of sets, but rather to the *rules (and resources)* that, in social reproduction, 'bind' time. Thus 'structure', as applied below, is first of all treated as a generic term; but structures can be identified as sets or matrices of rule-resource properties.

4.   The notion of structure applied by Lévi-Strauss is associated with the basic shortcomings I have identified in structuralist thought generally, in respect of semantic spacing as *Praxis*. I shall argue that, strictly speaking, there are no such things as 'rules of transformation'; *all social rules are transformational*, in the sense that structure is not manifested in empirical similarity of social items.[34]

5.   If structure exists (in time–space) only in its instances, it must include, it seems to me, reference to phenomena that are completely foreign to Lévi-Strauss's attempt to overcome formalism by emphasising form as the realisation of content: phenomena relating to *power*. I want to say that, in the senses in which I shall elaborate conceptions of domination and power, these concepts are logically presupposed by that of

agency, and by the agency/structure connections characterised below.

As I shall employ it, 'structure' refers to 'structural property', or more exactly, to 'structuring property', structuring properties providing the 'binding' of time and space in social systems. I argue that these properties can be understood as rules and resources, recursively implicated in the reproduction of social systems. Structures exist paradigmatically, as an absent set of differences, temporally 'present' only in their instantiation, in the constituting moments of social systems. To regard structure as involving a 'virtual order' of differences, as I have already indicated, does not necessitate accepting Lévi-Strauss's view that structures are simply models posited by the observer. Rather, it implies recognising the existence of: (a) knowledge – as memory traces – of 'how things are to be done' (said, written), on the part of social actors; (b) social practices organised through the recursive mobilisation of that knowledge; (c) capabilities that the production of those practices presupposes.

'Structural analysis' in the social sciences involves examining the structuration of social systems. The connotation of 'visible pattern' which the term 'social structure' ordinarily has, as employed in Anglo–American sociology, is carried in my terminology by the notion of system: with the crucial proviso that social systems are patterned in time as well as space, through continuities of social reproduction. A social system is thus a 'structured totality'. Structures do not exist in time–space, except in the moments of the constitution of social systems. But we can analyse how 'deeply-layered' structures are in terms of the historical duration of the practices they recursively organise, and the spatial 'breadth' of those practices: how widespread they are across a range of interactions. The most deeply-layered practices constitutive of social systems in each of these senses are *institutions*.

It is fundamental to understand that, when I speak of structure as rules and resources, I do not imply that we can profitably study either rules or resources as aggregates of isolated precepts or capabilities. From Saussure to Wittgenstein to Searle the game of chess appears in the philosophical literature as a reference point for illustrating features of linguistic and social rules. But, as I shall suggest below – especially in the way in which they are employed by philosophical authors – such game analogies can be highly misleading. Rules tend to be regarded as isolated formulae, to be related to particular 'moves'. Nowhere in the philosophical literature, to my knowledge, are either the history of chess (which has its origins in warfare), or actual games of chess, made the focus of study. Such study would, however, be much more relevant than the usual analogies for elucidating the standpoint I wish to suggest, which regards rules as media and outcome of the reproduction of social systems. Rules can only be grasped in the context of the historical development of social totalities, as recursively implicated in practices. This point is important in a twofold sense. (a) *There is not a singular relation between 'an activity' and 'a rule'*, as is sometimes suggested or implied by appeal to statements like 'the rule governing the Queen's move' in chess. Activities or practices are brought into being in the context of overlapping and connected sets of rules, given coherence by their involvement in the constitution of social systems in the movement of time. (b) Rules cannot be exhaustively described or analysed in terms of their own content, as prescriptions, prohibitions, etc.: precisely because, apart from those circumstances where a relevant lexicon exists, *rules and practices only exist in conjunction with one another*.

Rules and resources

The connections between the three concepts in Figure II.2 can be quickly stated at the outset. Social systems involve regularised relations of interdependence between individuals or groups, that typically can be best analysed as *recurrent social practices*. Social systems are systems of social interaction; as such they involve the

STRUCTURE	Rules and resources, organised as properties of social systems Structure only exists as 'structural properties'
SYSTEM	Reproduced relations between actors or collectivities, organised as regular social practices
STRUCTURATION	Conditions governing the continuity or transformation of structures, and therefore the reproduction of systems

Figure II.2

situated activities of human subjects, and exist syntagmatically in the flow of time. Systems, in this terminology, have structures, or more accurately, have structural properties; they are not structures in themselves. Structures are necessarily (logically) properties of systems or collectivities, and *are characterised by the 'absence of a subject'*. To study the structuration of a social system is to study the ways in which that system, via the application of generative rules and resources, and in the context of unintended outcomes, is produced and reproduced in interaction.

Each of these notions demands further elaboration, however, beginning with rules and resources. The idea of 'rule' of course, has been much discussed in the recent philosophical literature, and it is important to enter some major qualifications as to its use.

(1) I reject the distinction which is frequently made between 'constitutive' and 'regulative' rules (which can be traced back to Kant).[35] All social rules have both constitutive and regulative (sanctioning) aspects to them. The sort of prescription which is usually offered as an instance of a regulative rule is, for example, 'don't take the goods of another'; as contrasted to something like the aforementioned 'rule governing the Queen's move' in chess. But the first enters into the constitution of ideas of 'honesty', 'propriety', etc.; while the latter implies sanctions ('you mustn't/can't move the piece like that').

(2) We have to be very careful about using the rules of games – like chess – as illustrative of the characteristics of social rules in general. Only certain features of 'knowing a rule' are best exemplified in this way, because games like chess have clearly fixed, formalised rules that are established in a lexicon, as well as because the rules of chess are not generally subject to chronic disputes of legitimacy, as social rules may be. To know a rule, as Wittgenstein says, is to 'know how to go on', to know how to play according to the rule. This is vital, because it connects rules and practices. Rules generate – or are the medium of the production and reproduction of – practices. *A rule is thus not a generalisation of what people do, of regular practices.* These considerations are important in respect of the arguments of those authors (such as Ziff) who have been inclined to discard the notion of rule in favour of that of

dispositions.[36] The usual basis of this view is the idea that rules are foreign to most areas of social life, which are not organised prescriptively. One version is given by Oakeshott, who writes that, in language and in practical social life:

> No doubt . . . what is learnt (or some of it) can be formulated in rules and precepts; but in neither case do we . . . learn by learning rules and precepts . . . And not only may a command of language and behaviour be achieved without our becoming aware of the rules, but also, if we have acquired a knowledge of the rules, this sort of command of language and behaviour is impossible until we have forgotten them as rules and are no longer tempted to turn speech and action into the applications of rules to a situation.[37]

This, however, identifies knowing rules with knowing how to formulate rules, which are two different things. 'To know how to go on' is not necessarily, or normally, to be able to formulate clearly what the rules are. A child who learns English as a first language, when he or she can speak the language, knows the rules of English usage, whether or not he or she can formulate any of them. Oakeshott's argument does not compromise the general usefulness of 'rule', although it does focus attention upon the Wittgensteinian emphasis on the practical character of rule-following.

(3) Pursuing the implications of point 2, we may say that Wittgenstein's references to the rules of children's games are more illuminating in some key respects than discussions of games with fixed and determined rules like chess. He makes, in fact, virtually the same point as Oakeshott, when arguing that the rules involved in most forms of life resemble the former more than they do the latter: 'remember that in general we don't use language according to strict rules – it hasn't been taught us by means of strict rules, either'. In children's games, at least those which are practised by children's groups themselves, or transmitted informally from generation to generation, there is no lexicon of formal rules, and it may be an essential characteristic of the rules which do exist that they cannot be strictly defined. Such is the case, Wittgenstein argues, with most of

the concepts employed in ordinary language. We cannot clearly delimit them in a lexical sense: 'not because we don't know
their real definition, but because there is no real "definition" to
them. To suppose that there must be would be like supposing
that whenever children play with a ball they play a game
according to strict rules.'[38] It is worth making a point with
regard to ethno-semantics . . . at this juncture. The operations
of practical consciousness enmesh rules *and* the 'methodological' interpretation of rules in the continuity of practices.[39]
Garfinkel's conception of the interpretative work which is
always temporally involved in accountability is very important here. What Garfinkel calls 'ad hoc' considerations – the
'etcetera clause', 'let it pass', etc. [*sic*] – are chronically involved in the instantiation of rules, and are not separate from
what those rules 'are'.

In emphasising the importance of resources as structural properties of social systems, I mean to stress the centrality of the concept
of power to social theory. Like 'rule', power is not a description of a
state of affairs, but a capability. I think it true to say that few of the
major thinkers or traditions of thought in sociology have accorded
power as focal a place in social theory as is warranted. Those who
have recognised the essential importance of power, like Nietzsche
and Weber, have usually done so only on the basis of a normative
irrationalism which I want to repudiate (although I shall not give
the grounds for this here). If there is no rational mode of adjudging
'ultimate value' claims, as Weber held, then the only recourse open
is that of power or might: the strongest are able to make their
values count by crushing others.[40] More common are those standpoints which either treat power as secondary to the meaningful or
normative character of social life, or ignore power altogether. Such
is the case, for example, with the works of authors in traditions of
phenomenology (Schutz) or Wittgensteinian social thought
(Winch), just as much as with traditions to which they are opposed
in other respects (the functionalism of Durkheim or Parsons). It is
even true, in a certain, although a quite different, sense, of Marxism, in so far as Marx connected power directly to class interests,
with the possible inference that when class divisions disappear,
relations of power do also.
Among the many interpretations of power in social and political

theory, two main perspectives appear. One is that power is best conceptualised as the capability of an actor to achieve his or her will, even at the expense of that of others who might resist him – the sort of definition employed by Weber[41] among many other authors. The second is that power should be seen as a property of the collectivity: Parsons's concept of power, for instance, belongs to this latter category.[42] I wish to claim, however, that neither of these modes of conceiving power is appropriate in isolation; and that we should connect them together as features of the duality of structure. I shall treat resources as the 'bases' or 'vehicles' of power, comprising structures of domination, drawn upon by parties to interaction and reproduced through the duality of structure. Power is generated by definite forms of domination in a parallel way to the involvement of rules with social practices: and, indeed, as an integral element or aspect of those practices. [For an extended discussion of power and domination, see Giddens, *Central Problems in Social Theory*, pp.88–94.]

The theory of structuration

The concept of structuration involves that of the *duality of structure*, which relates to the *fundamentally recursive character of social life, and expresses the mutual dependence of structure and agency*. By the duality of structure I mean that the structural properties of social systems are both the medium and the outcome of the practices that constitute those systems. The theory of structuration, thus formulated, rejects any differentiation of synchrony and diachrony or statics and dynamics. The identification of structure with constraint is also rejected: structure is both enabling and constraining, and it is one of the specific tasks of social theory to study the conditions in the organisation of social systems that govern the interconnections between the two. According to this conception, the same structural characteristics participate in the subject (the actor) as in the object (society). Structure forms 'personality' and 'society' simultaneously – but in neither case exhaustively: because of the significance of unintended consequences of action, and because of unacknowledged conditions of action. Ernst Bloch says, *Homo semper tiro*: man is always a beginner.[43] We may agree, in the sense that every process of action is a production of something new, a fresh act; but at the same time all action exists in continuity with the past, which supplies the means of its initiation. *Structure thus is not to be conceptualised as a barrier to action, but as essentially involved in its production*: even in the most radical processes of social change which, like any others, occur in time. The most disruptive modes of social change, like the most rigidly stable forms, involve structuration. Hence there is no need, nor any room, for a conception of de-structuration such as that suggested by Gurvitch.[44] A notion of de-structuration is only necessary if we retain the idea that structure is simply equivalent to constraint, thereby counterposing structure and freedom (as Gurvitch does, and as Sartre does also).

It is important to accentuate this last point, because some authors who have emphasised the contingency of social life have done so only at the cost of adopting an overly voluntaristic viewpoint. One such example, its interesting contributions notwithstanding, is Shackle's economics. Shackle argues against determinism in human economic activities, stressing their temporal and contingent character: but he is led by this to attach an excessive importance to what he calls 'decision' in human social life. The past is dead and 'determined', but the present is always open to the free initiative of human actors.[45] Commendable as this perspective may be in some ways, it hardly allows us to grasp how the past makes itself felt in the present, even while the present may react back against the past. In this respect, Shackle's view seems to share a good deal in common with that elaborated by Sartre in *The Critique of Dialectical Reason* – indeed, it would not be too inaccurate to regard Shackle's work as a kind of Sartrean economic theory. For in spite of his accentuation of the importance of history to the understanding of the human condition, Sartre preserves a gulf between past and present, in the sense that while the past is 'given and necessary' the present is a realm of free, spontaneous creation: in that sense he fails to escape from a dualism of 'materiality' and '*Praxis*'.

According to the notion of the duality of structure, rules and resources are drawn upon by actors in the production of interaction, but are thereby also reconstituted through such interaction. Structure is thus the mode in which the relation between moment and totality expresses itself in social reproduction. This relation is distinct from that involved in the relation of 'parts' and 'wholes' in the co-ordination of actors and groups in social systems as posited in functionalist theory. That is to say, the differences which constitute social systems reflect a dialectic of presences and absences in space and time. But these are only brought into being and reproduced via the virtual order of differences of structures, expressed in the duality of structure. The differences that constitute structures, and are constituted structurally, relate 'part' to 'whole' in the sense in which the utterance of a grammatical sentence presupposes the absent corpus of syntactical rules that constitute the language as a totality. The importance of this relation of moment and totality for social theory cannot be exaggerated, since it involves a dialectic of presence and absence which ties the most minor or trivial forms of social action to structural properties of the overall society (and, logically, to the development of mankind as a whole).

It is an essential emphasis of the ideas developed here that institutions do not just work 'behind the backs' of the social actors who produce and reproduce them. Every competent member of every society knows a great deal about the institutions of that society: such knowledge is not *incidental* to the operation of society, but is necessarily involved in it. A common tendency of many otherwise divergent schools of sociological thought is to adopt the methodological tactic of beginning their analyses by discounting agents' reasons for their action (or what I prefer to call the rationalisation of action), in order to discover the 'real' stimuli to their activity, of which they are ignorant. Such a stance, however, is not only defective from the point of view of social theory, it is one with strongly-defined and potentially offensive political implications. It implies a *derogation of the lay actor*. If actors are regarded as cultural dopes or mere 'bearers of a mode of production', with no worthwhile understanding of their surroundings or the circumstances of their action, the way is immediately laid open for the supposition that their own views can be disregarded in any practical programmes that might be inaugurated. This is not just a question of 'whose side (as social analysts) are we on?'[46] – although there is no doubt that social incompetence is commonly attributed to people in lower socio-economic groupings by those in power-positions, or by their associated 'experts'.

It is not a coincidence that the forms of social theory which have made little or no conceptual space for agents' understanding of themselves, and of their social contexts, have tended greatly to exaggerate the impact of dominant symbol systems or ideologies upon those in subordinate classes: as in Parsons or Althusser. A good case can be made to the effect that only dominant class groups have ever been strongly committed to dominant ideologies.[47] This is not just because of the development of divergent 'sub-cultures' – for example, working-class culture as compared to bourgeois culture in nineteenth-century Britain – but also because *all social actors, no matter how lowly, have some degree of penetration of the social forms which oppress them.*[48] Where partially closed, localised cultures become largely unavailable, as is increasingly the case within advanced capitalism, scepticism about 'official' views of society often is expressed in various forms of 'distancing' – and in humour. Wit is deflationary. Humour is used socially both to attack and to defend against the influence of outside forces that cannot otherwise easily be coped with.

One must not overestimate the degree of conviction with which even those in dominant classes, or other positions of authority, accept ideological symbol-systems. But it is not implausible to suppose that, in some circumstances, and from some aspects, those in subordinate positions in a society might have a greater penetration of the conditions of social reproduction than those who otherwise dominate them. This is related to the *dialectic of control* in social systems . . . Those who in a largely unquestioning way accept certain dominant perspectives may be more imprisoned within them than others are, even though these perspectives help the former to sustain their position of dominance. The point at issue here has a definite similarity to Laing's thesis about schizophrenia: that notwithstanding the distorted nature of schizophrenic language and thought, in some respects the schizophrenic person 'sees through' features of day-to-day existence which the majority accept without demur.

These things having been said, we have to enter major qualifications about what is implied in the proposition that every competent actor has a wide-ranging, yet intimate and subtle, knowledge of the society of which he or she is a member. First, 'knowledge' has to be understood in terms of both practical and discursive consciousness: and even where there is substantial discursive penetration of institutional forms, this is not necessarily, nor normally, expressed in a propositional manner. Schutz in a sense makes this point when he calls typifications 'cookery book knowledge', and contrasts cookery book knowledge to the sort of abstract, theoretical knowledge called for by the relevances of the social scientist.[49] But this does not distinguish satisfactorily between practical consciousness, which is knowledge embodied in what actors 'know how to do', and discourse, that is, what actors are able to 'talk about' and in what manner or guise they are able to talk about it.

Second, every individual actor is only one among others in a society: very many others, obviously, in the case of the contemporary industrialised societies. We have to recognise that what an actor knows as a competent – but historically and spatially located – member of society, 'shades off' in contexts that stretch beyond those of his or her day-to-day activity. Third, the parameters of parctical and discursive consciousness are bounded in specifiable ways, that connect with the 'situated' character of actors' activities, but are not reducible to it. These can be identified [as] . . . : the unconscious conditions of action and the unintended consequences of action. All of these phenomena have to be related to problems of ideology . . .

(iv)   Structure, action, reproduction*

Structures, structural properties

. . . [T]he concept of structure may be used in a technical and in a more general way. Understood as rules and resources, structure is recursively implicated in the reproduction of social systems and is wholly fundamental to structuration theory. Used in a looser fashion, structure can be spoken of as referring to the institutionalized features (structural properties) of societies. In both usages 'structure' is a generic category involved in each of the structural concepts given below:

(1)   *structural principles*: Principles of organization of societal totalities;
(2)   *structures*: Rule-resource sets, involved in the institutional articulation of social systems;
(3)   *structural properties*: Institutionalized features of social systems, stretching across time and space.

---

* *The Constitution of Society* pp. 185–93.

The identification of structural principles, and their conjunctures in intersocietal systems, represents the most comprehensive level of institutional analysis. That is to say, the analysis of structural principles refers to modes of differentiation and articulation of institutions across the 'deepest' reaches of time-space. The study of structural sets, or *structures*, involves the isolating of distinct 'clusterings' of transformation/mediation relations implied in the designation of structural principles. Structural sets are formed by the mutual convertibility of the rules and resources implicated in social reproduction. Structures can be analytically distinguished within each of the three dimensions of structuration, signification, legitimation and domination, or across these. I have offered elsewhere an illustration,[50] on which I shall comment at rather greater length here. This is the example of private property in Marx's analysis of modern capitalism.

Consider what is involved in the following structural set:

> private property : money : capital : labour contract : profit

The structural relations indicated here mark out one of the most fundamental transmutations involved in the emergence of capitalism and hence contribute in a significant way to the overall structuration of the system. In feudalism (in my terminology, one among other types of class-divided society) private property in the means of production was based predominantly on ownership of land, and such ownership was hedged about with numerous qualifications upon alienability. In so far as these conversion relations pertained at all, they were confined to marginal sectors of the economy. In capitalism, by contrast, private ownership of the means of production takes on a different *form* – land becoming only one type among other resources mobilized within production – and a diversity of goods becomes freely alienable. Essential to this process, Marx demonstrates, is the universalizing of commodity form. The condition of such universalization is the development of a full-blown money economy. Money, Marx says, is 'the metamorphosed shape of all other commodities, the result of their general alienation'.[51] Money (M) represents, on the one side, a sold commodity (C) and, on the other, a commodity to be bought. M-C is a purchase but is at the same time C-M, a sale: 'the concluding metamorphosis of one commodity is the first metamorphosis of another' or, as Quesnay expressed the same thing in his *Maximes générales*, 'vendre est acheter'. The differentiation of commodities into commodities and money does not dissolve the material differences between commodities; it develops, Marx says, a *modus vivendi*, 'a form in which they can exist side by side'.[52]

C-M-C, the simplest form of the circulation of commodities, is the beginning point of capital. As contrasted with the landed property of feudalism, capital first takes the form of money – the capital of the merchant and the usurer. The first distinction between money and capital is simply a difference in the relation of transformation involved, expressed as M-C-M. This formula expresses the transformation of money into commodities and of commodities back into money – in other words, buying in order to sell. Money which has undergone this transformation has become capital. Like the other relation, M-C-M involves two linked phases of transmutation. In the first money is changed into a commodity; in the second the commodity is changed back again into money. But the combination of these phases, Marx argues, 'constitutes a single moment' whereby a commodity is bought in order to be sold. It might seem as though money has simply been exchanged for money – more or less, according to the success or otherwise of the transaction. But where money has been transformed into capital it has gone through a 'characteristic and original movement' quite distinct in type from that of, say, a peasant who sells corn and uses the money thus acquired to buy clothes. The transformations involved in M-C-M, as compared with C-M-C, differ more than in the mere difference in the 'direction' of change.

The difference is that in the C-M-C relation the money is converted into a use value, which is then 'consumed'. In the opposite form, M-C-M, the money is not spent; it is 'advanced' – the secret of the transformation of money into capital. In the C-M-C form the same element of money changes its place twice, completing the transaction. But the contrary is the case in the M-C-M relation: in this connection it is not the money that changes hands twice but the commodity. The transmutation of money into capital depends upon the renewal of the operation, its 'reflux', which only the M-C-M relation makes possible. M-C-M should thus more accurately be written as $M\text{-}C\text{-}M^1$, as an expansionary process. The circulation of commodities has here become separated off from a direct relation to use value. Capital trades not in use values but in exchange values.

M-C-M^1, however, can represent mercantile capital as well as industrial capital. It is therefore only the 'general formula for capital'. A further structural relation is implicated in the development of industrial or manufacturing capital, one which, like the altered nature of private property, presumes a major process of social change. This further relation is the possibility of the transformation of capital into labour and *vice versa*, something which presupposes a massive expropriation of workers from control of their means of production, such that they have to offer their labour power for sale on the market in order to attain a livelihood. Labour power is a commodity that has the peculiar feature, among others, of being a source of the creation of value. The capitalist labour contract is inherently involved with the transformation of money into an equivalent of labour power. 'This relation has no natural basis, neither is its social basis one that is common to all historical periods. It is clearly the result of a past historical development, the product of many economic revolutions, of the extinction of a whole series of older forms of social production.[53] Thus the isolation of such a connection helps to diagnose one of the key structural features of the novel institutional form constituted by capitalism. That labour power is a commodity is not given in the 'general formula for capital'.

The capitalist labour contract presumes that employer and worker 'meet in the market' in circumstances in which each is 'formally free'. This is a basic aspect of the class relations of capitalism. One is a buyer of labour power, the other a seller. The 'owner' of labour power sells it only for a definite period, as does the employer who 'takes on' labour. Slavery, in which some persons are owned by others, does not permit the commodification of labour power. The value of labour power, in common with that of other commodities, is governed by the labour time involved in its production and therefore by what is demanded to ensure the physical survival of those who supply labour. The transformation of the hire of labour power into profit, of course, is dependent upon the generation of surplus value. 'Necessary labour time' is that given over to the

level of abstraction ↑	structural principles	
	structural sets (structures)	social/system integration
	elements/axes of structuration	

sustaining of the source of labour power, the worker; surplus labour is the source of profit.

There is no definite cut-off point between the three levels of abstraction distinguished in the above diagram. The specification of structural sets, as indicated previously, is of basic importance to the elaboration of overall structural principles, but the one task obviously merges into the other. The same holds for the lowest level of abstraction, the isolating of elements or axes of structuration. Distinguishing elements of structuration preserves the *epoché* of institutional analysis, but brings the level of study closer to the direct examination of relations of co-presence. In order to preserve continuity with the preceding discussion, let me follow through Marx's discussion in respect of a major feature of capitalist production, the division of labour. It is an analysis with which I am largely in accord, although my main purpose here is an illustrative one.[54]

The division of labour, Marx seeks to show, is closely bound up with the nature of manufacture and therefore with the structural relations portrayed in the foregoing paragraphs of this extract. The division of labour links the broader structural characteristics of capitalism, as identified previously, with the more proximate organization of the industrial enterprise. Manufacture, a pre-eminent feature of capitalism that has advanced beyond commerce, is associated with two modes of the emergence of workshops. One is the assembling, under the control of a particular employer, of workers with different craft skills in a specific locale. These are co-ordinated in the making of a single product. But such co-ordination tends also progressively to strip away aspects of the skills originally possessed by workers, leading to the splitting up of tasks into 'detailed' processes, 'each of which crystallizes into the exclusive function of a particular workman, the manufacture, as a whole, being carried on by the men in conjunction'.[55] A second way in which manufacture arises is something of the reverse of this. It is the assembling within one locale of a number of workers who all do the same task, each worker making the entire commodity. However, 'external circumstances', Marx says, lead to changes in much the same direction as those occurring in the first type of setting. Labour is therefore redistributed; instead of workers all occupied in the same way side by side, operations become broken down into detailed tasks, organized in a co-operative fashion. The final form is thus the same in both cases: 'a productive mechanism whose parts are human beings'.[56]

The detailed division of labour is of major importance to the organization of the capitalist enterprise in several ways. It enhances the opportunities for direct surveillance of the workforce and the consolidation of labour discipline. But it also both expresses and makes possible the connection of labour, as labour power, with the technology of machine production. For the 'detail labourer' carries out a circumscribed number of repetitive operations that can be co-ordinated with the movements of mechanized production processes. Division of labour within the enterprise is not simply an aspect or extension of the division of labour outside, the 'division of labour in society', but these none the less react upon one another. The 'division of labour in society' depends upon the purchase and sale of products of different sectors of industry; the division of labour within the enterprise derives from the sale of the labour power of a plurality of workers to an employer who applies it in a co-ordinated fashion.

> Division of labour within the workshop implies the undisputed authority of the capitalist over men, that are but parts of a mechanism that belongs to him. The division of labour within the society brings into contact independent commodity-producers, who acknowledge no other authority but that of competition. . . . It is very characteristic [Marx adds caustically] that the enthusiastic apologists of the factory system have nothing more damning to urge against a general organization of the labour of society than that it would turn all society into one immense factory.[57]

To analyse the division of labour in this way is to elucidate an axis of structuration connecting the internal form of the enterprise with broader aspects of the societal totality, indicating at the same time contrasts with the 'division of labour in society'. Of course, these relations could be spelled out in very much greater detail. In institutional analysis this involves detailing the transformation/ mediation relations implicated in the 'clustering' of institutionalized practices across space and time. However, once we abandon the *epoché* of institutional analysis, all the structural relations indicated above, at whatever level, have to be examined as conditions of system reproduction. They help to pick out basic features of the *circuits of reproduction* implicated in the 'stretching' of institutions across space and time. Analysing circuits of reproduction, it should be clear, is not equivalent to identifying the sources of social stability alone. They serve indeed to indicate some of the main forms of change involved in the transition from one type of societal totality to another. What 'must happen' for certain conditions of system reproduction to occur is posed as a counterfactual question, not as a covert version of functionalism.

A reproduction circuit can be sketched in diagrammatic form (see Figure II.3).

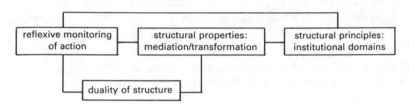

Figure II.3

The reintroduction of the duality of structure means leaving the virtual time–space of institutional analysis, thereby re-entering 'history'. All structural properties of social systems, to repeat a leading theme of structuration theory, are the medium and outcome of the contingently accomplished activities of situated actors. The reflexive monitoring of action in situations of co-presence is the main anchoring feature of social integration, but both the conditions and the outcomes of situated interaction stretch far beyond those situations as such. The mechanisms of 'stretching' are variable but in modern societies tend to involve reflexive monitoring itself. That is to say, understanding the conditions of system reproduction becomes part of those conditions of system reproduction as such.

We can trace these observations through more concretely by returning to the structural set discussed previously. The two opposed but complementary transformations C-M and M-C occur, of course, only through the activities of buyers and sellers acting in a range of divergent settings. According to Marx, the C-M-C relation brings into co-relation three '*dramatis personae*'. The owner of a commodity comes into contact with a possessor of money, the money becoming, in Marx's words, 'its transient equivalent-form'. Money, the 'final term of the first transmutation', is the origin of the third, the buying of another commodity.[58] But as Marx expresses it, this is unsatisfactory. For structural relations are not isomorphic to the acts of corresponding individuals who personify them. It is in just such tendencies of Marx's argument that one can see where Althusser derives textual corroboration for the view that human agents are no more than 'supports' for modes of production. Moreover, it is also easy to see how such a style of analysis slips over into functionalism. For if the relations between structural properties, once isolated, are treated as having their own 'inner dynamics', as functional necessities rather than as continually reproduced conditions, the activities of historically situated individuals do indeed seem rather redundant. The overall conditions of system reproduction are in no way 'guaranteed' by the structural relations upon which (counter-factually) they depend. Nor does analysing those relations in virtual time–space explain in any way why they came about. This means that it is highly important to shift conceptual gears when moving from such analysis to the study of the conditions of system reproduction.

By circuits of reproduction I mean fairly clearly defined 'tracks' of processes which feed back to their source, whether or not such feedback is reflexively monitored by agents in specific social positions. When Marx uses the term 'circuits of capital' he seems to have something of this sort in mind; however, I want to refer to actual conditions of social reproduction, while Marx sometimes uses the term in reference to what I have called structural sets. Reproduction circuits can always usefully be examined in terms of the regionalization of locales. There is no harm in thinking of such circuits as having something in common with electronic circuits, which can be traced out in a visual display – the graphic techniques of time-geography, in fact, might be relevant here. The reproduction circuits associated with the M-C-M^1 set as Marx himself makes clear – actually depend upon vast processes of change not just within societies but on an international scale. The concentration of the population in newly expanding (and internally transformed) urban areas is one of these processes of change. Others concern the nature of the workplace. But as important as any of these is the mechanization of transportation, the tremendous expansion of means of communication from the late eighteenth century onwards and the development of electronic communication dating from the invention of the Morse Code.

(v)   Lay knowledge and technical concepts*

Sociology and lay knowledge

In analysing what sociologists do, let me start from the observation that what seems obvious, or what 'everyone knows', may not only not be obvious at all, it might actually be wrong. Not many of us today belong to the flat-earth society, although it seems obvious enough when you look at it that the earth is as flat as any pancake. In the case of our presumed knowledge about social institutions, it might be argued, we are particularly inclined to error. At any rate, examples are very easy to find. It is commonly known – or believed – for example that there has been a steep rise in the number of 'broken homes' or one-parent families over the past century. Thus if we look back to Victorian times, we see a dramatic contrast between the stable, integrated families of that era and the disarray of the current period. In fact the proportion of one-parent families was possibly greater in the Victorian epoch than it is today – not as a result of divorce, but mainly as a consequence of higher rates of mortality in relatively youthful age-groups. Or again, it is common knowledge that the United Kingdom is particularly strike-prone, its tendency to industrial disruption even being taken by some to be the main origin of its shortcomings in respect of economic performance. However, in terms of any accepted measures, the incidence of strikes in Britain is not especially high as compared with various other industrially-developed countries. To take another example, it is well-known – or imagined – that Sweden has an extremely high rate of suicide. Something in the gloomy Nordic character, or the long years of having had to tolerate a socialist government, creates a disposition to melancholy or to despair. In actuality Sweden does not display a particularly elevated suicide rate, and never has done so.

One should not underestimate the contribution which social research can make to identifying false or slanted beliefs widely held

---

* *Social Theory and Modern Sociology*, pp. 4–21.

about social phenomena. For such beliefs may often take the form of prejudices, and hence contribute to intolerance and discrimination, or might inhibit social changes that would otherwise be seen as desirable. It surely must be one of the tasks of the sociologist to seek to discover how far commonly-held views about given aspects of social life are in fact valid, even if they appear obvious to everyone else. And this is bound to mean that the results of social research may now and then seem uninspiring, since what is thought to be obvious may indeed prove to be the case. It should not be forgotten, moreover, that a good deal of what is now taken to be among the things everyone knows about social institutions is the result of sociological analysis and social research. An enormous amount of social research – often carried out by government bodies or survey agencies, not only by sociologists in a university context – goes into the routine running of a modern society. We tend to take this for granted, but without it much that is involved in what everyone knows would not be part of our awareness at all. We all know that rates of divorce in most Western countries are higher that they were two or three decades ago; but we tend to forget the very considerable amount of continuing social investigation involved in charting such trends.

If this were all there were to sociology, there would probably not be too much to get excited about. Sociology is not just in the business correcting false beliefs which we may hold about social phenomena – although some of its advocates have in fact seen it only in this role. Let me return to the theorem I stated earlier. To be a human agent is to know, virtually all the time, under some description, what one is engaged in and why. There is a sense in which we cannot be wrong about what our actions are, or those actions would not exist. I cannot, for instance, write a cheque without knowing not only what it is I am doing, but without also knowing a complex array of concepts and rules, defining what 'credit' is, what 'having an account' is, what a 'bank' is, and so on. The formula that human agents always in a certain sense know what they are doing, and why, necessarily involves a range of elements in the broader institutional context within which a particular action is carried on. We do not need social research to tell us what these elements are, since not only do we know them already, we must know them already for the action in question to be possible at all.

This sort of knowledge – knowledge of the social conventions involved in the societies in which we live – cannot, therefore, be subject to illumination by sociology. Or so it might seem. Only a little reflection is required to see that such is not the case. I want to propose, in fact, that there are no less than four types of question that one might legitimately ask about social conduct, none of which contravenes the assertion that human individuals always know what their actions are and why they engage in them. These four kinds of enquiry, which have a logical unity with one another, supply the keys to understanding what sociologists do – to what the discipline of sociology is all about.

Consider again the example of signing a cheque. Everyone in a modern society knows what signing a cheque is, but someone from a culture in which there are no banks, and perhaps not even a monetary system at all, would not. What is familiar convention to one individual or group, in other words, is not necessarily so to another. This is true not only between different societies, or forms of society, but within them too. All of us live our lives within particular sectors of the societies of which we are members, and the modes of behaviour of those in other milieux may be largely opaque to us. Showing what it is like to live in one particular cultural setting to those who inhabit another (and vice versa) is a significant part of what the sociologist does. This might be called the anthropological moment of social research, and it is worthwhile noting some of its implications. Notice, for example, that the identification of the cultural diversity of social life is simultaneously often a means of disclosing the common rationality of human action. To provide an account of the conventions involved in a given cultural milieu, or a given community, allows a grasp of the intentions and reasons the agents have for what they do, which may entirely escape us in the absence of such an account.

There are complicated problems of a philosophical sort involved here, and I do not want to underestimate them. But it is fairly easy to develop the point. In a world riven with conflict and embedded hostilities, and yet increasingly interdependent, mutual comprehension across diverse cultural settings becomes of the first importance. The *sine qua non* of such cross-cultural communication is the effective prosecution of the ethnographic tasks of social research. This is just as true of the cultural distance which separates West Indian communities in Brixton from affluent white suburbs (and from Whitehall) as it is, for example, of that which separates the Islamic Revolution from the culture of the West. Of course, bridging the spaces of cultural dissimilarity does not inevitably lead to a reduction of pre-existing conflicts. The better one knows one's enemies, the clearer it may become that hostility towards them is justifiable or unavoidable. But this should not lead us to doubt what an elementary part the ethnography of culture plays in forging mutual understanding. Its natural counterpart on the level of academic disciplines is the close meshing of sociology and anthropology.

Without seeming unduly mercenary, let me revert to the instance of signing a cheque. We all know what it is to sign a cheque, but this is not the same as saying we know all there is to know about it. Would a cheque be valid if I wrote it on the back of a bus ticket, rather than on the printed slips the bank so thoughtfully provides? Most of the knowledge we have of the conventions which define our actions is not only contextual, it is basically practical and *ad hoc* in character. In order to have a bank account, and cash cheques on it, we are not required to have an elaborate understanding of the banking system. Nor could everyone necessarily put into words what a 'cheque' or an 'account' is, if asked to do so. We all know (in modern societies) what money is in the sense that we have no trouble handling monetary transactions in our day-to-day lives. But as any economist will attest, giving a clear definition of what money is tends to be far from unproblematic. As St Augustine remarked in the course of his celebrated observations about time, we all know what time is – until someone asks us.

Various inferences might be drawn from this, but I want to concentrate only upon one of them. This is that our discourse – what we are able to put into words – about our actions, and our reasons for them, only touches on certain aspects of what we do in our day-to-day lives. There is a highly complex non-discursive side to our activities which is of particular interest to sociology, and to other social sciences as well. It is not paradoxical here to say that sociology in this respect does study things we already know – although ordinarily we do not know them in the sense of being entirely aware of them. To put the matter another way, a good deal of our knowledge of social convention, as Wittgenstein famously observes, consists of being able to 'go on' in the multifarious contexts of social activity. The study of how we manage to accomplish this is a matter of great interest – and has potentially profound consequences, or so I shall try to indicate later.

We might offer as an illustration Erving Goffman's brilliant observations about body idiom.[59] To be a human agent, one must not only know what one is doing, but must also demonstrate this to others in visible fashion. We all expect each other to maintain a sort of 'controlled alertness' in our actions. We do this through the disciplined management of bodily appearance, control of bodily posture and of facial expression. Goffman shows how dazzlingly intricate are the bodily rituals whereby we 'exhibit presence' to others, and thereby routinely and chronically defend our status as agents. The best insights into how tightly controlled our public exhibition of self ordinarily is can be gained by analysing circumstances in which it lapses. Thus we might investigate the behaviour of young children from this point of view, because it takes children years to acquire the controlled bodily idiom of their elders. Or we might study inadvertent interruptions in body management – slips of the tongue, lapses in control of posture, facial expression or dress. In this regard there are intriguing connections between Goffman and Freud, although I shall not pursue them here.

The social world never seems the same again after having read Goffman. The most inoffensive gesture becomes charged with potential associations, not all of them pleasant. But why should this be? What accounts for the fact that, for most of his readers, Goffman's writings tend to produce a feeling of privileged insight into the mundane? It is, I think, because they deal with what is intimate and familiar, but from its non-discursive side. They enhance our understanding of ourselves precisely because they reveal what we already know and must know to get around in the social world, but are not cognisant of discursively. There is from this perspective no paradox in saying that what we already know warrants detailed study, yet that the outcome of such study is far from self-evident. We could make the same point about the investigation of language. Linguists spend their professional careers studying what we already know, and indeed must know to be competent language speakers at all. But this in no way compromises the importance of linguistics, or makes it less demanding than other areas of research.

I have so far distinguished two qualifications to the proposition that we all know most of the time what our actions are, and why we perpetrate them – that all of us inhabit restricted milieux within a culturally variegated world, and that we are normally able discursively to identify only little of the complex conventional frameworks of our activities. To these we now have to add a third: that our activities constantly, I would even say routinely, have consequences that we do not intend, and of which we might be quite oblivious when undertaking the behaviour in question.

Let us trudge once more up the High Street to the bank. A modern monetary system depends upon public confidence in the exchange transactions it regularizes in order to keep going. At a given point of time banks only possess coinage to cover a small fraction of the deposits that are lodged with them. Therefore although every individual creditor can withdraw the whole of his or her deposit at will, the same is not true of all creditors. If there is a run on a bank, a spiralling diminution in confidence in the bank's ability to pay up may ensue, leading perhaps to its collapse. Now it will probably be the case that few, and perhaps none, of the bank's customers had the intention of initiating such a spiral. The outcome may be one that none of them wanted, even if it came about through their agency. It was an unintended consequence of a large number of intentional actions. The bank-run example is a special case, but it is not that special. There is, for example, a general category of unintended consequences that sociologists have often labelled 'perverse consequences'. Consider the following illustration. The state government in Florida made the shooting or trapping of alligators illegal, in order to rescue them from imminent extinction. But swampland areas that had been marginally profitable for farmers, when used for the cultivation of alligators for game hunting, then became uneconomic. As a result, the farmers began to drain the land, in order eventually to produce crops from it. The consequence was that the habitat of the alligators disappeared, and they were wiped out in the very region, in which they were supposed to be conserved.[60]

Or consider an example taken from research carried out on urban renewal programmes. In some such programmes in the United States, legislation was introduced to force the owners of dilapidated buildings to bring them up to standard, especially where there were tenants in those buildings. As a consequence, some owners abandoned their buildings completely, while others only improved them insofar as they were able substantially to raise rents or turn them into non-rented accommodation. The end result was a diminution in the available amount of rented accommodation for low-income groups, coupled with a further deterioration in the housing stock in the areas involved.

Of course, not all unintended consequences are perverse. Schelling provides the following example. In the 1930s Federal deposit insurance was introduced to provide recompense for people losing their bank deposits.[61] By generating confidence, the effect of the insurance was precisely to tend to obviate the behaviour that led to the problem. Similarly those who act purely selfishly may unintentionally contribute to the collective well-being. Those who act from base motives may contribute to the good of everyone. They echo Goethe's Mephistopheles, who is 'a part of that force which always intends evil and always does good.' Perverse consequences are a particularly significant and interesting class of unintended consequences, partly because they have a certain irony, tragic in some instances, deliciously comic in others; but mainly because the boomerang effect they express is a common feature of social policy-making. My point, however, is not just to suggest that one of the things sociologists can and should do is to study the perverse effects that attempts at social intervention frequently bring in their train. It is to emphasise how fundamental the analysis of the unintended consequences of intended actions is to the whole sociological enterprise. For it is this more than anything else that entails that, while as social agents we are necessarily the creators of social life, social life is at the same time not our own creation.

The examples of unintended consequences I have given this far are instances in which there is a discrete and singular outcome. And of course many of the unintended consequences which preoccupy us in social analysis are of this form. No one intended the overall sequence of events that led up to the Russian Revolution of 1917, not even Lenin and the Bolsheviks, anxious as they were to propel history along certain rails. It is surely always true of cataclysmic social events, like the outbreak of the World Wars, that they are only marginally the outcomes of design. But the unintended consequences of actions are not confined to sequences of events having discrete outcomes. When I speak English in a syntactically correct way, it is not my intention to reproduce the structures of the English language. Such is nonetheless a consequence of my speaking correctly, even if my contribution to the continuation of the language is a rather modest one. Generalizing this observation, we may say that unintended consequences are deeply involved in the reproduction of social institutions, however much such reproduction is also governed by intention and contrivance; and the study of the intertwining of what is intended and what is not is the fourth type of task that is of elementary importance in sociology.

This needs a certain amount of commentary, because it allows us in some part to link together each of the aspects of sociological study. As a way of thinking about what is involved, take the example of a poverty cycle. In the deprived areas of inner cities we may be able to trace a continuity in underprivilege across the generations. These areas tend to have badly-equipped schools, with teachers who have to spend more time maintaining some degree of order in the classroom than in the formal business of teaching, addressing pupils whose motivation to follow the academic syllabus is less than overwhelming. Children from such schools inevitably tend to have limited opportunities in job markets when they leave the place of education. Hence they are likely to live in similarly deprived areas to those of their parents. These areas will have badly-equipped schools . . . and so the cycle continues. Such a poverty cycle is not intended by any of those affected by it, or by anyone else either. It can be explicated via a 'mix' of intentional actions and unintended consequences, but it should be noted that these have a feedback effect, so that they become conditions of further action. This is pervasively true of social life as a whole, and forms a point of connection with the contextuality or cultural diversity mentioned earlier. Given that all action is situated in limited time–space contexts, it follows that all of us are influenced by institutional orders that none of us taken singly – and perhaps none of us taken collectively – intentionally established.

All I do under some description I do intentionally and knowledgeably. However this scarcely makes me the master of my own fate. In following the routines of my day-to-day life I help reproduce social institutions that I played no part in bringing into being. They are more than merely the environment of my action since, as I have stressed previously, they enter constitutively into what it is I do as an agent. Similarly, my actions constitute and reconstitute the institutional conditions of action of others, just as their actions do of mine. The key concept tying together the several different endeavours of sociology which I have listed is that of what I like to call the recursive nature of social life. When I pursue the activities of my daily life, I draw chronically upon established convention – in a manner which is both largely tacit and at the same time extraordinarily complex – in order to do so. But this very process of drawing upon convention reconstitutes it, in some part as a binding influence upon the behaviour of others as well as that of myself. My activities are thus embedded within, and are constitutive elements of, structured properties of institutions stretching well beyond myself in time and in space.

In one of the most quoted methodological statements in sociology, Emile Durkheim observed: 'The system of signs that I employ to express my thoughts, the monetary system I use to pay my debts, the credit movements I utilise in my commercial relationships, the practices I follow in my profession, etc., all function independently of the use I make of them. Thus there are ways of acting, thinking and feeling which possess the remarkable property of existing outside the consciousness of the individual.'[62] There is nothing wrong with the general drift of the statement, but the conclusion is quite awry. For Durkheim was led effectively to deny that very sense of agency that all of us quite properly have. It is entirely possible to acknowledge the force of his point without drawing the implication that we are not after all the purposive reasoning agents we take ourselves to be.

Durkheim tended to argue as though only the study of the large-scale and the long-term were sufficiently important to warrant the attention of sociology. Yet – as a further element in drawing together the several strands of sociological endeavour I have identified – it can readily be demonstrated that the analysis of the apparently trivial or ephemeral can contribute in a basic way to understanding the more durable features of social institutions. Consider the following snippet of conversation. A husband and wife are conversing while idly watching television. The husband remarks that he is tired. After this, the conversation runs as follows:

W: 'How are you tired? Physically, mentally, or just bored?'
H: 'I don't know, I guess physically, mainly.'
W: 'You mean that your muscles ache, or your bones?'
H: 'What's the matter with you? You know what I mean.'
W: 'I wish you would be more specific.'
H: 'You know what I mean! Drop dead!'[63]

What is going on here? Well, what is going on is actually a piece of social research. The wife was a participant in a study designed to investigate the nature of ordinary language. Those involved in the study were asked simply to engage an acquaintance in conversation and to try to get the other to clarify the sense of commonplace remarks that he or she might make. On the face of things, it would be difficult to think of anything more trivial upon which to spend good research money, and indeed many within the sociological profession have concluded just that. I think such a judgement is quite wrong. The research is interesting from several different angles. The very severity of the responses elicited indicates that the deviation from certain accepted canons of small talk was perceived as a disturbing one. For breakdown in communication, and the assumption by the victim of what the researchers rather charmingly call a posture of 'righteous hostility', occurred very rapidly indeed. There is something in the tacit conventions of small talk which has a very powerful moral fixity. This something might be defined as unstated trust in the integrity of others, anchored in the assumed mutuality of what stays unsaid in the words of the conversation. The demand to supply precision of meaning was experienced as a breach of trust.

The apparent vagueness of ordinary language is expressive of the fact that it is geared to social practices, our tacit knowledge of the conventions that order those practices being the grounds of its meaningfulness. This is essentially the discovery that Wittgenstein made, by a very different route, when he forsook his earlier views in favour of the idea that language is what language does. Ordinary language cannot be tightened up and made into a simulacrum of scientific language. What remains unsaid – and, in a certain sense, unsayable – in day-to-day talk has largely to be taken on trust. For most of us this has become second nature. But imagine what the day-to-day social world would be like if no one ever felt secure that they could rely on the mutuality of the unstated conventions shared with others. That is to say, imagine a social universe in which every interaction was experienced by an individual as threatened by collapse in the manner brought about in the research setting. For how can I ever really be sure that the other party in a situation of interaction does not harbour malicious intentions towards me? Even the most harmless gesture may seem a possible threat. Now this is probably just how social life does look to some of those individuals whom we call mentally ill. There has been some very promising work done relating mental illness to the incapacity (or unwillingness) of certain types of person to take on trust what for most of us is only infrequently a source of serious worry. This connects back directly to Goffman's discussion of body idiom and its relation to continuity of self. Mental patients will often sit slackly, move jerkily rather than with the flow and control we ordinarily expect of agents, and may allow their clothing to become randomly disarrayed. They may avoid the gaze of another who talks to them, may flout the convention that one does not talk to oneself in public, and generally fail to observe other tacit conventions of talk and interaction.

The point is not that these characteristics are necessarily relevant in an aetiological sense to mental disorder, but that they drive home how important are apparently trivial features of micro-settings for broader institutions. The complex conventions we observe in day-to-day life are not just a superficial gloss upon large-scale social institutions, they are the very stuff of their continuity and fixity. That is why it is unsurprising that the French social historians, headed by Fernand Braudel, both concentrate upon the 'long duration' and are at the same time fascinated by the seemingly insignificant routines of mundane daily life. For the long-term institutional history that absorbs their interest is sedimented in the routine practices of day-to-day social activity. Among the things sociologists do, and must do, is to study long-term patterns of institutional stability and change. Although there may be differences of emphasis from the work of historians, with sociologists less concerned with recovering a sense of 'pastness' and more preoccupied with demonstrating the impact of the past on the present, the boundary-lines are, and should be, difficult to draw.

As an example, we may take the upsurge of recent work on the development of carceral institutions. This is one area among many others where there has been a marvellously fruitful cross-fertilization between sociology and history. In modern societies, certain categories of individuals are kept largely shut away from casual contact with the majority of the population. There are forms of structured concealment which separate from view a range of persons who in some way deviate from the normal run of activities in day-to-day life. These include the sick and the dying. The sight of death is not a common experience for the vast majority of those living in modern societies today. Ambulances typically have blacked out windows, concealing the potentially disturbing spectacle of injury or death from the onlooker:

> Closed like confessionals, they thread
> Loud noons of cities, giving back
> None of the glances they absorb.[64]

Sociologically most significant are prisons and asylums, 'total institutions' that sequester from the everyday world the criminal and the mentally ill. These are substantially creations of the eighteenth century and after. Prior to this period, as Foucault and, following him, many more scrupulous but less innovative historians have shown, incarceration was relatively rare. Thus to take the influence of crime, far from being hidden away, punishment – including capital punishment – was a spectacle, an open display. The anonymous, impersonal discipline of the prison, where the main sanctions are no longer public humiliation or the marking of the body through the imposition of physical pain, but the loss of 'freely controlled time', is something very different. Where it remains, even capital punishment is really a 'maximal loss of time', in which far from publicly demonstrating the process of putting to death, there is a more or less private execution, where pain is minimized as far as possible.

Current issues

So far, I have been analysing what sociologists do as if the discipline were an unchanging one, and as if there were complete agreement among its practitioners about its objectives and methods. Neither of these are the case, and in the next part of my discussion I want to indicate some of the changes going on in sociology today and where they look likely to lead us. Like the social sciences in general, sociology' has undergone a considerable mutation in recent years – were the term not so over-used in the wake of Kuhn's writings in the philosophy of science, we could with some justification speak of the occurrence of a revolution in sociological thought. The changes involved are both substantive and methodological.

The late eighteenth and nineteenth centuries set the substantive agenda for, as well as the methodological content of, sociology in the current century. Sociology has its origins in the coming of modernity – in the dissolution of the traditional world and the consolidation of the modern. Exactly what 'traditional' and 'modern' should be taken to mean is a matter of chronic debate. But this much is plain. With the arrival of industrialism, the transfer of millions of people from rural communities to cities, the progressive development of mass democracy, and other quite fundamental institutional changes, the new world was savagely wrenched away from the old. What began as a series of transformations substantially internal to Europe and North America has increasingly traversed the globe. The lurching juggernaut of change which the West launched is still careering erratically over the surface of the earth. Sociology was born of the attempt to track its path, but until well into the twentieth century was itself rather too strongly stamped by the context of its own origins.

For one thing, in contrasting modernity with tradition, the dominant schools of thought in sociology have tended too forcefully to emphasize trends and mechanisms presumed to be inherent in the industrialized societies themselves. As a result, whether they have been swallowed up in history, or continue to exist in other parts of the world, traditional societies have too often been seen as essentially uninteresting. They have been regarded as no more than a foil to the development of a triumphant industrial order. There thus came about an unhappy disjuncture between sociology and anthropology; the fracturing clash between modern and traditional simultaneously became a disciplinary schism. But it has surely become apparent by now that anthropology can no longer confine itself to a preoccupation with otherness, any more than sociology can afford not to examine that destructive connection which binds the modern to other forms of society.

Modernity in the twentieth century demonstrably stands revealed as world-historical in the true sense of that term. At the same time as we have to recognize that the institutions created by the advent of modernity are not cut of whole cloth, we see more and more clearly that our lives today are dominated by influences no one living anywhere in the world can any longer entirely escape. Yet, together with the rest of the social sciences, sociology is only now starting to come to terms with an increasingly interdependent global system. Moreover, we seem to be living through an accelerated phase of social change. As the twenty-first century approaches, we are experiencing a period of social transformation as spectacular as anything that has occurred in earlier phases of the modern era. It seems certain that some of the leading sociological theories and concepts will have to be substantially overhauled if we are to seek to comprehend both this and the consolidation of something like a world society. Among the changes which might be singled out for mention are: exceptionally rapid technological innovation, coupled with the impact of the computer and of robotics; an apparent erosion of the established manufacturing base of Western economies, associated with a transfer of basic industrial production Eastwards; the deepening involvement of all the industrialised societies within an increasingly integrated global division of labour; widespread political disaffection within Western democracies, associated with realignments in patterns of voting and political support; and the looming threat of the proliferation of nuclear weapons, conjoined with the continuing application of science and technology to the intensification of weapons systems.

The list is a formidable one, and I certainly do not want to claim that sociology is the only discipline relevant to tackling it. But daunting though the intellectual and practical problems facing us in the late twentieth century may be, it is surely indisputable that they are above all organizational and institutional in character. That is to say, they are in a fundamental sense sociological. The sociological enterprise is now even more pivotal to the social sciences as a whole, and indeed to current intellectual culture generally, than it has ever been before. We live today, not to put too fine a point on it, in a world on a knife-edge between extraordinary possibility and global disaster. We cannot even say with confidence which of these alternatives is the more likely. This is the residue of modernity for us all, and it is distant indeed from the scenarios laid out by the more optimistic of the eighteenth- and nineteenth-century founders of sociology. For they expected modernity to culminate, one way or another, in a humane and rational social order. In the light of trends of development in the current century, we must see these anticipations as at best premature and rash.

Nonetheless we must sustain the practical intent that underlay their writings. We must defend the ambition of sociology in a practical fashion to influence for the better the human condition. This thought both allows me to fashion a conclusion and also to return to the themes with which I opened. For in some degree the unsettling character of sociology derives from the special position it has in respect of the practical governance of social change. Sociology occupies a tensed zone of transition between diagnosis and prognosis; and this is another area in which a spate of controversies over the past few years has allowed us eventually to clarify what the role of sociology can and should be.

These controversies cannot be comprehended without an analysis of methodological problems in sociology – concerning which, it would be fair to say, sociologists recently have been rather radically reappraising what they themselves do. The majority of the early founders of sociology, in the late eighteenth and the nineteenth centuries, sought to derive the logic and the method of their field of study from the natural sciences. This view certainly never went unchallenged, for such an idea is difficult to reconcile with those features of human agency that I have discussed. Consequently the discipline – and in some considerable degree the whole of the social sciences – tended to be divided between the notion that a natural science of society is possible and the opposing view that sociology is essentially a type of humanism. For advocates of the former standpoint, everything short of a precisely specified corpus of laws about social life is a disappointment. In the eyes of the anti-naturalists on the other hand, the claims of sociology to emulate natural science are spurious and misleading. This methodological division was for many years given conceptual form by the contrast, drawn from German traditions of historiography, between *Verstehen* and *Erklären* – understanding versus explanation. It was accepted by both sides that the natural sciences have to do with explanation. The differences of opinion concerned whether the realm of *Erklären* could also be extended to the explication of human social institutions.

We know today that the separating of *Verstehen* from *Erklären* was a misleading way to characterize both social and natural science. Summarizing complicated matters briefly, advances in the philosophy of the natural sciences have made it plain that understanding or interpretation are just as elemental to these sciences as they are to the humanities. On the other hand, while generalizations in the social sciences are logically discrepant from those of natural science, there is no reason to doubt that they involve causal attributions. We must therefore discard the conceptual clothing of the

Verstehen versus *Erklären* debate. There is no harm done, and there are positive virtues, in continuing to use the phrase social 'sciences'. The social sciences share with natural science a respect for logical clarity in the formulation of theories and for disciplined empirical investigation. But social science is not a battered tramp steamer chugging along vainly in the wake of the sleek cruiser of the natural sciences. In large degree the two simply sail on different oceans, however much they might share certain common navigational procedures. There are thus profound differences between the social and natural sciences, but they do not concern the presence or absence of interpretation as such. Rather, they are bound up with what I have elsewhere, no doubt rather clumsily, called a 'double hermeneutic'.[65] As I have been at pains to emphasize earlier, the subjects of study in the social sciences and the humanities are concept-using beings, whose concepts of their actions enter in a constitutive manner into what those actions are. Social life cannot even be accurately described by a sociological observer, let alone causally elucidated, if that observer does not master the array of concepts employed (discursively or non-discursively) by those involved.

All social science, to put the issue bluntly, is parasitic upon lay concepts, as a logical condition of its endeavours. Sociologists invent their own conceptual metalanguages, and have to do so for reasons described earlier – that they seek to grasp aspects of social institutions which are not described by agents' concepts. However, unlike in natural science, in the social sciences there is no way of keeping the conceptual apparatus of the observer – whether in sociology, political science or economics – free from appropriation by lay actors. The concepts and theories invented by social scientists, in other words, circulate in and out of the social world they are coined to analyse. The best and most original ideas in the social sciences, if they have any purchase on the reality it is their business to capture, tend to become appropriated and utilized by social actors themselves. John Barnes expressed this aptly when he wrote that sociology makes it possible for us 'to take a more informed and more far-seeing view of the social scene' than is available to those 'who have not been trained to take a detached view of their own social institutions and who lack the opportunity to compare these carefully with alternative arrangements found in other societies'. Remarking that sociology is 'concerned with the regularities and the lack of regularity in institutions', he added: 'There is a two-way or dialectical relation between the conceptual apparatus of the sociologist and the world view of the people whose actions, sentiments and beliefs he [or she] seeks to understand.'[66] This two-way relation, however, deserves careful consideration, for grasping its nature leads us to a major reappraisal of the practical influence of sociology upon modern societies.

It is often thought that the social sciences – not only sociology – have been unsuccessful as policy-making aids. Perhaps this is even one final reason why their critics have found them wanting. After all, consider the impact that natural science has had, via the implementation of technology, in shaping our interactions with the material world. The natural sciences have plainly increased our capabilities of controlling the material contexts of our activities. For surely one cannot make a parallel claim for social science? For there just are not the social technologies that would allow us to control social life in the manner in which material technology permits us to harness the forces of nature.

However we can see the issue in an entirely different light if we follow through the implications of the double hermeneutic. Those who have discussed this problem, particularly philosophers of the social sciences, have tended to concentrate their attention upon the manner in which lay concepts obstinately intrude into the technical discourse of social science. Few have considered the matter the other way round. But the concepts of the social sciences are not produced about an independently constituted subject-matter, which continues regardless of what these concepts are. The 'findings' of the social sciences very often enter constitutively into the world they describe. Let me give examples from several of the social sciences to show how significant this point is.

When, in the early fifteenth century, Bodin, Machiavelli and others invented some novel ideas about political power and government, they did not simply describe an independently occurring series of social changes. They helped constitute the state forms that emerged from those changes. Modern states could not exist at all were not concepts such as 'citizen', 'sovereignty', and 'government' itself, mastered by the individuals who administer them and those subject to their rule. Political theory has ever after been reflexively tied to what it is about: the elucidation of the mechanics of government within modern states. Something very similar is true from the late eighteenth century onwards of both economics and sociology. The discourse of economics has not only made it possible for us to understand – within limits – the workings of modern economies, it has become basic to what those economies are. Shifts in the usage of terms like 'economic', or 'industrial' were in some part fostered by the writings of academic economists, helping to introduce into the newly-forming fields of economic activity the concepts that constitute what those fields have become. Economics has thereafter been reflexively implicated in processes of continuity and change in modern economic systems.

The same can be said of sociology in respect of a whole spectrum of modern social institutions. One of the best illustrations that can be given of this is the collation of social statistics. For statistical surveys might seem on the face of things to be furthest removed from incorporation into what they are about. Statistics on the distribution of population, patterns of birth and death rates, or marriage and the family, all might appear to be simply quantified analyses of objectively-given sets of phenomena. So, of course, in a sense they are. But as I emphasized at the beginning, the gathering of social statistics also enters in a fundamental way into the constitution of modern societies. Modern societies could not exist were their demographic characteristics not regularly charted and analysed. In the study of class divisions, bureaucracy, urbanism, religion, and many other areas, sociological concepts regularly enter our lives and help redefine them.

The inferences to be drawn from this are far from simple, but they are of very considerable importance. On the one hand we are able to see why even the most brilliantly innovative ideas in the social sciences risk becoming banal. Once they become constitutive of what we do, after all, they are part of the patterns of our daily activities and may become almost numbingly familiar. Every time I use a passport to travel abroad I demonstrate my practical grasp of the concept of sovereignty; far from being novel any longer, it has become an entirely routine part of modern life. Precisely because of its adoption within society itself, knowledge generated by the social sciences does not have a neatly cumulative form. By this I do not mean that we do not progressively learn more about social institutions than we knew before, or that there is not continual conceptual and theoretical innovation. But the achievements of the social sciences tend to become submerged from view by their very success. On the other hand, exactly because of this we can in all seriousness make the claim that the social sciences have influenced 'their' world – the universe of human social activity – much more strongly than the natural sciences have influenced 'theirs'. The social sciences have been reflexively involved in a most basic way with those very transformations of modernity which give them their main subject-matter.

There are no options in this regard. The practical impact of social sciences is both profound and inescapable. Modern societies, together with the organizations that compose and straddle them, are like learning machines, imbibing information in order to regularize their mastery of themselves. Because of the perversity of unintended consequences, and the very contingency of social change, we may presume that such mastery will always be less than complete. Yet upon our capabilities for social learning, in the world that is the legacy of modernity, we predicate our future. Only societies reflexively capable of modifying their institutions in the face of accelerated social change will be able to confront that future with any confidence. Sociology is the prime medium of such reflexivity. The degree, therefore, to which a society fosters an active and imaginative sociological culture will be a measure of its flexibility and openness.

(vi)   Structuration theory and empirical research*

These points suggest a number of guidelines for the overall orientation of social research.

First, all social research has a necessarily cultural, ethnographic or 'anthropological' aspect to it. This is an expression of what I call the double hermeneutic which characterizes social science. The sociologist has as a field of study phenomena which are already constituted as meaningful. The condition of 'entry' to this field is getting to know what actors already know, and have to know, to 'go on' in the daily activities of social life.[67] The concepts that sociological observers invent are 'second-order' concepts in so far as they presume certain conceptual capabilities on the part of the actors to whose conduct they refer. But it is in the nature of social

---

* *The Constitution of Society*, pp. 284–304.

science that these can become 'first-order' concepts by being appropriated within social life itself. What is 'hermeneutic' about the
double hermeneutic? The appropriateness of the term derives from
the double process of translation or interpretation which is involved. Sociological descriptions have the task of mediating the
frames of meaning within which actors orient their conduct. But
such descriptions are interpretative categories which also demand
an effort of translation in and out of the frames of meaning involved in sociological theories. Various considerations concerning
social analysis are connected with this:

(1)   Literary style is not irrelevant to the accuracy of social descrip-
      tions. This is more or less important according to how far a
      particular piece of social research is ethnographic – that is, is
      written with the aim of describing a given cultural *milieu* to
      others who are unfamiliar with it.
(2)   The social scientist is a communicator, introducing frames of
      meaning associated with certain contexts of social life to those
      in others. Thus the social sciences draw upon the same sources
      of description (mutual knowledge) as novelists or others who
      write fictional accounts of social life. Goffman is able quite
      easily to intersperse fictional illustrations with descriptions
      taken from social science research because he seeks very often
      to 'display' the tacit forms of mutual knowledge whereby
      practical activities are ordered, rather than trying to chart
      the actual distribution of those activities.
(3)   'Thick description' will be called for in some types of research
      (especially that of a more ethnographic kind) but not in others.
      It is usually unnecessary where the activities studied have
      generalized characteristics familiar to those to whom the
      'findings' are made available, and where the main concern of
      the research is with institutional analysis, in which actors are
      treated in large aggregates or as 'typical' in certain respects
      defined as such for the purposes of the study.

   Second, it is important in social research to be sensitive to the
complex skills which actors have in co-ordinating the contexts of
their day-to-day behaviour. In institutional analysis these skills may
be more or less bracketed out, but it is essential to remember that
such bracketing is wholly methodological. Those who take institu-

tional analysis to comprise the field of sociology *in toto* mistake a methodological procedure for an ontological reality. Social life may very often be predictable in its course, as such authors are prone to emphasize. But its predictability is in many of its aspects 'made to happen' by social actors; it does not happen in spite of the reasons they have for their conduct. If the study of unintended consequences and unacknowledged conditions of action is a major part of social research, we should none the less stress that such consequences and conditions are always to be interpreted within the flow of intentional conduct. We have to include here the relation between reflexively monitored and unintended aspects of the reproduction of social systems, and the 'longitudinal' aspect of unintended consequences of contingent acts in historically significant circumstances of one kind or another.

Third, the social analyst must also be sensitive to the time-space constitution of social life. In part this is a plea for a disciplinary coming together. Social scientists have normally been content to let historians be specialists in time and geographers specialists in space, while they maintain their own distinctive disciplinary identity, which, if it is not an exclusive concern with structural constraint, is bound up with a conceptual focus upon 'society'. Historians and geographers, for their part, have been willing enough to connive at this disciplinary dissection of social science. The practitioners of a discipline, apparently, do not feel secure unless they can point to a sharp conceptual delimitation between their concerns and those of others. Thus 'history' may be seen as about sequences of events set out chronologically in time or perhaps, even more ambiguously, about 'the past'. Geography, many of its representatives like to claim, finds its distinctive character in the study of spatial forms. But if, as I have emphasized, time-space relations cannot be 'pulled out' of social analysis without undermining the whole enterprise, such disciplinary divisions actively inhibit the tackling of questions of social theory significant for the social sciences as a whole. Analysing the time-space co-ordination of social activities means studying the contextual features of locales through which actors move in their daily paths and the regionalization of locales stretching away across time-space. As I have accentuated frequently, such analysis is inherent in the explanation of time-space distanciation and hence in the examination of the heterogeneous and complex nature assumed by larger societal totalities and by intersocietal systems in general.

In order to comment upon the empirical implications of the foregoing remarks, I shall consider several separate pieces of research. [In this extract, Giddens deals only with the first piece of research.] . . . I shall use as illustrative cases material to do with education and with the state. Since the modern state everywhere encompasses attempts to monitor institutional reproduction through influencing the nature of educational systems, these two 'areas' of research are, in fact, closely bound up with one another. The first example is a well-known study of conformity and rebellion in a working-class school in the Midlands of England. It is primarily ethnographic in character and contrasts in this respect, and in the country of its origin, with the second, a questionnaire study of educational mobility in Italy. The third and fourth examples draw upon empirical material directly concerned with the activities and involvements of modern states. One describes not so much a particular research project as the work of an author who has tried to combine empirical material with a theoretical explanation of the contradictory character of 'capitalist states'. The other refers to a specific piece of research – an attempt to analyse the origins of the divide between 'the City' and 'industry' that has been a notable feature of British society for some two centuries or more.

I shall use each piece of research to illustrate certain partly distinct conceptual issues. Looking to begin with at what I take to be in many respects an exemplary research report, I shall detail several of the main empirical emphases which connect with the major tenets of structuration theory. I shall subsequently concentrate upon three specific problems. How should we empirically analyse structural constraint? How might we give empirical flesh to the notion of structural contradiction? And what type of research is appropriate to the study of the *longue durée* of institutional change?

Two important qualifications must be made before moving on to the main content of the discussion. In specifying some of the connections between structuration theory and empirical research, I shall not be concerned with an assessment of the virtues and the drawbacks of different types of research method or technique. That is to say, I shall not seek to analyse whether ethnographic research is or is not superior to, say, the use of questionnaires. I shall, however, offer some comments upon the relation between so-called 'qualitative' research and 'quantitative' research. Moreover, I shall want to pursue the discussion in a direction not ordinarily held to be closely related to problems of empirical work – by indicating how social research is tied to social critique. . . .

These latter aspects of the discussion might seem, on the face of things, to move on quite a different plane from discussion of empirical research. But the connection is, in fact, a very close one indeed. For it will not do only to consider in what ways empirical study can be illuminated via the concepts developed in preceding parts of this book. All research is carried on in relation to explicit or implied explanatory objectives and has potential practical consequences both for those whose activities are investigated and for others. Elucidation of the character of these objectives and consequences is not easy, and demands coming to terms with some of the problems posed when a model based directly upon appeal to the logical form of natural science is abandoned. In examining these problems, I shall endeavour to limit as far as possible any forays into epistemology. My aim is to analyse what follows from the basic claim underlying all social research – that the researcher communicates new knowledge previously unavailable (in some sense or other) to the members of a social community or society.

The analysis of strategic conduct

According to structuration theory, two types of methodological bracketing are possible in sociological research. In institutional analysis structural properties are treated as chronically reproduced features of social systems. In the analysis of strategic conduct the focus is placed upon modes in which actors draw upon structural properties in the constitution of social relations. Since this is a difference of emphasis, there is no clear-cut line that can be drawn between these, and each, crucially, has to be in principle rounded out by a concentration upon the duality of structure. The analysis of strategic conduct means giving primacy to discursive and practical consciousness, and to strategies of control within defined contextual boundaries. Institutionalized properties of the settings of interaction are assumed methodologically to be 'given'. We have to take care with this, of course, for to treat structural properties as methodologically 'given' is not to hold that they are not produced and reproduced through human agency. It is to concentrate analysis upon the contextually situated activities of definite groups of actors. I shall suggest the following tenets as important in the analysis of strategic conduct: the need to avoid impoverished descriptions of agents' knowledgeability; a sophisticated account of motivation; and an interpretation of the dialectic of control.

Consider the research described by Paul Willis in his book *Learning to Labour*.[68] Willis was concerned to study a group of working-class children in a school located in a poor area of Birmingham. Although the group studied was quite small, Willis's research is both compelling in its detail and suggestive in drawing implications that range far beyond the context in which the study was actually carried out. As I shall try to show, it conforms closely to the main empirical implications of structuration theory. What gives the research these qualities? In some considerable part, at least, the answer is that Willis treats the boys concerned as actors who know a great deal, discursively and tacitly, about the school environment of which they form a part; and that he shows just how the rebellious attitudes which the boys take towards the authority system of the school have certain definite unintended consequences that affect their fate. When leaving school the boys take up unskilled, unrewarding jobs, thus facilitating the reproduction of some general features of capitalist-industrial labour. Constraint, in other words, is shown to operate through the active involvement of the agents concerned, not as some force of which they are passive recipients.

Let us look first of all at discursive and practical consciousness as reflected in Willis' study. Willis makes it clear that 'the lads' can say a great deal about their views on authority relations in the school and why they react to them as they do. However, such discursive capabilities do not just take the form of propositional statements; 'discourse' has to be interpreted to include modes of expression which are often treated as uninteresting in sociological research – such as humour, sarcasm and irony. When one of 'the lads' says of the teachers, 'They're bigger than us, they stand for a bigger establishment than we do',[69] he expresses a propositional belief of the sort familiar from responses to interview questions posed by researchers. But Willis shows that humour, banter, aggressive sarcasm – elements of the discursive stock in trade of 'the lads' – are fundamental features of their knowledgeable 'penetration' of the school system. The joking culture of 'the lads' both displays a very complex understanding of the basis of teacher's authority, and at the same time directly questions that authority by subverting the language in which it is normally expressed. As Willis points out, 'pisstakes', 'kiddings' and 'windups' are difficult to record on tape and especially to represent in the print of research reports. But these, and other discursive forms that rarely find their way into such reports, may show as much about modes of coping with oppressive social environments as more direct comments or responses. In the author's words:

> The space won from the school and its rules by the informal group is used for the shaping and development of particular cultural skills principally devoted to 'having a laff'. The 'laff' is a multi-faceted implement of extraordinary importance in the counter-school culture . . . the ability to produce it is one of the defining characteristics of being one of 'the lads' – 'We can make them laff, they can't make us laff.' But it is also used in many other contexts: to defeat boredom and fear, to overcome hardship and problems – as a way out of almost anything. In many respects the 'laff' is the privileged instrument of the informal, as the command is of the formal . . . the 'laff' is part of an irreverent marauding misbehaviour. Like an army of occupation of the unseen, informal dimension, 'the lads' pour over the countryside in a search for incidents to amuse, subvert and incite.[70]

On the level of both discursive and practical consciousness it might seem as though the conformist children – those who more or less accept the authority of the teachers and their educational goals, rather than rebelling against them – would be most knowledgeable about the social system of the school. However, Willis makes a good case to the effect that on both levels of consciousness 'the lads' are more knowledgeable than the conformists. Because they actively contest the authority relations of the school, they are adept at picking out where the bases of the teachers' claims to authority lie, and where their weakest points are as the wielders of discipline and as individual personalities. Opposition is expressed as a continuous nagging at what teachers expect and demand, usually stopping short of outright confrontation. Thus in the classroom the children are expected to sit still, to be quiet and to get on with their work. But 'the lads' are all movement, save when the teacher's stare might freeze one of them transitorily; they gossip surreptitiously or pass open remarks that are on the verge of direct insubordination but can be explained away if challenged; they are always doing something else other than the work required of them but are ready with some sort of spurious justification when it is required. They have invented 'experiments with trust' without, it seems, having read Garfinkel: '"Let's send him to Coventry when he comes", "Let's laugh at everything he says", "Let's pretend we can't understand, and say, 'How do you mean?' all the time."'[71]

How should one assess the motivational content of the oppositional activities of 'the lads'? This depends in some degree upon material which Willis did not set out directly to explore. But it is clear that regarding 'the lads' as skilled and knowledgeable agents suggests a different account of their motivation from that implied in the 'official' view of them, as 'louts' or 'wreckers' unable to appreciate the importance of the educational opportunities the school offers – the counterpart to the sociologese of 'imperfect socialization'. The motives which prompt their activities and underlie the reasons they have for what they do cannot be well-explicated as a result of a deficient understanding of the school system or its relations with other aspects of the social *milieux* that are the backdrop to their lives. Rather, it is because they know a great deal about the school and the other contexts in which they move that they act as they do. Such knowledge may be carried primarily in their practical activities or in discourse which is highly contextualized, although in Willis' account 'the lads' emerge as much more articulate than others in the school would probably acknowledge. However, the bounds of what they know about the circumstances in which they live out their lives are fairly confined. Certainly, they realize that their chances of getting anything other than inferior and unedifying jobs are poor, and this realization influences their rebellious attitudes towards the school. But they have at most an imprecise awareness of aspects of the wider society that influence the contexts of their own activity. It might be plausible to infer a general underlying motivational pattern – perhaps partly unconscious – of an attempt to establish modes of conduct which inject some kind of meaning and colour into a drab set of life prospects that are, however diffusely, accurately seen as such. We cannot satisfactorily understand the motivation of 'the lads' unless we see that they do grasp, although in a partial and contextually confined way, the nature of their position in society.[72]

Willis describes in a very insightful manner the dialectic of control within the school setting. Both 'the lads' and their teachers are specialists in the theory and practice of authority, but their respective views as to its necessity and formal objectives are deeply opposed. Teachers recognize that they need the support of the conformist children to make the sanctions available to them stick, and that power cannot be exercised effectively if punitive sanctions have to be applied frequently. The deputy head reveals himself as a dextrous Parsonian theorist of power when he comments that the running of a school depends mainly upon the existence of a certain moral consensus, which cannot be forcibly implanted in children. Punitive sanctions should be used only as a last resort because they are a sign of the failure of effective control rather than the basis of it: 'You can't go throwing suspensions around all the time. Like the football referees today, I mean they're failing because they're reduced to the ultimate so quickly, somehow . . . the yellow card comes out first of all, and once they've done that, they've either got to send the player off or ignore everything else he does in the game.'[73] Teachers know this, and 'the lads' know that they know it. Hence 'the lads' are able to exploit it to their own advantage. In subverting the mechanics of disciplinary power in the classroom, they assert their autonomy of action. Moreover, the fact that the school is somewhere in which they spend only part of the day and part of the year is vital to the 'counter-culture' which they have initiated. For it is out of school, away from the gaze of the teachers, that pursuits can be freely engaged in which would be anathema in the school setting.

Unintended consequences: against functionalism

Willis's research is not only a superb ethnographic study of an informal group within a school; it is also an attempt to indicate how the activities of 'the lads', within a restricted context, contribute to the reproduction of larger institutional forms. Willis' study is unusual, compared with a great deal of social research, because he stresses that 'social forces' operate through agents' reasons and because his examination of social reproduction makes no appeal

to all to functionalist concepts. His interpretation of the connection
between the school 'counter-culture' and wider institutional patterns, expressed concisely, runs as follows. The oppositional modes
of behaviour of 'the lads' while at school leads them to want to leave
school to go out to work. They want the financial independence
which work will provide; at the same time, however, they have no
particular expectations about any other types of reward that work
might offer. The aggressive, joking culture which they have developed within the school *milieu* actually quite strongly resembles that
of the shop-floor culture of the work situations into which they tend
to move. Hence they find the adjustment to work relatively easy,
and they are able to tolerate the demands of doing dull, repetitive
labour in circumstances which they recognize to be uncongenial.
The unintended and ironical consequence of their 'partial penetration' of the limited life chances open to them is actively to perpetuate the conditions which help to limit those very life chances. For
having left school with no qualifications and entered a world of low-
level manual labour, in work which has no career prospects and
with which they are intrinsically disaffected, they are effectively
stuck there for the rest of their working lives. 'The working-class
lad is likely to feel that it is already too late when the treacherous
nature of his previous confidence is discovered. The cultural cele-
bration has lasted, it might seem, just long enough to deliver him
through the closed factory doors'[74] – or, more often nowadays, to a
life of chronic unemployment or semiemployment.

Now, all of this could have been stated in a functionalist mode
and 'explained' in functional terms. Thus it could be argued that
industrial capitalism 'needs' large numbers of people either to work
in unrewarding manual labour or to be part of an industrial reserve
army of the unemployed. Their existence is then 'explained' as a
response to these needs, somehow brought about by capitalism –
perhaps as a result of some unspecified 'social forces' which such
needs call into play. The two types of account can be contrasted, as
below:

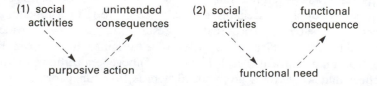

In (1), the sort of view developed by Willis, a given set of social activities (the oppositional behaviour of 'the lads') is interpreted as purposeful action. In other words, those activities are shown to be carried on in an intentional way, for certain reasons, within conditions of bounded knowledgeability. Specification of those bounds allows the analyst to show how unintended consequences of the activities in question derive from what the agents did intentionally. The interpretation involves an attribution of rationality and of motivation to the agents concerned. The actors have reasons for what they do, and what they do has certain specifiable consequences which they do not intend. In (2) little attempt is made to detail the intentionality of the agents' conduct. It is probably assumed that the conduct is intentional in some way, that it has, in Merton's terminology, manifest functions. But usually in functionalist interpretations this is not regarded as especially interesting because attention is concentrated upon attributing rationality to a social system, not to individuals. The identification of a functional need of the system is presumed to have explanatory value, calling into play consequences which in some way meet that need. Merton's functional interpretation of the Hopi rain ceremonial . . . fits this scheme exactly. The intentional features of Hopi participation in the ceremonial are given short shrift – the 'purpose' of the rain ceremonial is to bring rain, and this it does not do. On the face of things, participation in the ceremonial is an irrational activity. However, we can identify a functional need to which the ceremonial corresponds, generating a positively functional consequence. Small societies need a unitary value system to hold them together; participation in the rain ceremonial reinforces such a value system by regularly bringing the community together in circumstances in which adherence to group values can be publicly affirmed.

I have previously indicated why (2) will not do and why it is not an explanation at all of whatever activities are in question. Cohen has recently suggested an ingenious way in which it might be rescued, however.[75] This is by postulating what he calls 'consequence laws'. Interpretation (2) is not an explanation because it does not supply a mechanism linking the positing of a functional need and the consequences that are presumed to ensue for the wider social system in which the activities to be explained are involved. In establishing 'consequence laws' we set up generalizations to the effect that whenever a given social item is functional for another, the first social item is found to exist. Subsumption of a particular instance of social activity under a consequence law can be regarded as an 'unelaborated' functionalist explanation. But 'unelaborated' functionalist explanations are not explanations at all and, moreover, have the dangerous side-property of implying that a higher degree of cohesion exists than may in fact be the case in the social systems to which they refer. To say that (2) is 'unelaborated' is to admit ignorance of the causal connections which link the social item or activities concerned with their functional consequences. What would these connections be if discovered? They would be precisely of the sort given in (1) – a specification of intentional action (or types of intentional action) having unintended outcomes (or types of outcomes). In other words, (2) is viable only when transmuted into (1). But in (1) it is not necessary to use the term 'function' at all. The term 'function' implies some sorts of teleological quality that social systems are presumed to have: social items or activities are held to exist because they meet functional needs. But if the fact that they have functional outcomes does not explain why they exist – only an interpretation of intentional activity and unintended consequences does that – the activities may become more readily severed from those outcomes than 'consequence laws' would imply. The conduct of 'the lads' leads to consequences functional for the reproduction of capitalist wage labour as a result of their 'partial penetration' of their life circumstances. But this very 'partial penetration', as Willis argues, may be potentially radicalizing for the individuals involved, in which case it could lead to disruptive rather than cohesive consequences for the wider social system.

The work of functionalist authors has been very important in social research precisely because it has directed attention to the disparities between what actors intend to do and the consequences which ensue from what they do. But we can identify, and attempt to resolve, the issues involved more unambiguously by dispensing with functionalist terminology altogether. There are three types of circumstance in which functionalist language is commonly used. All are important in social analysis but can easily be expressed in non-functionalist terms.

Suppose we render Willis' findings in a functionalist mode, as follows: 'Education, in a capitalist society, has the function of allocating individuals to positions in the occupational division of labour.' First, such a statement is acceptable if understood as an implicit counterfactual.[76] Many functionalist assertions, or purported 'explanations', can be read in this way. In fact, they set up a relation which calls for explanation, rather than explaining it. We can express the statement in a different manner, without using 'function', as follows: 'In order for the occupational division of labour to be maintained, the educational system has to ensure that individuals are allocated differentially to occupational positions.' The force of 'has to' here is counterfactual; it involves identifying conditions that must be met if certain consequences are to follow. It sets up a research problem, and understood as asking a question rather than as answering one, it is entirely legitimate. But the use of the term 'function' can be misleading because it suggests that the 'has to' refers to some sort of need that is a property of the social system, somehow generating forces producing an appropriate (functional) response. We might suppose that we have resolved a research problem when all that has been done is actually to establish a problem that demands research. Second, the statement may be read as referring to a feedback process which depends wholly upon unintended consequences. As I have already indicated, to say 'Education . . . has the function of allocating individuals . . .' fudges over the differences between intended and unintended aspects of social reproduction. It is therefore not clear in such statements how far the processes in question are the result of 'causal loops', and how far they are incorporated in processes of what I have . . . called reflexive self-regulation. Social needs exist as causal factors implicated in social reproduction only when they are recognized as such by those involved at some point and acted upon by them. The educational system in which 'the lads' are involved was supposedly established in order to further equality of opportunity. Its substantive results, in respect of perpetuating immobility, run counter to this, but they are not so planned by the Ministry of Education or some other directive body of the state. If they were – if education were deliberately organized by powerful decision-makers in order to perpetuate the class system – the process concerned would be substantially different. Of course, this is a complex matter. All modern education systems involve attempts at reflexive regulation, which often lead to consequences that rebound upon those who initiate educational policies. But to leave these complexities unstudied is to fail to grasp the actual conditions of reproduction. The result can be some form of objectivism – whatever happens does so as the result of social forces as inevitable as laws of nature. Alternatively, however, there could be a tendency to accept some kind of conspiracy theory. Whatever happens does so because someone or other designed that it should. If the former, the characteristic view of functionalism, is associated with not according enough importance to intentional action, the second derives from failing to see that the consequences of activities chronically escape their initiators.

The duality of structure

I take it that it is clear from my discussion earlier in this book that the concept of the duality of structure, fundamental to structuration theory, is implicated in the ramified senses that the terms 'conditions' and 'consequences' of action have. All social interaction is expressed at some point in and through the contextualities of bodily presence. In moving from the analysis of strategic conduct to a recognition of the duality of structure, we have to begin to 'thread outwards' in time and space. That is to say, we have to try to see how the practices followed in a given range of contexts are embedded in wider reaches of time and space – in brief, we have to attempt to discover their relation to institutionalized practices. To pursue the illustration drawn from Willis' work, how far do 'the lads', in developing an oppositional culture within the school, draw upon rules and resources more broadly involved than in the immediate contexts of their action?

We can specify analytically what is involved in making the conceptual move from the analysis of strategic conduct to examination of the duality of structure as below (institutional analysis would begin at the other end, as the upward arrow indicates):

intersections of regions → spatial spread away
from the immediate contexts of interaction

routinization → temporal spread away from the
immediate contexts of interaction

time–space distanciation

forms of societal totality

Transferring analysis from the situated activities of strategically placed actors means studying, first, the connections between the regionalization of their contexts of action and wider forms of regionalization; second, the embeddedness of their activities in time – how far they reproduce practices, or aspects of practices, that are long-established; third, the modes of time–space distanciation which link the activities and relationships in question to features of overall societies or to inter-societal systems.

Willis actually provides a very perceptive discussion of some of these phenomena, even if his terminology is different. The formal hierarchy of the school, of course, incorporates modes of conduct and normative expectations that are broadly spread across different sectors of the society, although strongly influenced by class divisions. The school as a locale is physically separate from the workplace and is temporally separated from the experience of work in the life spans of children. While school and workplace share overall patterns of disciplinary power, they are not merely aspects of a single institutional form. As Willis points out, the discipline of the school has a strongly moralized tone to it, which is lacking in the workplace. School discipline embodies an 'abstract educational paradigm, maintaining and reproducing what it makes possible'.[77] The moral character of this axis of authority, or the normative claims on which it is focused, influences the nature of the rebellious subculture. In their manifest disregard for the minutiae of school routines 'the lads' do more than deviate behaviourally from what is expected of them; they show their rejection of the moral prerogatives upon which the teachers' authority supposedly rests. The resources available to the staff in seeking to assert their authority, however, at the same time involve more than these claims to legitimation. The staff are 'resource centres' for the distribution of knowledge, recognized as a scarce commodity by the conformist children, if not by 'the lads', and they have the more direct control over the timing and spacing of activities that make up the organization of classrooms and of the school timetable as a whole. Of course, in all this the teaching staff are drawing indirectly upon entrenched sources of institutional support in the wider society.[78]

For their part, the attitudes and conduct of 'the lads' are certainly not wholly invented *de novo* by them; they draw upon a fund of experience built into their lives outside the school and built up historically within working-class communities in general. Children who disaffiliate themselves from the norms and expected behaviour of the school environment are able to make use of this fund of experience. In transforming elements of it and bringing them to bear upon the school *milieu*, they help to reproduce those very characteristics in the wider context, although they use it innovatively, not in a mechanical fashion. The neighbourhood and the street provide symbolic forms of youth culture that are also in a more direct way the source of themes articulated in the counter-school culture. Willis mentions too the importance of stories related by adults about life on the shop floor, especially those concerned with attitudes towards authority. Parents help to transmit working-class culture to their children, but obviously they do not all behave in an identical fashion or share the same views. Moreover, there is a considerable degree of independent fashioning of outlook between parents and children. Some parents express attitudes quite similar to those of 'the lads', while others disapprove strongly and forcibly of their behaviour. Yet others, who are wary of the values of the school or are hostile to them, have children who conform closely to expected standards of school conduct. The interchange between the activities of 'the lads' and influences from the broader society, in other words, is one which is 'worked upon' by all involved.

As a reflexively monitored social phenomenon, the national school system makes use of sociological research and psychology. Both have filtered down into the practical organization of this particular school (no doubt the teachers there are now thoroughly familiar with Willis' own study). There has been a move towards a somewhat more 'progressive' outlook in respect of the organization of the curriculum and of classroom teaching arrangements. One of the main contexts in which 'the lads' come into direct contact with academic research drawn from the wider society is in relation to vocational guidance, which there is now a statutory requirement for all schools to provide. Careers guidance is influenced mostly by psychological theory and psychological testing and is taken seriously inside the school. As Willis shows, despite a certain egalitarian aura, careers guidance strongly reflects middle-class values and aspirations. Centred upon 'work', the views promulgated tend to contrast rather vigorously with the attitudes and ideas about work which – in their own particular appropriation – 'the lads' have picked up from parents and others in the neighbourhood and community. They make fun of, or are indifferent towards, the material provided in careers lessons. But this response is not simply a negative one. They consider that they have insights into the true character of work denied to the conformist children – and perhaps they have. The conformists have to do things the 'hard way', through acquiring qualifications, because they have not the wit to do better. Survival in the world of work demands guts, determination and an eye to the main chance.

It is not hard to see how these views, picked up and elaborated from established working-class environments of labour, help to plunge 'the lads' into those very environments when they leave school. The sources of discontinuity with the 'official' norms of the school in some part offer continuity, unofficially, with the contexts of work. It is the counter-school culture which provides the main guide that 'the lads' follow in going out to work. Often in the views of both the boys and their parents there is a direct connection between authority relations in the school and at work, providing cognitive and emotive links between the two that are quite different from those 'officially' sanctioned in either. We can see in this a temporally long-established and spatially widespread basis of experience, renewed in varying ways by each generation for whom the disparate and physically separate social worlds of school and work are bridged. The views of 'the lads' towards the school orient them towards the future, but they see the future as 'flat' – more of the same – rather than as having any of the progressive qualities associated with the essentially middle-class notion of a career. They are not interested in choosing particular jobs, and they drift into what they do rather than deliberately confronting a range of alternatives and then opting for one among them. 'The lads', as Willis makes clear, commit themselves to a life of generalized labour. They do not have any such notion of 'generalized labour' in mind. Motivated by a desire for the best wages that can be got immediately and by the presumption that work is essentially disagreeable, they make such a commitment in their conduct.

Looked at in a wider time–space framework, then, there is a process of the regeneration of working-class culture which both helps give rise to, and is effected through, the situated activities of groups like 'the lads'. As Willis comments:

The informal and formal processes of the school are obviously vital in preparing labour power in a certain way, but the home, family, neighbourhood, media and non-productive working-class experience in general are equally vital for its continuous reproduction and daily application to the labour process. In a converse way it is important to assess the degree to which the shop floor, both in its objective dimensions and in the oppositional culture it throws up, reacts back upon the non-productive sites of the reproduction of labour power and influences them in a certain way so that, as we have seen with the counter-school culture, there may be an unseen and often unintended circle of meaning and direction which acts ultimately to preserve and maintain a particular configuration – perhaps again at a tangent to the intentions of official policy.[79]

In raising the question of labour power a connection is provided with the transformation/mediation relations I discussed on pp. 128–34 above . . . I shall not cover this ground again but shall simply indicate how the structural relations involved may be worked through analytically in terms of the situated activities of the counter-school culture. Other structural sets, besides that discussed previously, implicated in the reproduction of industrial capitalism as an overall societal totality, can be represented as follows:[80]

```
private property : money : capital : labour contract : industrial authority
```

```
private property : money : educational advantage : occupational position
```

The transformations on the left-hand side of the first set are the same as analysed before. However, the convertibility of the structural properties towards the right-hand side depend upon ways in which the labour contract is 'translated' into industrial authority. As Marx showed in great detail, the form of the capitalist labour contract is quite different from the ties of fealty which existed between lord and serf in the feudal order. The capitalist labour contract is an economic relation between employer and employee, the meeting of two 'formally free' agents in the labour market. One main aspect of the new form of labour contract is that the employer hires not 'the worker' but the worker's labour power. The equivalence of labour power is essential – as is that provided by the

unitary exchange medium of money – to the structural transforma
tions involved in the existence of industrial capitalism as a generic
type of production system. Abstract labour is quantifiable in equivalent units of time, making the qualitatively different tasks that
individuals carry out in the various branches of industry interchangeable to the employer. The labour contract is transformed into
industrial authority via the economic power which employers, as
a class, are able to exert over workers once the vast majority of the
latter are rendered propertyless.

According to Marx, for these relations to exist 'the owner of
money must meet in the market with the free labourer, free in the
double sense, that as a free man he can dispose of his labour power
as his own commodity, and that on the other hand he had no other
commodity for sale, is short of everything necessary for the realisation of his labour power'.[81] Now the 'must' here could be read or
implying a functional 'explanation' of the phenomena in question,
as if the statement explains why those phenomena come about.
There certainly are strong functionalist leanings in Marx's formulation of some of the key arguments in his account of capitalist
development. But let us agree to interpret the 'must' in the way
which I have suggested is unobjectionable, as posing a question
to be answered. Such questions can be asked not just in relation
to the early origins of capitalism but also in regard of its continued
reproduction as an overall institutional order – there are no mechanical forces which guarantee that reproduction from day to day or
from generation to generation.

What Willis's research helps to indicate, in the situated contexts
of action of 'the lads', is how the structural relations identified
above are sustained in, and reproduced by, that action. Because
of their very 'partial penetration' of the school system, their indif-
ference to the character of work, yet willingness to enter the world
of labour, 'the lads' constitute themselves as 'abstract labour power'. The assumption that all work is the same confirms the conditions of the exchangeability of labour power structurally involved in
the capitalist labour contract. There is pathos here, because if
Willis's account is valid, the oppositional culture of 'the lads'
effectively leads them to integrate their activities more closely, in
some respects, with the institutions of the order they oppose than
do the conformists. However, in the very complexity of this relationship we can see the importance of not attempting merely to

'read off' action from structure or vice versa – of resisting, in other words, the dualism of objectivism and of subjectivism. The situated activities of 'the lads', complicated as they are in respect of the meshing of intended and unintended consequences, are only one tiny corner of a massively complex overall process of institutional reproduction. The same conclusion has to be reached if we consider the right-hand side of the other structural set, the institutional features making for the convertibility of educational advantage into differentiated occupational positions. There are some relatively direct ways in which possession of money can be converted into educational advantage, that in turn can be translated into privileged occupational position. Thus private education can be purchased, yielding higher possibilities of achieving occupational rewards than are open to those moving through the state educational sector. But the translation of one into the other for the most part involves much more complex reproduction circuits.

The identification of structural sets is a very useful device for conceptualizing some of the main features of a given institutional order. But, as I have emphasized previously, structures refer to a virtual order of relations, out of time and space. Structures exist only in their instantiation in the knowledgeable activities of situated human subjects, which reproduce them as structural properties of social systems embedded in spans of time-space. Examination of the duality of structure, therefore, always involves studying what I have earlier called dimensions or axes of structuration.

Notes

1. For more detailed discussions of the basic concepts of structuration theory, the reader should turn to Anthony Giddens, *New Rules of Sociological Method* especially Chapters 2 and 3; Giddens, *Central Problems in Social Theory* and *A Contemporary Critique of Historical Materialism*, Chapters 1 and 2.
2. *Central Problems in Social Theory*, pp. 56–7.
3. *Central Problems in Social Theory*, Chapter 1.
4. Donald Davidson, 'Agency', in Davidson, *Essays on Actions and Events* (Oxford: Clarendon Press, 1980) p. 45.
5. *New Rules of Sociological Method*, Chapter 2.
6. Joel Feinberg, 'Action and responsibility', in Max Black, *Philosophy in America* (Ithaca: Cornell University Press, 1965). On the problem of what are 'consequences', see Lars Bergström, *The Alternatives and Consequences of Actions* (Stockholm: Almqvist, 1966).

7. Thomas Schelling, 'On the ecology of micromotives', *The Public Interest*, vol. 25, 1971; 'Dynamic models of segregation', *Journal of Mathematical Sociology*, vol. 4, 1971. See also the discussion in Raymond Boudon, *The Unintended Consequences of Social Action* (London: Macmillan, 1982) pp. 43ff.
8. Giddens, *New Rules of Sociological Method*, p. 76.
9. Merton, however, favours the term, 'unanticipated' rather than unintended consequences. In my analysis 'intention' presumes knowledge of the likely consequences of action and therefore anticipation. Of course, one can anticipate that something will happen without intending it to happen, but one cannot intend something to happen without anticipating that it might happen. R.K. Merton, 'The unanticipated consequences of purposive social action'. *American Sociological Review*, vol. 1, 1936; Merton 'Manifest and latent functions', in Merton *Social Theory and Social Structure* (Glencoe: Free Press, 1963).
10. Merton, 'Manifest and latent functions', p. 51.
11. Merton, 'Manifest and latent functions', pp. 64–5.
12. For a fuller discussion, see Giddens, *Central Problems in Social Theory*, Chapter 6.
13. Max Weber, *The Methodology of the Social Sciences* (Glencoe: Free Press, 1949).
14. Mancur Olson, *The Logic of Collective Action* (Cambridge, Mass.: Harvard University Press, 1965); Boudon, *The Unintended Consequences*; Jon Elster, *Logic and Society, Contradictions and Possible Worlds* (Chichester: Wiley, 1978); Elster, *Ulysses and the Sirens* (Cambridge: Cambridge University Press, 1979).
15. Boudon, *The Unintended Consequences*, Chapter 2.
16. Maurice Merleau-Ponty, *In Praise of Philosophy* (Evanston: Northwestern University Press, 1963) p. 54.
17. Cf. Barbara Hall Partee, 'Opacity, coreferences and pronous', in Donald Davidson and Gilbert Harman, *Semantics of Natural Language* (Dordrecht Reidel, 1972) (published in US by Reidel Publications).
18. Cf. Goffman on puns, riddles, jokes, etc.: 'Wordplay seems to celebrate the power of the content to disqualify all but one reading, more than it disconfirms the workings of this force'. Erving Goffman, *Frame Analysis* (New York: Harper & Row, 1974) p. 443.
19. Paul Ziff, 'Natural and formal languages', in Sidney Hook, *Language and Philosophy* (New York: New York University Press, 1969); see also Hook, *Semantic Analysis* (Ithaca: Cornwell University Press, 1960).
20. Michael Polanyi, *Personal Knowledge* (London Routledge, Wegan Paul, 1958). 'Experience and the perception of pattern', in Kenneth M. Sayre and Frederick J. Crosson. *The Modelling of Mind* (New York: Simon & Schuster, 1968).
21. I borrow this example again from Ziff, 'What is said', in Davidson and Gilbert Harman Donald, *Semanties of Natural Language* (Dordrecht: Seidel, 1972). For an interesting relevant discussion, cf. Dell

Hynes, 'Sociolinguistics and the ethnography of speaking', in Edwin Ardener, *Social Anthropology and Language* (Tavistock: Tavistock Publications, 1971) (published in US by Humanities Press).

22. Cf. Joseph Weizenbaum, 'Contextual understanding by computers', *Communications of the ACM*, Vol. 10, 1967; Herbert Dreyfus, *Alchemy and Artificial Intelligence* (Santa Monica: Rand Corporation 1965); for more recent work, Roger C. Schank and Kenneth Mark Colby, *Computer Models of Thought and Language* (San Francisco: Freeman 1973).

23. Cf. Barbara Stanesz, 'Meaning and Interpretation', *Semiotoca*, vol. 11, 1974, p. 356.

24. George Henrik von Wright, *Norm and Action* (London: Routledge, Wegan Paul, 1963).

25. Karl Löwith, *From Hegel to Nietzsche* (London: Constable, 1964) p. 321.

26. Karl Marx, *Grundrisse der Kritik der politischen Ökonomie* (Berlin: Dietz-Verlag, 1953) p. 265.

27. Max Weber, *Economy and Society* (New York: Bedminster Press, 1968) vol. 1, p. 224.

28. Cf. Anthony Giddens, ' "Power" in the recent writings of Talcott Parsons', *Sociology*, vol. 2, 1968.

29. Henri Lefèbvre. *Everyday Life in the Modern World* (London: Allen Lane, 1971.

30. Merton, 'Manifest and latent functions', for comments see Anthony Giddens, 'Functionalism: *après la lutte*' (*Studies* in *Social and Political Theory*).

31. For example, Lévi-Strauss's formulation of the major features of structural analysis in Claude Lévi-Strauss, *Structural Anthropology*, vol. 1 (London: Allen Lane, 1968).

32. Raymond Firth, *Elements of Social Organisation* (London: Watts, 1956) pp. 30 and 39 (my italics).

33. Lévi-Strauss, *Structural Anthropology*, vol. 1, p. 271.

34. The conception of structure I advance seems to me close to that advocated by Bauman, save that he uses 'structure' as more or less synonymous with 'culture'. Zygmunt Bauman, *Culture as Praxis* (London: Routledge, 1973).

35. See, for instance, John R. Searle, *Speech Acts* (Cambridge: Cambridge University Press, 1969) pp. 33ff. Raymond D. Gumb, *Rule-governed Linguistic Behaviour* (The Hague: Mouton, 1972) reaches the same conclusion that I do, in respect of language rules: 'all linguistic rules have both a regulative and a constitutive aspect' (p. 25). For other relevant considerations, see Joan Safran Ganz, *Rules, a Systematic Study* (The Hague: Mouton, 1971); and Hubert Schwyzer, 'Rules and practices', *Philosophical Review*, vol. 78, 1969.

36. See Paul Ziff, *Semantic Analysis* (Ithaca: Cornell University Press, 1960); also Pierre Bourdieu, *Outline of a Theory of Practice* (Cambridge: Cambridge University Press, 1977). It might be noted that the notion of rule appears frequently in the symbolic interactionist litera-

ture, but with very little cross-referencing to the parallel literature in philosophy to do with rules. See, for instance, the various contributions to George J. McCall *et al.*, *Social Relationships* (Chicago: Aldine, 1970).

37. Michael Oakeshott, *Rationalism in Politics* (London: Methuen, 1967).
38. Wittgenstein, *The Blue and Brown Books* (Oxford: Blackwell, 1972) p. 25.
39. Wittgenstein, *Philosophical Investigations* (Oxford: Blackwell, 1972) pp. 80–1.
40. Cf. Georg Lukács, *Die Zerstörung der Vernunft* (Berlin: Aufbau-Verlag, 1955).
41. The nature of Weber's conceptualisation of power is still a matter of some controversy. Weber says 'Macht bedeutet jede Chance, innerhalb einer sozialen Beziehung den eigenen Willen auch gegen Widerstreben durchzusetzen, gleichviel worauf diese Chance beruht' (*Wirtschaft und Gesellschaft*, Tübingen: Möhr-Siebeck, 1956, p. 28). Although most English translations render *Chance* as 'capacity', it has been argued that, understood as 'chance' or 'possibility', the definition is less individualistic than appears to be the case. See Niklas Luhmann, *Macht* (Stüttgart: Enke, 1975).
42. ' "Power" in the writings of Talcott Parsons', in Giddens, *Studies in Social and Political Theory*.
43. Ernst Bloch, *A Philosophy of the Future* (New York: Herber, 1970) p. viii.
44. Georges Gurvitch, *Déterminismes sociaux et liberté humaine* (Paris: Presses Universitaires, 1955).
45. G.L.S. Shackle, *Decision, Order and Time* (Cambridge: Cambridge University Press, 1969).
46. Cf. Howard S. Becker, *Sociological Work* (London: Allen Lane, 1971).
47. See Nicholas Abercrombie and Bryan S. Turner, 'The dominant ideology thesis', *British Journal of Sociology*, vol. 29, 1978.
48. For one of the most acute pieces of research reporting around this theme, see Paul Willis, *Learning to Labour* (Farnborough: Saxon House, 1977).
49. Alfred Schutz, *Reflections on the Problem of Relevance* (New Haven: Yale University Press, 1970) pp. 120ff and *passim*.
50. Giddens, *Central Problems in Social Theory*, pp. 104–5.
51. Karl Marx, *Capital*, vol. 1 (London: Lawrence & Wishart, 1970) p. 110.
52. Marx, *Capital*, vol. 1, pp. 110 and 103.
53. Marx, *Capital*, vol. 1, p. 168.
54. For an earlier version of some of these points, see Anthony, Giddens, *The Class Structure of the Advanced Societies*, Chapter 6.
55. Marx, *Capital*, vol. 1, p. 337.
56. Marx, *Capital*, vol. 1, p. 338.
57. Marx, *Capital*, vol. 1, p. 356.
58. Marx, *Capital*, vol. 1, p. 111.

59. Erving Goffman, *Behaviour in Public Places* (New York: Free Press, 1963) and other writings.
60. Sam D. Sieber, *Fatal Remedies* (New York: Plenum Press, 1981) p. 59.
61. Thomas C. Schelling, *Choice and Consequence* (Cambridge, Mass.: Harvard University Press, 1984) p.8.
62. Emile Durkheim, *The Rules of Sociological Method* (London: Macmillan, 1982) p.51.
63. From Harold Garfinkel: 'A conception of, and experiments with, "trust" as a condition of stable concerted actions', in O.J. Harvey, *Motivation and Social Interaction* (New York: Ronald Press, 1963) p. 222. I have shortened the interchange slightly.
64. Philip Larkin, *The Whitsun Weddings* (London: Faber & Faber, 1971) p. 33.
65. Anthony Giddens, *The Constitution of Society*.
66. J.A. Barnes, *Sociology in Cambridge* (Cambridge: Cambridge University Press, 1970) p. 19.
67. Cf. Giddens, *New Rules of Sociological Method*, Chapter 3.
68. Willis, *Learning to Labour*.
69. Willis, *Learning to Labour*, p. 11.
70. Willis, *Learning to Labour*, pp. 29–30.
71. Willis, *Learning to Labour*, p. 33.
72. Cf. especially Willis, *Learning to Labour*, Chapter 5.
73. Quoted in Willis, *Learning to Labour*, p. 64.
74. Willis, *Learning to Labour*, p. 107.
75. G.A. Cohen, *Karl Marx's Theory of History, a Defence* (Oxford: Clarendon Press, 1978).
76. Here I draw upon my discussion in 'Commentary on the debate', a debate about functionalism, in *Theory and Society*, vol. II, 1982.
77. Willis, *Learning to Labour*, p. 66.
78. Willis, *Learning to Labour*, pp. 68ff.
79. Willis, *Learning to Labour*, p. 107.
80. See Giddens, *Central Problems in Social Theory*, pp. 104–6.
81. Marx, *Capital*, vol. 1, p. 169.

Chapter III
Time and Space

(i) Time–space, structure, system*

Time–space relations

. . . [I]t is a basic mistake to identify time and social change, and we can now pursue this further by looking more closely at temporal aspects of the constitution of social systems. In the context of doing so, I want to lodge a further claim, which is that most forms of social theory have failed to take seriously enough *not only the temporality of social conduct but also its spatial attributes*. At first sight, nothing seems more banal and uninstructive than to assert that social activity occurs in time and in space. But neither time nor space have been incorporated into the centre of social theory; rather, they are ordinarily treated more as 'environments' in which social conduct is enacted. In regard of time, this is primarily because of the influence of synchrony/diachrony differentiations: the assimilation of time and change has the consequence that time can be treated as a sort of 'boundary' to stable social orders, or at any rate as a phenomenon of secondary importance[1] The suppression of space in social theory derives from different origins, probably in some part from the anxiety of sociological authors to remove from their works any hint of geographical determinism. The importation of the term 'ecology' into the social sciences has done little to help matters, since this tends both to encourage the confusion of the spatial with other characteristics of the physical world that might influence social life, and to reinforce the tendency to treat spatial

---

* *Central Problems in Social Theory*, pp. 201–10.

characteristics as in the 'environment' of social activity, rather than as integral to its occurrence.

. . . I have argued [elsewhere] that social systems may be treated as systems of interaction, and have discussed some of the characteristics of systemness. But it is important at this point to consider some features of interaction passed over fairly cursorily there. Most schools of social theory, but especially functionalism, have failed to situate interaction in time, because they have operated within a synchronic/diachronic division.[2] A synchronic image of a social system writes out social reproduction, or at least takes it for granted: the other side of the assimilation of time and change, as I have noted above, is the equation of the a-temporal or the static with stability. When social analysts writing in this vein speak of systems of interaction as 'patterns' they have in mind, often in a fairly vague way, a sort of 'snapshot' of relations of social interaction. The flaw in this is exactly the same as that involved in the presumption of 'static stability': such a snapshot would not in fact reveal a pattern at all, because *any patterns of interaction that exist are situated in time*; only when examined over time do they form 'patterns' at all. This is most clear, perhaps, in the case of individuals in face-to-face encounters. Whatever else the concern of ethnomethodological writers with 'turn-taking' in conversations might or might not have illuminated, it points up something important: the seriality of the activities of the participants.[3] It is not just a trivial and obvious feature of conversational talk that only one person usually speaks at a time; or at least, it has not been obvious to most social analysts. If ethnomethodological examinations of turn-taking appear trivial, it is because their authors have not pursued their implications by connecting them in a broad way to temporality and social reproduction. The ethnomethodological study of conversation has, however, made a significant contribution in stressing that the 'managing' of talk by social actors routinely employs the location of a conversation in time as a mode of organising that conversation.[4]

The distinction commonly made between 'micro-' and 'macro-sociological' studies does not really help to elucidate some of the key differences between face-to-face interaction and other types of interactive relation in terms of which social systems are constituted. The term *face-to-face*, however, does convey a sense of the importance of the positioning of the body in space in social interaction.

The face is of course normally the focus of attention in social encounters, and as the most expressive part of the body is chronically monitored by actors in checking upon the sincerity of the discourse and acts of others. Not all interaction which takes place in the presence of others, where sensibility of that presence influences that interaction, is 'face-to-face': some instances of crowd behaviour may be an exception to this. But most such examples are quite marginal: it is striking how far, even in large-scale assemblies, the term 'face-to-face' still applies in a significant way. In assemblies, lectures, concerts, etc., the positioning of the audience is nearly always such that the members of the audience collectively face the performers.

In face-to-face interaction, the presence of others is a major source of information utilised in the production of social encounters. The micro- versus macro-sociological distinction puts an emphasis upon contrasting small groups with larger collectivities or communities; but a more profound difference is between *face-to-face interaction and interaction with others who are physically absent* (and often temporally absent also). The extension of social systems in space and in time is an evident feature of the overall development of human society. The extension of interaction in time . . . is opened out in a fundamental way by the development of writing. Tradition in non-literate cultures incorporates the sum of the cultural products of past generations; but the emergence of the text makes possible communication with the past in a much more direct way, and in a fashion which bears certain similarities to interaction with physically present individuals.[5] The access to the past that is opened up by the material existence of texts is however a distanciated interaction, if we contrast it to the presence of others in face-to-face interaction. The development of writing greatly extends the scope of distanciated interaction in space as well as in time. In cultures which do not have writing, contact both within the cultural group as well as with other groups is perforce always of a face-to-face kind. Of course in these circumstances actors themselves can act as mediators between others. But writing alters the nature of the transactions that can be carried out: the letter by-passes its carrier, and 'speaks' directly to its recipient. It should be noticed that the extension of interaction in space expressed in the transmitting of a letter from a sender to a recipient also involves the temporal absence of the sender, *vis-à-vis* the moment of communication when the letter is opened and read. The temporal gap between an exchange of letters is obviously much greater than that in the 'turn-taking' of conversations; on the other hand, of course, one of the main features of modern technologies of communication is that they no longer allow distance in space to govern temporal distance in mediated interaction. The telephone recaptures the immediacy of face-to-face interaction across spatial distance, at the cost of the restriction of the sensory context of communication; television and video communication restore considerably more, by returning distanciated interaction to a face-to-face form. If some of McCluhan's claims as to the significance of television and video are extreme, they none the less raise some salient questions about transmutations that might be occurring in structures of signification in the contemporary world.[6]

Time, space and repetition are closely intertwined. All known methods of assessing or calculating time involve repetition: the cyclic movement of the sun, the hands on a watch, the vibration of quartz crystals, etc.; all involve motion in space.[7] It is difficult to speak of time without reference to spatial metaphors – although if Whorf is right this may be in some part derivative of particular characteristics of the Indo-European languages. My argument in previous paragraphs attests to the closeness of the connections between time, space and repetition in social life. The cyclical character of repetition or social reproduction in societies governed by tradition is geared indirectly to the experience and mapping of time. But the experience of time probably never entirely sheds its cyclical guise, even when 'linear time consciousness' comes to predominate. Just as calendars and clocks interpolate cycles into the sequential movement of time, so daily, weekly and annual periods of time continue to maintain cyclical aspects in the organisation of social activities within contemporary societies. The same is true of the life-span of the individual, which we still continue aptly to call the 'life-cycle'.

The extension of social life in time and space has already been mentioned, as an overall characteristic of social development: time-scales of social activity are altered by the transmutation of communication over distance (cf. Heidegger's 'de-severance' – making the farness vanish). The interconnection of time and space can be explored in terms of the participation of social actors in cycles of social activity as well as at the level of the transformation of society itself.[8] Time-geography deals with the time–space 'choreography' of individuals' existence over given time periods: the day, week, year or the whole life-time. A person's daily routine of activities, for example, can be charted as a path through time–space. Thus the social transition involved in leaving home to go to work is also a movement through space. Social interaction from this point of view can be understood as the 'coupling' of paths in social encounters, or what Hägerstrand calls 'activity bundles'. 'Activity bundles' occur at definite 'stations' – buildings or other territorial units – where the paths of two or more individuals coincide; these encounters dissolve as actors move off in space and time to participate in other activity bundles. The interest of this conception of social activity as 'a weaving dance through time-space'[9] does not depend upon Hägerstrand's particular formulation of it, to which various objections can be made; its general importance is that it emphasises the co-ordination of movement in time and space in social activity, as the coupling of a multiplicity of paths or trajectories. The same conception can be applied to much broader problems of social change, to which I shall turn later: change in society can also be understood in terms of time–space paths. *Social development characteristically involves spatial as well as temporal movement*: the most significant form of which, in our times, concerns the world-wide expansion of Western industrial capitalism.

Spatial presence and absence

The fact that the concept of social structure ordinarily applied in the social sciences – as like the anatomy of a body or the girders of a building – has been so pervaded by spatial imagery, may be another reason, together with the fear of lapsing into geographical determinism, why the importance of space itself has rarely been sufficiently emphasised in social theory. The significance of spatial elements for social analysis can be illustrated in numerous ways, . . . first of all by referring to class theory.

In class society, spatial division is a major feature of class differentiation. In a fairly crude, but nevertheless sociologically significant, sense, classes tend to be regionally concentrated. One can easily instance the contrasts between the north and south of England, or west and east in Scotland, to make the point. Such spatial

differentiations always have to be regarded as time–space formations in terms of social theory. Thus one of the important features
of the spatial differentiation of class is the sedimentation of divergent regional 'class cultures' *over time*: class cultures which today,
of course, are partly dissolved by new modes of transcending time–
space distances.

The most consequential connections of class and space, however,
are both more far-flung and more immediately confined. On the
one hand, the class-character of capitalism incorporates international systems of centre and periphery; on the other, class domination is strongly influenced and reproduced by patterns of rural/
urban difference, and by the differentiation of neighbourhoods
within cities.[10] Neighbourhood segregation, in capitalist society, is
not predominantly a managed process: rather, it is the result of
class struggle in housing markets.[11] The social management of
space is none the less in definite ways a feature of all societies.
Virtually all collectives have a *locale* of operation, spatially distinct
from that associated with others. 'Locale' is in some respects a
preferable term to that of 'place', more commonly employed in
social geography: for it carries something of the connotation of
space used as a *setting* for interaction. A setting is not just a spatial
parameter, and physical environment, in which interaction 'occurs':
– it is these elements mobilised as part of the interaction. Features
of the setting of interaction, including its spatial and physical
aspects, . . . are routinely drawn upon by social actors in the
sustaining of communication – a phenomenon of no small importance for semantic theory.

If the notion of locale is combined with the influence of physical
presence/absence (this being understood as potentially both temporal and spatial), we can characterise the *small community* as
one in which there is only short distance in time–space separations. That is to say, the setting is such that all interaction has
only a small 'gap' to carry over in crossing time and space. It is
not just physical presence in immediate interaction which matters in
'small-scale' interaction: it is the temporal and spatial *availability* of
others in a locale.

No one has analysed such phenomena more perceptively than
Goffman, who in all his writings has brought out the significance
of space and place – or what in his first work he called 'regions'.[12] A
region, in Goffman's sense, is part of what I have called a locale,

which places bounds upon one or other of the major features of presence. Regions differ in terms of how they are confined or demarcated, as well as in terms of which features of presence they might 'let through'. A thick glass screen in a broadcasting studio can be used to isolate a room aurally but not visually. Regions are usually defined, he points out, in terms of time–space relations: the separation of 'living space' from 'sleeping space' in homes is also differentiation in times of use.

Goffman's contrast between *front and back regions* in which social performances are carried on is one of great interest – and one which has been unjustifiably ignored in the literature of social theory (Goffman's own works excepted). The spatial and social separation of back and front regions, as distinguished by Goffman – whereby various potentially compromising features of interaction are kept absent or hidden – can be connected in an illuminating way to practical consciousness and the operation of normative sanctions. The sustaining of a spatial discrimination between front and back is a prominent feature of the use of locale within the reflexive monitoring of action in discursive and practical consciousness.

On various occasions . . . I have sought to criticise Parsons's theorems about the relation he presumes between the 'internalisation of values' and normative constraints. One of my concerns has been to emphasise the importance of modes of normative conformity and deviance other than those given prominence by Parsons – without relapsing into the sort of futile confrontation between 'consensus' and 'conflict theory' which for a time held sway in discussions of such issues. One such mode of conformity is that of 'pragmatic acceptance' (grudging, semi-cynical, distanced through humour) of normative prescriptions as 'facts' of the circumstances of action. The front/back region contrast helps to demonstrate how such pragmatic acceptance is sustained through *control of the setting*.

The normative significance of the difference between front and back regions of interaction is well analysed by Goffman. Performances in front regions typically involve efforts to create and sustain the appearance of conformity to normative standards to which the actors in question may be indifferent, or even positively hostile, when meeting in the back. The existence of front/back discriminations normally indicates substantial *discursive penetration* of the institutional forms within which interaction is carried on. It is easy to relate this again to issues of class theory and the legitimation of structures of domination. Workers on the shop-floor work in a setting, for instance, in which it is often possible to turn spatial separation from management supervision into a practical back region, which becomes fully frontal [*sic*] only when management or other supervisors are immediately present. An example quoted by Goffman, describing the attitudes of workers in a shipyard, is a good illustration:

> It was amusing to watch the sudden transformation whenever word got around that the foreman was on the hull or in the shop or that a front-office superintendent was coming by. Quartermen and leadermen would rush to their groups of workers and stir them to obvious activity. 'Don't let him catch you sitting down', was the universal admonition, and where no work existed a pipe was busily bent and threaded, or a bolt which was already firmly in place was subjected to further and unnecessary tightening.[13]

It is important to see, as the author of the quotation in fact points out, that both sides in such a situation are usually aware, to greater or lesser degree, of what is occurring. Such recognition on the part of management is an acknowledgement of the limits of its power, and hence such spatial – social interchanges are highly important in the dialectic of control in organisations.

The shop-floor is usually physically demarcated as a spatial setting from the 'office'.[14] But of course similar kinds of opportunities for the translation of spatial separations into regions, in Goffman's sense, occur throughout the locales in which organisations operate. Weber's characterisation of modern bureaucracies as involving hierarchies of offices applies to the differentiation of physical space as well as to the differentiation of authority. Spatial separation of offices permits various sorts of back-region activities which involve control of information moving 'upwards', and thus serve to limit the power of those in the higher echelons.[15] But of course the controlled use of front/back differentiations is not confined to those in formally subordinate positions in organisational locales. The capability of controlling settings is one of the major prerogatives of power itself: the board-room, for instance, may be characteristically a front region in which activities displayed for public gaze conceal more significant manipulations that are withheld from view.

Absence and presence in small communities, or in collectivities involving only time–space separations of short distance, are primarily expressed through the physical characteristics and perceptual abilities of the human organism. The media of availability of presence in locales of large-scale collectivities are necessarily different. They include the various ways in which individuals can 'make themselves available' to others as a distance – via, for example, electronic communication. The front/back region opposition seems to hold mainly on the level of social integration, where the setting of locales is controlled directly in the reflexive monitoring of face-to-face interaction. But something of a similar effect can occur in less calculated fashion in cities, which in contemporary societies are the major intermediate locales between those of short-term presence-availability and the nation-state. The slum areas of a city, for example, may be 'hidden away' from the time–space paths which others who use the city, but do not live in those areas, follow.

The rise of the modern nation-state, with its clearly defined territorial boundaries, exemplifies the significance of control of space as a resource generating power differentials. Much has been written about this; the control of time as a resource in structures of domination has been far less studied. One of the themes of *Capital* . . . is that the economic order of capitalism depends upon the exact control of time: labour-time becomes a key feature of the exploitative system of class domination. Time remains today at the centre of capital–labour disputes, as the employers' weapon of time-and-motion studies, and the workers' riposte of go-slows, readily attest. The control of time as a resource employed in structures of domination, however, may be historically more significant than even Marx believed. The invention of the calendar seems to have been closely associated with the emergence of writing, and both in turn were bound up with the exploitation of 'human machines' in the early Near East. In the origins of modern capitalism, Mumford has suggested, the clock rather than the steam engine should be regarded as the prototype of the era of mechanised production. The applying of quantitative methods to the analysis of nature, he claims, was first of all manifested in the quantification of time. Power-machines had existed well before the invention of clocks: in the latter we find 'a new kind of power-machine, in which the source of power and its transmission were of such a nature as to ensure the even flow of energy throughout the works and to make possible regular production and a standardised product'.[16]

(ii)   Time–space distanciation*

The structuration of every social system, however small or large occurs in time and space, but none the less also 'brackets' time–space relations. This intermingling of presence and absence is inherent in the nature of the constitution of social systems: every society participates in some form of dissolution of the restraints of time and space. The study of how such a dissolution is achieved is the proper concern of the analysis of time–space distanciation . . . I shall be concerned here with how time–space distanciation is involved with the generation of power.

According to the theory of structuration . . ., power is generated in and through the reproduction of structures of domination, which includes the dominion of human beings over the material world (allocative resources) and over the social world (authoritative resources). Here, I shall concentrate attention upon modes in which authoritative resources are implicated in distanciation, taking the time–space edges between tribal and class-divided societies as my main empirical focus.

The underlying thread of my argument is as follows. Power is generated by the transformation/mediation relations inherent in the allocative and authoritative resources comprised in structures of domination. These two types of resource may be connected in different ways in different forms of society. It certainly is a mistake to suggest, as at least some interpretations of Marx's 'materialist conception of history' would have us believe, that the accumulation of allocative resources is the driving principle of all major processes of societal change. On the contrary, in non-capitalist societies it seems generally to be the case that the co-ordination of authoritative resources is the more fundamental lever of change. This is because – or so I shall argue – authoritative resources are the prime carriers of time–space distanciation.

* *A Contemporary Critique of Historical Materialism*, pp. 91–7.

Consider the time–space organisation of the smallest of human societies, band societies of hunters and gatherers. Such societies, of course, are marked by the predominance of presence, or of very high presence-availability. Extension in space occurs via the foraging activity of individuals who may spend periods of up to several days away from the remainder of the group. But the main, and distinctive, mode of spatial organisation is to be found in the perambulatory activity of the group as a whole. The spatial movement of hunting and gathering societies, it should be made clear, is not adequately understood as simply concerned with the production of material goods. These groups, like larger nomad societies, may lack fixed settlements but they do typically lay claim to the legitimate control of a domain as their 'territory of operation'. The periodic movement of the whole society may be seen as one way in which the members of that society transcend spatial limitations of presence. If 'territoriality' is taken to mean first and foremost the formation of a type of authoritative resource – claim to legitimate dominion over a given spatial extension – it must not be associated only with the settlement of villages or cities. Still less would it be correct to suppose that claim to legitimate control over territory is only found where there is some kind of state apparatus; what normally appears in this case is the insistence upon clear-cut administrative control of a territorial area (developed to its fullest extent only in nation-states).

Extension in time in band societies is achieved primarily via two overlapping sets of phenomena: the grounding of legitimation in tradition, and the fundamental part played by kinship in societal structuration. Kin relations are embedded in time, in that they link living individuals to the dead, whether or not this is formalised in lineage systems or ancestor worship.[17] But kin relations also help locate the living temporally, by marking phases of the life-cycle. The kinship system, together with religion, provide the main axes around which tradition coagulates. The connections between tradition, time and time-consciousness in non-literate societies are so important that it is worth spelling them out in a little detail. Tradition, which is the most elemental form of social reproduction, involves a particular type of time-consciousness, but it would probably be mistaken to regard it as involving a particular type of consciousness of time as such. In societies that are dominated by tradition, neither 'tradition' nor 'time' tend to be distinguished as separate from the continuity of events which they help to mould. We must have some reservations about Max Weber's conception of the 'traditional' as a type of legitimation. According to Weber, in this type 'legitimacy is claimed . . . and believed in by virtue of the sanctity of age-old rules and powers'.[18] This formulation, particularly in the context of Weber's contrast with more 'rational' modes of organisation, is a potentially misleading one. It suggests that tradition is itself a legitimising force, and thereby implies that 'traditional legitimation' has no rational basis; that what is done today is done merely because it is 'age-old', because it has always been done. But people do not generally believe in the age-old for its own sake: they believe in it because they regard it as embodying distinctive and precious value-standards and forms of knowledge. This is why 'tradition' as such is a chimera, seen apart from the concrete beliefs and practices which are embedded in it.

The level of time–space distanciation characteristic of band societies is low. The mobile character of the society does not involve a mediated transcendence of space: that is to say, it does not, as in large societies, involve regularised transactions with others who are physically absent. The differentiation of presence and absence is not incorporated in the structuration of the societal community. The distanciation in time that can be secured in any non-literate society is similarly quite restricted. Tradition in a broad way maintains contact with a distant past, in the sense that similar beliefs and practices are continued across the generations. But the influence of tradition specifically acts to overcome a severance of 'present' and 'past': the past is not recoverable except in so far as it is implicated in the present (more accurately, in the continuity of 'presencing').

These considerations point to the importance of *storage capacity* to time–space distanciation and the generation of power. We may distinguish two forms of storage, corresponding to the two types of resources that enter into structures of domination. One is the more obvious of the two: the storage of 'material' or allocative resources. Storage capacity is much more important to the production of a 'surplus' than technological change in the instruments of production. But the storage of allocative resources turns out also to be less significant than the storage of authoritative resources as a whole. I shall try to amplify these claims shortly. To talk of 'storage' of material resources is more complex than may appear at first sight.

Storage here involves not simply the physical containment of material goods (which is its least interesting form). The term should rather be understood as implying a range of time–space control. The two types of productive system most often mentioned in the archaeological literature as associated with the formation of 'civilisations' – agriculture in general, and irrigation agriculture in particular – each increase storage capacity, as contrasted to hunting and gathering. In agriculture the earth itself is regarded as a 'store' of potential produce; the garnering of products here involves biting quite deeply into time, since even relatively rudimentary forms of agriculture necessitate advance planning of a regularised character. Irrigation agriculture, where it involves the human construction of waterways, canals, etc., both demands and makes possible a greater co-ordination of time–space relations.

Storage of authoritative resources involves above all *the retention and control of information or knowledge*. There can be no doubt that the decisive development here is the invention of writing and notation. In non-literate societies knowledge is stored through its incorporation in traditional practices, including myth-telling: the only storage 'container' in such circumstances is the human memory. The time–space distanciation made possible by writing (and, in modern times, by mechanical printing) is much greater. There have, of course, been civilisations without writing – most notably the Inca, who employed *quipus*, knotted cords, as a mnemonic device. But such examples are exceptional. Writing seems everywhere to have orginated as a direct mode of storage: as a means of recording information relevant to the administration of societies of an increasing scale. In the early phases of development of Sumer, for example, writing seems to have been used exclusively to record and tally administrative details: 'Tallies and tokens, wage-lists and ration lists, lists of supplies and monthly accounts – these are the documents we have in tens of thousands.'[19] Listing, collating – what are these but the first origins, and always the main foundation, of what Foucault calls 'surveillance'? The keeping of written 'accounts' – regularised information about persons, objects and events – generates power that is unavailable in oral cultures. The list is the most elementary form of information coding, and therefore of information storing. The significance of lists, and of the differences between them and oral communication, have been well brought out by Goody.[20] A list is a particular type of 'container', not just an aid to the memory, but a definite means of encoding information. Lists do not represent speech in any sort of direct way, and contrast with the flow of oral communication; the early development of writing thus signals a sharper break with speech than might be imagined if we suppose that writing originated as a visual depiction of the spoken word.[21] In Sumer, listing led eventually to the further development of writing as a mode of chronicling events of a 'historical' nature. Kings adopted it in order to list or record their achievements in government and in war. These 'event lists' form the first known 'written histories', and eventually built up to span a large number of generations.

If storage of allocative and authoritative resources plays an essential underlying role in the promotion of time–space distanciation so also does the differentiation of centre/periphery relations. The *city*, as a religious, ceremonial and commerical centre, is a distinctive feature of all societies characterised by extensive time–space distanciation. When Spengler wrote that 'World history is city history' he may have been overstating the case, but not too unduly. Suppose we set out an over-all classification of major types of society as follows:

Band societies
Settled agricultural communities
City-states   ⎫
Empires   ⎬ 'Civilisations' (class-divided societies)
Feudal societies ⎭
Capitalist societies ⎫
Socialist societies ⎬ Industrialised societies

In *all* these forms of society, following the first emergence of civilisations, the city, in divergent relations with the countryside, has played an influential role. In the light of the pervading influence of evolutionary theories it is worth again emphasising the significance of time–space edges in societal development. It is not just the case, for instance, that hunting and gathering societies have coexisted with early agricultural communities or city-states: each of the types of society indicated above has coexisted simultaneously with every one of the others (with the possible exception of feudalism, depending upon how narrowly the concept of 'feudal society' is formulated).

The city, as Mumford has shown brilliantly, may be regarded as a special form of 'container', a crucible for the generation of power on a scale unthinkable in non-urban communities. In his words,

> the first beginning of urban life, the first time the city proper becomes visible, was marked by a sudden increase in power in every department and by a magnification of the role of power itself in the affairs of men. A variety of institutions had hitherto existed separately, bringing their numbers together in a common meeting place, at seasonable intervals: the hunters' camp, the sacred monument or shrine, the palaeolithic ritual cave the neolithic agricultural village – all of these coalesced in a bigger meeting place, the city . . . The original form of this container [the city] lasted for some six thousand years; only a few centuries ago did it begin to break up.[22]

The enclosure of cities by walls enhances the metaphor of the container. How far is Mumford correct, however, to presume that the agricultural village preceded the origin of the city? Mumford's work has done a good deal to free us from the misleading presumption that the expansion of 'productive forces' is the chief mobilising factor in social change. But in one respect he might not have gone far enough in questioning established views in archaeology.

(iii)   Analysing social change*

[In explaining social change no single and sovereign mechanism can be specified; there are no keys that will unlock the mysteries of human social development, reducing them to a unitary formula, or that will account for the major transitions between societal types in such a way either.][23]

The foregoing considerations do not mean that we cannot generalize about social change and do not imply that we should relinquish all general concepts in terms of which change might be analysed. Five concepts are particularly relevant in this respect . . . [In addition to] structural principles, time–space edges and intersocietal systems . . . I want to add the notions of *episodic characterization* (or, more briefly, episodes) and *world time*.[24]

---

* *The Constitution of Society*, pp. 244–56.

Structural principles	Analysis of modes of institutional articulation; and of factors involved in the overall institutional argument of a society or type of society[25]
Episodic characterizations	Delineation of modes of institutional change of comparable form
Intersocietal systems	Specification of relations between societal totalities
Time–space edges	Indication of connections between societies of differing structural type
World time	Examination of conjunctures in the light of reflexively monitored 'history'

All social life is episodic, and I intend the notion of episode, like most of the concepts of structuration theory, to apply to the whole range of social activity. To characterize an aspect of social life as an episode is to regard it as a number of acts or events having a specifiable beginning and end, thus involving a particular sequence. In speaking of large-scale episodes I mean identifiable sequences of change affecting the main institutions within a societal totality, or involving transitions between types of societal totality. Let us take as an example the emergence of agrarian states. To treat the formation of a state as an episode means analytically cutting into 'history', that is, identifying certain elements as marking the opening of a sequence of change and tracing through that sequence as a process of institutional transmutation. State formation has to be studied in the context of the involvement of a pre-existing society in broader intersocietal relations (without, of course, neglecting endogenous forms of change), examined in the context of the structural principles implicated in the relevant societal totalities. Thus the accumulation of surplus production on the part of spatially proximate village communities in areas of high potential fertility may be one type of pattern leading to the emergence of a state combining those communities under a single order of administration. But it is only one among others. In many cases the co-ordination of military power used coercively to establish a rudimentary state apparatus is the most important factor. Agrarian states always exist along time–space edges in uneasy relations of symbiosis and conflict with, and partial domination over, surrounding tribal societies, as well, of course, with other states which may struggle for hegemony over a given area. To insist that social change be studied in 'world time' is to emphasize the influence of varying forms of intersocietal system upon episodic transitions. That is to say, it depends upon conjunctions of circumstances and events that may differ in nature according to variations of context, where context (as always) involves the reflexive monitoring by the agents involved of the conditions in which they 'make history'.

We can categorize modes of social change in terms of the dimensions represented below, these being combined in the assessment of the nature of specific forms of episode. In analysing the origins of an episode, or series of episodes studied in a comparative fashion, various sorts of consideration are ordinarily relevant. In the modern world the expansion in the time–space distanciation of social systems, the intertwining of different modes of regionalization involved in processes of uneven development, the prominence of contradictions as structural features of societies,[26] the prevalence of historicity as a mobilizing force of social organization and transmutation – all these factors and more supply a backdrop to assessing the particular origins of an episode.

In referring to the type of social change involved in an episode I mean to indicate both how intensive and how extensive it is – that is to say, how profoundly a series of changes disrupts or reshapes an existing alignment of institutions and how wide-ranging such changes are. One idea that is relevant here, which I have outlined

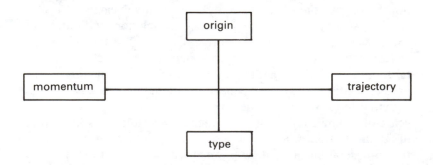

in some detail in other sources,[27] is that there may be 'critical thresholds' of change characteristic of transitions between overall societal types. A set of relatively rapid changes may generate a long-term momentum of development, that development being possible only if certain key institutional transformations are accomplished initially. 'Momentum' refers to the rapidity with which change occurs in relation to specific forms of episodic characterization, while 'trajectory' concerns the direction of change, as mentioned earlier.

Let us look briefly at the problem of the emergence of agrarian states in order to illustrate the concepts just introduced. How far can the development of such states be regarded as a single type of episode? Even such an apparently innocuous question turns out to be much harder to answer than is suggested by the relative simplicity of most theories which have been put forward about such states – for example, that they have their origins in warfare, in irrigation schemes, in the rapid accumulation of surplus production and so on. To make an episodic characterization, as I have mentioned, means making a number of conceptual decisions: about what social form is the 'starting point' of a presumed sequence of change, about what the typical trajectory of development is and about where the 'end point' is said to be.

First of all, we might register that the term 'state' is an ambiguous one. It can refer either to the overall form of a 'state based society' or to governmental institutions of a definite type within such a society. To simplify the issue, I shall take 'state' for this purpose to mean the second of these alternatives. The initial characterization problem, then, becomes one of deciding the main contrasts being looked for in juxtaposing circumstances in which certain political institutions exist to those in which they do not. This question does seem to admit of an answer, although not an uncontroversial one. Following Nadel, we may suppose that a state exists when the following conditions are found: (a) centralized organs of government, associated with (b) claims to legitimate territorial control and (c) a distinct dominant elite or class, having definite modes of training, recruitment and status attributes.[28] Such a formulation, or one very much like it, has been adopted by many prominent contributors to the field, notably in the case of classic discussion of Fortes and Evans-Pritchard.[29] What is the obverse, the type of social situation from which states develop? The answer might be thought to be self-evident – societies which do not possess state institutions as defined above. But matters are not, in fact, so obvious, or they are so only if we unthinkingly apply an endogenous model. For it is probably not usually the case that state institutions develop within an already constituted 'society' that remains more or less unchanged. On the contrary, the development of states very often fuses previously unarticulated social entities and may at the same time break up others that have existed hitherto.

We have to bear this point in mind when distinguishing states from chiefdoms. It may be that the latter are usually the antecedents of the former (and remain when states are destroyed or collapse), but the one rarely derives simply from the 'expansion' or 'internal differentiation' of the other. The distinction between states and chiefdoms is by no means as easy to make as is seemingly often presumed in the anthropological literature. The normal basis of the distinction has to do with centralization. In contrast to states, chiefdoms have a range of equivalent office holders, under the chief; these offices entail more or less the same power and status. There is no doubt that this distinction does help to order the relevant empirical materials. None the less, the dividing line can be variously placed. Consider, for example, the case of Tahiti.[30] Here there were three endogenous descent groups, stratified in some degree by status and political responsibility. Chiefs, presided over by a paramount chief, were drawn from the upper of these groups within different parts of the island. But are these groups worth calling 'states'? Claessen says yes,[31] but the author who has devoted most energy to studying ancient Tahitian society, Oliver, says no.[32]

The difference of opinion is not so much empirical as conceptual. It is important because it is symptomatic of the difficulties involved in specifying classes of social objects. My view is that Claessen makes the criteria for the existence of states too lax. Of course, it is apparent enough that criteria of classification and the predication of definite mechanisms of institutional articulation are not independent issues. One cannot start out with a theoretically neutral taxonomy and then later inject a theoretical interpretation into it. Thus on the basis of a survey of twenty-one 'early states' Claessen claims that there is no specific association between such states and urbanism. But, in fact, nearly all of the examples cited to reach this conclusion belong to his category of 'inchoate states', which would seem to me to be more accurately designated as chiefdoms.[33]

How should we specify the trajectory of change to be looked at? As posed in the existing literature, this question is often answered not only within an endogenous framework but also with regard to implicitly evolutionary premises. That is to say, it is posed in a unidirectional way, as to do only with the development of states, the existence of the state being taken as the end-point of the process. But why should episodes involving agrarian states be thought of exclusively, even primarily, in this fashion? The development of a state in one particular region very often coincides with, and perhaps brings about, the dissolution or attenuation of other neighbouring states. The dissolution of states is no less common an occurrence than their initial formation, and there is little rationale for concentrating on the one process to the exclusion of the other – especially in so far as they are recurrently linked together. I would therefore be inclined to characterize the issue as follows. In understanding processes of institutional change affecting agrarian states, we are seeking to analyse the conditions giving rise to the intersecting relations between chiefdoms and state forms.

Expressed in this way, it should be clear why such a position is at odds with the usual concentration on the 'origins' of the state. It is also unsurprising that the large literature on the 'origins' of the state has not come up with support for the sorts of all-enveloping generalization that have often been ventured. These fall into various types, according to the causal forces given priority.[34] Probably the most influential are those which emphasize demographic factors, war and the growth of the forces of production. Childe's writings have had a substantial impact upon theories which are in the third of these categories; in archaeology his work has probably been a more important source of Marxist influence than the writings of Marx and Engels themselves. Theories of this type tend to be strongly evolutionary and to presume that the 'origins' of the state are associated with either sheer technological change or the accumulation of surplus production. Where such views do not amount to false functionalist 'explanations', they are simply inconsistent with empirical data. There are some cases which come close to fitting the bill – that is to say, where surplus accumulation precedes the development of a state and where an emergent ruling class 'pushes' towards state formation. But these are exceptional.[35]

Phases of state formation are often connected with declining pro-ductivity and wealth rather than the reverse, although sometimes goods may be plundered from surrounding areas.

The 'warfare theory' has attracted many adherents because if there is one aspect of agrarian (and industrialized) states which is more or less chronic, it is participation in war. Spencer's version of evolutionism, of course, attributed great significance to warfare prior to the development of the industrial age. War is definitely very commonly involved in the formation and the disintegration of states – which, as I have stressed, is often one and the same process. But it is one thing to say that states frequently engage in warlike activities; it is another to say that such activities play a dominant or determinant role in the origins of those states and yet another to say that they play this role in the formation (or decline) of all agrarian states. The first statement is unobjection-able. The second is at best only partially valid. The third is simply erroneous. Demographic theories scarcely fare better. They usually suggest that population increase, the result of increasing birth rates in populations whose available living space is relatively confined, creates pressure leading to centralization of authority and differen-tiation of power.[36] Certainly, state-based societies are larger, often very much larger, than tribal orders. Demographic theories are often associated with the idea that the 'neolithic revolution' stimu-lates population increase, leading to state formation. But this does not work on either a general or a more specific level. The beginning of the neolithic is distant from the development of any known state-based societies. In more specific terms, it does not turn out that those states which were formed in physically confined areas always follow a build-up of population pressure. There are some instances that seem to accord fairly well with the theory, but many do not. Thus, examining state formation in the Valley of Mexico and in Mesopotamia, Dumont reaches the conclusion that population growth cannot explain the development of state forms, although the former is associated with the latter.[37] Other research indicates that population may decline in the period prior to state formation.[38]

Some accounts of state formation emphasize relations between societies other than that of war. Thus Polanyi has studied the impact of long-distance trade on the development of states.[39] To my knowledge, no one has offered this as a generalized theory of state formation; if anyone did, it would fare even worse than those

mentioned above. This sort of viewpoint does at least call attention
to aspects of the importance of intersocietal systems in processes of
state formation and decay. However, the mention neither of war
nor of trade confronts the analytical issue of the nature of intersocietal systems . . . It will not do to think of such systems only as a
series of relations linking clearly delimited societal wholes. To study
such systems means at the same time to discard the assumption that
the question of what a 'society' is admits of a ready and easy
answer. Consider again the sorts of example discussed by Eberhard. In a single geographical arena numerous societies may exist
in relatively close physical proximity but without much direct contact between them, although all are nominally or actually subject to
political rule from a centre.[40] By contrast, in such an arena there
may exist interlaced groupings quite differently located in time–
space – this is one of the phenomena I have in mind in speaking
of 'time–space edges'. Thus, as in traditional China, in Moghul
India the bulk of the Indian farmers had virtually no contact with
the Moghuls. Their languages, customs and religion were different.
The big merchants were only peripherally part of 'Moghul society',
but most of their contacts and affiliations with groups were distributed over large distances, stretching across the subcontinent and
the whole of the Near East. Much the same was true of the priests,
who belonged to associations spanning the subcontinent and sometimes beyond.

> We should not be astonished to find certain folk tales in the
> whole Near East, in some parts of South Asia and, finally, on
> the Fu-kien coast of China, while we do not find them in the
> Philippines or on Hainan Island. Miao tribes in Kui-chou for
> centuries preserved their own customs, beliefs and tales in spite
> of Chinese settlements only a few miles away in which other
> customs, beliefs and tales were propagated. Miao and Chinese
> in such places did not interact, as a rule, except in the fields of
> economic exploitation or military aggression. But the Miao in
> Kui-chou might have had the same customs as Miao in Viet-
> nam because – as we can often prove – some contacts were
> maintained even over long distances and long periods.[41]

The points made so far suggest that theories of the 'origins' of the
state tend to suffer from shortcomings deriving from the character-

ization of episodes in an endogenous and/or evolutionary form and
a failure to examine societal organization and change in the context
of intersocietal systems. But to these have to be added a neglect of
the impact of 'world time'. Putting these together, we can come to
see that the type of theory often looked to as explaining 'state
origins' turns out to be a chimera. In speaking of the influence of
'world time', I do not mean the arranging of events or happenings
in a calendar of world history. I mean two things referred to by
Eberhard in his use of the phrase (although these are not clearly
distinguished by him). Each concerns factors limiting generalizations that might be made about types of episode. One refers to
conjunctures, the other to the influence of human knowledgeability
on social change. By 'conjunctures' I mean the interaction of
influences which, in a particular time and place, have relevance to
a given episode – in this case, state formation or decline. The
conjuncture of circumstances in which one process of development
occurs may be quite different from that of another, even if their
'outcomes' – e.g. the consolidation of a similar type of state apparatus – are similar. In order to understand how this may come about,
it is essential to consider human reflexivity – and this is exactly what
many theories of state formation do not do. Conjunctural conditions could be treated as comparable with the 'boundary conditions' of laws were it not the case that they can enter into the
thinking, and therefore the conduct, of human actors who are
aware of them.

   Adopting bits of each of the theories previously mentioned
above, Claessen and Skalnik list the following elements as relevant
to explaining state formation, although these are not always found,
they say, and their relative importance may vary from instance to
instance:

(1)   population growth or pressure;
(2)   war, conquest or their threat;
(3)   technological progress or the production of a surplus;
(4)   ideology and legitimation;
(5)   the influence of already existing states.[42]

While these are offered as if they were 'factors' of equivalent
logical status, (5) is, in fact, different from the others. Taking (5)
seriously means coping with all the issues I have mentioned

previously in regard to intersocietal systems, time–space edges and 'world time'. It is simply absurd to compress these into a single additional 'factor' to be added to the other ones mentioned.

We can begin to unpack some of the problems involved by considering the distinction introduced by Fried, and widely adopted since then, between 'pristine' and 'secondary' states.[43] Pristine or primal states are those which develop in areas where no state forms have previously existed; secondary states are those developing in areas where others have existed before them or are to be found nearby. The differences between these supply at least one main axis in 'world time' and bring intersocietal relations directly into play. I take it that my previous discussion has indicated that the empirical identification of primal states is exceedingly difficult. It is not possible to define primal states as those which have become formed in geographically isolated environments. For the influence of forms of political organization which are simply 'known about' are enough to make a state a secondary state. Thus Egypt of the Old Kingdom is sometimes regarded as a primal state on the basis that it apparently developed in a geographically protected *milieu* (although the archaeological evidence on this is, in fact, very meagre). But all that this means is that no previous state form is known to have existed there. The impact of pre-existing Mesopotamian states certainly cannot be discounted.[44]

The implication I wish to draw is that the categories of primal and secondary states are highly imbalanced. Instances of primal states are hard to come by, and in the nature of the case we are never going to be able to be sure that cases which look to be plausible candidates for belonging in the category are any more than that. For it may be, of course, that traces of prior state influences have simply disappeared. It certainly follows that, while there is no bar to speculating about the modes of development of primal states, it may be quite misleading to treat what is known about them as a basis for theorizing about processes of state formation in general. It is likely to be very much more fruitful to regard 'secondary states' as prototypical – that is to say, states which develop in a world, or in regions of the world, where there are already either states or political formations having a considerable degree of centralization.

In a world of already existing states there is no difficulty in explaining the availability of the idea of the state, or of models of state formation, that could be followed by aspiring leaders and their followerships. We are all familiar with the fact that the leaders of Japan in recent times quite deliberately – although after a good deal of external pressure from the West – decided to adopt a certain model of industrial development derived from prior European and American experience. While this example is no doubt unusual in so far as the changes initiated were quite sudden and very far-reaching, it is hardly only in recent times that human beings in one context have been concerned to emulate, or borrow from, those in another in order to offset their power or influence. The steps involved in state formation, in other words, have probably hardly ever been unknown to those who have played leading parts in such a process. It is enough to surmise that state builders have almost always been aware of major aspects of the nature and basis of power of centralized political formations in order to explain a good deal about how states have come into being and declined. We do not have to imagine that it was ever common for individuals or groupings to have overall organizational plans in mind for social change and then to set about implementing them. That is very largely a phenomenon of the modern era.

What, then, might a theory of state formation look like, recast in these terms? First of all, we have to remember the point that the operation of generalized 'social forces' presumes specifiable motivation on the part of those influenced by them. To speak of, for example, 'population expansion' as a contributing cause of state formation implies certain motivational patterns prompting definite sorts of response to that expansion (and involved in bringing it about). Second, the influence of 'world time' means that there are likely to be considerable differences in respect of the major influences upon state formation; an overall account which will fit in some cases will not do so in others. This does not mean that generalizations about state formation as a type of episode are without value. However, they will probably apply to a more limited range of historical contexts and periods than the originators of most of the more prominent theories have had in mind.

Carneiro's theory might be taken as an example. A formal representation of it can be given as in Figure III.1. Carneiro emphasizes the importance of warfare in the origin of states. But warfare is more or less chronic in societies of all kinds, he says, and is thus not a sufficient explanation of state formation. War tends to lead to the

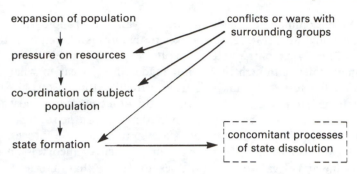

Figure III.1

formation of states, he claims, when those involved are penned into physically cirumscribed areas of agricultural land, such as the Nile, Tigris–Euphrates and Indus valleys, the Valley of Mexico or the mountain and coastal valleys of Peru. In such circumstances warfare may come to set up a pressure upon scarce resources where migration out of the area is unlikely to occur. Established ways of life come under strain, inducing some groups to seek military ascendancy over others and fostering attempts to centralize control over production. Population growth tends to be a highly important contributory factor both in stimulating conflicts over resources and in promoting centralization of administrative authority.[45] An entire valley eventually becomes unified under a single chiefdom, which, with further concentration of administrative resources, becomes distinguishable as a state. The state may then push its own boundaries outwards to conquer and absorb surrounding peoples. It is here (although Carneiro does not say so) that the theory presumes the primacy of certain types of motive – and, we can add, the likely influence of strategies, models or diffuse influences from pre-existing political forms. It has to be inferred that in the face of pressure on resources and established modes of conduct, those involved do not alter such modes of conduct so as to renew social co-operation. Unequal division of resources does not follow mechanically from population pressure. Also, tendencies towards the strengthening of centralized control will not happen willy-nilly in such a situation. They are likely to involve some sort of reflexive understanding of 'social needs' by actors engaged in policies that strengthen such control, although no one might intend the outcomes which actually come about.

As is common in much of the relevant anthropological and archaeological literature, Carneiro's discussion is offered as a theory of the 'origin of the state'. The phrase normally tends to refer to primal states, although this is not made wholly clear in what the author has to say. I think it is more valuable, for reasons already mentioned, to move away from the distinction between primary and secondary states. The very same pattern as Carneiro treats as involved in the 'origin' of the state may also be a process of political dissolution or fragmentation. Carneiro's theory is an interesting and elegant one, but it does not follow that in order to be defended it has to apply to all known cases of state formation, even if it were possible easily to distinguish primal from secondary states. Carneiro admits that cases can be readily found which the theory does not seem to fit. He then tries to modify it in such a way as to give it universal application, believing that if it does not have such a universal character there must be something wrong with the theory. States do not always develop in physically confined geographical areas. To cover such cases, Carneiro introduces a concept of what he calls 'resource concentration'. Where natural resources are particularly concentrated within any given area, people tend to become drawn to that area, leading to a crowding of population within it. Once there is a fairly dense population within the area in question, the pattern of state development will tend to occur. However, thus extended the theory no longer looks as plausible, and it is surely best to conclude that it only covers certain types of cases of state formation, not all. Of course, it is very important to seek to discover just where the limits of its validity lie. But the fact that it serves to illuminate only a given range of instances does not necessarily imply that it is logically flawed.

(iv)　The production of everyday life*

In the theory of structuration, social life is taken to consist in regularised social practices. Life is not experienced as 'structures', but as the *durée* of day-to-day existence, in the context of conventions ordered above all on the level of practical consciousness. The continuity of daily life is not a 'directly motivated' phenomenon,

---

* *A Contemporary Critique of Historical Materialism*, pp.150–6.

but assured in the routinisation of practices.[46] In tribal and class-divided societies the routinisation of daily life is governed above all by tradition. There is no doubt that the significance of tradition in purely oral cultures is different from those in which some form of writing exists. Besides expanding the level of time–space distanciation, writing also opens the way for those divergences of interpretation which in modern historiography have come to be called 'hermeneutics'. Writing gives rise to texts that enjoy an 'objectified' existence independent of the sustaining of oral traditions in daily social practices. The 'conflict of interpretations' engendered by texts is very closely related to ideology, and illustrations of this can be seen very early in the history of the Near Eastern civilisations: in, for instance, the struggles of priestly groups in Sumer to protect one version of the scriptual past against that favoured by an increasingly independent and powerful monarchy.

But in all class-divided societies literacy was the monopoly of the few, and inevitably for the majority of the population the routinisation of daily life was carried in orally based tradition. Tradition, it is important to reaffirm, in tribal and class-divided societies is a source of legitimacy: daily social practices, and the *durée* of experience itself, are moralised through their antiquity (although not through that alone). The 'meaningfulness' of the day-to-day organisation of social life is a taken-for-granted feature of human existence, and guaranteed by tradition. The routinisation of daily life, it should be pointed out, is immediately and necessarily connected with the succession of the generations. The temporality of the *durée* of daily existence appears only to the sociologist to be a separate phenomenon from the temporality of the life-cycle, of the replacement of one generation by another. The continuity of routinisation controlled by tradition extends to the practices which influence the life-passages conventionally labelled as 'socialisation'.

The dissolution of the pervading influence of tradition in post-medieval Europe was undoubtedly the result of a number of divergent factors, not all of which can in any specific way be explained as deriving from the rise of capitalism. Equally certainly, however, the transformations of labour and property that assume concrete (*sic*) form in the emergence of capitalist urbanism are the chief origin of a radical weakening of tradition as the main source of the routinisation of day-to-day life. The 'pulverising and macadamising tendency of modern history' of which Maitland once spoke can be derived in a direct manner from Marx's analysis of capitalism as a system of commodity production founded in the labour contract . . . In my opinion this is just as consequential for social theory, in respect of those conceptions of the modern world which focus upon the notion of 'mass society', as it is when juxtaposed to the 'theory of industrial society'. According to most theorists of 'mass society', in the contemporary industrialised societies human beings feel vulnerable, chronically anxious and often 'alone in the crowd'. This is supposed to be the result of the sheer scale of such societies, but is more generally traced to the eradication of 'community' by the growth of urbanism. In this respect there are considerable overlaps between accounts of 'mass society' and conceptions of urbanism such as that offered by Wirth.

If such accounts are correct, these circumstances are neutral in respect of class theory: they are not, in any significant way at least, dependent upon the constitution of capitalism as a class system. I have no quarrel with the descriptions of the 'rootless' way of life offered by the 'mass-society' theorists, but consider it highly important to take issue with their diagnoses of the origins of the phenomena thus referred to. Marx's analysis of the commodity, it should be emphasised, opens out in two directions, one more familiar than the other. The first, the most discussed by Marx himself and by the majority of his followers, is that the commodification of social relations leads to the loss of control by workers over the labour they carry out and over the products they make. The second, while by no means completely separable substantively from the social changes referred to by the first, leads precisely in the direction of the 'meaninglessness' of modern social life – to the themes that figure so prominently in the writings of the 'mass-society' theorists – for commodification, as I have stressed, depends upon the transformation of substance into form. Less provocatively expressed, commodities have a 'double existence' as objects or phenomena having definite qualities on the one hand, and on the other as pure transformation/mediation relations. Now tradition always has a content, and is geared into the qualities of definite activities characteristic of the temporality of tribal and class-divided societies; temporality itself directly reflects an 'ontological security' that invokes a normatively secured continuity between the *durée* of presence and the *longue durée* of established institutions.

The ontological security of tradition (which should not be construed as a purely positive phenomenon) is fundamentally undermined by three of the sets of transformations . . . :

(a)   *The commodification of labour via its transformation into labour-power* as the medium of the production of surplus value. It follows from Marx's analysis that this is a major point of connection between the two themes mentioned above: loss of control over the labour process and of the fruits of production, and the undermining of the 'meaningfulness' of labour. The latter phrase is not a precise one, and it would be foolish merely to contrast forms of labour in capitalist economies with craft skills that have now disappeared. Marx was not prone to romanticise peasant labour, and neither should we.[47] But, however hard and unrewarding it may be in many contexts, peasant labour, as Marx emphasises in the *Formen*, was always carried on as an inherent element of a broader series of communal practices, and of course maintained the worker in an intimate and knowledgeable interrelation with nature.

(b)   *The transformation of the 'time–space paths' of the day*, through its centring upon a defined sphere of 'work' physically separate from the household and separated in objectified time from 'leisure' or 'private time'. The capitalistic labour contract is explicitly drained of the moralised rights and obligations which (in principle at least) typically accompanied the exploitation of labour in class-divided societies. This is attended by technological innovations affecting labour (often but by no means always leading to the 'deskilling' of labour) on a scale quite without precedent in world history. This does not imply that work in capitalist industry is devoid of 'meaning' for workers, a matter that in any case varies widely within the high diversification of the division of labour in capitalist production. But there are no longer any guaranteed normative connections between the distinct time-encapsulated sphere of work and the remainder of social life, which itself becomes substantially disembedded from traditionally established practices. The converse of the 'public time' introduced by the rule of the clock is the 'private time' that is freely disposable by the individual, but remains objectified time in the sense that it has been severed from an integral involvement with the situated practices of social life.

(c)   *The commodification of urban land, resulting in the 'created space'* that is the day-to-day habitat of the majority of the population in the developed capitalist societies. 'Created space' is long distant from the associations with nature characteristic in substantial degree even of cities in class-divided civilisations. Capitalist cities are almost wholly manufactured environments, in which an architectural functionalism produces the prosaic physical surroundings that become the settings in which the bulk of urban life is carried on. As Lefebvre writes,

> with the Incas, the Aztecs, in Greece or in Rome, every detail (gestures, words, tools, utensils, costumes, etc.) bears the imprint of a *style;* nothing had as yet become prosaic, not even the quotidian; the prose and the poetry of life were still identical . . . [the capitalist city], anti-nature or non-nature yet second nature, heralds the future world, the world of the generalised urban.[48]

In the phrase 'the production of everyday life', 'everyday life' has to be understood as having something of a technical sense: as being distinct from the more generic terms 'day-to-day life', 'daily life', etc., that I have employed. Everyday life refers to routinised day-to-day activities in which the routinisation of those activities is not strongly embedded normatively in frameworks of tradition.

Routinisation in this context certainly embodies residual traditions, as all social life must do; but the moral bindingness of traditionally established practices is replaced by one geared extensively to habit against a background of economic constraint.[49] The pervasiveness of everyday life in capitalist–industrial urbanism has to be understood as a historical product, not as the 'given' or existential conditions under which social life is universally carried on. This is in specific contrast, however, to how these conditions are experienced by the mass of the population. Large areas of the time–space organisation of day-to-day social life tend to be stripped of both a *moral* and a *rational* content for those who participate in it. There seems little doubt that the psychological implications and consequences of this, which naturally vary widely between different societies, classes and regional and other social groupings, are potentially severe and important to the experience of authority. If the theory of the unconscious I have suggested elsewhere is correct, the maintenance of ontological security in the routinisation of daily life is inherently involved with the control by ego and super-ego of repressed anxieties. In the everyday life of capitalist society ontological security is relatively fragile as a result of the purely habitual character of the routinisation of many day-to-day activities. In such circumstances, particularly in times of severe social or economic dislocation, large segments of the population are potential recruits for demagogic leaders or authoritarian political movements.[50] In terms of its consequences, therefore, the analysis of capitalistic everyday life supports important elements of the views of those who have written of 'mass society'.

Most self-professedly Marxist authors, as I have mentioned previously, have taken up the implications of Marx's analysis of commodification only in the direction of the loss of control of the worker of the labour process and its products. This is even true, I think, though in a more attenuated sense, of those who have been most preoccupied with the discussion of commodification as a general concept, such as Lukács (although not Adorno).[51] For them, the commodification of social relations is a highly pervasive feature of capitalist societies. But they link commodification above all to reification. This is defined in somewhat different ways, but in the main the burden of their accounts is that social relations as a whole (rather than labour as such) escape the control of their creators, human beings in society. For the Lukács of *History and Class Consciousness*, reification is 'the central structural problem of capitalist society in all respects'.[52] Whatever the abiding importance and subtlety of aspects of Lukács's dissection of reification – and in spite of the hostile reception the book provoked from Communist orthodoxy – the theme of reification continues Marx's major preoccupation with control of the production of material life as the main thread of history. Reification, as presented by Lukács, is basically an elaboration of the conception of the fetishism of commodities introduced in *Capital*. It leaves unquestioned the principal constituents of historical materialism as an evolutionary theory of history, though Lukács does, however, lay considerable emphasis upon the distinctive features of capitalism as contrasted to preceding types of society.

. . . Thus far I have rejected historical materialism, as an over-all theory of history, for two reasons: 'modes of the production of material life' are not, in tribal or class-divided societies, the chief motor of social change, neither is class struggle; and historical materialism rests upon an ambiguous and badly flawed mixture of an ethnocentrically biased evolutionary scheme and a philosophical conception of history in which 'mankind always sets itself only such tasks as it can solve'. To this I would add a third, one with profound consequences for the critical theory of contemporary capitalism and for theories of socialism. Expressed bluntly, it is that Marx was wrong to regard human beings as above all tool-making and using animals, and to treat this as the single most important criterion distinguishing the 'species being' of humanity from that of the animals. Human social life neither begins nor ends in production. When Mumford calls man 'a mind-making, self-mastering, and self-designing animal', and when Frankel sees in human life a 'search for meaning', they are closer to supplying the basis for a philosophical anthropology of human culture than Marx was.[53] Such pronouncements are undeniably heretical to anyone close to orthodox Marxism, but I believe them to be compatible with acceptance of an important core of Marx's analysis of capitalism.

Notes

1. Cf. however, Shils: 'Time provides not only a setting which permits the state of one moment to be compared heuristically with that of another moment. Time is also a constitutive property of society. Society is only conceivable as a system of varying states occurring at moments in time. Society displays its characteristic features not at a single moment in time but in various phases assuming various but related shapes at different and consecutive moments of time.' Edward Shils, *Center and Periphery* (Chicago: Chicago University Press, 1975) p. xiii.
2. Cf. 'Functionalism: *après la lutte*', in Anthony Giddens, *Studies in Social and Political Theory*.
3. Harvey Sacks and Emmanuel A. Schegloff, 'A simplest systematics for the organisation of turn-taking in conversation', *Language*, vol. 50, 1974.
4. Harold Garfinkel, *Studies in Ethnomethodology* (Englewood Cliffs: Prentice-Hall, 1967).
5. Cf. Paul Ricoeur, 'The model of the text: meaningful action considered as a text', *Social Research*, vol. 38, 1971, which explores some of these similarities.

6. Marshall McCluhan, *The Gutenberg Galaxy* (Toronto: Toronto University Press, 1962).

7. Cf. Whitman: 'It seems that, however accurate the repetitive control elements of the clock may be, one can never arrive at a concept of standard time-duration without prior reference to space congruence. In fact, the more accurate the clock, the more complex are the spatio–temporal physical laws which have to be known and utilised.' Michael Whitman, *Philosophy of Space and Time* (London: Allen & Unwin, 1967) p. 71.

8. On the development of time and space concepts with the decay of feudalism, see Agnes Heller, *Renaissance Man* (London: Routledge, 1978) pp. 170–96.

9. Alan Pred, 'The choreography of existence: comments on Hägerstrand's time-geography and its usefulness', *Economic Geography*, vol. 53, 1977, p. 208.

10. Only fairly recently has a literature begun to develop which treats these issues with some sophistication. See especially the writings of Harvey and Castells.

11. John Rex and Robert Moore, *Race, Community and Conflict* (London: Oxford University Press, 1967).

12. Erving Goffman, *The Presentation of Self in Everyday Life* (New York: Doubleday, 1959); for the same author's more recent views on some overlapping issues, see Goffman, *Frame Analysis* (New York: Harper & Row, 1974).

13. Kathleen Archibald, *Wartime Shipyard* (Berkeley: University of California Press, 1947) p. 159.

14. Cf. David Lockwood, *The Blackcoated Worker* (London: Allen & Unwin, 1958) for a discussion in the context of broader issues of class theory.

15. Cf. R.E. Pahl and J.T. Winkler, 'The economic elite: theory and practice', in Philip Stanworth and Anthony Giddens, *Elites and Power in British Society* (Cambridge: Cambridge University Press, 1974).

16. Lewis Mumford, *Interpretations and Forecasts* (London: Secker & Warburg, 1973) p. 272.

17. No one has done more to illuminate this than Meyer Fortes in his various writings. See, for instance, his *Kinship and the Social Order* (London: Routledge & Kegan Paul, 1970). Cf. also Jack Goody, *The Character of Kinship* (Cambridge: Cambridge University Press, 1973).

18. Max Weber, *Economy and Society*, vol. I (Berkeley: University of California Press, 1978) p. 226.

19. Ruth Whitehouse, *The First Cities* (Oxford: Phaidon, 1977) p. 66.

20. Jack Goody, *The Domestication of the Savage Mind* (Cambridge: Cambridge University Press, 1977) Chapter 5.

21. See I.J. Gelb, *A Study of Writing* (Chicago: University of Chicago Press, 1963) and David Diringer, *Writing* (London: Thames & Hudson, 1962), which contains a useful bibliography.

22. Lewis Mumford, 'University City', in Carl H. Kraeling and Robert M. Adams (eds), *City Invincible* (Chicago: University of Chicago Press, 1960) p. 7.
23. Anthony Giddens, *The Constitution of Society*, p. 243.
24. The second of these concepts I take from Eberhard. See Wolfram Eberhard, *Conquerors and Rulers* (Leiden: Brill, 1965).
25. Giddens, *The Constitution of Society*, p. 193.
26. Anthony Giddens, *A Contemporary Critique of Historical Materialism*, Chapter 10.
27. Anthony Giddens, *The Class Structure of the Advanced Societies*; Giddens, *Central Problems in Social Theory*, pp. 228ff.
28. S.F. Nadel, *A Black Byzantium* (London: Oxford University Press, 1942).
29. M. Fortes and E.E. Evans-Pritchard, *African Political Systems* (London: Oxford University Press, 1940).
30. Douglas L. Oliver, *Ancient Tahitian Society* (Honolulu: University of Hawaii Press, 1974).
31. Henri J.M. Claessen, 'The early state in Tahiti', in Henri J.M. Claessen and Peter Skalnik, *The Early State* (The Hague: Mouton, 1978).
32. Oliver, *Ancient Tahitian Society*.
33. Henri J.M. Claessen; 'The early state: a structural approach', in Claessen and Skalnik, *The Early State*.
34. See Ronald Cohen, 'State origins: a reappraisal', in Claessen and Skalnik, *The Early State*; Robert L. Carneiro, 'A theory of the origin of the state', *Science*, no. 169, 1970; Morton H. Fried, *The Evolution of Political Society* (New York: Random House, 1967); W. Koppers, 'L'Origine de l'état', *6th International Congress of Anthropological and Ethnological Sciences*, vol. 2, Paris, 1963; Lawrence Krader, *Formation of the State* (Englewood Cliffs: Prentice-Hall, 1968); G. Lenski, *Power and Privilege* (New York: McGraw-Hill, 1966); Robert Lowie, *The Origin of the State* (New York: Harcourt, Brace, 1927); Elman R. Service, *Origins of the State and Civilization* (New York: Norton, 1975).
35. Cf. Service, *Origins of the State and Civilization*.
36. Carneiro, 'A theory of the origin of the state'.
37. Louis Dumont, 'Population growth and cultural change', *South-western Journal of Anthropology*, vol. 21, 1965; Service, *Origins of the State and Civilization*.
38. Henry T. Wright and Gregory Johnson, 'Population, exchange and early state formation in southwestern Iran', *American Anthropologist*, vol. 77, 1975.
39. Karl Polanyi, *Trade and Markets in Early Empires* (Glencoe: Free Press, 1957).
40. Eberhard, *Conquerors and Rulers*, pp. 9ff.
41. Eberhard, *Conquerors and Rulers*, p. 10.
42. Henri J.M. Claessen and Peter Skalnik, 'Limits, beginning and end of the early state', in Claessen and Skalnik, *The Early State*, p. 625.
43. Fried, *The Evolution of Political Society*.

44. Compare the judgements of Wilson and Kelley: John A. Wilson, *The Culture of Ancient Egypt* (Chicago: University of Chicago Press, 1951); Allyn L. Kelley, 'The evidence for Mesopotamian influence in pre-dynastic Egypt', *Newsletter of the Society for the Study of Egyptian Antiquities*, vol. 4, no. 3, 1974.

45. Carneiro, 'A theory of the origin of the state'.

46. Cf. Anthony Giddens, *Central Problems in Social Theory*, pp. 216–22. See also Pierre Bourdieu, *La Distinction, critique sociale du judgement* (Paris: Minuit, 1979) pp. 190ff.

47. For an imaginative discussion of this, see John Berger, *Pig Earth* (London: Writers and Readers Co-operative, 1979).

48. Henri Lefèbvre, *Everyday Life in the Modern World* (London: Allen Lane, 1971) p. 29; and *The Survival of Capitalism* (London: Allison & Busby, 1976) pp. 14–15. My endorsement of this quotation does not, however, involve accepting Lefèbvre's view that the 'urban society' is a phase beyond industrial capitalism. For a critique, see Manuel Castells, *The Urban Question* (London: Arnold, 1977) pp. 86–95. For a partly convergent analysis of 'everyday life', see Agnes Heller, *Das Alltagsleben, Versuch einer Erklärung der individuellen Reproduktion* (Frankfurt: Suhrkamp, 1978). She, however, treats *Alltagsleben* as the basis of social life in every form of society, rather than giving the term a historically specific sense.

49. An important body of critical urban theory relevant to these matters has arisen over the past ten years, especially as represented by the writings of Richard Sennett. See his *The Uses of Disorder* (New York: Vintage, 1970) and *The Fall of Public Man* (Cambridge: Cambridge University Press, 1977).

50. Giddens, *Central Problems in Social Theory*, pp. 120–30.

51. Cf. David Held, *Introduction to Critical Theory, Horkheimer to Habermas* (London: Hutchinson, 1980).

52. Georg Lukács, *History and Class Consciousness* (London: Merlin, 1971) p. 94.

53. Lewis Mumford, *The Myth of the Machine* (London: Secker & Warburg, 1967) p. 9; Viktor E. Frankel, *Man's Search for Meaning* (New York: Washington Square Press, 1963).

Chapter IV

Domination and Power

(i) Parsons on power*

'Power' in the writings of Talcott Parsons

As the most eminent modern representative of functionalism, Talcott Parsons has been consistently attacked for his neglect of issues of conflict and power.[1] It is therefore of some interest that Parsons should have devoted a number of his more recent writings to a discussion of power and related phenomena, explicit reference to which is conspicuous by its relative absence in the bulk of his earlier works.[2]

Parsons's work on power involves a conscious modification of his previous views, where he accepted what he calls the 'traditional' view of power. This newer theory of power is an attempt to develop a set of concepts which will overcome what he sees as important defects in the 'traditional' notion. One of the first places where Parsons explicitly confronted these issues was in a review article of C. Wright Mills' *The Power Elite*, published in 1957. There Parsons proffered a variety of criticisms of Mills' book, but also took issue with the conception of power which he saw as underlying Mills' work. Mills' thesis, Parsons argued, gains weight from a 'misleading and one-sided' view of the nature of power, which Parsons labelled the 'zero-sum' concept of power. That is, power is conceived to be possessed by one person or group to the degree that it is not possessed by a second person or group over whom the power is wielded. Power is thus defined in terms of mutually exclusive objectives, so that a party is conceived to hold power in

---

* *Studies in Social and Political Theory*, pp. 333–49.

so far as it can realize its own wishes at the expense of those of others. In terms of game theory, from which the phrase 'zero-sum' is taken, to the degree that one party wins, the other necessarily loses. According to Parsons, this tends to produce a perspective from which all exercise of power appears as serving sectional interests.[3] Parsons then went on to suggest that power is more adequately conceived by analogy with a non-zero-sum game: in other words, as a relation from which both sides may gain.

Power, Parsons proposed, can be seen as being 'generated' by a social system, in much the same way as wealth is generated in the productive organization of an economy. It is true that wealth is a finite quantity, and to the degree that one party possesses a proportion of a given sum of money, a second party can only possess the remainder; but the actual amount of wealth produced varies with the structure and organization of different types of economy. In an industrial society, for example, there is typically more for all than in an agrarian one. Power similarly has these two aspects, and it is the collective aspect which is most crucial, according to Parsons, for sociological analysis. Parsons summed up his objections to Mills' views as follows:

> to Mills, power is not a facility for the performance of function in, and on behalf of, the society as a system, but is interpreted exclusively as a facility for getting what one group, the holders of power, wants by preventing another group, the 'outs', from getting what it wants.
>
> What this conclusion does is to elevate a secondary and derived aspect of a total phenomenon into the central place.[4]

Much of the substance of Parsons' later writings on power consists of a reaffirmation of this position, and an elaboration of the analogy between power and money.[5] The parallels which Parsons develops between the two are based upon the supposition that each has a similar role in two of the four 'functional sub systems' of society which Parsons has distinguished in previous works. Power has a parallel function in the polity (goal-attainment subsystem) to that of money in the economy (adaptive subsystem). The main function of money in the modern economy is as a 'circulating medium': that is, as a standardized medium of exchange in terms of which the value of products can be assessed and compared.

Money itself has no intrinsic utility; it has 'value' only in so far as it is commonly recognized and accepted as a standard form of exchange. It is only in primitive monetary systems, when money is made of precious metal, that it comes close to being a good in its own right. In a developed economy, precious metal figures directly only in a very small proportion of exchange transactions. The sense in which the economy is 'founded' upon its holdings of gold is really a symbolic and an indirect one, and gold forms a 'reserve' to which resource is made only when the stability of the economy is for some reason threatened.

Power is conceived by Parsons as a 'circulating medium' in the same sense, 'generated' primarily within the political subsystem as money is generated in the economy, but also forming an 'output' into the three other functional subsystems of society. Power is defined, therefore, as 'generalized capacity to serve the performance of binding obligations by units in a system of collective organization when the obligations are legitimized with reference to their bearing on collective goals'.[6] By 'binding obligations' Parsons means the conditions to which those in power, and those over whom power is exercised, are subject through the legitimation which allows them that power; all power involves a certain 'mandate', which may be more or less extensive, which gives power-holders certain rights and imposes on them certain obligations towards those who are subject to their power. The collective goals rest upon the common value-system, which sets out the major objectives which govern the actions of the majority in a society. Thus American society is, according to Parsons, characterized by the primacy of values of 'instrumental activism', which entails that one main 'collective goal' of the society is the furtherance of economic productivity.

Just as money has 'value' because of common 'agreement' to use it as a standardized mode of exchange, so power becomes a facility for the achievement of collective goals throught the 'agreement' of the members of a society to legitimize leadership positions – and to give those in such positions a mandate to develop policies and implement decisions in the furtherance of the goals of the system. Parsons emphasizes that this conception of power is at variance with the more usual 'zero-sum' notion which has dominated thinking in the field. In Parsons' view, the net 'amount' of power in a system can be expanded 'if those who are ruled are prepared to place a considerable amount of trust in their rulers'. This process is conceived as a parallel to credit creation in the economy. Individuals 'invest' their 'confidence' in those who rule them – through, say, voting in an election to put a certain government in power; in so far as those who have thus been put into power initiate new policies which effectively further 'collective goals', there is more than a zero-sum circular flow of power. Everybody gains from this process. Those who have 'invested' in the leaders have received back, in the form of the effective realization of collective goals, an increased return on their investment. It is only if those in power take no more than 'routine' administrative decisions that there is no net gain to the system.

Power is thus for Parsons directly derivative of authority: authority is the institutionalized legitimation which underlies power, and is defined as 'the institutionalization of the rights of "leaders" to expect support from the members of the collectivity'.[7] By speaking of 'binding obligations', Parsons deliberately brings legitimation into the very definition of power, so that, for him, there is no such thing as 'illegitimate power'. As Parsons expresses it:

> the threat of coercive measures, or of compulsion, without legitimation or justification, should not properly be called the use of power at all, but is the limiting case where power, losing its symbolic character, merges into an intrinsic instrumentality of securing compliance with wishes, rather than obligations.[8]

In line with his general approach, Parsons stresses that the use of power is only one among several different ways in which one party may secure the compliance of another to a desired course of action. The other ways of obtaining compliance should not be regarded, Parsons stresses, as forms of power; rather it is the case that the use of power (i.e., the activation of 'binding obligations') is one among several ways of ensuring that a party produces a desired response. Parsons distinguishes two main 'channels' through which one party may seek to command the actions of another, and two main 'modes' of such control, yielding a four-fold typology. Ego may try to control the 'situation' in which alter is placed, or try to control alter's 'intentions'; the 'modes' of control depend upon whether sanctions which may be applied are positive (i.e. offer something which alter may desire), or negative (i.e. hold out the threat of punishment):

(1) Situational channel, positive sanction: the offering of positive advantages to alter if he follows ego's wishes (*inducement*, e.g. the offering of money).
(2) Situational channel, negative sanction: the threat of imposition of disadvantages if alter does not comply (the use of *power*: in the extreme case, the use of force).
(3) Intention channel, positive sanction: the offering of 'good reasons' why alter should comply (the use of *influence*).
(4) Intention channel, negative sanction: the threat that it would be 'morally wrong' for alter not to comply (the appeal to *conscience* or other moral commitments).[9]

There is, Parsons points out, an 'asymmetry' between positive and negative sanctions. When compliance is secured through positive sanctions, because there is some definite reward, the sanctions are obvious. But, in the case of negative sanctions, compliance entails that the sanction is not put into effect; the operation of negative sanctions is generally symbolic rather than actual. In most cases where power is being used, there is no overt sanction employed (instances where force is used, for example, are relatively rare in the exercise of power). It is quite misleading, Parsons emphasizes, to speak of the use of power only when some form of negative sanction has actually been used: some writers who take the 'zero-sum' notion of power tend to do this, speaking of 'power' only when some form of coercion has been applied. As Parsons says:

> [When things are 'running smoothly'] to speak of the holder of authority in these circumstances as not having or using power is, in our opinion, highly misleading. The question of his capacity to coerce or compel in case of non-compliance is an independent question that involves the question of handling unexpected or exceptional conditions for which the current power system may or may not be prepared.[10]

It is particularly necessary to stress, Parsons argues, that possession and use of power should not be identified directly with the use of force. In Parsons' view, force must be seen as only one means among several, in only one type among several, modes of obtaining compliance. Force tends to be used in stable political systems only as a last resort when other sanctions have proved ineffective. Again using the analogy between money and power, Parsons draws a parallel between centralization of state control over gold, and state monopoly over the instruments of organized force in 'advanced and stable' societies. In the economy, there sometimes occur deflations, in which loss of confidence in the value of money leads to increasing reliance upon gold reserves in order to maintain the stability of the economy. In a similar way, Parsons holds, 'power deflation' can occur when a progressive decrease of confidence in the agencies of political power develops. Such a 'loss of confidence' produces increasing reliance by such agencies upon force to preserve political integration. In both the economic and political case, the undermining of the confidence which is the foundation of money and of power produces a 'regression' towards a 'primitive' standard.[11]

In the subsequent discussion, my principal interest will be to comment on Parsons' analysis of power as such. I shall not attempt to assess in any detail the accuracy of the parallels which Parsons attempts to specify between the polity and economy as 'functional subsystems' of society. If Parsons' conceptual scheme, and the assumptions which underlie it, cannot satisfactorily handle problems of power, then many of these 'parallels' must in any case be declared either invalid or misleading.[12]

Parsons' critique of the 'zero-sum' concept of power does contain a number of valuable contributions and insights. There is no doubt that Parsons is correct in pointing out that the 'zero-sum' concept of power sometimes reinforces a simplistic view which identifies power almost wholly with the use of coercion and force. Such a perspective tends to follow from, although it is not at all logically implied by, the Weberian definition of power, which has probably been the most influential in sociology. In Weber's familiar definition, power is regarded as 'the chance of a man or of a number of men to realize their own will in a communal action even against the resistance of others who are participating in the action'.[13] Such a definition tends to lead to a conception of power relations as inevitably involving incompatible and conflicting interests, since what is stressed is the capacity of a party to realize its *own* (implicitly, sectional) aims, and the main criterion for gauging the 'amount' of power is the 'resistance' which can be overcome.

As Parsons correctly emphasizes, this can be extremely misleading, tending to produce an identification of power with the sanctions that are or can potentially be used by the power-holder. In fact, very often it is not those groups which have most frequent recourse to overt use of coercion who have most power; frequent use of coercive sanctions indicates an insecure basis of power. This is particularly true, as Parsons indicates, of the sanction of force. The power position of an individual group which has constant recourse to the use of force to secure compliance to its commands is usually weak and insecure. Far from being an index of the power held by a party, the amount of open force used rather is an indication of a shallow and unstable power base.

However, to regard the use of force in itself as a criterion of power is an error which only the more naive of social analysts would make. It is much more common to identify the power held by a party in a social relation with the coercive sanctions it is *capable* of employing against subordinates if called upon to do so – including primarily the capacity to use force. Again Parsons makes an important comment here, pointing out that a party may wield considerable power while at the same time having few coercive sanctions with which to enforce its commands if they are questioned by subordinates. This is possible if the power-holding party enjoys a broad 'mandate' to take authoritative decisions ceded or acquiesced in by those subject to the decisions – i.e., if those over whom the power is exercised 'agree' to subject themselves to that power. In such circumstances, the party in power depends, not on the possession of coercive sanctions with which it can override non-compliance, but sheerly upon the recognition by the subordinate party or parties of its legitimate right to take authoritative decisions. The latter in some sense acquiesce in their subordination. Thus when subordinates 'agree' to allow others to command their actions, and when at the same time those who receive this 'mandate' have few coercive sanctions to employ if their directives are not obeyed, then there exists a situation of power not based upon control of means to coerce. It is because of such a possibility that Parsons emphasizes that the question of 'how much' power a party holds, and the question of what sanctions it is able to bring into play in case of disobedience, are analytically separable. And it must be conceded that lack of capacity to command a defined range of sanctions does not necessarily entail a lack of power; the 'amount' of power held by a party cannot be assessed simply in terms of the effective sanctions it is able to enforce if faced with possible or actual non-compliance.[14] At the same time, it should be pointed out that the 'amount' of power wielded in any concrete set of circumstances, and the effective sanctions that can be used to counter non-compliance, are usually closely related. Studies of all types of social structures, from small groups up to total societies, show that power-holders usually do command or develop sanctions which reinforce their position: in any group which has a continued existence over time, those in power face problems of dissensus and the possibility of rebellion. The very fact of possession of a 'mandate' from those subordinated to a power relation allows the dominant party to use this 'good will' to mobilize sanctions (even if only the scorn, ridicule, etc., of the conforming majority) against a deviant or potentially deviant minority. If a power-holding party does not possess sanctions to use in cases of disobedience, it tends rapidly to acquire them, and can in fact use its power to do so.

What Parsons is concerned to point out, then, is that the use of power frequently represents a facility for the achievement of objectives which *both* sides in a power relation desire. In this sense, it is clear that the creation of a power system does not *necessarily* entail the coercive subordination of the wishes or interests of one party to those of another. Nor is the use of power inevitably correlated with 'oppression' or 'exploitation'. Quite clearly, in any type of group, the existence of defined 'leadership' positions does 'generate' power which may be used to achieve aims desired by the majority of the members of the group. This possibility is, of course, envisaged in classic Marxist theory, and in most varieties of socialist theory, in the form of 'collective' direction of the instruments of government.

As Parsons recognizes, this kind of power is necessarily legitimate, and so he makes legitimacy part of his very definition of power. Parsons thus rejects the frequently-held conception that authority is a 'form' of power, or is 'legitimate power'. This is again a useful emphasis. To regard authority as a 'type' of power leads to a neglect of its principal characteristic: namely that it concerns the *right* of a party to make binding prescriptions. Authority refers to the legitimate position of an individual or group, and is therefore properly regarded as a *basis* of power (for Parsons, the only basis of power), rather than as a kind of power. It is precisely the confusion of the forms with the bases of power which causes Parsons to specify a very restricted definition of power. Authority is no more a form of power than force is a form of power.

A further valuable aspect of Parsons' analysis is the introduction of a typology of compliant behaviour. It is still quite common for social analysts naively to assert or to assume that conformity to any specific course of social action is founded *either* on 'internalization' of appropriate moral values *or* upon some form of coercion. This tendency is strong in the works both of those who follow Parsons and those who are highly critical. The isolation of various modes of securing compliance does allow for other mechanisms of conformity. The importance of the typology is diminished by the lack of any attempt to specify how these different ways of securing compliance are related together in social systems. Nevertheless, within the general context of Parsonian theory, this typology has some significance, marking a more definite recognition of the role of non-normative factors in social action.[15]

But there are other respects in which Parsons' discussion of power shares some of the basic difficulties and deficiencies of his general theory, and is at least as one-sided as the conception which he wishes to replace. Parsons is above all concerned to emphasize that power does not necessarily entail the coercive imposition of one individual or group over another, and he does indeed point to some valuable correctives for the mainstream of sociological thinking on problems of power. But what slips away from sight almost completely in the Parsonian analysis is the very fact that power, even as Parsons defines it, is always exercised *over* someone! By treating power as necessarily (by definition) legitimate, and thus *starting* from the assumption of consensus of some kind between power-holders and those subordinate to them, Parsons virtually ignores, quite consciously and deliberately, the necessarily hierarchical character of power, and the divisions of interest which are frequently consequent upon it. However much it is true that power can rest upon 'agreement' to cede authority which can be used for collective aims, it is also true that interests of power-holders and those subject to that power often clash. It is undoubtedly the case that some 'zero-sum' theorists tend to argue as if power differentials *inevitably* entail conflicts of interest, and produce overt conflicts –

and fail to give sufficient attention to specifying the conditions under which no conflict of either type is present. But it is surely beyond dispute that positions of power offer to their incumbents definite material and psychological rewards, and thereby stimulate conflicts between those who want power and those who have it. This brings into play, of course, a multiplicity of possible strategies of coercion, deceit and manipulation which can be used to either acquire, or hold on to, power. If the use of power rests upon 'trust' or 'confidence', as Parsons emphasizes, it also frequently rests upon deceit and hypocrisy.[16] Indeed this is true of all social life; all stable social action, except perhaps for all-out total war, depends upon some kind of at least provisional 'trust' – but this very fact makes possible many sorts of violations and rejections of 'confidence'. *L'enfer c'est les autres*. 'Deceit' and 'mistrust' only have meaning in relation to 'trust' and 'confidence': the former are as ubiquitous a part of social life as the latter are, and will continue to be as long as men have desires or values which are exclusive of each other, and as long as there exist 'scarce resources' of whatever kind. Any socio-logical theory which treats such phenomena as 'incidental', or as 'secondary and derived', and not as structurally intrinsic to power differentials, is blatantly inadequate. To have power is to have potential access to valued scarce resources, and thus power *itself* becomes a scarce resource. Though the relationships between power and exploitation are not simple and direct, their existence can hardly be denied.

Parsons escapes dealing with such problems largely through a trick of definition, by considering only as 'power' the use of author-itative decisions to further 'collective goals'. Two obvious facts, that authoritative decisions very often do serve sectional interests and that the most radical conflicts in society stem from struggles for power, are defined out of consideration – at least as phenomena connected with 'power'. The conceptualization of power which Parsons offers allows him to shift the entire weight of his analysis away from power as expressing a relation *between* individuals or groups, towards seeing power solely as a 'system property'. That collective 'goals', or even the values which lie behind them, may be the outcome of a 'negotiated order' built on conflicts between parties holding differential power is ignored, since for Parsons 'power' assumes the prior existence of collective goals. The implica-tions of this are clearly demonstrated in Parsons' short book,

Societies, in which he tries to apply some of these ideas to social change in actual historical settings. Social change in its most general aspect, Parsons makes clear, is fundamentally cultural evolution – i.e., change in values, norms and idea-systems. And the basic *sources* of change are to be traced to changes in cultural values, and norms *themselves*, not to any sort of 'lower-level' factors, which at the most exert a 'conditioning' effect on social change. In spite of various qualifications and assertions to the contrary, Parsons's theory, as he applies it here, comes down to little more than a kind of idealist orthodoxy. History is moved, societies change, under the guiding direction of cultural values, which somehow change, independently of other elements in the structure of social systems, and exert a 'cybernetic control' over them. This is hardly consonant with Parsons' conclusion that 'once the problem of causal imputation is formulated analytically, the old chicken and egg problems about the priorities of ideal and material factors simply lose significance'.[17] There is a great deal of difference between the sort of interpretation of social and historical change which Parsons presents in *Societies*, and one which follows a Marxist standpoint. Parsons' account is based very largely upon an examination of value-systems, and changes in them, and displays practically no concern with non-normative factors as causative agencies in their formation, maintenance and diffusion. As in Parsons' more general theoretical expositions, such factors are formally recognized as of some importance, but no systematic discussion of the interplay between them and values is presented. As a consequence, Parsons tends to argue as if to show that some kind of logical relationship or 'fit' between a specific value, norm, or pattern of behaviour, and some more general value or set of values, constitutes an 'explanation' of the former. This is characteristic also of Parsons' theoretical analysis of power and social change. Thus, for example, at one point in his discussion of political power, he traces 'political democracy' – i.e., universal franchise – to 'the principle of equality before the law', which is a 'subordinate principle of universalistic normative organization', as if this were to explain why or how universal franchise came into being.

In Parsons' conceptualization of power there is one notion which has an explicitly dynamic reference: that of 'power deflation'. This does at least make a conceptual *niche* in the Parsonian system for the possibility of social revolution.[18] It is characteristic, however, that this concept depends upon the prior assumption of consensual 'confidence' in the power system. Power deflation refers to a spiralling diminution of 'confidence' in the agencies of power, so that those subordinate to them come increasingly to question their position. Parsons does not suggest any answers to why power deflations occur, except to indicate that once they get under way they resemble the 'vicious circle' of declining support characteristic of economic crisis. Now the parallel with economic deflation, in the terms in which Parsons discusses it, shows clearly that he conceives the process as basically a psychological one, which is a kind of generalization of the picture of deviance presented in *The Social System*. Power deflation is deviance writ large and in so far as it is focused on legitimate authority.[19] Thus the possibility of explaining power deflation in terms of the mutual interaction of interest-groups is excluded. The opportunity for theoretically tying such factors to the mechanics of power deflation, via the typology of means of obtaining compliance, is left aside. The parallels which Parsons is determined to pursue between the polity and the economy serve, in fact, to separate political and economic processes from one another. That economic and other 'material' factors themselves play a key part in power deflation is ignored because Parsons is above all concerned to show how the polity and economy are 'analytically' similar, not how they intertwine. Parsons' many discussions of the relationships between sociology and economics, including his and Smelser's *Economy and Society*, are all stated in terms of highly formal typological categories, and rarely suggest any substantive generalizations linking the two. Parsons' method is well illustrated by the entirely abstract character of his typology of modes of securing compliance. A distinction is made between 'inducement' and 'power'. The rationale for the distinction is that these can be considered parallel 'media' in the subsystems of the economy and the polity. Now such a typological distinction might be useful, but the important sociological problem is to apply it. How do inducement and power operate as systematic properties of societies or other social structures? Obviously inducement is often a *basis* of power; and the reverse also may frequently be true – a person or group holding power is often in a position allowing access to various forms of inducement, including the offer of financial reward. The relationship between 'positive' and 'negative' sanctions may be quite complicated as they actually operate in social systems. Thus inducements, offering some definite rewards in exchange for compliance, always offer the possibility of being transformed into negative sanctions; the *withholding* of a reward represents a punishment, and represents a definite form of coercion. But Parsons makes no attempt to draw out such possibilities and apply them to the analysis of power deflation, and in view of this, the process of power deflation is conceived purety as one of psychological 'loss of confidence' in the existing system.

Perhaps it is significant that Parsons makes very little mention of what factors produce 'power inflation' – i.e., the process whereby 'confidence' in a power system is *developed and expanded* in societies. It is just in this area that some of the most crucial problems in the study of power lie, and where conflict and coercion may play a major part. In Parsons' treatment of power, coercion and force are pictured as along the end of the line of a progression of corrective sanctions which can be applied to counter any tendency towards power deflation. Force is the sanction which is applied when all else has failed. It is only when the system shows a lack of 'confidence' that open use of power becomes frequent. Thus, Parsons argues, stable power systems are only based indirectly, or 'symbolically', on the use of force. But in power 'inflation', coercion and force may be the foundation of a consensual order in quite a different way. The history of societies shows again and again that particular social forms are often at first implemented by force, or by some other form of definite coercion, and coercive measures are used to *produce* and reinforce a new legitimacy. It is in this sense that power can grow out of the barrel of a gun. Force allows the manipulative control which can then be used to diminish dependence upon coercion. While this has been in previous ages probably only in part the result of conscious manipulation, in recent times, through the controlled diffusion of propaganda it can become a much more deliberate process. But whether deliberate or not, it is not only the fact that stable power systems rest upon stable legitimation of authority which is the key to the analysis of power but, as the 'zero-sum' theorists have always recognized, just how legitimation is *achieved*. Through defining power as the activation of legitimate obligations, Parsons avoids dealing with the processes whereby legitimacy, and thereby authority and power, are established and maintained. Consensus is assumed, and power conceived to be derivative of it; the determinants of the consensual basis of power are regarded as non-problematic.

This means also that Parsons tends to accept the operations of authority at their face-value, as if all 'obligations' of importance were open, public, and legitimate. But it is an accepted fact of political life that those who occupy formal authority positions are sometimes puppets who have their strings pulled from behind the scenes. It is in the hidden processes of control that some of the crucial operations of power in modern societies are located. By defining power as 'the activation of *legitimate* obligations' Parsons would seem to have to classify those processes as not involving 'power'. But the puppeteers behind the scenes may be the people who hold real control, and it is not a helpful concept of power which does not allow us to explore the often complicated relations which pertain between the 'unrecognized' or illegitimate, and the legitimate, in systems of power.

This may not necessarily stem from Parsons' definition of power *per se*, since it could be held that those who are *in fact* 'activating legitimate obligations' are those who are using the individuals in formal authority positions as a front – that it is the men behind the scenes who really control those 'legitimate obligations', and thus who really hold 'power'. But, at any rate, Parsons' own analysis shows an ingenuous tendency to see nothing beyond the processes which are overt. Parsons' account of how political support is derived, for example, is given in terms of a *prima facie* comparison between government and banking:

> political support should be conceived of as a generalized grant of power which, if it leads to electional success, puts elected leadership in a position analogous to a banker. The 'deposits' of power made by constituents are revocable, if not at will, at the next election.[20]

Thus those in positions of political power have the legitimized right to 'use' the power 'granted' to them by the electorate in the same way as a banker can invest money deposited with him. Parsons is presumably only arguing that these two processes are 'analytically' parallel, and would no doubt recognize the many substantive differences between them. But nevertheless his anxiety to develop formal similarities between the polity and economy, and correspondingly between money and power, seems to have blinded him to the realities of political manipulation.

It is apparent that Parsons' treatment of power, while marking in a few respects a greater formal recognition of the role of 'interests' in social action,[21] in the main represents a strong retrenchment of his general theoretical position as set out in *The Social System*. Power now becomes simply an extension of consensus, the means which a society uses to attain its 'goals'. But this is surely inadequate. We must assert that power extends as deeply into the roots of social life as do values or norms; if all social relationships involve normative elements, so also do all social relationships contain power differentials.

Remarks on the theory of power

In the 'normative functionalism' of Durkheim and Parsons, the concept of interest tends to be conceived of only in relation to a traditional dichotomy of the individual and society, rather than as concerning divisions between groups within the social totality. Thus this type of social theory finds difficulty in allowing a conceptual space for the analysis of power as the instrument of sectional group interests. Power is conceived as the 'power of society' confronting the individual. While this type of theory, as is shown in Durkheim's political writings, can yield an account of the domination of the state over civil society, it cannot conceive of society itself as a system of power founded in entrenched divergencies of interest. However, the notions that power is not adequately treated as being a fixed quantum, and that it has no necessary tie with the existence of conflict, are important. But neither is dependent upon the sort of formulation of the concept that Parsons gives. The 'expandable' character of power actually has no logical connection with its conceptualization as directed to the achievement of 'goals' of the collectivity. It is possible, and indeed necessary, to sustain the substance of Parsons' critique of the zero-sum conception of power without following the same route that he does in developing a reconstruction of the notion.

In the theory of structuration, power is recognized as an integral element in the reproduction of systems of interaction; but it can also be shown, in an even more basic way, that power is a logical component of the idea of 'action' itself. I wish to claim that we can distinguish a broad and narrow sense of the term power, and that these parallel the differentiation between 'action' and 'interaction', where the latter refers to mutually oriented forms of conduct between two or a plurality of actors. Action or agency implies the intervention (or refraining) of an individual in a course of events in the world, of which it would be true to say that 'he could have done otherwise'. Defined in this way, action involves the application of 'means' to secure outcomes, these outcomes constituting the intervention in the on-going course of events. Let us now define power as the use of resources, of whatever kind, to secure outcomes. Power then becomes an element of action, and refers to the *range* of interventions of which an agent is capable. Power in this broad sense is equivalent to the *transformative capacity* of human action: the capability of human beings to intervene in a series of events so as to alter their course. In this sense, power is closely bound up with the notion of *Praxis*, as relating to the historically shaped, and historically mutable, conditions of social and material existence.

The production and reproduction of interaction of course involves power as transformative capacity: but in interaction we can distinguish a narrower, 'relational' sense of power, since action taken with intentions of securing particular outcomes then involves the responses, or the potential behaviour, of others (including their resistance to a course of action that one party wants to bring about). Power here is domination, but it would be quite mistaken to suppose, as zero-sum theories of power suppose, that even in this narrower sense the existence of power logically implies the existence of conflict, whether that latter term is taken to mean opposition of interest or actual struggle of some sort between two or more combatants. It is precisely the concept of interest that is most immediately linked to those of conflict and solidarity. The use of power is frequently accompanied by struggle; this is not because of a logical relation between the two, but because of a lack of coincidence of actors' interests in circumstances of the application of power. (In saying this, I do not want to propose the view that people are always aware of what their interests are, although the identification of interests on the part of the theorist always involves the imputation of wants to those persons. Nor do I want to claim either that division of interest always leads to open conflict, or conversely that the existence of such conflict *ipso facto* presupposes division of interest.) The concept of interest has to be understood as a metatheoretical one. That is to say, it has to be freed from any association with human needs in a state of nature, or for that matter with any unique connection to class divisions in society. The first leads to a situation in which interest is conceived solely in reference to the interests of the 'individual' as opposed to those of 'society' (or the state). The second, on the other hand, as expressed in certain readings of Marx, carries the implication that, with the transcendence of classes, divisions of interest in society thereby disappear. While we must recognize that particular interest oppositions may always be transcended by social transformation, this is altogether distinct from the presumption that divisions of interest in a society may be superseded altogether.

The same point applies to domination. Specific forms of domination, as historically located systems of power, are in every instance open to potential transformation. Since power, according to the theory of structuration, is held to be intrinsic to all interaction, there can be no question of transcending it in any empirical society. It would be possible to develop a model of emancipation based upon the achievement of equality of power in interaction. But taken alone, this would be quite inadequate. For it does not come to terms with the significance of power, in the guise of transformative capacity, as the medium of the realization of collective human interests. From this aspect, freedom from domination in systems of interaction appears as a problem of the achievement of rationally defensible forms of authority.

(ii)   Critique of Foucault*

Rather than discussing the writings of the new philosophers in any detail, I propose to concentrate my attention upon Foucault. In 1977 Jean Baudrillard published a little book called *Oublier Foucault*. But in the English-speaking world there could hardly be any question of forgetting Foucault because I think it would be true to say that he has only just been discovered – the Foucault of power, at any rate, rather than the cryptic Foucault of metahistory. In this essay I shall discuss critically certain of the themes

* *Profiles and Critiques in Social Theory*, pp. 218–25.

that have come to the fore in Foucault's work, returning at the end to the challenge posed by the new philosophers.

Foucault's more recent writings, those that are primarily preoccupied with power, do of course preserve some of the emphases of his earlier ones. His historical studies are informed by what he calls 'genealogy', by which he means 'a form of history which accounts for the constitution of knowledges, discourses, domains of objects, etc., without having to refer to a subject, whether it be transcendental in relation to the field of events or whether it chase its empty identity throughout history'.[22] Foucault is often bracketed to 'poststructuralism', in spite of his dislike of the term. And one can see some reason for this. Foucault continues, and indeed elaborates upon, the theme of the decentring of the subject that was introduced by Saussure and by Lévi-Strauss. In Foucault's work, the decentring of the subject becomes both a methodological and, in a certain sense, a substantial phenomenon. History is constituted in epistemes, or more latterly in fields of power, through which human subjects are disclosed; and, in the current age, we are moving away from an era dominated by a particular type of constitution of subjectivity. We are witnessing the 'end of the individual', a phrase which has a poignant contrast with that employed increasingly by Horkheimer and Adorno towards the ends of their lives.

To my mind, Nietzschean themes are strongly prominent in Foucault's later writings, although they are deployed in quite a different (and in some ways much more interesting) way from that of others of his contemporaries in France – even those with whom he has been closely associated, like Deleuze. These themes include not only the all-enveloping character of power, its priority to values and to truth, but also the idea that the body is the surface upon which power impinges. Power, for Foucault, is declaredly the opposite of that haunted and hunted spectre which it appears as in Marxist theory – a noxious expression of class domination, capable of being transcended by the progressive movement of history. Power, says Foucault, is not inherently repressive, not just the capability to say no. If this is all power were, Foucault asks, would we really consistently obey it? Power has its hold because it does not simply act like an oppressive weight, a burden to be resisted. Power is actually the means whereby all things happen, the production of things, of knowledge and forms of discourse, and of pleasure.

This theory of power forms the axis of Foucault's as yet only partly begun history of sexuality. 'Sexuality', as we understand that phenomenon in contemporary Western society, is a product of power rather than power being repressive of sexuality. Sex has a specific political significance in modern times because it concerns characteristics and activities that are at the intersection between the discipline of the body and control of the population. There are evident connections here with Foucault's account of the origins of the prison, which I find to be his most brilliant work, the focus of most of what he has to say of importance about power. I presume a familiarity with this work, and shall not seek to reproduce its arguments in any detail. According to Foucault, the widespread adoption of the prison in Western societies in the nineteenth century signals a major transition in fields of power. In the sphere of punishment, incarceration replaces public executions, torturing, or other 'spectacles'. A 'double process' of change is involved: the disappearance of the spectacle, and the elimination of pain in favour of the deprivation of liberty and correctional discipline. This epitomises the disappearance of one type of social order, based upon 'the representative, scenic, signifying, public, collective model', and the emergence of another, 'the coercive, corporal, solitary, secret model of the power to punish'.[23]

Discipline and surveillance are key aspects of the prison, according to Foucault; and in his view it is essential to see that these are not peculiar to prisons. On the contrary, they pervade a range of other organisations that also come to the fore in nineteenth-century industrial capitalism: factories, offices and places of work, hospitals, schools, barracks, and so on. Discipline, Foucault says, dissociates power from the body, the contrary of traditional practices, in which the body was marked – in the case of punishment, publicly branded in some way. At the same time, the emphasis is placed upon the 'interiorisation' of power. Disciplinary power, in Foucault's phrase, is 'exercised through its invisibility'; those who experience it acquiesce in this new technology of power, and their acquiescence is an essential part of that new technology. It is not difficult in such a context to see how these notions might connect to the analysis of authority that Sennett has developed in his work – and I mean here not just the book *Authority*, but earlier work also. By the 'hidden injuries' of class, Sennett means, I take it, not simply that the 'injuries' of class domination are 'hidden', but that it is in the nature of class domination in contemporary capitalism that it is 'exercised through its invisibility'.

But the invisibility of disciplinary power, Foucault allows, has a visible counterpart, and sustaining mechanism, in surveillance. The idea that individuals should be constantly 'under observation', he argues, is the natural correlate of discipline, once the latter is manifested externally in regularity of conduct by 'docile bodies'. Thus the type case of the layout of the prison is Bentham's plan of the Panopticon, with its central observation tower. But this is only an 'ideal' form of the physical layout that inevitably accompanies the discipline/surveillance relationship. For disciplinary power involves the specified enclosure of space, the partitioning of space according to specialised criteria of identification or activity. Such spatial sequestration is so much a part of factories, offices and the other organisations I have mentioned that we should not be surprised to find they all resemble prisons. Perhaps it would not be stretching things too far to say that, for Foucault, it is the prison and the asylum which above all exemplify the modern age, not the factory or place of production as it was for Marx. And this contrast, one might add, in turn expresses Foucault's particular version of the displacement of Marx by Nietzsche.

Now we should not miss the significance of Foucault's work, which in my assessment is perhaps the most important contribution to the theory of administrative power since Max Weber's classic texts on bureaucracy. None the less, it is equally important not to fall too easily under its sway: it is at this juncture I want to begin a series of observations that lead in the end to a rejection of the 'Nietzschean resurgence' in social theory. I want to make several major objections to what Foucault has to say about power, discipline and surveillance; and these will eventually lead us back to issues raised by the perorations of the new philosophers. I believe that the points I shall make both have relevance to social theory as a whole, as it currently exists, and to questions of politics.

(1) I think it very important to break with the 'post-structuralist' style of thought in which Foucault stands. Foucault seems to link the expansion of disciplinary power with the rise of industrial capitalism, but he does so only in a very general way. Like the 'epistemic transformations' documented in his earlier works, the transmutation of power emanates from the dark

and mysterious backdrop of 'history without a subject'. Now I accept that 'history has no subject', if that phrase refers to a Hegelian view of the progressive overcoming of self-alienation by humanity; and I accept the theme of the decentring of the subject, if this means that we cannot take subjectivity as a given. But I do not at all accept the idea of a 'subject-less-history', if that term is taken to mean that human social affairs are determined by forces of which those involved are wholly unaware. It is precisely to counter such a view that I have developed the tenets of the theory of structuration.[24] Human beings, in the theory of structuration, are always and everywhere regarded as knowledgeable agents, although acting within historically specific bounds of the unacknowledged conditions and unintended consequences of their acts. Foucault's 'genealogical method', in my opinion, continues the confusion which structuralism helped to introduce into French thought, between history without a *transcendental subject* and history without *knowledgeable human subjects*. These are two very different things, however. We must disavow the first, but recognise the cardinal significance of the second – that significance which Marx expressed pithily in the famous observation that 'men make history, but not in conditions of their own choosing'.

(2)   This first objection has concrete implications for the analyses that Foucault has produced of the prison and the clinic. 'Punishment', 'discipline', and especially 'power' itself, are characteristically spoken of by him as though they were agents – indeed the real agents of history. But the development of prisons, clinics and hospitals was not a phenomenon that merely appeared 'behind the backs' of those who designed them, helped to build them, or were their inmates. Ignatieff's work on the origins of prisons is in this respect a useful counterbalance to Foucault.[25] The reorganisation and expansion of the prison system in the nineteenth century was closely bound up with the perceived needs of state authorities to construct new modes of controlling miscreants in large urban spaces, where the sanctioning procedures of the local community could no longer apply.

(3)   Foucault draws too close an association between the prison and the factory. There is no doubt that prisons were in part

consciously looked to as models by some employers in the early years of capitalism in their search for the consolidation of labour discipline. Unfree labour was actually sometimes used. But there are two essential differences between the prison and the factory. 'Work' only makes up one sector, albeit normally the most time-consuming one, of the daily life of individuals outside prisons. For the capitalistic work-place is not, as prisons are, and clinics and hospitals may be, a 'total institution', in Goffman's term. More important, the worker is not forcibly incarcerated in the factory or office, but enters the gates of the work-place as 'free wage-labour'. This gives rise to the historically peculiar problems of the 'management' of a labour force that is formally 'free', analysed interestingly by Pollard among others.[26] At the same time, it opens the way for forms of worker resistance (especially unionisation and the threat of collective withdrawal of labour) that are not part of the normal enactment of prison discipline. The 'docile bodies' which Foucault says discipline produces turn out very often to be not so docile at all.

(4)   In line with his Nietzschean 'hermeneutics of suspicion', by treating the prison as the exemplar of power as discipline, Foucault to my mind produces too negative a view of 'bourgeois' or 'liberal freedoms', and of the reformist zeal they helped to inspire. We are all well aware of the Marxian 'hermeneutics of suspicion', which sees liberal freedoms as an ideological cloak for coercive and exploitative class domination. No one can plausibly deny that the freedom of 'free wage-labour' in the early years of industrial capitalism was largely a sham, a means to the exploitation of labour power in conditions not controlled by the worker. But the 'mere' bourgeois freedoms of freedom of movement, formal equality before the law, and the right to organise politically, have turned out to be very real freedoms in the light of the twentieth-century experience of totalitarian societies in which they are absent or radically curtailed. Foucault says of the prison that 'prison reform' is born together with the prison itself: it is part of its very programme. But the same point could be made, and in less ironic vein, about various of the political and economic transformations introduced with the collapse of feudalism. Liberalism is not the same as despotism, absolut-

ism or totalitarianism, and the bourgeois ethos of rational, universalised justice has the same double-edged character as prisons and their reform. With this major difference: prisoners are denied just those rights which the remainder of the population formally possess. Taken together, freedom of contract and freedom to organise politically have helped generate the rise of labour movements that have been both a challenge to, and a powerful force for change within, the political and economic orders of capitalism.

(5)   There is a surprising 'absence' at the heart of Foucault's analyses – thus far at any rate – an absence shared with Marxism. It is . . . an account of the state. In Marx, as I have commented, this lack is in some part to be traced to his involvement with political economy. In Foucault, one suspects, it is related to the very ubiquity of power as discipline. The state is what Foucault describes as the 'calculated technology of subjection' writ large, *the* disciplinary matrix that oversees the others. If Foucault does believe this, it is to my mind at best a partial truth. There can, in the contemporary world, no longer be a theory of 'the state', but only a theory of *states*; and this has implications both 'internally' and 'externally'. 'Internally', whatever the new philosophers may say or imply, it seems to me nonsense to claim that the very existence of 'the state' negates both liberal and socialist principles. Diffuse talk of the prevalence of power and the unchallengeable might of the state generates a quiescence which is every bit as weakly founded as glib Marxist chatter about the transcendence of 'the state'.

'Externally', it seems to me of the first importance to follow Tilly and others in emphasising the significance of the association between the rise of capitalism and the pre-existing European state system. Foucault writes as follows:

> If the economic take-off of the West began with the techniques that made possible the accumulation of capital, it might perhaps be said that the methods for administering the accumulation of men made possible a political take-off in relation to the traditional, ritual, costly, violent forms of power, which soon fell into disuse and were superseded by a subtle, calculated technology of subjection.[27]

But this analysis can very easily be misleading, like all talk of the state in general. There has never been a 'capitalist state', there have always been capitalist nation-states, in which the internal processes of pacification of which Foucault speaks have been accompanied by a fearsome concentration of the means of violence in the hands of the state. In a book I have recently completed, I have tried to show that there are direct relations between the capitalist labour contract, as a medium of class domination, and the appropriation of the means of violence by the state.[28] The capitalist labour contract begins as a purely economic relation, in which the employer possesses neither moral sanctions nor sanctions of violence to secure the compliance of the labour force in the work-place. This 'extrusion' of the means of violence from the labour contract meant that compliance was secured in substantial degree through the novel technology of power which Foucault describes. But one could hardly argue that 'costly, violent forms of power' were thereby done away with, in the context of the relations between nation-states. Rather, the twentieth century has seen an escalation of violence upon a level unparalleled in prior history.

(ii) Class structuration*

It is useful, initially, to distinguish the *mediate* from the *proximate* structuration of class relationships. By the former term, I refer to the factors which intervene between the existence of certain given market capacities and the formation of classes as identifiable social groupings, that is to say which operate as 'overall' connecting links between the market on the one hand and structured systems of class relationships on the other. In using the latter phrase, I refer to 'localised' factors which condition or shape class formation. The mediate structuration of class relationships is governed above all by the distribution of mobility chances which pertain within a given society. Mobility has sometimes been treated as if it were in large part separable from the determination of class structure. According to Schumpeter's famous example, classes may be conceived of as

* *The Class Structure of the Advanced Societies*, pp. 107–12.

like conveyances, which may be constantly carrying different 'passengers' without in any way changing their shape. But, compelling though the analogy is at first sight, it does not stand up to closer examination, especially within the framework I am suggesting here.[29] In general, the greater the degree of 'closure' of mobility chances – both intergenerationally and within the career of the individual – the more this facilitates the formation of identifiable classes. For the effect of closure in terms of intergenerational movement is to provide for the *reproduction* of common life experience over the generations; and this homogenisation of experience is reinforced to the degree to which the individual's movement within the labour market is confined to occupations which generate a similar range of material outcomes. In general we may state that the structuration of classes is facilitated *to the degree to which mobility closure exists in relation to any specified form of market capacity*. There are three sorts of market capacity which can be said to be normally of importance in this respect: ownership of property in the means of production; possession of educational or technical qualifications; and possession of manual labour-power. In so far as it is the case that these tend to be tied to closed patterns of inter- and intragenerational mobility, this yields the foundation of *a basic three-class system* in capitalist society: an 'upper', 'middle', and 'lower' or 'working' class. But as has been indicated previously, it is an intrinsic characteristic of the development of the capitalist market that there exist no legally sanctioned or formally prescribed limitations upon mobility, and hence it must be emphasised that there is certainly never anything even approaching complete closure. In order to account for the emergence of structured classes, we must look in addition at the proximate sources of structuration.

There are three, related, sources of proximate structuration of class relationships: the division of labour within the productive enterprise; the authority relationships within the enterprise; and the influence of what I shall call 'distributive groupings'. I have already suggested that Marx tended to use the notion of 'division of labour' very broadly, to refer both to market relationships and to the allocation of occupational tasks within the productive organisation. Here I shall use the term only in this second, more specific, sense. In capitalism, the division of labour in the enterprise is in principle governed by the promotion of productive efficiency in relation to the maximisation of profit; but while responding to the same exigencies as the capitalist market in general, the influence of the division of labour must be analytically separated as a distinctive source of structuration (and as a significant influence upon class consciousness). The division of labour, it is clear, may be a basis of the fragmentation as well as the consolidation of class relationships. It furthers the formation of classes to the degree to which it creates homogeneous groupings which cluster along the same lines as those which are fostered by mediate structuration. Within the modern industrial order,[30] the most significant influence upon proximate structuration in the division of labour is undoubtedly that of technique. The effect of industrial technique (more recently, however, modified by the introduction of cybernetic systems of control) is to create a decisive separation between the conditions of labour of manual and non-manual workers. 'Machine-minding', in one form or another, regardless of whether it involves a high level of manual skill, tends to create a working environment quite distinct from that of the administrative employee, and one which normally enforces a high degree of physical separation between the two groupings.[31]

This effect of the division of labour thus overlaps closely with the influence of the mediate structuration of class relationships through the differential apportionment of mobility chances; but it is, in turn, potentially heavily reinforced by the typical authority system in the enterprise. In so far as administrative workers participate in the framing, or merely in the enforcement, of authoritative commands, they tend to be separated from manual workers, who are subject to those commands. But the influence of differential authority is also basic as a reinforcing agent of the structuration of class relationships at the 'upper' levels. Ownership of property, in other words, confers certain fundamental capacities of command, maximised within the 'entrepreneurial' enterprise in its classical form. To the extent to which this serves to underlie a division at 'the top', in the control of the organisation (something which is manifestly influenced, but not at all destroyed, if certain of the suppositions advanced by the advocates of the theory of the separation of 'ownership and control' are correct) it supports the differentiation of the 'upper' from the 'middle' class.

The third source of the proximate structuration of class relationships is that originating in the sphere of consumption rather than production. Now according to the traditional interpretations of class structure, including those of Marx and Weber, 'class' is a phenomenon of production: relationships established in consumption are therefore quite distinct from, and secondary to, those formed in the context of productive activity. There is no reason to deviate from this general emphasis. But without dropping the conception that classes are founded ultimately in the economic structure of the capitalist market, it is still possible to regard consumption patterns as a major influence upon class structuration. Weber's notions of 'status' and 'status group' . . . confuse two separable elements: the formation of groupings in consumption, on the one hand, and the formation of types of social differentiation based upon some sort of non-economic value providing a scale of 'honour' or 'prestige' on the other. While the two may often coincide, they do not necessarily do so, and it seems worthwhile to distinguish them terminologically. Thus I shall call '*distributive groupings*' those relationships involving common patterns of the consumption of economic goods, regardless of whether the individuals involved make any type of conscious evaluation of their honour or prestige relative to others; 'status' refers to the existence of such evaluations, and a 'status group' is, then, any set of social relationships which derives its coherence from their application.[32]

In terms of class structuration, distributive groupings are important in so far as they interrelate with the other sets of factors distinguished above in such a way as to reinforce the typical separations between forms of market capacity. The most significant distributive groupings in this respect are those formed through the tendency towards community or neighbourhood segregation. Such a tendency is not normally based only upon differentials in income, but also upon such factors as access to housing mortgages, etc. The creation of distinctive 'working-class neighbourhoods' and 'middle-class neighbourhoods', for example, is naturally promoted if those in manual labour are by and large denied mortgages for house buying, while those in non-manual occupations experience little difficulty in obtaining such loans. Where industry is located outside of the major urban areas, homogeneous 'working-class communities' frequently develop through the dependence of workers upon housing provided by the company.

In summary, to the extent to which the various bases of mediate and proximate class structuration overlap, classes will exist as distinguishable formations. I wish to say . . . that *the combination of the sources of mediate and proximate structuration distinguished here, creating a threefold class structure, is generic to capitalist society.* But the mode in which these elements are merged to form *a specific class system*, in any given society, differs significantly according to variations in economic and political development. It should be evident that structuration is never an all-or-nothing matter. The problem of the existence of distinct class 'boundaries', therefore, is not one which can be settled *in abstracto*: one of the specific aims of class analysis in relation to empirical societies must necessarily be that of determining how strongly, in any given case, the 'class principle' has become established as a mode of structuration. Moreover, the operation of the 'class principle' may also involve the creation of forms of structuration within the major class divisions. One case in point is that which Marx called the 'petty bourgeoisie'. In terms of the preceding analysis, it is quite easy to see why ownership of small property in the means of production might come to be differentiated both from the upper class and from the ('new') middle class. If it is the case that the chances of mobility, either inter- or intragenerationally, from small to large property ownership are slight, this is likely to isolate the small property-owner from membership of the upper class as such. But the fact that he enjoys directive control of an enterprise, however minute, acts to distinguish him from those who are part of a hierarchy of authority in a larger organisation. On the other hand, the income and other economic returns of the petty bourgeois are likely to be similar to the white-collar worker, and hence they may belong to similar distributive groupings. A second potentially important influence upon class formation is to be traced to the factor of skill differential within the general category of manual labour. The manual worker who has undergone apprenticeship, or a comparable period of training, possesses a market capacity which sets him apart from the un-skilled or semi-skilled worker. There are certain factors promoting structuration on the basis of this differentiation in market capacity (e.g., that the chances of intergenerational mobility from skilled manual to white-collar occupations are considerably higher than they are from unskilled and semi-skilled manual occupations).

So far I have spoken of structuration in a purely formal way, as though class could be defined in terms of relationships which have no 'content'. But this obviously will not do: if classes become social realities, this must be manifest in the formation of common patterns of behaviour and attitude. Since Weber's discussion of classes and status groups, the notion of 'style of life' has normally come to be identified as solely pertaining to the mode whereby a status group expresses its claim to distinctiveness. However, in so far as there is marked convergence of the sources of structuration mentioned above, classes will also tend to manifest common styles of life.

An initial distinction can be drawn here between 'class awareness' and 'class consciousness'.[33] We may say that, in so far as class is a structurated phenomenon, there will tend to exist a common awareness and acceptance of similar attitudes and beliefs, linked to a common style of life, among the members of the class. 'Class awareness', as I use the term here, does *not* involve a recognition that these attitudes and beliefs signify a particular class affiliation, or the recognition that there exist other classes, characterised by different attitudes, beliefs, and styles of life; 'class consciousness', by contrast, as I shall use the notion, does imply both of these. The difference between class awareness and class consciousness is a fundamental one, because class awareness may take the form of *a denial of the existence or reality of classes.*[34] Thus the class awareness of the middle class, in so far as it involves beliefs which place a premium upon individual responsibility and achievement, is of this order.

Within ethnically and culturally homogeneous societies, the degree of class structuration will be determined by the interrelationship between the sources of structuration identified previously. But many, if not the majority, of capitalist societies are not homogeneous in these respects. Traditionally, in class theory, racial or religious divisions have been regarded as just so many 'obstacles' to the formation of classes as coherent unities. This may often be so, where these foster types of structuration which deviate from that established by the 'class principle' (as typically was the case in the battles fought by the rearguard of feudalism against the forces promoting the emergence of capitalism). The idea that ethnic or cultural divisions serve to dilute or hinder the formation of classes is also very explicitly built into Weber's separation of (economic) 'class' and 'status group'. But this, in part at least, gains its cogency from the contrast between estate, as a legally constituted category, and class, as an economic category. While it may be agreed, however, that the *bases* of the formation of classes and status groups (in the sense in which I have employed these concepts) are different, nonetheless the tendency to class structuration may receive a considerable impetus *where class coincides with the criteria of status group membership* – in other words, where structuration deriving from economic organisation 'overlaps' with, or, in Dahrendorf's terms, is 'superimposed' upon, that deriving from evaluative categorisations based upon ethnic or cultural differences.[35] Where this is so, status group membership itself becomes a form of market capacity. Such a situation frequently offers the strongest possible source of class structuration, whereby there develop clear-cut differences in attitudes, beliefs and style of life between the classes. Where ethnic differences serve as a 'disqualifying' market capacity, such that those in the category in question are heavily concentrated among the lowest-paid occupations, or are chronically unemployed or semi-employed, we may speak of the existence of an *underclass*.[36]

(iv) Class and power*

Power, the dialectic of control and class structuration

In this discussion I shall seek to draw some connections between certain aspects of the theory of structuration and the analysis of class structure in capitalist societies. The theory of structuration is based upon the following claims: that social theory (which I take to be relevant equally to each of the social scientific disciplines: sociology, anthropology, psychology and economics, as well as history) should incorporate an understanding of human behaviour as *action*; that such an understanding has to be made compatible with a focus upon the *structural components* of social institutions or societies; and that notions of *power* and *domination* are logically, not just contingently, associated with the concepts of action and structure as I conceptualise them.[37] I shall not be concerned to substantiate these claims, but shall attempt rather to trace out a few of their implications for issues that I take to be important to class analysis.

Let me pursue here the theme of the relation between action and power. I wish to distinguish two aspects of this issue:

---

* *Profiles and Critiques in Social Theory*, pp. 197–212.

(1)   The general implications of the logical relation between agency and power.

(2)   The mode in which power relations may be analysed as a chronically reproduced feature of social systems.

Of (1) we can say the following: to be a human agent is to have power, to be able to 'make a difference' in the world. This has direct consequences for (2), because it follows that, in any relationship which may be involved in a social system, the most seemingly 'powerless' individuals are able to mobilise resources whereby they carve out 'spaces of control' in respect of their day-to-day lives and in respect of the activities of the more powerful. One way of examining (1) is to consider instances which lie on the margins of action. These both help to explicate what it means to be an agent, and show how intimately this is related to power. But such examples also serve to demonstrate how closely (1) connects to (2), a connection which, I shall suggest, can best be handled by the concept of the 'dialectic of control'.

Consider first an instance where *A* is injected with a drug by *B*, rendering *A* unconscious and immobile. Such a case clearly lies outside the scope of the agency/power relation: *A* ceases to be an agent, and while *B* potentially has power over *A*'s fate, *A* has been rendered powerless. This apparently banal example is not without interest, however. If *B* can do more or less what he or she desires with *A*'s body, including ending *A*'s life altogether, it may appear that *B*'s power over *A* is absolute or unconditional. And so in a sense it is, for *A* is incapable of resisting. Complete though it may be in one aspect, it is very limited in others. For by killing or immobilising *A*, *B* is necessarily deprived of whatever goods or services *A* might render within a continuing social relationship. The threat to do violence to another may be very often a major sanction helping to enforce modes of domination, but the actual destruction of one agent by another can hardly be regarded as the type case of the use of social power.

Consider a second example that one might suppose to be near the margins of whether or not a person remains an agent: someone in solitary confinement in a prison. Now it is clear that in such an instance the person does retain the capability of 'making a differ- ence'. Such a capability includes not just the chance to invent modes of occupying the mind in circumstances of extreme tedium; the solitary prisoner normally possesses at least some resources that can be brought to bear against his or her captors. 'Dirty protests' or hunger strikes in Northern Ireland are familiar illustrations. There are many ways in which the seemingly powerless, in particular contexts, may be able to influence the activities of those who appear to hold complete power over them; or in which the weak are able to mobilise resources against the strong. There are few social relations, of course, which are as markedly imbalanced in respect of power as that between prisoners in solitary confinement and their jailors. But such examples serve to highlight the points I have in mind. These can be stated as follows. Anyone who participates in a social relationship, forming part of a social system produced and reproduced by its constituent actors over time, necessarily sustains some control over the character of that relationship or system. Power relations in social systems can be regarded as relations of autonomy and dependence; but no matter how imbalanced they may be in terms of power, actors in subordinate positions are never wholly dependent, and are often very adept at converting whatever resources they possess into some degree of control over the conditions of reproduction of the system. In all social systems there is a dialectic of control, such that there are normally continually shifting balances of resources, altering the overall distribution of power. While it is always an empirical question just what power relations pertain within a social system, the agency/power connection, as a connection of logical entailment, means that an agent who does not participate in the dialectic of control *ipso facto* ceases to *be* an agent.[38]

I believe it true to say that in large areas of the social sciences – particularly (but not exclusively) in those dominated either by a general 'objectivist' position or more specifically by functionalism or by structuralism – human beings are not treated as knowledgeable, capable agents. This is perhaps most notoriously the case with Althusser's 'structuralist Marxism' and in the writings of those influenced by it: human agents are mere 'bearers of modes of production'. But, as I have argued elsewhere, a theory of action is also lacking in the functionalist sociology of Talcott Parsons, in spite of Parsons' labelling of his theoretical scheme as 'the action frame of reference'. Although Parsons may have moved towards a more objectivist stance in his later writings, as is often asserted, this was not a movement away from the concept of action as I have proposed it should be understood: for such a concept was not there in the first place. Garfinkel is quite right to say that in Parsons' theory human beings appear as 'cultural dopes', as impelled by 'internalised cultural values' that govern their activity.[39]

In the subsequent sections of this discussion, I want to try to show that, however abstract they may appear, these general considerations have direct consequences for quite fundamental issues of class analysis. I shall not concern myself with either Althusser or Parsons, but rather with two authors, one 'classic' and one more recent, whose works have made a strong imprint upon the study of classes. First, Weber's discussion of the nature of bureaucratic organisation, and its association with the expansion of capitalism. The second is Braverman's investigation of the division of labour in his *Labour and Monopoly Capital*.[40] Although Weber's views are in certain key respects explicitly anti-Marxist, while Braverman claims to defend a Marxist standpoint, there are some major similarities between the conclusions which each author tends to reach. These similarities – or so I shall claim – derive in some substantial part from deficiencies which can be analysed in terms of the concept of the dialectic of control.

Weber: bureaucracy and capitalism

Marx and Weber are widely regarded as the two most pre-eminent contributors to general problems of class analysis. It is sometimes supposed that Weber's main divergence from Marx consists in expanding upon, and modifying, Marx's views by adding the concept of 'status group' or *Stand*, and that of 'party' to that of 'class'. Others point out that, by apparently identifying the notion of class with market relations, Weber fails to pursue the Marxian theme that class divisions are founded in the relations of production. But each of these comparisons is relatively superficial. Much more significant are the differences between Weber's conception of capitalism and that of Marx; the former's interpretation of bureaucratisation, of course, plays a pivotal role in these differences. When Marx wrote about 'bureaucracy' (in, for example, his early critical discussions of Hegel), he used the term in its traditional sense, to refer to the administrative apparatus of government. One of Weber's major theoretical innovations was to provide a compelling rationale for extending the notions of 'bureaucracy' and 'bureau-cratisation' to a whole variety of social organisations.

Lying behind this terminological difference, of course, is Weber's conviction that the 'steel-hard cage' of rational–legal organisation is a necessary feature of the expansion of capitalism – and that the bars of the cage would become even more confining were capitalism to be replaced by socialism. Marxists have quite rightly seen We-ber's sombre projection of an increasingly bureaucratised social world – in which the alienation that Marx saw as involved for the wage-worker in the capitalist labour process would become the ineluctable lot of everyone – as constituting a direct challenge to Marx's ideas. Marxist writers have attacked Weber's conceptions of capitalism and bureaucracy from various different angles. But most such attacks have converged upon a single standpoint: the traits that Weber attributed to an overall process of 'bureaucratisation' are in fact the specific outcome of capitalist class domination, and hence will be transcended with the advent of socialism.

I do not want to say that these critical views are without founda-tion, and shall later argue that Braverman's work contributes in an important fashion to them; but I do think they are seriously limited because they characteristically accept *too much* of what Weber has to say about the nature and consequences of bureaucratisation. That is to say, the common tendency among Weber's Marxist critics is to accept the essential elements of Weber's characterisa-tion of bureaucracy, while declaring bureaucratic domination to be a specific outcome of the class system of capitalism. But Weber's conception of bureaucracy has to be confronted in a more direct way than this. Below, I distinguish four respects (among others which I shall not discuss here) in which the overall interpretation of bureaucracy that Weber offered has major weaknesses.

Weber's portrayal of bureaucracy and bureaucratisation is so well known that it is necessary to give no more than the briefest representation of it here. Weber sometimes uses the term 'bureau-cracy' as a general descriptive type (when talking of the traditional 'Chinese bureaucracy', etc.). But his most important formulation is as an 'ideal type': the more an organisation conforms to the features of the ideal type, the more 'bureaucratised' it can be said to be. The ideal type of bureaucratic organisation involves the following prin-cipal features: a formally delimited hierarchy, with the duties of distinct 'offices' being specified by written rules; staffing by means of full-time, salaried officials; and selection and allocation of officials by impersonal criteria on the basis of 'qualifications'. Weber avers that:

> Experience tends universally to show [that] the purely bureaucratic type of administrative organisation . . . is, from a purely technical point of view, capable of attaining the highest degree of efficiency and is in this sense formally the most rational known means of exercising authority over human beings. It is superior to any other form in precision, in stability, in the stringency of its discipline, and in its reliability.[41]

But the 'technical effectiveness' of bureaucracy exacts a heavy price. It is the source of the alienated character of bureaucratic tasks.

Weber's talk of 'precision', 'stability' and 'reliability' points to the direct connection between bureaucracy and mechanisation that he sometimes makes quite explicit. Bureaucracy, he says, is a 'human machine': the formal rationality of technique applies with equal relevance to human social organisation as to the control of the material world. A vital corollary to this is the theme that the more an organisation approaches the ideal type, the more power becomes centralised in the hands of those at the apex of the organisation. The expropriation of the worker from control of the means of production (or 'the means of administration') is a process that inevitably and irreversibly accompanies the expansion of bureaucratisation. Although Weber did not coin the phrase 'the iron law of oligarchy', his ideas strongly influenced Michels and there is no doubt that the theorem 'bureaucracy means oligarchy' is there in his writings.

Weber's specification of bureaucracy as an ideal type creates difficulties in assessing his views, since it seems to offer a mode of deflecting criticism. For if it is proposed that his conception of bureaucracy does not in fact provide a wholly valid or useful interpretation of the phenomenon with which it is concerned, the response can be made that, as it is an ideal type, one should feel no particular qualms if it does not conform to social reality. Weber adds fuel to such a rejoinder when he comments that ideal types 'do not contain hypotheses', that they are no more than a 'one-sided accentuation' of reality.[42] I do not have the space here to discuss the notion of ideal types; but however it may be most aptly described, Weber's conception of bureaucracy certainly does contain hypotheses (concerning technical effectiveness, etc.) that can be adjudged in terms of how well they cope with the subject-matter they relate to. And I want to argue that they can be placed seriously in question.

My objections each relate to the idea of the dialectic of control which I have introduced previously; they are as follows.

(1)   Weber seeks to draw a generalised contrast (in an 'ideal–typical' manner) between traditional and bureaucratic organisations, in which the 'steel-hard cage' of the latter denies to individuals the autonomy and spontaneity of behaviour possible in a non-bureaucratised social world. But this 'philosophy of history'[43] is surely not particularly convincing. Some forms of traditional organisation have scarcely allowed much autonomy of conduct to their members: not in spite of, but because of their nature as small, localised community forms. One can detect in Weber's writing here the influence of a Romanticism that also resonates through Tönnies' opposition between *Gemeinschaft* and *Gesellschaft*.[44] In this regard, Weber's approach can usefully be balanced by a chord struck by Durkheim in the latter's discussion of so-called 'mechanical solidarity'.[45] Although communities dominated by mechanical solidarity offer the person a secure moral haven, the individual is none the less subject to what Durkheim refers to as the 'tyranny of the group'. The range of possible activities of the individual is severely curtailed by the norms of the collectivity, backed by 'repressive' sanctions. I am no more persuaded by Durkheim's account of the consequences of the expansion of the division of labour than I am by Weber's interpretation of bureaucratisation. But I think that the former author is correct in claiming that the movement away from *gemeinschaftlich* forms of organisation towards more large-scale, diversified ones is frequently in some part a liberating phenomenon.

(2)   The 'iron law of oligarchy' is not a law at all; or rather it is a spurious one. The 'law' states that the increasing centralisation or co-ordination of activities which accompanies bureaucratisation necessarily means that power becomes more and more consolidated in the hands of a minority in an organisation.

Stated as a universal tendency, however, such is simply not the case. It is easy enough to demonstrate this. The British economy today is considerably more highly centralised than was the case fifty years ago. But the very fact of such increased centralisation entails that certain nominally subordinate groupings of workers actually have more power now than they were able to wield previously. This is true, for example, of workers in public utilities, in the oil industry, etc. It is precisely *because* of the increased interdependence of everyone in a strongly centralised economic order that strategically placed categories of workers are able, through the threat of withdrawal of their labour power, to increase their power. What applies within the economy or the state as a whole applies in more specific organisations also. An excellent illustration of this is work on a production line. What could be a better example of a highly 'formally rational' system, in which human beings and machines are strictly co-ordinated with one another? But again the strongly co-ordinated nature of such a production process, while it undeniably reduces labour to dull, repetitive tasks, in some respects increases rather than limits the power of workers involved in it. For a highly centralised production process tends to be much more vulnerable to disruption by small groups of workers than one in which labour tasks are less interdependent.

I don't mean to suggest by these illustrations that the centralisation involved in bureaucracy leads to the opposite situation to that suggested by the 'iron law of oligarchy': that is, that more centralisation entails the greater dependence of those in formal positions of authority upon their subordinates, and hence that the result is the diffusion of power downwards. Such a conclusion would of course be more fatuous than the famous 'iron law' itself. What I do mean to say is that there is no simple movement of power 'upwards' or 'downwards' with increasing bureaucratisation; normally there are various kinds of possible 'trade-offs' in the resources which can be actualised by groupings at different levels of an organisation.

(3)   The implications of point (2) are that bureaucratic organisations do not in fact look very much like Weber presents them in his 'ideal type'. It is useless to respond to this by replying

that ideal types by definition only approximate more or less closely to reality; the point at issue is how far Weber's formulation provides an apposite model for analysing contemporary forms of social organisation. And in fact there is good reason to suppose that, in modern bureaucratic systems, those in nominally subordinate positions usually have considerably greater control over the nature of their labour task than Weber allows. Although some of the work by Blau and others on the significance of 'informal relations' within bureaucratic hierarchies is worth mentioning here,[46] more directly relevant is that of Crozier.[47] As Crozier shows, the social (and often physical) distance between offices allows spaces of potential control for sub-ordinates that are not available in smaller, more traditional communities. A formal authority system of an organisation that approaches the characteristics of Weber's 'ideal-type', in fact, can often be more successfully circumvented or manipulated by subordinates than one in which those traits are less developed.[48] No doubt Weber was right to underscore the importance of written rules as a feature of bureaucracy. But the formal codification of procedures rarely conforms to actual practice; the 'rule book' may be subject to divergent interpretations, and hence can focalise conflicts which subordinates may turn to their own advantage. The irony of the idea of 'working to rule' is certainly not lost upon those who invoke the practice as a strategy in the dialectic of control.

(4)   The above considerations place seriously in question Weber's theorem that the 'purely bureaucratic' type of organisation is the most 'formally rational' mode of exercising authority over human beings. This theorem is so important to Weber's association of bureaucracy with capitalism, and to his critique of socialism, that it is worthwhile emphasising the point rather strongly. For it is the basis of Weber's cultural pessimism, and of his diagnosis of an antithesis between bureaucracy and democracy. Bureaucratic domination, in which the mass of the population are largely powerless to influence the decisions that govern the course of their day-to-day lives, is for Weber quite literally an irresistible force that sweeps us all along. Attempts to stem the tide merely succeed in giving it a greater force. But such pessimism is misplaced if Weber's character-

isation of the main elements of bureaucracy is a misleading one. This should not in any way be taken to imply that the sorts of problems Weber connected to bureaucratic domination can be ignored. Quite the contrary. They remain of great significance; but when we attempt to tackle them, on either a sociological or a political level, we have to disentangle ourselves from a good deal of what has become received Weberian wisdom.

How does such a critique of Weber's conception of bureaucracy connect with the methodological arguments I made in the opening section of the paper? For Weber was not by any streak of the imagination an 'objectivist'; rather, he stressed the 'subjective meaning' of human conduct as integral to social analysis. Without pursuing this issue in any detail, it can be said that, in respect of bureaucratic organisation, Weber associated 'meaning' with *legitimacy*. Consequently his account of bureaucracy is very much written 'from the top'; the ideal type of bureaucratic organisation is heavily weighted towards how the 'legitimate order of a rational-legal form' is sustained.

Braverman: class domination and capitalism

Braverman writes as a Marxist, and the starting-point of his analysis of capitalistic organisations is the sale of labour power as a commodity. In the sale of their labour power to the capitalist, workers cede control of the labour process; capitalists, for their part, seek to consolidate this control through 'management'. Workers have to be 'managed' without employers being able to rely either upon the moral ties of fealty involved in feudal class relations, or upon the use of physical force to make workers obey; their only real sanction is the economic constraint of the need of workers to find paid employment in order to make a living. The crux of Braverman's thesis is that managerial control is obtained above all via the effects of the division of labour. It is mistaken, Braverman argues, to talk about the division of labour in general. The 'social division of labour', which is found in all societies, has to be clearly distinguished from the 'technical division of labour', which is specific to capitalism. While the social division of labour involves the separation of tasks devoted to the making of whole products, the technical

division of labour fragments the labour task into repetitive operations carried out by different individuals. The expansion of the
technical division of labour, in Braverman's view, is the most basic
element extending managerial control over the labour, because
knowledge of and command over the labour process are thereby
progressively 'expropriated' from workers.

Braverman lays a great deal of stress upon the contribution of
Taylorism, or 'scientific management', to this process. In Taylorism
the operations carried out by the worker are integrated into the
technical design of production as a whole. 'Scientific management' may seem in most countries to have made only limited
inroads into industry, and to have been generally superseded by
the 'human-relations' approach of Elton Mayo and his associates
in the USA.[49] But Braverman claims that the impact of the 'human-
relations' view has been of relatively marginal significance. Taylorism serves as the chief set of organising principles of capitalist
production.

Braverman's analysis, in my opinion, stands as a major corrective
to some of the elements of Weber's account of bureaucratisation.
Braverman shows that the rationality of technique in modern industrial enterprise is not neutral in respect of class domination. It
would be difficult to exaggerate the significance of this. For if
Braverman's argument is correct, industrial technique embodies
the capital/wage-labour relation in its very form. Class domination
appears as the absent centre of the linkage Weber drew between the
rationality of technique and the rationality of the (formally) most
'technically effective' type of organisation, bureaucracy. It would
follow that bureaucratic domination, and the concomitant power-
lessness of workers, are not inevitable features of contemporary
organisations; the transformation of the class relations incorporated within the 'technical division of labour' could in principle
furnish the basis for the democratic reorganisation of the labour
process. Braverman's work should therefore provide for a more
optimistic assessment of the possibilities of unlocking Weber's
'steel-hard cage' than Weber's own gloomy vision of the future
allows for. In fact, however, the process of the sieving off of
control of the labour process that Braverman describes appears
to have just the same inevitable, irreversible character about it as
the processes of bureaucratisation portrayed by Weber. The factors
responsible for this, I want to argue, do in some respects have

similarities to the shortcomings I have pointed to in Weber's treatment of bureaucracy; but this time they are very closely connected to an 'objectivist' methodological position that Braverman declaredly embraces towards the beginning of his book.

Labour and Monopoly Capital, he claims, is only concerned with the ' "objective" content of class', and not with the ' "subjective will" '.[50] The result is a work which, notwithstanding its self-professed Marxist standpoint, certainly drastically underestimates the knowledgeability and the capability of workers faced with a range of management imperatives. Braverman is mistaken to say that his work is unconcerned with 'subjective will': the 'subjective will' of *management*, as expressed in Taylorist strategies of control, is more than adequately represented in the book. What is lacking is a parallel discussion of the reactions of workers, as themselves knowledgeable and capable agents, to the technical division of labour and to Taylorism. Braverman bases his severance of the 'objective' from the 'subjective' components of class upon Marx's famous distinction between a class 'in itself' and a class 'for itself'. But it is important to see that this distinction conceals a possible ambiguity. For the differentiation could be taken to imply that 'class consciousness' can be equated with class 'for itself', and therefore that the 'objective' features of class can be examined without reference to consciousness (discursive or practical). This is evidently mistaken. All class relations obviously involve the conscious activity of human agents. But this is different from groups of individuals being conscious of being members of the same class, of having common class interests and so on.[51] It is quite possible to conceive of circumstances in which individuals are not only not cognisant of being in a common class situation, but where they may actively deny the existence of classes – and where their attitudes and ideas can nevertheless be explained in terms of class relationships. Such is characteristically the case, as I have argued elsewhere,[52] with certain categories of white-collar workers.

Braverman's surprising disinclination to treat workers as capable and knowledgeable agents seriously compromises the validity of some of his conclusions. The implications of Braverman's analysis, which in emphasising the class character of managerial control begins from different premises to those of Weber, appear every bit as pessimistic as those of that author. For although Braverman's study is an explicitly Marxist one, there is no indication at all that the working class is likely to rise against its oppressors, or even that workers are able in some part to stem the advance of the processes that rob them of control over their labour. On the contrary, the spread of de-skilling, and the sieving off of control over the labour task from the worker, appear to have much the same implacable force about them as the advance of bureaucracy depicted by Weber.

The revolution may be as far off as ever; but one can certainly doubt that the processes described by Braverman are either as clear cut or categorical as his discussion suggests. One reason for this is that the technological changes constantly taking place in capitalist economies seem more complicated, in their effects upon the labour process, than Braverman allows. Certainly old craft skills are for the most part eliminated, but new types of skilled activity, albeit different in character, are continually created. Of course, what counts as 'skill' is a complicated matter, as Braverman and a host of subsequent commentators have recognised. But the factor of human knowledgeability again enters in here. For what counts as 'skilled work', or a 'skilled trade', depends in some substantial degree upon what can be *made* to count as such. There are many examples where workers have proved able to sustain the definition of themselves as 'skilled' in spite of changes in the nature of the labour task. A classic mode in which this has been achieved is via the 'balkanisation' of the labour market: where access to the occupation has been kept strictly limited by the union or the workers' association.

Equally important are the various forms of worker resistance whereby workers have succeeded in maintaining a significant amount of control over the labour process itself. Historical studies of the American working class indicate not only that Taylorism had consistently less impact than Braverman claims, in large degree because of worker resistance, but that the expansion of 'human-relations' ideology was partly due to working-class opposition to Taylorism.[53] It is perhaps worth adding that opposition to Taylorism was not confined to those most directly affected by it, the working class. Many employers and managers, in the USA and elsewhere (in contrast to the attitude of Lenin!), were either sceptical of scientific management or openly hostile to it, on a mixture of pragmatic and humanitarian grounds. In adopting such attitudes, even on purely practical grounds, managers were in fact being quite realistic. For those who attempt to control a labour force are by no means impervious to understanding the Marxist adage that 'labour power is a commodity that refuses to be treated like any other commodity'.

This is where the point that, in capitalist economies, workers have to be 'managed', without the moral or military sanctions possessed by exploiting classes in prior types of society, becomes particularly important. In other types of class-divided society, the dominant class has normally had direct possession of the means of violence, and hence of disciplining recalcitrant labour where necessary. But in capitalism (a) regularised labour discipline is more integral to work than in most contexts (especially that of the peasant producer) of production in earlier forms of society, and (b) the chief coercive sanction employers possess to ensure the compliance of the workforce is that the latter is propertyless, and hence compelled to find employment in order to make a living. It is quite right, I think, to argue that the significance of these phenomena can best be analysed in terms of the capitalist labour contract. But the contractual encounter between capital and wage-labour has to be seen as providing axes of chronic struggle in which the working class is by no means always and inevitably the loser.

There are, I consider, two connecting axes or 'sites' of class struggle in the capitalist societies. One is class struggle in the workplace, the main focus of Braverman's attention. As I have argued, I do not think Braverman adequately acknowledges the significance of such struggle on the level of day-to-day practices on the shop-floor. Braverman's work can here be usefully complemented by studies such as that of Friedman.[54] Friedman argues that not only Braverman but Marx himself, in anticipating the progressive homogenisation of labour through the undermining of skill differentials, fails to give sufficient weight to the influence of worker resistance at the level of the firm, and the need of employers or managers to incorporate the fact of such resistance into their own strategies. Friedman distinguishes two principal types of managerial strategy that are commonly used to control the labour force. One such strategy is that of 'responsible autonomy'.[55] Workers in these circumstances are allowed considerable independence of activity in the work situation, so that they are encouraged to co-operate in accepting technological changes in ways which conform to the over-all aims of management. This can be contrasted with the strategy of 'direct control'. Such a strategy approximates to that which Braverman takes to be prevalent throughout industry. Here managers attempt to obtain the compliance of the labour force by close supervision of the labour process, and the sustaining of discipline by minimising worker responsibility through Taylorist techniques. Braverman, says Friedman, exaggerates the scope and the effectiveness of the second of these strategies. This over-emphasis follows from 'a failure to appreciate the importance of worker resistance as a force provoking accommodating changes in the mode of production', a mistake which 'leads to a technological deterministic view of capitalist development'.[56] Part of the importance of distinguishing different types of managerial strategy in this way is that it becomes possible to connect the analysis to the study of dual or segmented labour markets. Those in weak positions in segmented labour markets are probably usually less able to resist incorporation within managerial strategies of 'direct control'. Such workers include particularly ethnic minorities – and women.

The second site of class struggle involves the pitting of labour movements against the organised power of employers and of the state. Here we have a prime example of the operation of the dialectic of control. In the early years of the development of capitalism, as Marx showed, the capitalist labour contract was a medium of bolstering the power of the emerging entrepreneurial class. By dissolving feudal bonds of fealty and obligation, the capitalist labour contract allowed for the 'freedom' of employers to buy, and workers to sell, labour power, at its exchange value. By making the relation between employers and workers a purely economic one, abstract 'political' rights were confined to a separate sphere of the polity, a separation first of all supported by property qualifications on the franchise. The capitalist labour contract, however, in the context of parliamentary government, allowed the creation of labour movements based upon the power generated by the threat or actuality of the withdrawal of labour. In my opinion, the struggles of labour movements to improve the general economic conditions of the working class, and to realise 'citizenship rights', have helped profoundly to alter the characteristics of the capitalist societies of the West.

Braverman is not directly concerned with such issues in his book, but again I do not believe they can be wholly separated from the problems he discusses. For the achievements of Western labour movements have undoubtedly acted to counter the kind of mono-

lithic triumph of capitalism suggested by the style of analysis
Braverman develops. Just as Braverman underestimates the significance of worker resistance in the work-place, many other Marxists
have been dismissive of the part played by labour movements in
transforming what C.B. Macpherson calls the 'liberal' state of the
nineteenth century into the 'liberal democratic' state of the twentieth.[57] The worst of these analyses incorporate the flaws of both
'objectivistic' social science and of functionalism:[58] whatever citizenship rights the working class may have obtained are the result of
'adjustments' of the capitalist system protecting its source of labour
supply. Consider the judgement of Müller and Neusüss on the
welfare state: 'By establishing a minimum subsistence level
(through workmen's protection and social security systems) the
material existence of wage-labourers is ensured during the times
when they cannot sell their labour-power on the market (sickness,
old age, unemployment).'[59] Such assessments not only ignore the
long-term battles workers have had to conduct in most countries to
attain political and welfare rights, but once more treat workers as
mere dupes of the system. Evaluations of such a kind have about as
much validity as contrary assertions of the sort often heard from
conservative sectors of the British press, that 'the country is run by
the unions'. At least this second viewpoint does accept that the
organised working-class has achieved a considerable measure of
power in the liberal democratic state, even if it wildly exaggerates
the scope of such power.

Conclusion: agency and alienation

In this essay I have concentrated upon indicating that abstract
issues of social theory do have a definite bearing upon concrete
problems of social analysis. In emphasising the notion of the dialectic of control, I do not mean to imply that those in subordinate
positions in social systems are chronically driven, or are able, to
overthrow those who dominate them. I am not suggesting some sort
of revised version of Hegel's master–slave dialectic. But I do think
the critique of Weber's interpretation of the expansion of bureaucracy (directed against Marxist class analysis) and of works such as
that of Braverman (written supposedly precisely from a standpoint
of Marxist class analysis) allows a more satisfactory analysis of

issues of the relation between class domination and authority systems than their writings provide.[60] In concluding this analysis, however, I want to return to a more philosophical plane.

If my arguments about human agency and power in the opening part of the essay are correct, they can be related, I think, to Marx's discussion of the alienated character of capitalist production. To be an agent is to have the capability of 'making a difference', of intervening in the world so as to influence events which occur in that world. To be a *human* agent is to be a highly knowledgeable and skilled individual, who applies that knowledgeability in securing autonomy of action in the course of day-to-day life. By 'alienated labour' Marx refers to work situations in which the worker becomes an appendage of a machine – Braverman's study is about 'alienated labour' in this sense, although he barely mentions the term itself. In my terminology the connection of alienation with the 'human-ness' of our 'species-being' can be expressed simply and coherently in a single sentence. The more a worker comes close to being an 'appendage of a machine', the more he or she ceases to be a human agent. As Marx puts it, 'The animal becomes human and the human becomes animal.'[61] The interest of this analysis for a philosophical anthropology of labour, however, should not make us forget that, precisely because they are not machines, wherever they can do so human actors devise ways of avoiding being treated as such.

(v)   Administrative power and the nation-state*

The nation-state, let me repeat, is the sociologist's 'society'. The nonchalant use of the term 'society' in the literature of sociology belies the complexity of the changes creating that bounded and unitary whole that is its usual referent. I say this not in order to prohibit use of the concept in the social sciences but to point to a range of problems it ordinarily conceals. Unlike traditional states, the nation-state is a power-container whose administrative purview corresponds exactly to its territorial delimitation. How is this administrative power generated? This will be the topic that will [initially] occupy my attention. But it leads on to further issues.

---

* *The Nation-State and Violence*, pp. 172–81.

For the creation of such administrative capabilities is immediately related to the combined influences of industrialism and urbanism. And it is important in turn to analyse how these connect to key aspects of the nation-state as a capitalist society, which means elucidating the nature of class structure in relation both to sovereignty and democracy. A word of warning to the reader: . . . I shall assume greater familiarity with ideas introduced in the first volume of this work [A *Contemporary Critique of Historical Materialism*;] . . . although they are essential to the arguments deployed, there is not room enough to provide a full justification of them.

Administrative power: communication and information storage

Several factors concerned with the extension of communication are deeply involved with the consolidation of the administrative unity of the nation-state. They include: the mechanization of transportation; the severance of communication from transportation by the invention of electronic media; and the expansion of the 'documentary' activities of the state, involving an upsurge in the collection and collation of information devoted to administrative purposes. However, the second and third of these have increasingly merged in the twentieth century as electronic modes of the storage of information have become more and more sophisticated. Moreover, electricity becomes increasingly involved in the means of mechanical propulsion. All three are tied together in terms of the scheme of concepts that inform this book. Each represents a mode of biting into time and space, providing the means of radically increasing the scope of time–space distanciation beyond that available in class-divided societies.

The simplest, and most effective way of analysing the direct impact of innovations in transportation is via the notion of time-space convergence.[62] Somewhere about the middle of the eighteenth century, was initiated a series of innovations in modes of transportation, paring down the time taken to make journeys from one point to another. In all traditional states there were road systems of some kind, often of a fairly complex sort, as in the Roman Empire. Small bands of individuals could move quite rapidly over long distances, particularly if there were staging-posts where fresh horses could be obtained. The Vikings were able to make very fast –

as well as on occasion very long – voyages, which compare favourably with anything achieved later, until the advent of mechanically powered vessels. However, the main impetus underlying such forms of (relatively) swift transportation was very often military, commercial long haulage being slow and usually confined to rivers or seas. Until the eighteenth century, Europe was no different from anywhere else in these respects. Roads were generally extremely poor, except for a few highways between major cities and ports. In Britain, a 'turnpike boom' began about the middle of the eighteenth century, prior to which 'the roads throughout the Kingdom were extremely bad and almost impassable, so that it was very difficult to convey from place to place either bulky or heavy articles. Wheel carriages could be little used, and pack horses were the general means of conveyance.'[63]

Not until around the turn of the nineteenth century was there a cohesively organized network of turnpikes, providing for reasonably cheap commercial transportation, in which respect they were in any case undercut for bulk transport by the rapidly developing canal system. The stage-coach system was the first modern rapid-transit form of transportation operating regularly and over a wide spatial pattern. It was also the first to be organized in terms of a time-table, even if those in use well into the nineteenth century were very haphazard and poorly co-ordinated by the standards of subsequent rapid-transit systems. A timetable is one of the most significant of modern organizational devices, presuming and stimulating a regulation of social life by quantified time in a manner quite unknown to prior types of society. Timetables are not just means of using temporal differences in order to identify and specify regularized events – the arrival and departure of coaches, trains, buses or planes. *A time-table is a time–space ordering device, which is at the heart of modern organizations.*[64] All organizations, up to and including the world system today, operate by means of time-tables, through which the sequencing of activities in time–space is choreographed. Organizations have always involved some sort of time-table – the invention of the calendar, for example, was a characteristic feature of traditional states. But only within regularized time–space settings, organized via 'clock time', can time-tables assume a more precise form. The monastery may have been the earliest example of such a setting,[65] but the commodified time inherent in capitalist production undoubtedly was its most decisive propagator. Time–space convergence provides, then, a dramatic index of the phenomenon of which it is by now barely possible to speak without relapsing into cliché – the shrinking world. But lying behind time–space convergence there is the more diffuse, but profoundly important, phenomenon of the increasingly precise co-ordination of the time–space sequencing of social life.

It is somewhat specious to focus mainly upon the mechanization of transportation in interpreting the dissolution of the segmental character of class-divided societies. The effects of such mechanization would have been much more limited were it not for its conjunction with the invention of electronic communication. Without the telegraph, and subsequent electronic communication modes, rapid-transit transportation would be confined to a few journeys per day for a small minority and a tiny proportion of manufactured goods. Mass transportation demands precisely timed and 'spaced' movement, which in turn presumes the capability of communicating 'ahead of time' what is planned. Only given these can an overall traffic system be reflexively monitored and thus comprehensively 'organized'. Thus, rather than the steam train, it is Bradshaw's directory, co-ordinated by telegraphic communication, that epitomizes modern transportation. Contemporaries understandably enough were awed by the railway, 'a plexus of red, a veritable system of blood circulation, complicated, dividing, and reuniting, branching, splitting, extending, throwing out feelers, offshoots, taproots, feeders'.[66] But the combination of the railway and the telegraph was what brought this complex into being, not the locomotive and its rails on their own.

Most historians and sociologists perhaps do not recognize the extended process that was involved in the spread of mechanized modes of transportation, a process that did not culminate until the introduction of world standard time in 1884. At the Prime Meridian Conference held in Washington during that year, following a series of acerbic political debates, Greenwich was adopted as the zero meridian. The globe was partitioned into twenty-four time zones, each one hour apart, and an exact beginning of the universal day was fixed.[67] In some states, railways and other transport time-tables were quite quickly brought into line with these delimitations, but in others more chaotic practices prevailed. How far one or the other was the case depended substantially upon the pre-existing system. As late as 1870 in the USA there were some eighty different railway times.[68] However, in 1883 representatives of the railroads met to establish a uniform time, referred to as 'the day of two noons', since in the eastern part of each region clocks were put back at midday.[69] When the Washington Conference was held, France – whose delegates were the most bitter opponents of the choice of Greenwich as the zero meridian – still had four different regional times, none of which was readily convertible to Greenwich time. Paris time, nine minutes and twenty-one seconds in front of Greenwich, was adopted as the time of the railways, and in 1891 this was made the statutory time for the whole of France. Curiosities remained. The trains were in fact scheduled to run five minutes behind their 'official' times, so as to give passengers opportunity to board in a leisured way. Nonetheless, it was the French who initiated the International Conference on Time, held in Paris in 1912; this was the congress that set up a uniform method of specifying accurate time signals and transmitting them around the world.[70]

The separation of communication from transportation which the telegraph established is as significant as any prior invention in human history. It reduces to a minimum what geographers call the 'friction of distance'. Separation in distance had always been not only separation in time, but had been directly correlated with the expenditure of costs and effort. More or less instantaneous communication may not eliminate either cost or effort, but it does break the coincidence of these with spatial segregation. Postal networks are, of course, a major supplement to the telegraph and its successor, the telephone. Figures IV.1 and IV.2 show the increasing time-space convergence between New York and San Francisco.[71]

Postal services of a national and international type originated in the eighteenth century. But early postal communications were both slow and sporadic. Prior to the mid-nineteenth century, mail was rarely transported at more than ten miles an hour over lengthy distances.[72] The point already made about modern transportation systems in general – that co-ordination in time–space is as important as the mechanization of the actual channel of movement – applies to postal services as a transport communication device. But highly efficient postal systems certainly antedate their telephone counterparts. In the USA, a fully national telephone service has only existed since the laying of the first transcontinental cable in 1915. Even then trunk-calling was time-consuming compared with later on. In 1920, some quarter of an hour was needed to make such a call, involving

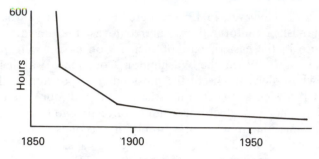

Figure IV.2 Telephone time–space convergence between New York and San Francisco

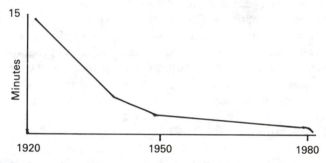

Figure IV.1 Postal time–space convergence between New York and San Francisco

the collaboration of as many as eight operators. As Figure IV.2 indicates, by 1930 improvements in network connections cut down the average service time to two minutes; the introduction of automatic switching equipment reduced this to one minute in 1950. The coming of direct long distance dialling reduced this to as long as it takes to compose the number and for someone to answer the call.

In telephone communications there is almost complete time–space convergence both within states and internationally. There is small difference between placing a local call and one across thousands of miles.[73] Of course the telephone is only one among a range of electronic media that permit more or less instantaneous (or, if it is preferred, delayed) communication over indefinite distances. Television has developed as a 'one-way' medium of communication, but there is no intrinsic reason why it should remain so, since various forms of two-way link are in principle, and in some cases in practice, possible. Facsimile, video and computer transmission represent more novel forms of actual and potential communication, the likely impact of which on social life is still largely unknown, but which will undoubtedly further extend processes of time–space convergence.

I mention these phenomena here not in order to attempt to bring the discussion of the nation-state through to the present day. My point is to emphasize the significance to the consolidation of the nation-state in the latter part of the nineteenth and early twentieth centuries of the separation of the communication of information from transportation. The initial leap forward in the administrative power generated by the nation-state was accomplished prior to the development of electronic communication. But modern societies have been 'electronic societies' longer than we ordinarily imagine and 'information societies' since their inception. There is a fundamental sense, as I have argued, in which *all* states have been 'information societies', since the generation of state power presumes reflexively monitored system reproduction, involving the regularized gathering, storage, and control of information applied to administrative ends. But in the nation-state, with its peculiarly high degree of administrative unity, this is brought to a much higher pitch than ever before.

In discussing traditional states, Innis makes a distinction between communication media which 'emphasise time' and those which 'emphasise space'.[74] The former are durable but heavy, and are the main textual materials of the earlier civilizations. Stone, clay and parchment belong in this category. They carry the marks of the written word over very lengthy passages of time but are not conducive to the generation of administrative power across wide spans of space. Papyrus and paper tend to be less long-lasting but are light, more easily transportable and also more easily reproducible. The Roman conquest of Egypt, according to Innis, was peculiarly important to the expansion of the Empire, not primarily because of the territory thus acquired, but because it allowed access to large supplies of papyrus which were then used widely to carry administrative documentation. Following the fall of Rome, the European states reverted to the use of the parchment codex, papyrus virtually disappearing after the eighth century. Paper was initially used mainly for commercial purposes, as credit documents and bills of exchange. Texts of any length, including scholarly texts, continued to be inscribed on parchment until the development of the printing press. The invention of printing was a phenomenon as important to the formation of the absolutist state as the other factors mentioned [previously: i.e. the commodification of land and products; the emergence of a guaranteed, centralized legal order permitting a range of contractual rights and obligations; the development of a monetary system; and the formation of a centrally organized taxation system.[75] It would be difficult to overestimate the generalized impact of printing in the shaping of modernity.[76] Printing is the first major step in the mechanization of communication and, in making documents and texts widely available, it initiated the process of drawing European culture away from mimetic imagery in material, intellectual and artistic domains.

So far as the state is concerned, the most important consequence of the easy and cheap availability of printed materials was an enlargement of the sphere of the 'political'. The growth of a 'public sphere' of state administration is inseparable from textually mediated organization. The discursive arena thereby opened up is quite mistakenly described if it is regarded as one in which 'free speech' is in principle possible. It is not primarily speech which is at issue, however important debating chambers might become. Rather it is the 'intertextuality' of the exchange of opinions and observations via texts that are 'freely available' – in Ricoeur's terms, distanciated from their authors – that marks the decisive shift in the lurch towards a new form of state . . . I want to concentrate upon the implications for the enlargement of the administrative power of the state. What printing made possible, and what it was increasingly used for during the phase of the consolidation of absolutism, was a very profound furtherance of the surveillance operations of the state. It was essential to the codification of law upon which Weber rightly places so much stress. Laws had long been in some part written but in the preceding scribal culture their influence was necessarily limited and diffuse. Printed codes of law, within an increasingly literate culture, made for the increasing integration of 'interpreted' law within the practice of state administration and for a much more consistent and direct application of standardized juridical procedures to the activities of the mass of the population. But the sphere of the law is only one area in which such changes can be observed. Records, reports and routine data collection become part of the day-to-day operation of the state, although of course not limited to it.

As good a single index as any of the movement from the absolutist to the nation-state is the initiation of the systematic collection of
'official statistics'. In the period of absolutism, such data-gathering
was particularly concentrated in two areas, at least as regards the
internal affairs of states. One was that of finance and taxation, the
other the keeping of population statistics – which tended, however,
until the eighteenth century to be localized rather than centralized.
The first bears witness to the significance of fiscal management,
already alluded to. The second is to do with a . . . preoccupation
of the centralizing state with maintaining internal 'order' in respect
of rebellion, vagabondage and crime. The official statistics that all
states began to keep from about the middle of the eighteenth
century onwards maintain and extend these concerns. But they also
range over many sectors of social life and, for the first time, are
detailed, systematic and nearly complete. They include the centralized collation of materials registering births, marriages and deaths;
statistics pertaining to residence, ethnic background and occupation; and what came to be called by Quételet and others 'moral
statistics', relating to suicide, delinquency, divorce and so on.

There is a very important point to be made about official statistics. From the time of their first beginnings onwards students of
society have regarded them as offering a fund of material that can
be used to chart the characteristics of social organization and social
change. The origins of empirical social research in the social sciences are closely bound up with the use of official statistics as an
index of processes of social activity.[77] Durkheim's *Suicide* is only
one among many nineteenth-century works to have relied upon the
analysis of such statistics to substantiate its conclusions. Now it
might well be accepted that, given certain reservations about the
manner of their collection, official statistics are an invaluable source
of data for social research. But they are not just 'about' an independently given universe of social objects and events, *they are in
part constitutive of it*. The administrative power generated by the
nation-state could not exist without the information base that is the
means of its reflexive self-regulation. Other implications also derive
from this. Social science, even its earliest formulations did not come
fresh-faced and innocent to an ordered array of empirical data. The
collection of official statistics is impossible without those involved
having a systematic understanding of the subject-matter that is the
concern of those statistics. Such an understanding is progressively

monitored, in the modern state, by much the same methods as 'independent' social scientists use to analyse the data thus produced. From this it follows that the social sciences have themselves been persistently implicated in the phenomena they set out to analyse. The connections involved here are in some part empirical (because the collection of modern statistics normally involves learning processes used to 'systematize' and 'improve' them) but also conceptual or theoretical. The discourses of social science are recurrently absorbed into what it is that they are about, at the same time as they (logically) draw upon concepts and theories already employed by lay actors.[78]

Social science, in other words, has from its early origins in the modern period been a constitutive aspect of that vast expansion of the reflexive monitoring of social reproduction that is an integral feature of the state. In the period of absolutism, two forms of discourse were particularly relevant in this respect. One, which I have previously mentioned, was the discourse of early political theory, constitutively entangled in the formation of the modes of sovereignty that distinguish the absolutist state from traditional ones. The other, belonging to a slightly later phase, is the discourse of early economic theory, which helped to give the modern senses to 'economic', 'economy', 'industry' and a whole set of surrounding terms. However, these usages only became firmly established in the nineteenth century and it is economics, together with sociology and psychology, that have been most deeply involved with the rise of the administrative power of the nation-state. In saying this, I do not mean to claim that the social sciences cannot in some part stand outside that power and subject it to analysis and critique, as I consider myself to be doing in this text. But we should recognize that one of the features of the modern state – and of modern organizations in general – is the systematic study and utilization of materials relevant to their own reproduction.

(vi) The nation-state and military power*

When nineteenth-century thinkers contrasted the emerging order of 'industrial society' with 'military society', they established some of

---

* *The Nation-State and Violence*, pp. 244–54.

the main parameters of modern social science . . . I have set out to question some of the chief suppositions thus developed. But how far should such a questioning lead us to reject altogether the idea that, in the modern world, military power declines in relative importance, as compared to specifically political and economic sources of social organization and social change? Do we in the West still, in fact, live in 'military societies', albeit ones in which the nature of military power and its relations to other sources of power, have been radically altered?

Although Marxist accounts of the expansion of capitalism and rival interpretations of 'industrial society' still predominate, some theories give military power a prominent role. Thus Lasswell's analysis of the 'garrison-state', originally formulated in the 1930s, reverses the usual type of thesis found in the social sciences. According to him, in the nineteenth century industrial organization and administrative rationalization pervaded the development of the European countries and the USA. But subsequently there has developed a trend towards 'military-police dominance', which threatens increasingly to expand in the impending future.[79] The garrison-state is a phenomenon that is coming into being, not one that already exists. In Lasswell's view, the trend towards the garrison-state has to be understood against the background of the development of a world military order. The garrison-state emerges in a garrisoned world, in which resort to the threat or use of organized violence is more-or-less chronically present. It is not necessarily undemocratic or non-polyarchic, since it leaves open the possibility that a majority might participate in the internal political process. Nonetheless, Lasswell's views were formulated in the context of his fears for the future of Western liberal democracy in the face of 'the explosive growth of modern science and technology and the connection of these developments with the control of large population and resource basins suitable for huge capital accumulation'.[80]

In assessing the significance of military power today, several distinguishable questions can be posed. How far are Western nation-states currently dominated by military imperatives in terms of their basic economic organization? Are patterns of military rule likely to become more, rather than less, common and what can be said about the conditions making for civil rather than military government? On a global level, what is the nature of the 'world military order' and how does it connect with other characteristics of the modern world system? In spite of the persistent tendency of the social sciences, particularly sociology to skirt these issues, it hardly takes a giant leap of the imagination to see how relevant they are to current paths of development of modern societies. They are evidently too complex to be addressed in detail here and I shall only attempt to offer schematic answers to them, concentrating my attention mainly upon the industrialized countries.

Of one thing there can be no doubt – the stupendous scale of military expenditures in the world economy as a whole. As indexed by officially published statistics, such expenditures amounted to $159 billion in 1966, $200 billion in 1973, and currently stand at some $600 billion. Taken on their own, such figures do no more than dazzle or depress and it is perhaps of greater use to consider some more comparative figures. Thus world military expenditure is greater than the Gross National Product of the whole of the African continent, South Africa included. It is more than that of the whole of Asia, if Japan is excluded. The GNP of Japan, the third largest in the world, is only about twice the size of the wealth dispensed for military ends globally. As one author puts it, 'It is as if half a "Japan" existed within the world economy, but was unrecognised diplomatically.'[81]

How far the industrialized countries should really be regarded as 'military-industrial' societies, however, depends in part upon appraising the role of military expenditure within their national economies. The most commonly employed statistical method of doing this is to analyse the ratio of military spending to GNP. As measured in these terms, the level of military expenditure is generally low, although perhaps not lower than would be the case in traditional states if some sort of comparable mode of computation could be devised.[82] While there are occasional instances of as much as a third of GNP being allocated for military purposes (Israel), for the industrialized states the total is mostly between 3–5 per cent, including the cases of both the USA and the Soviet Union, although there is good reason to be sceptical about the official figures connected with the latter. But there are considerable problems with this mode of measurement and it is more effective to analyse military expenditure as a proportion of total government expenditure. Judged by this index, the ratio of 'defence' to other spending in the industrialized countries varies between 11 and 30 per cent (although it has generally declined over the past twenty years). Such figures surely do indicate that the channelling of production to-wards military ends is a more significant feature of industrialism than the GNP ratio would indicate. But they do not as such reveal much about the 'military-industrial complex' involved in modern production; nor do they document its nature. The idea that such a phenomenon is to be found in most or all industrialized societies is, as usually represented, a fairly vague one. Eisenhower originally employed the term in the context of trying to promote the con-certed and systematic application of science and technology to military production, later using it to refer critically to what he came to see as threatening aspects of its development. At least two types of approach can be distinguished using the concept or something similar. One argument, of the kind favoured by C. Wright Mills in his earlier writings, holds that an integration has taken place of the main institutional spheres of power in society – the political, economic and military. In this view, bureaucratic centralization is the main organizing impulsion involved. The other argument is a quasi-Marxist one. Although it is elaborated in varying forms, the main claim is that military production is explic-able in terms of the economic imperatives of capitalist enterprise.[83] The 'military-industrial complex' is the concrete expression of the social changes fostered by these imperatives.

However, neither of these positions stands up well to scrutiny. If a 'military-industrial complex' can be said to *dominate* the econ-omy, it has to be the case that there are sharply defined links of interdependence between military production and other areas of production; and that modern economies are so reliant upon the maintenance of these ties that those holding political power find themselves compelled to acquiesce in such production needs. Now, in some of the major Western countries, 'defence' contractors do rank highly among the largest corporations. Thus some three quar-ters of the most sizeable military contractors in the USA are to be found in the list of the five hundred largest American corpora-tions.[84] In the Soviet Union, arms-related industries outstrip all other industrial sectors in terms of the sophisticated application of science to technological advancement and there is a range of agencies devoted to ensuring that processes of technical transfer are readily accomplished. But it does not follow that the main productive organizations in either economy are substantially dependent upon military-related activities for their prosperity. The proportion of such production engaged in by most of the large corporations in the USA is low, with one or two notable exceptions.[85] Moreover, those firms that are involved in military production show a defined tendency to move in and out of the area according to shifts in the political and economic climate. Thus, in the post-Vietnam period, the largest twenty-five military contractors in the USA changed from having some 40 per cent of their business in 'defence' in the late 1950s to under 10 per cent in the middle 1970s.[86] Such a situation certainly does not pertain in the Soviet Union, but in that society decisions taken by political planners have at various periods significantly altered investment policies in respect of military expenditure.

These observations indicate that the 'military-industrial complex' is not in the ascendancy in the economies of the industrialized societies. The production of 'defence'-related goods and services is a major part of most of those economies and expenditure on them a prime concern of most governments. Consequently, both military leaders and manufacturers are often able to wield considerable influence, directly and indirectly, over certain policies. But not even military leaders and manufacturers constitute a solitary grouping, let alone those whose main involvements are with government or with other sectors of economic life. The very nature of industrialized war in a certain sense ensures a diversity of interests and concerns. In traditional states, a militaristic ruling class could dominate the state, its control over the means of violence being dependent upon the mustering of soldiery rather than upon their sway over production. The means of waging industrialized war necessitate reliance upon a broad productive infrastructure. But just as it has been remarked of politics that 'in capitalism the dominant class does not rule', so also it could be added that it does not make war. So far as economic factors are concerned, it is undoubtedly the case in the modern world that military expenditure can help generate favourable conditions of production both for manufacturers and for an overall national economy. But – quite apart from the unacceptable functionalist cast of an argument that suggests that whatever is the case happens because of a beneficial end it secures – the conclusion cannot be drawn from this that such factors dominate other influences. On the contrary, the military expenditures of the contemporary nation-states have to be seen as mainly bound up with their political involvements within the global nation-state system. To be sure, it is not at all easy to discern where economic interests or concerns leave off and specifically political ones begin. But that is not the same thing at all as the claim that no distinctions can be drawn between them, or that one in some general sense underlies the other.

Especially in the two super-powers and other nuclear states, the modern military has access to destructive capabilities on a stupendous scale. The material wealth produced in the industrialized countries is so immense, compared with even the largest of traditional states, that even the use of a small proportion of available resources can generate prodigious military strength. Moreover, in most areas of the world, the military confront already largely pacified populations. In considering military 'intervention' in politics, therefore, there is some sense in posing the question, Why are governments everywhere in the modern world not 'military governments'? For, as Finer remarks, 'The armed forces have three massive political advantages over civilian organisations: a marked superiority in organisation, a highly emotionalised symbolic status, and a monopoly of arms. They form a prestigious corporation or Order, enjoying overwhelming superiority in the means of applying force. The wonder, therefore, is not why this rebels against its civilian masters but why it ever obeys them.'[87] The answer Finer goes on to provide is more or less the same as 'mine, although I shall develop it in terms of the themes and concepts of this book.

Two elements have to be separated in considering the nature of modern military rule. One is how far military personnel compose, or are the dominant part of, the higher councils of government; the other is how far the monopoly of the means of violence which the armed forces, together with the police, enjoy is used directly to sustain administrative power. While it is the former issue that has tended to brook large in the literature concerned with military 'intervention' in politics, it is the latter that is in some main respects more significant. Those governments in which military leaders have a prime role may often be, but are not necessarily, ones in which the monopoly of the means of violence is extensively used in a repressive way.

A modern army, as Finer points out, is in a certain sense a microcosm of the state as a whole.[88] The armed forces possess their own specialized systems of supply, engineering, communications and education. In countries of a low level of industrialization, they may be more advanced organizationally and technologically than the civil sector and may consequently be used to mobilize resources for economic development. But in industrialized societies the armed forces both tend to be separated from the rest of the population in virtue of their specialized training, as a distinct 'professional' group and, at the same time, are dependent upon a variety of productive and administrative resources which they cannot directly control. Administrative specialization is one factor inhibiting military direction of government or the economy, the strong pressure towards polyarchy another. 'Praetorian states' are rarely if ever wholly governed solely by military leaders in their higher councils, let alone in the more executive levels of administrative authority. Military governments have usually only managed to maintain some degree of stability in their composition and their rule where they have acknowledged reciprocal relations of polyarchy and have legitimized their position by successfully mobilizing the support of major segments of the subject population. Perlmutter's threefold typology of military regimes is useful here.[89] What he calls an 'arbitrator regime' is a mode of government in which the headquarters of the armed forces is taken over by a cabal of officers and where this group shares power with civilian political authorities. The military leadership 'arbitrates' policy decisions taken by those authorities by broadly overseeing them, but without attempting directly to take the reins of government. This type tends to be unstable, as either the political sector tends effectively to regain power or the military leadership seeks increasingly to control policy-making. In the second type, the 'ruler regime', a military council is established to directly control the executive with, however, the headquarters being composed of 'non-political' officers. Such a form of government can be more enduring, but only if it gains a considerable measure of popular legitimacy. The more it achieves such legitimacy, the more it becomes enmeshed in an administrative order distinct from the military sphere through which governmental control was obtained. Hence it tends to devolve into a third type, the 'part-army regime', or into a purely civil administration. The party-army regime is a military dictatorship, in which the military leader, supported by the high command in the headquarters, furthers a military party that dominates the loftiest councils of the state. The ruling party nevertheless has to acquire a strong level of popular support for the system to show any sort of stability. This is difficult to achieve, especially where the dictatorial element is marked. In such circumstances, the military must constantly 'patrol' the society, becoming the main policing agency, but only temporarily being able to contain the oppositional movements that develop.

We can derive from this analysis the following generalized conclusions. The structural basis for the existence of military governments in Third World states is their relative lack of development of internal administrative co-ordination, compared with the more industrialized societies. Because they often are in a significant sense 'state-nations', most such states lack the degree of centralized administrative integration achieved in the Western nation-state. Compared with traditional states, the military forces nonetheless face substantially pacified populations. The more successful the military is in 'governing', however – where 'successful governing' means that the state apparatus is increasingly able to influence the day-to-day activities of the mass of the population – the more likely it is to succumb to polyarchic pressures. In First and Second World states, those pressures tend to be all-enveloping. The military may step into the 'political arena' in various ways, but chronic military government is more or less a contradiction in terms. The most common direct relation between the military and government tends to be via the polyarchic appeal a popular military leader may secure. But this is not military rule; it is the use of the symbolic trappings of military leadership to generate political legitimacy in a polyarchic setting.

The issues raised by the existence of the modern military must concern not just the distinction between civil and military regimes, but *the use of force in the process of governing*. As Luckham says, there is no shortage of states in which 'civil liberties have been curtailed, the media browbeaten, trade unions deprived of the right to strike, opponents of the regime repressed . . . be they formally under civilian governments or under the military and whether the regime is of a conservative or progressive political tendency'.[90] What is involved here is an association of the curtailing of citizenship rights, the concentration of certain types of surveillance activity, and the systematic use of force based on the state's monopoly of the means of violence. I shall argue subsequently that in such relations can be discerned the origins of totalitarianism – a phenomenon specific to the modern state. As this comment indicates, however, tendencies towards totalitarian power do not derive from the role of the military alone, or even of the military combined with the police. Since this is a matter I shall take up in the final chapter, let me turn at this point to a consideration of the world military order.

There are three key institutional dimensions of the world military order today: super-power hegemony; the arms trade; and systems of military alliance. These each relate quite directly to one another, since the super-powers not only have the most powerful military presence but also dominate the arms trade and have constructed global systems of alliance, often involving the military training of the armies of allied states.[91] In the Lend-Lease Programme initiated during the Second World War, the Truman Doctrine that followed the War, and the McNamara reforms, the USA began to integrate military aid with the forging of a global security network. Accurate statistics on the arms trade are difficult to come by but what is clear is the increasing commerce in weaponry between the industrialized and Third World countries, some two-thirds of such commerce now moving in this direction.[92] A high proportion of this consists of major weapons systems, rather than small arms and support equipment.[93] In the period just after the Second World War, much of the weaponry exported to Third World states was of kinds being phased out of the US armed forces. But today, even in the field of the most sophisticated weapons systems, some Third World countries possess equipment as advanced as that of the American military. Whereas US policy in terms of defence transfers formerly concentrated upon states bordering the Soviet Union, increasingly arms transfers have been made to any states not directly tied by treaty to the Soviets. Several leading Western industrial powers are major arms exporters and have maintained the capacity to produce advanced military technology. But they are also heavily dependent upon US military supplies for certain basic types of advanced equipment. The USSR is easily the second largest arms exporter, although lagging some way behind the USA: the USA supplies arms to some seventy Third World countries, the Soviet Union to thirty-two.[94] Something like a third of Soviet arms transfers go to its allies in the Warsaw Pact. The two main pact systems, in fact, consume nearly three-quarters of combined world military expenditure.

However, a considerable number of countries outside the main industrialized states are also producers of advanced weapons systems, for themselves and as exporters, with others currently seeking to follow the same course. Particularly important is the potentiality of these states for the construction of nuclear weapons. Although there are only six countries known to have exploded a nuclear device, there are many more that have separable plutonium sufficient to build nuclear weaponry.[95] The Non-Proliferation Treaty of 1968 bans the transfer of nuclear weapons by nuclear states to others and has been signed by over 100 countries, although a group of governments have refused to be signatories. The treaty does not of course bar nuclear weapons for states that already possess them and does not prevent the dissemination of nuclear technology and materials for non-military uses. It is mainly because reprocessing or enrichment methods make it possible to convert the waste products from nuclear generating plants into weapons that such weaponry is likely to be available soon to a range of states. Nuclear reactors are already either in operation or in the process of being built in 48 of the 106 member states of the International Atomic Energy Agency.[96]

Bilateral and unilateral military treaties have supplied a new dimension to the international division of labour, since they increasingly go along with co-operation in the training and recruitment of military personnel and the development of military technology. The global system of alliances built up by the USA integrates these various activities. NATO, the Rio Treaty in Latin America, SEATO in South-East Asia (subsequently dissolved) and ANZUS with Australia and New Zealand, were designed to form an encircling chain of treaties across the world. To the countries thus involved the USA has since the Second World War provided some $80,000 million in assistance for military projects in the form of loans or grants.[97] Under these and other treaties the USA has made available many kinds of training personnel. It has been estimated that in the late 1960s, in Third World countries alone, there were American military advisers in contact with 88 military establishments.[98] Soviet military assistance is, so far, much less and less widespread too. The Soviets have focused attention upon Eastern Europe and upon a few strategically important clients, particularly in the Middle East, but to these they have provided very large stocks of armaments.

It is in this third sense – the world-wide diffusion of the means of waging industrialized war – that we live today in 'military societies'. There is thus some substance, given a number of strong qualifications, to the nineteenth-century thesis of the replacement of military societies by ones based upon industrialism or economic exchange relations more generally. The more highly industrialized a state is, and the more unified its administrative system, the less it tends to be the case either that production for military ends predominates over other sectors, or that direct military rule can be sustained save in short-term periods. Unfortunately and unhappily these limitations upon the scope of military power do not in themselves imply the imminence of a world without war. On the contrary, the combined spread of industrialism and of the nation-state system has served to ensure that virtually every state across the globe now possesses armed strength far in excess of that of any traditional empire.

That the world military order is influenced by capitalistic mechanisms there is no doubt. But to suppose that it is explicable wholly or even primarily as an expression of the global involvements of capitalist enterprise is plainly foolish. The nation-state is the prime vehicle of political organization in the contemporary world, recognized as holding legitimate monopoly of the means of violence by its own subject population and by other nation-states. As the possessor of the means of waging industrialized war, in a global context of the continuing application of science to the advancement of military technology, the state participates in and furthers a generalized process of militarization within the world system as a whole. Whether this can at some future point be contained, or will eventuate in a more frightful conflict than either of the preceding World Wars is, of course, still completely undetermined.

Notes

1. See, for instance – one among many – Ralf Dahrendorf, *Class and Class Conflict in Industrial Society* (Stanford: Stanford University Press, 1959).
2. The most important of these recent publications are: 'On the concept of political power', *Proceedings of the American Philosophical Society*, vol. 107, 1963, pp. 232–62; 'Some reflections on the place of force in social process', in Harry Eckstein, *Internal War*, (Glencoe: Free Press, 1964); 'On the concept of influence'. *Public Opinion Quarterly*, vol. 27,

1963, pp. 37–62; 'The political aspect of social structure and process', in David Easton, *Varieties of Political Theory* (Englewood Cliffs: Prentice-Hall, 1966). See also an earlier paper: 'Authority, legitimation and political action', reprinted in Parsons, *Structure and Process in Modern Societies* (Glencoe: Free Press, 1960) pp. 170–98. Parsons' review of Mills' book, entitled 'The distribution of power in American society', can be found in the same volume, pp. 199–225.

3. Thus Mills, in Parsons' view, shows a 'tendency to think of power as presumptively illegitimate; if people exercise considerable power, it must be because they have somehow usurped it where they had no right and they intend to use it to the detriment of others'. 'The distribution of power', p. 221.

4. Parsons, 'The distribution of power', p. 220.

5. Parsons stresses that this analysis of power marks a shift from the views set down in *The Social System*, where he states he still accepted the 'traditional' (i.e., the 'zero-sum') conception. This also means that his view of what constitutes 'political science' has also changed; whereas previously in *The Structure of Social Action* he accepted the idea that political science is a synthetic discipline, it now becomes seen as a relatively autonomous analytical discipline on a par with economics.

6. Parsons, 'On the concept of political power', p. 237.

7. Parsons, 'Authority, legitimation and political action', p. 181.

8. Parsons, 'On the concept of political power', p. 250.

9. Parsons, 'Some reflections on the place of force'.
   This typology obviously links up with the functional subsystems of society. As in most of Parsons' schemes involving the four 'functional subsystems', a regressive set of subclassifications is possible for each of the four 'media' of interaction. In the case of 'influence', for example, the pattern would look like this:

(I = integration; GA = goal-attainment; A = adaptation; PM = pattern-maintenance)

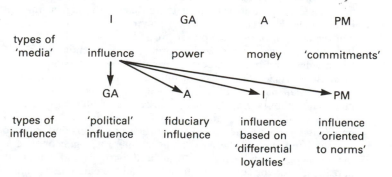

	I	GA	A	PM
types of 'media'	influence	power	money	'commitments'
	GA	A	I	PM
types of influence	'political' influence	fiduciary influence	influence based on 'differential loyalties'	influence 'oriented to norms'

10. Parsons 'Some reflections on the place of force', p. 52.
11. Parsons, 'Some reflections on the place of force', pp. 63ff.
12. These parallels are discussed in James S. Coleman's 'Comment on "On the Concept of Influence"', *Public Opinion Quarterly*, vol. 27, 1963, pp. 63–82.
13. Hans H. Gerth and C. Wright Mills (eds), *From Max Weber: Essays in Sociology* (New York: Galaxy 1958) p. 180.
14. Cf. some of Michael Crozier's comments in 'Pouvoir et organisation', *European Journal of Sociology*, vol. 5, 1964, pp. 52–64.
15. Parsons claims these concepts 'bridge the gap between the normative and factual aspects of the system in which they operate'. 'On the concept of influence', p. 45.
16. In commenting on Parsons' article on influence, Raymond Bauer writes: 'In advertising, in courtship, in all our relations, there is without doubt a large amount of nontruth, or irrelevance masking as relevant truth. The disparity between this circumstance and Parsons's position should not be regarded as a contradiction, but rather as a subject of investigation.' 'Communication as a transaction: a comment on "On the concept of influence"', *Public Opinion Quarterly*, vol. 27, 1963, p. 84.

    It is certainly true that deceit presupposes trust, but there is also a sense in which trust presupposes deceit. Neither has any meaning without the other, and to say that social life 'rests' upon the first is just as true, and misleading, as to say that it depends upon the second. If trust is 'expansionable', so is deceit; trust and deceit feed upon and intertwine with, one another.
17. Talcott Parsons, *Societies: Evolutionary and Comparative Perspectives* (Englewood Cliffs: Prentice-Hall, 1966) p. 115.
18. Cf. the attempt by Johnson to use some of Parsons' concepts together with others to produce a general theory of revolution. Chalmers Johnson, *Revolutionary Change* (Boston: Little, Brown, 1966).
19. Cf. Parsons' comment: 'We can say that the primary function of superior authority is to clearly define the situation for the lower echelons of the collectivity. The problem of overcoming opposition in the form of dispositions to non-compliance then arises from the incomplete institutionalization of the power of the higher authority holder.' 'On the concept of political power', p. 243.
20. 'On the concept of political power', p. 254.
21. Parsons has always recognized in principle the essential linkage between values and interests. See, for example, the discussion in one of his earliest articles: 'The place of ultimate values in sociological theory', *International Journal of Ethics*, vol. 45, 1935, pp. 282–316. In a much later publication, Parsons remarks, presumably with reference to Lockwood: 'I do not think it is useful to postulate a deep dichotomy between theories which give importance to beliefs and values on the one hand, and to allegedly 'realistic' interests, e.g. economic, on the other. Beliefs and values are actualized, partially and imperfectly, in realistic situations of social interaction and the outcomes are *always*

codetermined by the values and the realistic exigencies. 'Authority, legitimation and political action', p. 173. There is clearly a sense in which 'values' are prior to 'interests': to have an 'interest', an individual or group must have some kind of selective motivation, which presumes in turn some kind of 'value'. But this is very different from saying that in an *explanatory* sense values are necessarily prior to interests. And this is precisely what the whole of Parsons' theory is predicated upon. Parsons's recognition of the role of non-normative interests has not led to a systematic theoretical treatment of the interaction of values and interests. The point is that not only are the 'outcomes in realistic situations of social interaction' codetermined by values and 'realistic exigencies', but that the latter play an (often crucial) part in the *formation* and degree of 'actualization' of values.

22. Michel Foucault, *Power, Truth, Strategy* (Sydney: Feral Publications, 1979) p. 35.
23. Foucault, *Discipline and Punish: the Birth of the Prison* (London: Allen Lane, 1977) p. 131.
24. Anthony Giddens, *Central Problems in Social Theory*.
25. Michael Ignatieff, *A Just Measure of Pain* (London: Macmillan, 1978).
26. Sidney Pollard, *The Genesis of Modern Management* (London: Arnold, 1965).
27. Foucault, *Discipline and Punish*, pp. 220–1.
28. Anthony Giddens, *A Contemporary Critique of Historical Materialism*.
29. We may, however, agree with Schumpeter that 'The family, not the physical person, is the true unit of class and class theory' (Joseph Schumpeter, *Imperialism, Social Classes*, Cleveland: A.M. Welley, 1961). This is actually completely consistent with the idea that mobility is fundamental to class formation.
30. See Anthony Giddens, *The Class Structure of the Advanced Societies*, pp. 264–9.
31. David Lockwood, *The Blackcoated Worker* (London, Allen & Unwin 1958).
32. It might be pointed out that it would easily be possible to break down the notion of status group further: according, for example, to whether the status evaluations in question are made primarily by others outside the group, and rejected by those inside it, etc.
33. This is not, of course, the same as Lukács' 'class-conditioned unconsciousness'; but I believe that Lukács is correct in distinguishing qualitatively different 'levels' of class consciousness. Georg Lukács, *History and Class Consciousness* (London: Merlin Press, 1971) p. 52ff.
34. Cf. Nicos Poulantzas, *Pouvoir, politique et classes sociales de l'etat capitaliste* (Paris: F. Maspero, 1970). It is misleading, however, to speak of *classes sans conscience*, as Crozier does. See Michel Crozier, 'Classes sans conscience ou préfiguration de la société sans clas-

ses', *Archives européenes de sociologie*, 1, 1960; also 'L'ambiguité de la conscience de classe chez les employés et les petits fonctionnaires', *Cahiers internationaux de sociologie*, 28, 1955.

35. Or, to use another terminology, where there is 'overdetermination' (Louis Althusser, *For Marx*, London: Penguin, 1969, pp. 89–128).

36. Marx's *Lumpenproletariat*, according to this usage, is only an underclass when the individuals in question tend to derive from distinctive ethnic back-grounds. Leggett has referred to the underclass as the 'marginal working class', defining this as 'a sub-community of workers who belong to a subordinate ethnic or racial group which is usually proletarianised and highly segregated' (John C. Leggett, *Class, Race, and Labor*, New York: Oxford University Press 1968, p. 14).

37. See Anthony Giddens, *New Rules of Sociological Method; Studies in Social and Political Theory; Central Problems in Social Theory*.

38. Giddens, *Central Problems in Social Theory*, pp. 145 ff.

39. See Giddens, *New Rules of Sociological Method*.

40. Harry Braverman, *Labour and Monopoly Capital* (New York: Monthly Review Press, 1974).

41. Max Weber, *Economy and Society* (Berkeley: University of California Press, 1978) vol. 1, p. 223.

42. Weber, *The Methodology of the Social Sciences* (Glencoe: Free Press, 1949).

43. Wolfgang Mommsen, *The Age of Bureaucracy* (Oxford: Blackwell, 1974).

44. Cf. Arthur Mitzman, *The Iron Cage* (New York: Grosset & Dunlop, 1971).

45. Emile Durkheim, *The Division of Labour in Society* (Glencoe: Free Press, 1968).

46. Peter M. Blau, *The Dynamics of Bureaucracy* (Chicago: University of Chicago Press, 1967); see also the important discussion in Martin Albrow, *Bureaucracy* (London: Pall Mall, 1970).

47. Michel Crozier, *The Bureaucratic Phenomenon* (London: Tavistock, 1964).

48. Giddens, *Central Problems in Social Theory*, pp. 147 ff.

49. Cf. Reinhard Bendix, *Work and Authority in Industry* (New York: Harper, 1963).

50. Braverman, *Labour and Monopoly Capital*, p. 27.

51. See Russell Jacoby's review of *Labour and Monopoly Capital*, in *Telos*, no. 29, 1976; and Gavin Mackenzie, 'The political economy of the American working class', *British Journal of Sociology*, vol. 28, 1977.

52. Giddens, *The Class Structure of the Advanced Societies*, p. 111.

53. Cf. Bryan Palmer, 'Class, conception and conflict: the thrust for efficiency, managerial views of labour and working class rebellion, 1903–22', *Review of Radical Political Economy*, vol. 7, 1975; H.G.J. Aitken, *Taylorism at Watertown Arsenal* (Cambridge, Mass.: Harvard University Press, 1960); Stanley Aronowitz, *False Promises* (New York: McGraw-Hill, 1973), and 'Marx, Braverman, and the logic of capital', *Insurgent Sociologist*, Winter 1978–9.

54. Andrew L. Friedman, *Industry and Labour* (London: Macmillan, 1977).
55. Cf. Michael Buraway, *The Manufacture of Consent* (Chicago: University of Chicago Press, 1980).
56. Friedman, *Industry and Labour*, p. 7.
57. C.B. Macpherson, *The Real World of Democracy* (Oxford: Clarendon Press, 1966).
58. For a critique of functionalism, in the light of the conception of structuration, see 'Functionalism: *après la lutte*', in Giddens, *Studies in Social and Political Theory*.
59. Wolfgang Müller and Christel Neusüss, 'The "welfare-state illusion" and the contradiction between wage-labour and capital', in John Holloway and Sol Piciotto (eds), *State and Capital: a Marxist Debate* (London: Arnold, 1978) p. 34.
60. For the elements of such analysis, see Anthony Giddens, *A Contemporary Critique of Historical Materialism*.
61. T.B. Bottomore, *Karl Marx: Early Writings* (New York: McGraw-Hill, 1964) p. 125.
62. D.G. Janelle, 'Central place development in a time–space framework', *Professional Geographer*, vol. 20, 1968. See also Don Parkes and Nigel Thrift, *Times, Spaces and Places* (Chichester: Wiley, 1980), Chapter 7.
63. J. Bischoff, *A Comprehensive History of the Woollen and Worsted Manufactures* (London, 1842) p. 428. This passage is quoted and criticized in some part by Derek Gregory, who suggests that the road system was in fact rather better than it implies. See his *Regional Transformation and Industrial Revolution* (London: Macmillan, 1982, pp. 54–5).
64. Cf. Evitar Zerubavel, *Hidden Rhythms* (Chicago: University of Chicago Press, 1981).
65. Lewis Mumford, *Interpretations and Forecasts* (London: Secker & Warburg, 1973).
66. Frank Norris, *The Octopus* (London: Grant Richards, 1901) p. 42.
67. Cf. Zerubavel, *Hidden Rhythms*.
68. Derek Howse, *Greenwich Time and the Discovery of the Longitude* (New York: Oxford University Press, 1980) p. 121.
69. Stephen Kern, *The Culture of Time and Space 1880–1918* (London: Weidenfeld, 1983) p. 12.
70. Kern, *The Culture of Time*, p. 13.
71. Figures IV.1 and IV.2 from Ronald Abler, 'Effects of space-adjusting technologies on the human geography of the future', in Abler *et al.*, *Human Geography in a Shrinking World* (North Scituate: Duxbury, 1975) pp. 39 and 41.
72. Abler, 'Effects of space-adjusting technologies', p. 40.
73. Ithiel da Sola Pool, *The Social Impact of the Telephone* (Boston: MIT Press, 1977).
74. H.A. Innis, *Empire and Communications* (Oxford: Clarendon Press, 1950) p. 7.
75. Anthony Giddens, *The Nation-State and Violence*, Chapter 6.

76. Although it could be claimed McLuhan managed to do so. For a more sober, yet instructive, appraisal see in particular Elizabeth L. Eisenstein, *The Printing Revolution in Early Modern Europe* (Cambridge: Cambridge University Press, 1983).
77. Cf. Anthony Oberschall, *The Establishment of Empirical Social Research in Germany* (The Hague: Mouton, 1965). On the growth of state documentation, see B.R. Mitchell, *European Historical Statistics, 1750–1970* (New York: Columbia University Press, 1975).
78. Cf. Giddens, *The Constitution of Society*, Chapter 6.
79. Harold D. Lasswell, 'The garrison-state hypothesis today', in Samuel P. Huntingdon, *Changing Patterns of Military Politics* (Glencoe: Free Press, 1962) p. 51; H. Elan, 'H.D. Lasswell's developmental analysis', *Western Political Quarterly*, vol. 11, 1958. The thesis was first set out in Lasswell's *World Politics and Personal Insecurity* (New York: McGraw-Hill, 1935).
80. Lasswell, 'The garrison-state hypothesis', p. 54.
81. Gavin Kennedy, *Defense Economics* (London: Duckworth, 1983) p. 45. For calculations on world military expenditure, see the *World Armaments and Disarmament Yearbook, 1984* (London: Taylor & Francis).
82. Cf. Michael Mann, 'Capitalism and Militarism', in Martin Shaw, *War, State and Society* (London: Macmillan, 1984).
83. Mills's analysis is concentrated on the USA, and he does not claim that it holds in its entirety for other industrialized countries. C. Wright Mills, *The Power Elite* (New York: Oxford University Press, 1956). For versions of the 'economic' view see, for example, Paul A. Baran and Paul A. Sweezy, *Monopoly Capital* (New York: Monthly Review Press, 1966); Ernest Mandel, *Marxist Economic Theory* (London: Merit Publishers, 1968); Michael Kidron, *Western Capitalism Since the War* (London: Weidenfeld & Nicolson, 1968).
84. Kennedy, *Defense Economics*, p. 156.
85. Cf. Stanley Lieberson, 'An empirical study of military–industrial linkages', in Sam C. Sarkesian, *The Military–Industrial Complex: a Reassessment* (Beverly Hills: Sage, 1972).
86. Jacques Gansler, *The Defence Industry* (Cambridge, Mass: MIT Press, 1980).
87. S.E. Finer, *The Man on Horseback* (London: Pall Mall, 1962) p. 6.
88. Finer, *The Man on Horseback*, p. 15ff.
89. A. Perlmutter, *The Military and Politics in Modern Times* (New Haven: Yale University Press, 1977) p. 141ff.
90. Cf. Robin Luckham, 'Militarism: force, class and international conflict', in Mary Kaldor and Asbjorn Eide, *The World Military Order* (London: Macmillan, 1979) p. 245.
91. Cf. Ralph E. Lapp. *The Weapons Culture* (New York: Norton, 1968).
92. Jan Oberg, 'The new international military order: a threat to human security', in Asbjorn Eide and Marek Thee, *Problems of Contemporary Militarism* (London: Croom Helm, 1980) p. 47.
93. Mary Kaldor, *The Baroque Arsenal* (London: Deutsch, 1982) p. 133ff.

94. Kaldor and Eide, *The World Military Order*, p. 5.
95. Francis A. Beer, *Peace Against War* (San Francisco: Freeman, 1981) p. 310.
96. Cf. W. Epstein, *The Last Chance: Nuclear Proliferation and Arms Control* (New York: Free Press, 1975).
97. Kaldor, *The Baroque Arsenal*, p. 132.
98. Miles D. Wolpin, *Military Aid and Counter Revolution in the Third World* (Lexington, Mass.: Lexington Books, 1972).

Chapter V

The Nature of Modernity

(i) A 'discontinuist' approach*

The idea that human history is marked by certain 'discontinuities' and does not have a smoothy developing form is of course a familiar one and has been stressed in most versions of Marxism. My use of the term has no particular connection with historical materialism, however, and is not directed at characterising human history as a whole. There undoubtedly are discontinuities at various phases of historical development – as, for example, at the points of transition between tribal societies and the emergence of agrarian states. I am not concerned with these. I wish instead to accentuate that particular discontinuity, or set of discontinuities, associated with the modern period.

The modes of life brought into being by modernity have swept us away from *all* traditional types of social order, in quite unprecedented fashion. In both their extensionality and their intensionality the transformations involved in modernity are more profound than most sorts of change characteristic of prior periods. On the extensional plane they have served to establish forms of social interconnection which span the globe; in intensional terms they have come to alter some of the most intimate and personal features of our day-to-day existence. Obviously there are continuities between the traditional and the modern, and neither is cut of whole cloth; it is well known how misleading it can be to contrast these two in too gross a fashion. But the changes occurring over the past three or four centuries – a tiny period of historical time – have been so dramatic and so comprehensive in their impact that we get only limited

___
* *The Consequences of Modernity*, pp. 4–10.

assistance from our knowledge of prior periods of transition in trying to interpret them.

The long-standing influence of social evolutionism is one of the reasons why the discontinuist character of modernity has often not been fully appreciated. Even those theories which stress the importance of discontinuist transitions, like that of Marx, see human history as having an overall direction, governed by general dynamic principles. Evolutionary theories do indeed represent 'grand narratives', although not necessarily ones which are teleologically inspired. According to evolutionism, 'history' can be told in terms of a 'story line' which imposes an orderly picture upon the jumble of human happenings. History 'begins' with small, isolated cultures of hunters and gatherers, moves through the development of crop-growing and pastoral communities and from there to the formation of agrarian states, culminating in the emergence of modern societies in the West.

Displacing the evolutionary narrative, or deconstructing its story line, not only helps to clarify the task of analysing modernity, it also refocuses part of the debate about the so-called post-modern. History does not have the 'totalised' form attributed to it by evolutionary conceptions – and evolutionism, in one version or another, has been far more influential in social thought than the teleological philosophies of history which Lyotard and others take as their prime objects of attack. Deconstructing social evolutionism means accepting that history can not be seen as a unity, or as reflecting certain unifying principles of organisation and transformation. But it does not imply that all is chaos or that an infinite number of purely idiosyncratic 'histories' can be written. There are definite episodes of historical transition, for example, whose character can be identified and about which generalisations can be made.[1]

How should we identify the discontinuities which separate modern social institutions from the traditional social orders? Several features are involved. One is the sheer *pace of change* which the era of modernity sets into motion. Traditional civilisations may have been considerably more dynamic than other pre-modern systems, but the rapidity of change in conditions of modernity is extreme. If this is perhaps most obvious in respect of technology, it also pervades all other spheres. A second discontinuity is the *scope of change*. As different areas of the globe are drawn into interconnection with one another, waves of social transformation crash across virtually the whole of the earth's surface. A third feature concerns the intrinsic *nature of modern institutions*. Some modern social forms are simply not found in prior historical periods – such as the political system of the nation-state, the wholesale dependence of production upon inanimate power sources, or the thoroughgoing commodification of products and wage labour. Others only have a specious continuity with pre-existing social orders. An example is the city. Modern urban settlements often incorporate the sites of traditional cities, and it may look as though they have merely spread out from them. In fact, modern urbanism is ordered according to quite different principles from those which set off the pre-modern city from the countryside in prior periods.[2]

In pursuing my enquiry into the character of modernity, I want to concentrate a substantial portion of the discussion upon the themes of *security versus danger* and *trust versus risk*. Modernity, as everyone living in the closing years of the twentieth century can see, is a double-edged phenomenon. The development of modern social institutions and their worldwide spread have created vastly greater opportunities for human beings to enjoy a secure and rewarding existence than any type of pre-modern system. But modernity also has a sombre side, which has become very apparent in the present century.

On the whole, the 'opportunity side' of modernity was stressed most strongly by the classical founders of sociology. Marx and Durkheim both saw the modern era as a troubled one. But each believed that the beneficent possibilities opened up by the modern era outweighed its negative characteristics. Marx saw class struggle as the source of fundamental schisms in the capitalistic order, but at the same time envisaged the emergence of a more humane social system. Durkheim believed the further expansion of industrialism would establish a harmonious and fulfilling social life, integrated through a combination of the division of labour and moral individualism. Max Weber was the most pessimistic among the three founding fathers, seeing the modern world as a paradoxical one in which material progress was obtained only at the cost of an expansion of bureaucracy that crushed individual creativity and autonomy. Yet even he did not fully anticipate how extensive the darker side of modernity would turn out to be.

To take an example, all three authors saw that modern industrial work had degrading consequences, subjecting many human beings to the discipline of dull, repetitive labour. But it was not foreseen that the furthering of the 'forces of production' would have large-scale destructive potential in relation to the material environment. Ecological concerns do not brook large in the traditions of thought incorporated into sociology, and it is not surprising that sociologists today find it hard to develop a systematic appraisal of them.

A second example is the consolidated use of political power, particularly as demonstrated in episodes of totalitarianism. The arbitrary use of political power seemed to the sociological founders to belong primarily to the past (although sometimes having echoes in the present, as indicated in Marx's analysis of the rule of Louis Napoleon). 'Despotism' appeared to be mainly characteristic of pre-modern states. In the wake of the rise of fascism, the Holocaust, Stalinism, and other episodes of twentieth-century history, we can see that totalitarian possibilities are contained within the institutional parameters of modernity rather than being foreclosed by them. Totalitarianism is distinct from traditional despotism, but is all the more frightening as a result. Totalitarian rule connects political, military, and ideological power in more concentrated form than was ever possible before the emergence of modern nation-states.[3]

The development of military power as a general phenomenon provides a further case in point. Durkheim and Weber both lived to witness the horrendous events of the First World War, although Durkheim died before the war reached its conclusion. The conflict shattered the anticipation Durkheim had previously held that a pacific, integrated industrial order would naturally be promoted by industrialism and proved impossible to accommodate within the intellectual framework he had developed as the basis of his sociology. Weber gave more attention to the role of military power in past history than did either Marx or Durkheim. Yet he did not elaborate an account of the military in modern times, shifting the burden of his analysis towards rationalisation and bureaucratisation. None of the classical founders of sociology gave systematic attention to the phenomenon of the 'industrialisation of war'.[4]

Social thinkers writing in the late nineteenth and early twentieth centuries could not have foreseen the invention of nuclear weaponry.[5] But the connecting of industrial innovation and organisation to military power is a process that dates back to the early origins of modern industrialisation itself. That this went largely unanalysed in sociology is an indication of the strength of the view that the newly emergent order of modernity would be essentially pacific, in contrast to the militarism that had characterised previous ages. Not just the threat of nuclear confrontation, but the actuality of military conflict, form a basic part of the 'dark side' of modernity in the current century. The twentieth century is the century of war, with the number of serious military engagements involving substantial loss of life being considerably higher than in either of the two preceding centuries. In the present century thus far, over 100 million people have been killed in wars, a higher proportion of the world's population than in the nineteenth century, even allowing for overall population increase.[6] Should even a limited nuclear engagement be fought, the loss of life would be staggering, and a full superpower conflict might eradicate humanity altogether.

The world in which we live today is a fraught and dangerous one. This has served to do more than simply blunt or force us to qualify the assumption that the emergence of modernity would lead to the formation of a happier and more secure social order. Loss of a belief in 'progress' of course, is one of the factors that underlies the dissolution of 'narratives' of history. Yet there is much more at stake here than the conclusion that history 'goes not where'. We have to develop an institutional analysis of the double-edged character of modernity. In so doing, we must make good some of the limitations of the classical sociological perspectives, limitations which have continued to affect sociological thought in the present day.

(ii)   Dynamic tendencies of modernity*

. . . I use the term 'modernity' [here] in a very general sense, to refer to the institutions and modes of behaviour established first of all in post-feudal Europe, but which in the twentieth century increasingly have become world-historical in their impact. 'Modernity' can be understood as roughly equivalent to 'the industrialised world', so long as it be recognised that industrialism is not its only institutional dimension.[7] I take industrialism to refer to the social relations implied in the widespread use of material power and

---

* *Modernity and Self-Identity*, pp.14–21.

machinery in production processes. As such, it is one institutional axis of modernity. A second dimension is capitalism, where this term means a system of commodity production involving both competitive product markets and the commodification of labour power. Each of these can be distinguished analytically from the institutions of surveillance, the basis of the massive increase in organisational power associated with the emergence of modern social life. Surveillance refers to the supervisory control of subject populations, whether this control takes the form of 'visible' supervision in Foucault's sense, or the use of information to coordinate social activities. This dimension can in turn be separated from control of the means of violence in the context of the 'industrialisation of war'. Modernity ushers in an era of 'total war', in which the potential destructive power of weaponry, signalled above all by the existence of nuclear armaments, becomes immense.

Modernity produces certain distinct social forms, of which the most prominent is the nation-state. A banal observation, of course, until one remembers the established tendency of sociology to concentrate on 'society' as its designated subject-matter. The sociologist's 'society', applied to the period of modernity at any rate, is a nation-state, but this is usually a covert equation rather than an explicitly theorised one. As a sociopolitical entity the nation-state contrasts in a fundamental way with most types of traditional order. It develops only as part of a wider nation-state system (which today has become global in character), has very specific forms of territoriality and surveillance capabilities, and monopolises effective control over the means of violence.[8] In the literature of international relations, nation-states are often treated as 'actors' as 'agents' rather than 'structures' – and there is a definite justification for this. For modern states are reflexively monitored systems which, even if they do not 'act' in the strict sense of the term, follow coordinated policies and plans on a geopolitical scale. As such, they are a prime example of a more general feature of modernity, the rise of the *organisation*. What distinguishes modern organisations is not so much their size, or their bureaucratic character, as the concentrated reflexive monitoring they both permit and entail. Who says modernity says not just organisations, but organisation – the regularised control of social relations across indefinite time–space distances.

Modern institutions are in various key respects *discontinuous* with the gamut of pre-modern cultures and ways of life. One of the most obvious characteristics separating the modern era from any other period preceding it is modernity's extreme dynamism. The modern world is a 'runaway world': not only is the *pace* of social change much faster than in any prior system, so also is its *scope*, and the *profoundness* with which it affects pre-existing social practices and modes of behaviour.[9]

What explains the peculiarly dynamic character of modern social life? Three main elements, or sets of elements, are involved – and each of them is basic to the arguments deployed in this book. The first is what I call the *separation of time and space*. All cultures, of course, have possessed modes of time-reckoning of one form or another, as well as ways of situating themselves spatially. There is no society in which individuals do not have a sense of future, present and past. Every culture has some form of standardised spatial markers which designate a special awareness of place. In pre-modern settings, however, time and space were connected *through* the situatedness of place.

Larger pre-modern cultures developed more formal methods for the calculation of time and the ordering of space – such as calendars and (by modern standards) crude maps. Indeed, these were the prerequisites for the 'distancing' across time and space which the emergence of more extensive forms of social system presupposed. But in pre-modern eras, for the bulk of the population, and for most of the ordinary activities of day-to-day life, time and space remained essentially linked through place. 'When' markers were connected not just to the 'where' of social conduct, but to the substance of that conduct itself.

The separation of time from space involved above all the development of an 'empty' dimension of time, the main lever which also pulled space away from place. The invention and diffusion of the mechanical clock is usually seen – rightly – as the prime expression of this process, but it is important not to interpret this phenomenon in too superficial a way. The widespread use of mechanical timing devices facilitated, but also presumed, deeply structured changes in the tissue of everyday life – changes which could not only be local, but were inevitably universalising. A world that has a universal dating system, and globally standardised time zones, as ours does today, is socially and experientially different from all pre-modern eras. The global map, in which there is no privileging of place (a universal projection), is the correlate symbol to the clock in the 'emptying' of space. It is not just a mode of portraying 'what has always been there' – the geography of the earth – but is constitutive of quite basic transformations in social relations.

The emptying out of time and space is in no sense a unilinear development, but proceeds dialectically. Many forms of 'lived time' are possible in social settings structured through the separation of time and space. Moreover, the severance of time from space does not mean that these henceforth become mutually alien aspects of human social organisation. On the contrary: it provides the very basis for their recombination in ways that coordinate social activities without necessary reference to the particularities of place. The organisations, and organisation, so characteristic of modernity are inconceivable without the reintegration of separated time and space. Modern social organisation presumes the precise coordination of the actions of many human beings physically absent from one another; the 'when' of these actions is directly connected to the 'where', but not, as in pre-modern epochs, via the mediation of place.

We can all sense how fundamental the separation of time from space is for the massive dynamism that modernity introduces into human social affairs. The phenomenon universalises that 'use of history to make history' so intrinsic to the processes which drive modern social life away from the hold of tradition. Such historicity becomes global in form with the creation of a standardised 'past' and a universally applicable 'future': a date such as the 'year 2000' becomes a recognisable marker for the whole of humanity.

The process of the emptying of time and space is crucial for the second major influence on modernity's dynamism, the *disembedding* of social institutions. I choose the metaphor of disembedding in deliberate opposition to the concept of 'differentiation' sometimes adopted by sociologists as a means of contrasting pre-modern with modern social systems. Differentiation carries the imagery of the progressive separation of functions, such that modes of activity organised in a diffuse fashion in pre-modern societies become more specialised and precise with the advent of modernity. No doubt this idea has some validity, but it fails to capture an essential element of the nature and impact of modern institutions – the 'lifting out' of social relations from local contexts and their rearticulation across indefinite tracts of time–space. This 'lifting out' is exactly what I mean by disembedding, which is the key to the tremendous acceleration in time–space distanciation which modernity introduces.

Disembedding mechanisms are of two types, which I term 'symbolic tokens' and 'expert systems'. Taken together, I refer to these as *abstract systems*. Symbolic tokens are media of exchange which have standard value, and thus are interchangeable across a plurality of contexts. The prime example, and the most pervasively important, is money. Although the larger forms of pre-modern social system have all developed monetary exchange of one form or another, money economy becomes vastly more sophisticated and abstract with the emergence and maturation of modernity. Money brackets time (because it is a means of credit) and space (since standardised value allows transactions between a multiplicity of individuals who never physically meet one another). Expert systems bracket time and space through deploying modes of technical knowledge which have validity independent of the practitioners and clients who make use of them. Such systems penetrate virtually all aspects of social life in conditions of modernity – in respect of the food we eat, the medicines we take, the buildings we inhabit, the forms of transport we use and a multiplicity of other phenomena. Expert systems are not confined to areas of technological expertise. They extend to social relations themselves and to the intimacies of the self. The doctor, counsellor and therapist are as central to the expert systems of modernity as the scientist, technician or engineer.

Both types of expert system depend in an essential way on *trust*, a notion which, as has been indicated, plays a primary role in this book. Trust is different from the form of confidence which Georg Simmel called the 'weak inductive knowledge' involved in formal transactions.[10] Some decisions in life are based on inductive inferences from past trends, or from past experience believed in some way to be dependable for the present. This kind of confidence may be an element in trust, but it is not sufficient in itself to define a trust relation. Trust presumes a leap to commitment, a quality of 'faith' which is irreducible. It is specifically related to absence in time and space, as well as to ignorance. We have no need to trust someone who is constantly in view and whose activities can be directly monitored. Thus, for example, jobs which are monotonous or unpleasant, and poorly paid, in which the motivation to perform the work conscientiously is weak, are usually 'low-trust' positions. 'High-trust' posts are those carried out largely outside the presence

of management or supervisory staff.[11] Similarly, there is no requirement of trust when a technical system is more or less completely
known to a particular individual. In respect of expert systems, trust
brackets the limited technical knowledge which most people possess
about coded information which routinely affects their lives.

Trust, of varying sorts and levels, underlies a host of day-to-day
decisions that all of us take in the course of orienting our activities.
But trusting is not by any means always the result of consciously
taken decisions: more often, it is a generalised attitude of mind that
underlies those decisions, something which has its roots in the
connection between trust and personality development. We *can*
make the decision to trust, a phenomenon which is common because of the third underlying element of modernity (already mentioned, but also further discussed below): its intrinsic reflexivity.
But the faith which trust implies also tends to resist such calcula-
tive decision-making.

Attitudes of trust, in relation to specific situations, persons or
systems, and on a more generalised level, are directly connected
to the psychological *security* of individuals and groups. Trust and
security, risk and danger: these exist in various historically unique
conjunctions in conditions of modernity. The disembedding mechanisms, for example, purchase wide arenas of relative security in
daily social activity. People living in the industrialised countries,
and to some extent elsewhere today, are generally protected from
some of the hazards routinely faced in pre-modern times – such as
those emanating from inclement nature. On the other hand, new
risks and dangers are created through the disembedding mechanisms themselves, and these may be local or global. Foodstuffs
purchased with artificial ingredients may have toxic characteristics
absent from more traditional foods; environmental hazards might
threaten the ecosystems of the earth as a whole.

Modernity is essentially a post-traditional order. The transformation of time and space, coupled with the disembedding mechanisms,
propel social life away from the hold of pre-established precepts or
practices. This is the context of the thoroughgoing *reflexivity* which
is the third major influence on the dynamism of modern institutions. The reflexivity of modernity has to be distinguished from the
reflexive monitoring of action intrinsic to all human activity. Modernity's reflexivity refers to the susceptibility of most aspects of
social activity, and material relations with nature, to chronic revi-

sion in the light of new information or knowledge. Such information or knowledge is not incidental to modern institutions, but
constitutive of them – a complicated phenomenon, because many
possibilities of reflection about reflexivity exist in modern social
conditions. As the discussion of *Second Chances* indicated, the
social sciences play a basic role in the reflexivity of modernity: they
do not simply 'accumulate knowledge' in the way in which the
natural sciences may do.

Separation of time and space: the condition for the articulation
of social relations across wide spans of time–space, up to and
including global systems

Disembedding mechanisms: consist of symbolic tokens and
expert systems (these together = abstract systems);
disembedding mechanisms separate interaction from the
particularities of locales

Institutional reflexivity: the regularised use of knowledge about
circumstances of social life as a constitutive element in its
organisation and transformation

Figure V.1 The dynamism of modernity

In respect both of social and natural scientific knowledge, the
reflexivity of modernity turns out to confound the expectations of
Enlightenment thought – although it is the very product of that
thought. The original progenitors of modern science and philosophy believed themselves to be preparing the way for securely founded knowledge of the social and natural worlds: the claims of
reason were due to overcome the dogmas of tradition, offering a
sense of certitude in place of the arbitrary character of habit and
custom. But the reflexivity of modernity actually undermines the
certainty of knowledge, even in the core domains of natural science.
Science depends, not on the inductive accumulation of proofs, but
on the methodological principle of doubt. No matter how cherished, and apparently well established, a given scientific tenet
might be, it is open to revision – or might have to be discarded
altogether – in the light of new ideas or findings. The integral
relation between modernity and radical doubt is an issue which,
once exposed to view, is not only disturbing to philosophers but
is *existentially troubling* for ordinary individuals.

(iii)   Trust and risk in social life*

If there are features of the psychology of trust which are universal, or near-universal, there are also fundamental contrasts between the conditions of trust relations in pre-modern cultures and those of the modern world. It is not only trust that we have to consider here, but broad aspects of the connections between trust and risk, and between security and danger. It is a risky business in itself to draw generalised contrasts between the modern era and the whole gamut of pre-modern social orders. The abruptness and extent of the discontinuities between modernity and pre-modern institutions, however, justifies the attempt, although inevitably over-simplifications are involved. Table V.I provides an overall orientation to the distinctions I want to make between environments of trust and of risk.

In all pre-modern cultures, including the large agrarian civilisations, for reasons already discussed, the level of time-space distanciation is relatively low as compared with conditions of modernity. Ontological security in the pre-modern world has to be understood primarily in relation to contexts of trust, and forms of risk or danger, anchored in the local circumstances of place. Because of its inherent connection with absence, trust is always bound up with modes of organising 'reliable' interactions across time-space.

Four localised contexts of trust tend to predominate in pre-modern cultures, although each of these has many variations according to the particular social order in question. The first context of trust is the kinship system, which in most pre-modern settings provides a relatively stable mode of organising 'bundles' of social relations across time and space. Kinship connections are often a focus of tension and conflict. But however many conflicts they involve and anxieties they provoke, they are very generally bonds which can be relied upon in the structuring of actions in fields of time-space. This is true on the level of both fairly impersonal and more personal connections. In other words, kinspeople can usually be relied upon to meet a range of obligations more or less regardless of whether they feel personally sympathetic towards the specific individuals involved. Moreover, kinship often does provide a stabilising network of amicable or intimate

---

* *The Consequences of Modernity*, pp.100–11.

Table V.1 Environments of trust and risk in pre-modern and modern
cultures

Pre-modern *General context*: overriding importance of localised trust	Modern *General context*: trust relations vested in disembedded abstract systems
1. *Kinship relations* as an organising device for stabilising social ties across time–space	1. *Personal relationships* of friendship or sexual intimacy as means of stabilising social ties
2. *The local community* as a *place*, providing a familiar *milieu*	2. *Abstract systems* as a means of stabilising relations across indefinite spans of time–space
3. *Religious cosmologies* as modes of belief and ritual practice providing a providential interpretation of human life and of nature	3. *Future-oriented*, counter-factual thought as a mode of connecting past and present
4. *Tradition* as a means of connecting present and future; past-oriented in reversible time	
1. Threats and dangers emanating from *nature*, such as the prevalence of infectious diseases, climatic unreliability, floods, or other natural disasters	1. Threats and dangers emanating from the *reflexivity* of modernity
2. The threat of *human violence* from marauding armies, local warlords, brigands, or robbers	2. The threat of *human violence* from the industrialisation of war
3. Risk of a *fall from religious grace* or of malicious magical influence	3. The threat of *personal meaningless* deriving from the reflexivity of modernity as applied to the self

relations which endure across time-space. Kinship, in sum, provides
a nexus of reliable social connections which, in principle and very
commonly in practice, form an organising medium of trust relations.

Much the same can be said of the local community. We should
avoid the romanticised view of community which has often surfaced
in social analysis when traditional cultures are compared to the
modern. I mean here to stress the importance of *localised*

relations organised in terms of *place*, where place has not yet become transformed by distanciated time-space relations. In the large majority of pre-modern settings, including most cities, the local *milieu* is the site of clusters of interweaving social relations, the low spatial span of which provides for their solidity in time. Migrations of population, nomadism, and the long-distance journeys of merchants and adventurers were common enough in pre-modern times. But the large majority of the population were relatively immobile and isolated, as compared to the regular and dense forms of mobility (and awareness of other ways of life) provided for by modern means of transportation. The locality in pre-modern contexts is the focus of, and contributes to, ontological security in ways that are substantially dissolved in circumstances of modernity.

A third influence is that of religious cosmology. Religious beliefs can be a source of extreme anxiety or despair – so much so that they must be included as one of the main parameters of (experienced) risk and danger in many pre-modern settings. But in other respects religious cosmologies provide moral and practical interpretations of personal and social life, as well as of the natural world, which represent an environment of security for the believer. The Christian deity commands us, 'Trust in me, for I am the one true God!' While most religions are not so monotheistic, the idea of reliance upon supernatural beings or forces is a common feature of many otherwise different religious beliefs. Religion is an organising medium of trust in more than one way. Not only deities and religious forces provide providentially dependable supports: so also do religious functionaries. Most important of all, religious beliefs typically inject reliability into the experience of events and situations and form a framework in terms of which these can be explained and responded to.

As with the other contexts of trust in pre-moder orders, I place the emphasis here upon religion as something that generates a sense of the reliability of social and natural events, and thus contributes to the bracketing of time–space. It is possible that religion is connected psychologically to trust mechanisms in terms of the personages and forces it represents in such a way that these are directly expressive of trust – or its absence – in parental figures. Certainly Freud suggested as much,[12] and many other authors influenced by psychoanalysis have agreed. Erikson is a case in point: the 'faith' which trust presupposes and which first of all is vested in the infant's caretakers, he says, has its 'institutional safe-guard' in organised religion.

> Trust born of care is, in fact, the touchstone of the *actuality* of a given religion. All religions have in common the periodical childlike surrender to a provider or providers who dispense earthly fortune as well as spiritual health . . . [and] the insight that individual trust must become a common faith, individual mistrust a commonly formulated evil, while the individual's restoration must become part of the ritual practice of many, and must become a sign of trustworthiness in the community.[13]

Even given the extraordinary diversity of the world's religions, it is difficult to resist the conclusion that there must be some element of validity in this view; however, the standpoint I wish to develop here does not depend primarily upon it.

The fourth main context of trust relations in pre-modern cultures is tradition itself. Tradition, unlike religion, does not refer to any particular body of beliefs and practices, but to the manner in which those beliefs and practices are organised, especially in relation to time. Tradition reflects a distinct mode of structuring temporality (which also has direct implications for action across space). Lévi-Strauss's notion of 'reversible time' is central to understanding the temporality of traditional beliefs and activities. Reversible time is the temporality of repetition and is governed by the logic of repetition – the past is a means of organising the future. The orientation to the past which is characteristic of tradition does not differ from the outlook of modernity only in being backward-looking rather than forward-looking; this is in fact too crude a way to express the contrast. Rather, neither 'the past' nor 'the future' is a discrete phenomenon, separated from the 'continuous present,' as in the case of the modern outlook. Past time is incorporated into present practices, such that the horizon of the future curves back to inter-sect with what went before.

Tradition is routine. But it is routine which is intrinsically mean-ingful, rather than merely empty habit for habit's sake. Time and space are not the contentless dimensions they become with the development of modernity but are contextually implicated in the nature of lived activities. The meanings of routine activities lie in the general respect or even reverence intrinsic to tradition and in the connection of tradition with ritual. Ritual often has a compulsive aspect to it, but it is also deeply comforting, for it infuses a given set of practices with a sacramental quality. Tradition, in sum, contributes in basic fashion to ontological security in so far as it sustains trust in the continuity of past, present, and future, and connects such trust to routinised social practices.

To specify these various contexts of trust in pre-modern cultures is not to say that traditional settings were comforting and psychologically snug, while modern ones are not. There are some definite respects in which levels of ontological insecurity are higher in the modern world than in most circumstances of pre-modern social life, for reasons I shall try to identify. Yet the settings of traditional cultures were in a generic way fraught with anxieties and uncertainties. I refer to these, taken together, as the environment of risk characteristic of the pre-modern world.

The risk environment of traditional cultures was dominated by the hazards of the physical world. Hobbes's celebrated observation that, in a state of nature, human life would be 'nasty, brutish, and short' is not inaccurate if it is read as a description of the real life circumstances of many individuals in pre-modern cultures. Rates of infant mortality as well as death of women in childbirth were by modern standards extremely high. For those who survived childhood, life expectancy was relatively low and many people suffered from chronic illnesses as well as being vulnerable to infectious diseases of different kinds. There is some evidence that hunters and gatherers, especially those inhabiting naturally bountiful areas, may have been less subject to infectious illness than individuals living in fixed local communities or urban areas in larger premodern societies,[14] but even they were certainly not free from the range of endemic illnesses which abounded in pre-modern times. All types of pre-modern social order were affected, often in drastic ways, by the vagaries of climate and had little protection against natural disasters such as floods, storms, excessive rainfall, or drought.

To the unstable nature of social life in relation to the physical world we have to add, as a further source of insecurity, the prevalence of human violence. The major contrasts to be drawn here are between the larger pre-modern social orders and the modern social universe. The level of violence within and between hunting and gathering cultures appears generally to have been quite low, and there were no specialised warriors. With the appearance of armed soldiery, the situation is quite different. Most agrarian states were based in a very direct way upon military power. Yet, as was mentioned earlier, in such states the monopoly of control of the means of violence on the part of the ruling authorities was always far from complete. Such states were never internally pacified by the standards of modern nation-states. Few groups in the population could feel safe for lengthy periods from violence or the threat of violence from invading armies, marauders, local warlords, brigands, robbers, or pirates. Modern urban *milieux* are often considered dangerous because of the risk of being attacked or mugged. But not only is this level of violence characteristically minor as compared with many pre-modern settings; such *milieux* are only relatively small pockets within wider territorial areas, in which security against physical violence is vastly greater than ever was possible in regions of comparable size in the traditional world.

Finally we have to draw special attention to the dual influence of religion. If religious beliefs and practices commonly provide a refuge from the tribulations of day-to-day life, they can also, as noted, be an intrinsic source of anxiety and mental apprehension. In part this is due to the fact that religion permeates many aspects of social activity – the threats and dangers of nature, for example may be experienced through the codes and symbols of religion. Mainly, however, it is because religion normally occupies the very psychological site of potential existential anxiety. How far religion creates its own specific terrors at this site is no doubt widely variable. Probably those forms of religious belief and practice which Weber called 'salvation religions' are most prone to infect daily life with existential fears, invoking as they do a tension between sin and the promise of salvation in an afterlife.

With the development of modern social institutions, something of a balance between trust and risk, security and danger persists. But the main elements involved are quite different from those which predominated in the pre-modern era. In conditions of modernity, just as in all cultural settings, human activities remain situated and contextualised. But the impact of the three great dynamic forces of modernity – the separation of time and space, disembedding mechanisms, and institutional reflexivity – disengages some basic forms of trust relation from the attributes of local contexts.

None of the four main foci of trust and ontological security in pre-modern settings have a comparable importance in circumstances of modernity. Kinship relations, for the majority of the population, remain important, especially within the nuclear family, but they are no longer the carriers of intensively organised social ties across time–space. Such a statement is indisputably valid, in spite of the caution with which the thesis that modernity produces the decline of the family has to be viewed and in spite of the fact that some local *milieux* continue to be the hub of substantial kinship networks of rights and obligations.

The primacy of place in pre-modern settings has been largely destroyed by disembedding and time–space distanciation. Place has become phantasmagoric because the structures by means of which it is constituted are no longer locally organised. The local and the global, in other words, have become inextricably intertwined. Feelings of close attachment to or identification with places still persist. But these are themselves disembedded: they do not just express locally based practices and involvements but are shot through with much more distant influences. Even the smallest of neighbourhood stores, for example, probably obtains its goods from all over the world. The local community is not a saturated environment of familiar, taken-for-granted meanings, but in some large part a locally-situated expression of distanciated relations. And everyone living in the different locales of modern societies is aware of this. Whatever security individuals experience as a result of the familiarity of place rests as much upon stable forms of disembedded relations as upon the particularities of location. If this is more obvious when one shops at the local supermarket than at the corner grocery, the difference is not a fundamental one.[15]

The declining impact of religion and tradition has been so frequently discussed in the literature of the social sciences that we can deal with this quite briefly. Secularisation is no doubt a complex matter and does not seem to result in the complete disappearance of religious thought and activity – probably because of the purchase of religion upon some of the existential questions previously referred to. Yet most of the situations of modern social life are manifestly incompatible with religion as a pervasive influence upon day-to-day life. Religious cosmology is supplanted by reflexively organised knowledge, governed by empirical observation and logical thought, and focused upon material technology and socially applied codes. Religion and tradition were always closely linked, and the latter is even more thoroughly undermined than the former by the reflexivity of modern social life, which stands in direct opposition to it.

The pre-modern 'environment of risk' similarly becomes transformed. In conditions of modernity, the dangers we face no longer derive primarily from the world of nature. Of course, hurricanes, earthquakes, and other natural disasters still occur. But for the most part our relations with the physical world are radically different from those of previous ages – especially in the industrialised sectors of the globe, but in some degree everywhere. At first glance, the ecological dangers that we confront today might seem similar to the hazards of nature encountered in the pre-modern era. The contrast, however, is a very marked one. Ecological threats are the outcome of socially organised knowledge, mediated by the impact of industrialism upon the material environment. They are part of what I shall call a new *risk profile* introduced by the advent of modernity. By a risk profile I mean the particular portmanteau of threats or dangers characteristic of modern social life.

The threat of military violence remains part of the risk profile of modernity. However, its character has changed substantially, in conjunction with the altered nature of control of the means of violence in relation to war. We live today in a global military order in which, as a result of the industrialisation of war, the scale of the destructive power of the weaponry now diffused across the world is massively greater than has ever existed before. The possibility of nuclear conflict poses dangers no previous generations have had to face. Yet this development has coincided with processes of internal pacification within states. Civil war has become a relatively uncommon, if by no means unknown, phenomenon in developed nations; but in premodern times, at least after the first development of state organisations, something akin to civil war – divisions of military power, accompanied by frequent outbreaks of conflict – was more like the norm than the exception.

Risk and danger, as experienced in relation to ontological security, have become secularised along with most other aspects of social life. A world structured mainly by humanly created risks has little place for divine influences, or indeed for the magical propitiation of cosmic forces or spirits. It is central to modernity that risks can in principle be assessed in terms of generalisable knowledge about potential dangers – an outlook in which notions of *fortuna* mostly survive as marginal forms of superstition. Where risk is *known* to be risk, it is experienced differently from circumstances in which notions of *fortuna* prevail. To recognise the existence of a risk or set of risks is to accept not just the possibility that things might go wrong, but that this possibility cannot be eliminated. The phenomenology of such a situation is part of the cultural experience of modernity in general, discussed in more detail below. Even where the hold of traditional religion becomes relaxed, however, conceptions of fate do not wholly disappear. Precisely where risks are greatest – either in terms of the perceived probability that an unwelcome happening will occur or in terms of the devastating consequences that ensue if a given event goes awry – *fortuna* tends to return.

(iv) Modernity and self-identity*

Transformations in self-identity and globalisation, I want to propose, are the two poles of the dialectic of the local and the global in conditions of high modernity. Changes in intimate aspects of personal life, in other words, are directly tied to the establishment of social connections of very wide scope. I do not mean to deny the existence of many kinds of more intermediate connections – between, for example, localities and state organisations. But the level of time–space distanciation introduced by high modernity is so extensive that, for the first time in human history, 'self' and 'society' are interrelated in a global milieu.

Various factors, in circumstances of high modernity, directly influence the relation between self-identity and modern institutions . . . Modernity introduces an elemental dynamism into human affairs, associated with changes in trust mechanisms and in risk environments. I do not think it is true that, as some have suggested, the modern age is specifically one of high anxiety, as contrasted to preceding eras. Anxieties and insecurities have plagued other ages besides ours, and there is probably little justification for the assumption sometimes made that life in smaller, more traditional cultures had a more even tenor than that of today. But the content and form of prevalent anxieties certainly have become altered.

---

* *Modernity and Self-Identity*, pp.32–4.

The reflexivity of modernity extends into the core of the self. Put in another way, in the context of a post-traditional order, the self becomes a *reflexive project*. Transitions in individuals' lives have always demanded psychic reorganisation, something which was often ritualised in traditional cultures in the shape of *rites de passage*. But in such cultures, where things stayed more or less the same from generation to generation on the level of the collectivity, the changed identity was clearly staked out – as when an individual moved from adolescence into adulthood. In the settings of modernity, by contrast, the altered self has to be explored and constructed as part of a reflexive process of connecting personal and social change. This is a clear emphasis in Wallerstein and Blakeslee's study [Judith Wallerstein and Sandra Blakeslee, *Second Chances*, (London: Bantam, 1989)], and their work is not only a document about such a process, but also a constitutive contribution to it. The 'new sense of self' which, as they say, an individual has to cultivate after marital separation, is built as part of a process of pioneering innovative social forms, such as those involved in modern step-parenting (the very term 'parenting' is a relatively recent invention, helping to constitute what it now describes). The process of 'reaching back to one's early experiences' which Wallerstein and Blakeslee analyse is precisely part of a reflexive mobilising of self-identity; it is not confined to life's crises, but a general feature of modern social activity in relation to psychic organisation.

In such circumstances, abstract systems become centrally involved not only in the institutional order of modernity but also in the formation and continuity of the self. The early socialisation of children, for example, tends increasingly to depend on the advice and instruction of experts (paediatricians and educators), rather than on the direct initiation of one generation by another – and this advice and instruction is itself reflexively responsive to research in process. As academic disciplines, sociology and psychology are thus bound up in a direct way with the reflexivity of the self. Yet the most distinctive connection between abstract systems and the self is to be found in the rise of modes of therapy and counselling of all kinds. One way of interpreting the development of therapy is in purely negative fashion, as a response to the debilitating effects of modern institutions on self-experience and the emotions. Modernity, it might be said, breaks down the protective framework of the small community and of tradition, replacing these with much larger, impersonal organisations. The individual feels bereft and alone in a world in which she or he lacks the psychological supports and the sense of security provided by more traditional settings. Therapy offers someone to turn to, a secular version of the confessional.

I do not want to say that this standpoint should be dismissed altogether, since no doubt it contains elements of validity. But there is good reason to suppose that it is substantially inadequate. Self-identity becomes problematic in modernity in a way which contrasts with self–society relations in more traditional contexts; yet this is not only a situation of loss, and it does not imply either that anxiety levels necessarily increase. Therapy is not simply a means of coping with novel anxieties, but an expression of the reflexivity of the self – a phenomenon which, on the level of the individual, like the broader institutions of modernity, balances opportunity and potential catastrophe in equal measure . . .

(v) Love and sexuality*

Intimacy as democracy

A democratisation of the private sphere is today not only on the agenda, but is an implicit quality of all personal life that comes under the aegis of the pure relationship. The fostering of democracy in the public domain was at first largely a male project – in which women eventually managed, mostly by dint of their own struggle, to participate. The democratisation of personal life is a less visible process, in part precisely because it does not occur in the public arena, but its implications are just as profound. It is a process in which women have thus far played the prime role, even if in the end the benefits achieved, as in the public sphere, are open to everyone.

The meaning of democracy

First of all it might be worth considering what democracy means, or can mean, in its orthodox sense. There is much debate about the

---

* *The Transformation of Intimacy*, pp.184–96.

specifics of democratic representation and so forth, but I shall not concern myself with these issues here. If the various approaches to political democracy be compared, as David Held has shown, most have certain elements in common.[16] They are concerned to secure 'free and equal relations' between individuals in such a way as to promote certain outcomes:

(1)   The creation of circumstances in which people can develop their potentialities and express their diverse qualities. A key objective here is that each individual should respect others' capabilities as well as their ability to learn and enhance their aptitudes.

(2)   Protection from the arbitrary use of political authority and coercive power. This presumes that decisions can in some sense be negotiated by those they affect, even if they are taken on behalf of a majority by a minority.

(3)   The involvement of individuals in determining the conditions of their association. The presumption in this case is that individuals accept the authentic and reasoned character of others' judgements.

(4)   Expansion of the economic opportunity to develop available resources – including here the assumption that when individuals are relieved of the burdens of physical need they are best able to achieve their aims.

The idea of autonomy links these various aspirations. Autonomy means the capacity of individuals to be self-reflective and self-determining: 'to deliberate, judge, choose and act upon different possible courses of action'.[17] Clearly autonomy in this sense could not be developed while political rights and obligations were closely tied to tradition and fixed prerogatives of property. Once these were dissolved, however, a movement towards autonomy became both possible and seen to be necessary. An overwhelming concern with how individuals might best determine and regulate the conditions of their association is characteristic of virtually all interpretations of modern democracy. The aspirations that compose the tendency towards autonomy can be summarised as a general principle, the 'principle of autonomy':

individuals should be free and equal in the determination of the conditions of their own lives; that is, they should enjoy equal rights (and, accordingly, equal obligations) in the specification of the framework which generates and limits the opportunities available to them, so long as they do not deploy this framework to negate the rights of others.[18]

Democracy hence implies not just the right to free and equal self-development, but also the constitutional limitation of (distributive) power. The 'liberty of the strong' must be restrained, but this is not a denial of all authority – or it only becomes so in the case of anarchism. Authority is justifiable to the degree that it recognises the principle of autonomy, in other words, to the extent to which defensible reasons can be given as to why compliance enhances autonomy, either now or in the future. Constitutional authority can be understood as an implicit contract which has the same form as conditions of association explicitly negotiated between equals.

It is no good proposing a principle of autonomy without saying something about the conditions of its realisation. What are those conditions? One is that there must be equality in influencing outcomes in decision-making – in the political sphere this is usually sought after by the 'one person one vote' rule. The expressed preferences of each individual must have equal ranking, subject in certain instances to qualifications made necessary by the existence of justified authority. There must also be effective participation; the means must be provided for individuals to make their voices heard.

A forum for open debate has to be provided. Democracy means discussion, the chance for the 'force of the better argument' to count as against other means of determining decisions (of which the most important are policy decisions). A democratic order provides institutional arrangements for mediation, negotiation and the reaching of compromises where necessary. The conduct of open discussion is itself a means of democratic education: participation in debate with others can lead to the emergence of a more enlightened citizenry. In some part such a consequence stems from a broadening of the individual's cognitive horizons. But it also derives from an acknowledgement of legitimate diversity – that is, pluralism – and from emotional education. A politically educated contributor to dialogue is able to channel her or his emotions in a positive way: to reason from conviction rather than engage in ill-thought through polemics or emotional diatribes.

Public accountability is a further basic characteristic of a democratic polity. In any political system decisions must often be taken on behalf of others. Public debate is normally only possible in relation to certain issues or at particular junctures. Decisions taken, or policies forged, however, must be open to public scrutiny should the need arise. Accountability can never be continuous and therefore stands in tandem with trust. Trust, which comes from accountability and openness, and also protects them, is a thread running through the whole of democratic political order. It is a crucial component, although not exhaustive of, political legitimacy.

Institutionalising the principle of autonomy means specifying rights and obligations, which have to be substantive, not just formal. Rights specify the privileges which come with membership of the polity but they also indicate the duties which individuals have *vis-à-vis* each other and the political order itself. Rights are essentially forms of empowerment, they are enabling devices. Duties specify the price that has to be paid for the rights accorded. In a democratic polity, rights and duties are negotiated and can never be simply assumed – in this respect they differ decisively from, for example, the mediaeval *droit de seigneur* or other rights established simply by virtue of an individual's social position. Rights and duties thus have to be made a focus of continual reflexive attention.

Democracy, it should be emphasised, does not necessitate sameness, as its critics have often asserted. It is not the enemy of pluralism. Rather, as suggested above, the principle of autonomy encourages difference – although it insists that difference should not be penalised. Democracy is an enemy of privilege, where privilege is defined as the holding of rights or possessions to which access is not fair and equal for all members of the community. A democratic order does not imply a generic process of 'levelling down', but instead provides for the elaboration of individuality.

Ideals are not reality. How far any concrete political order could develop such a framework in full is problematic. In this sense there are utopian elements in these ideas. On the other hand, it could also be argued that the characteristic trend of development of modern societies is towards their realisation. The quality of utopianism, in other words, is balanced by a clear component of realism.[19]

The democratising of personal life

The possibility of intimacy means the promise of democracy: this is the theme I have suggested in earlier chapters . . . The structural source of this promise is the emergence of the pure relationship, not only in the area of sexuality but also in those of parent–child relations, and other forms of kinship and friendship. We can envisage the development of an ethical framework for a democratic personal order, which in sexual relationships and other personal domains conform to a model of confluent love.

As in the public sphere, the distance between ideals and reality is considerable. In the arena of heterosexual relations in particular, . . . there are profound sources of strain. Deeply embedded psychological, as well as economic, differences between the sexes stand in the way. Yet utopianism here can again readily be offset by realism. The changes that have helped transform personal environments of action are already well advanced, and they tend towards the realisation of democratic qualities.

The principle of autonomy provides the guiding thread and the most important substantive component of these processes. In the arena of personal life, autonomy means the successful realisation of the reflexive project of self – the condition of relating to others in an egalitarian way. The reflexive project of self must be developed in such a fashion to permit autonomy in relation to the past, this in turn facilitating a colonising of the future. Thus conceived, self-autonomy permits that respect for others' capabilities which is intrinsic to a democratic order. The autonomous individual is able to treat others as such and to recognise that the development of their separate potentialities is not a threat. Autonomy also helps to provide the personal boundaries, needed for the successful management of relationships. Such boundaries are transgressed whenever one person uses another as a means of playing out old psychological dispositions, or where a reciprocal compulsiveness, as in the case of codependence, is built up.

The second and third conditions of democracy in the public sphere noted above bear very directly upon the democratisation of personal life. Violent and abusive relationships are common in the sexual domain and between adults and children. Most such violence comes from men and is directed towards beings weaker than themselves. As an emancipatory ideal of democracy, the prohibition of violence is of basic importance. Coercive influences in relationships, however, obviously can take forms other than physical violence. Individuals may be prone, for example, to engage in emotional or verbal abuse of one another; marriage, so the saying goes, is a poor substitute for respect. Avoidance of emotional abuse is perhaps the most difficult aspect of the equalising of power in relationships; but the guiding principle is clearly respect for the independent views and personal traits of the other. 'Without respect', as one guide to intimacy puts it, 'ears turn deaf, attitudes sour, and eventually you can't figure out what you're doing living with someone so incompetent, stupid, unreliable, insensitive, ugly, smelly, untidy . . . It makes you wonder why you chose your partner in the first place. "I must have been out of my mind".'[20]

'The involvement of individuals in determining the conditions of their own association' – this statement exemplifies the ideals of the pure relationship. It expresses a prime difference between traditional and present-day marriage and gets to the heart of the democratising possibilities of the transformation of intimacy. It applies, of course, not just to the initiation of a relationship but to the reflexivity inherent in its continuance – or its dissolution. Not just respect for the other, but an opening-out to that person, are needed for this criterion to be met. An individual whose real intentions are hidden from a partner cannot offer the qualities needed for a cooperative determination of the conditions of the relationship. Any and every therapeutic text on the subject of relationships will demonstrate why revelation to the other – as a means of communication rather than emotional dumping – is a binding aspiration of democratically ordered interaction.

Rights and obligations: as I have tried to make clear, in some part these define what intimacy actually is. Intimacy should not be understood as an interactional description, but as a cluster of prerogatives and responsibilities that define agendas of practical activity. The importance of rights as means for the achievement of intimacy can easily been seen from the struggle of women to achieve equal status in marriage. The right of women to initiate divorce, to take one instance, which seems only a negative sanction, actually has a major equilibrating effect. Its balancing consequences do more than empower escape from an oppressive relationship, important though this is. They limit the capability of the husband to impose his dominion and thereby contribute to the translation of coercive power into egalitarian communication.

No rights without obligations – this elementary precept of political democracy applies also to the realm of the pure relationship. Rights help dissolve arbitrary power only in so far as they carry responsibilities towards the other which draw privileges into an equilibrium with obligations. In relationships as elsewhere, obligations have to be treated as revisable in the light of negotiations carried on within them.

What of accountability and its connection to authority? Both accountability and authority – where it exists – in pure relationships are deeply bound up with trust. Trust without accountability is likely to become one-sided, that is, to slide into dependence; accountability without trust is impossible because it would mean the continual scrutiny of the motives and actions of the other. Trust entails the trustworthiness of the other – according 'credit' that does not require continual auditing, but which can be made open to inspection periodically if necessary. Being regarded as trustworthy by a partner is a recognition of personal integrity, but in an egalitarian setting such integrity means also revealing reasons for actions if called upon to do so – and in fact having good reasons for any actions which affect the life of the other.

Authority in pure relationships between adults exists as 'specialisation' – where one person has specially developed capabilities which the other lacks. Here one cannot speak of authority over the other in the same sense as in parent–child relations, particularly where very young children are involved. Can a relationship between a parent and young child be democratic? It can, and should be, in exactly the same sense as is true of a democratic political order.[21] It is a right of the child, in other words, to be treated as a putative equal of the adult. Actions which cannot be negotiated directly with a child, because he or she is too young to grasp what is entailed, should be capable of counterfactual justification. The presumption is that agreement could be reached, and trust sustained, if the child were sufficiently autonomous to be able to deploy arguments on an equal basis to the adult.

Mechanisms

In the political sphere democracy involves the creation of a constitution and, normally, a forum for the public debate of policy issues. What are the equivalent mechanisms in the context of the pure relationship? So far as heterosexual relationships go, the marriage contract used to be a bill of rights, which essentially formalised the 'separate but unequal' nature of the tie. The translation of marriage into a signifier of commitment, rather than a determinant of it, radically alters this situation. All relationships which approximate to the pure form maintain an implicit 'rolling contract' to which appeal may be made by either partner when situations arise felt to be unfair or oppressive. The rolling contract is a constitutional device which underlies, but is also open to negotiation through, open discussion by partners about the nature of the relationship.

Here is a 'rule book', drawn up in a self-help manual aimed at helping women to develop more satisfying heterosexual relationships. The individual, the author suggests, should first of all catalogue the problems that have arisen for her in previous relationships – those she sees mainly as her own doing and those perpetrated by her previous lovers. She should share the rule book with her partner, who should develop a convergent set of rules:

> *Rule 1*: When I find myself trying to impress a man I like by talking so much about myself that I'm not asking him any questions, I'll stop performing and focus on whether he is right for me.
> *Rule 2*: I'll express my negative feelings as soon as I become aware of them, rather than waiting until they build up – even if it means upsetting my partner.
> *Rule 3*: I'll work on healing my relationship with my ex-husband by looking at how I set myself up to be hurt, and I won't talk about him as if I'm the victim and he's the villain.
> *Rule 4*: When my feelings are hurt, I'll tell my partner how I'm feeling rather than pouting, getting even, pretending I don't care or acting like a little girl.
> *Rule 5*: When I find myself filling in the blanks ['dead' areas in the relationship], I'll stop and ask myself if my partner has given back much to me lately. If the hasn't, I'll ask him for what I need rather than making things better myself.
> *Rule 6*: When I find myself giving unsolicited advice or treating my partner like a little boy, I'll stop, take a deep breath, and let him figure it out on his own, unless he asks for help.[22]

Such a list appears at first blush not only embarrassingly naive, but also likely to be quite counter-productive. For stating rules as rules, as Wittgenstein impressed upon us, alters their nature. The making explicit of such prescriptions, it can be argued, might rob them of all chance of having a positive effect, since only if they are taken for granted could a relationship proceed harmoniously. Yet such a view, I think, would miss the point. Differential power which is sedimented in social life is likely to stay unchanged if individuals refuse reflexively to examine their own conduct and its implicit justifications. Such rules, however unsophisticated they might seem, if successfully applied help prise the individual's actions away from an unconsciously organised power game. In principle, they serve to generate increased autonomy at the same time as they demand respect from the other.

A rolling contract does not deal in ethical absolutes. This one derives from a specific 'relationship problem list' where there were previously 'negatives'. The individual in question felt that she had been overly concerned to impress men in whom she was interested, was afraid to upset her partner by revealing her fears and needs, tended to mother him, and so forth. A 'constitution' of this sort, of course, is only democratic if it is integrated with the other elements mentioned above; it has to reflect a meeting of autonomous and equal persons.

The imperative of free and open communication is the *sine qua non* of the pure relationship; the relationship is its own forum. On this point we come round full circle. Self-autonomy, the break with compulsiveness, is the condition of open dialogue with the other. Such dialogue, in turn, is the medium of the expression of individual needs, as well as the means whereby the relationship is reflexively organised.

Democracy is dull, sex is exciting – although perhaps a few might argue the opposite way. How do democratic norms bear upon sexual experience itself? This is the essence of the question of sexual emancipation. Essentially, such norms sever sexuality from distributive power, above all from the power of the phallus. The democratisation implied in the transformation of intimacy includes, but also transcends, 'radical pluralism'. No limits are set upon sexual activity save for those entailed by the generalising of the principle of autonomy and by the negotiated norms of the pure relationship. Sexual emancipation consists in integrating plastic sexuality with the reflexive project of self. Thus, for example, no prohibition is necessarily placed on episodic sexuality so long as the principle of autonomy, and other associated democratic norms, are sustained on all sides. On the other hand, where such sexuality is used as a mode of exploitative domination, covertly or otherwise or where it expresses a compulsiveness, it falls short of the emancipatory ideal.

Political democracy implies that individuals have sufficient resources to participate in an autonomous way in the democratic process. The same applies in the domain of the pure relationship, although as in the political order it is important to avoid economic reductionism. Democratic aspirations do not necessarily mean equality of resources, although they clearly tend in that direction. They do involve including resources within the charter of rights reflexively negotiated as a defining part of the relationship. The importance of this precept within heterosexual relationships is very plain, given the imbalance in economic resources available to men and women and in responsibilities for childcare and domestic work. The democratic model presumes equality in these areas; the aim, however, would not necessarily be complete parity so much as an equitable arrangement negotiated according to the principle of autonomy. A certain balance of tasks and rewards would be negotiated which each finds acceptable. A division of labour might be established, but not one simply inherited on the basis of pre-established criteria or imposed by unequal economic resources brought to the relationship.

There are structural conditions in the wider society which penetrate to the heart of the pure relationships; conversely, how such relationships are ordered has consequences for the wider social order. Democratisation in the public domain, not only at the level of the nation-state, supplies essential conditions for the democratising of personal relationships. But the reverse applies also. The advancement of self-autonomy in the context of pure relationships is rich with implications for democratic practice in the larger community.

A symmetry exists between the democratising of personal life and democratic possibilities in the global political order at the most extensive level. Consider the distinction between positional bargaining and principled negotiation prominent in the analysis of global strategies and conflicts today. In positional bargaining – which can be equated with a personal relationship in which intimacy is lacking

– each side approaches negotiation by taking up an extreme stance. Through mutual threats and attrition, one side or other is worn down and an outcome achieved – if the process of negotiation has not by then broken down completely. Global relations ordered in a more democratic manner would move towards principled negotiation. Here the interaction of the parties begins from an attempt to discover each other's underlying concerns and interests, identifying a range of possible options before narrowing down upon a few of them. The problem to be resolved is separated from antagonism towards the other, so that it is possible to be firm about the substance of the negotiation while being supportive of and respectful towards the other party. In sum, as in the personal sphere, difference can become a means of communication.

Notes

1. Anthony Giddens, *The Constitution of Society*, Chapter 5.
2. Anthony Giddens, *A Contemporary Critique of Historical Materialism*.
3. Anthony Giddens, *The Nation-State and Violence*.
4. William McNeill, *The Pursuit of Power* (Oxford: Blackwell, 1983).
5. Yet, writing in 1914, just before the outbreak of the Great War, H.G. Wells did make such a prediction, influenced by the physicist Frederick Soddy, a collaborator of Ernest Rutherford. Wells' book, *The World Set Free*, recounts the story of a war which erupts in Europe in 1958, from there spreading throughout the world. In the war, a terrible weapon is used, constructed from a radioactive substance called Carolinum. Hundreds of these bombs, which Wells called 'atomic bombs,' are dropped on the world's cities, causing immense devastation. A time of mass starvation and political chaos follows, after which a new world republic is set up, in which war is forever prohibited.
6. See the statistics provided in Ruth Leger Sivard, *World Military and Social Expenditures* (Washington, D.C.: World Priorities, 1983).
7. A fuller explanation of the major points of the next few sections can be found in Anthony Giddens, *The Consequences of Modernity*.
8. Giddens, *The Nation-State and Violence*.
9. See Anthony Giddens, *The Consequences of Modernity*.
10. Georg Simmel, *The Philosophy of Money* (London: Routledge, 1978), p.179.
11. Alan Fox, *Beyond Contract* (London: Faber, 1974). For one of the few generalised discussions of trust in systems, see Susan P. Schapiro, 'The

social control of impersonal trust', *American Journal of Sociology*, vol. 93, 1987.

12. Sigmund Freud, *The Future of an Illusion* (London: Hogarth, 1962).
13. Erik H. Erikson, *Childhood and Society* (Harmondsworth: Penguin, 1965) p.242.
14. Donald L. Patrick and Graham Scambler (eds), *Sociology as Applied to Medicine* (New York: Macmillan, 1982).
15. See Joshua Meyrowitz, *No Sense of Place* (Oxford: Oxford University Press, 1985); Robert D. Sack, 'The Consumer's World: Place as Context', *Annals of the Association of American Geographers*, vol.78, 1988.
16. I follow closely Held's thought [here]. See David Held, *Models of Democracy* (Cambridge: Polity Press, 1986).
17. Held, *Models* of *Democracy*, p.270.
18. Held, *Models* of *Democracy*, p.271.
19. Giddens *The Consequences of Modernity*, pp.154–8.
20. C. Edward Crowther *Intimacy. Strategies for Successful Relationships* (New York: Dell, 1988) p.45.
21. Allison James and Alan Prout *Constructing and Reconstructing Childhood* (Brighton: Falmer, 1990). The 'new paradigm' James and Prout suggest for studying childhood relates closely to the ideas developed here.
22. Barbara De Angelis, *Secrets About Men Every Woman Should Know* (London: Thorsons, 1990), p.274.

Chapter VI

Critical Theory

(i)   Max Weber on facts and values*

The metaphysical principle of the logical separation of 'facts' and 'values' has always been closely associated with positivistic philosophies. In the social sciences, however, its strongest and most influential advocate has been Max Weber, who derived it from Kant rather than from Hume. In Weber's writings, the implications of the fact/value dichotomy (or his version of it)[1] are rigorously traced out in respect of a series of problems; I shall treat here only those concerning the logical status of the differentiation of facts and values, and the relation of values within 'calculi' or 'hierarchies' of values.

Weber's insistence upon the logical gulf between facts and values was oriented to the rejection of two sorts of competing ethical views: theories of natural right, and Marxist theories of the rational progress of history. According to the first, in Weber's words, 'what was normatively right was identical . . . with the immutably existent', while according to the second the 'normatively right' is to be discovered in 'the inevitably emergent'. Each involves an illegitimate extension of the significance of empirical knowledge, for 'it can never be the task of an empirical science to provide binding norms and ideals from which directives for immediate practical activity can be derived'; or alternatively expressed, 'An empirical science cannot tell anyone what he *should* do – but rather what he *can* do – and under certain circumstances – what he wishes to do'.[2] This does not mean to say that empirical knowledge is irrelevant to the pursuit of values. The relevance of the one to the other, Weber

---

* *Studies in Social and Political Theory*, pp. 89–95.

holds, can be explicated in terms of the categories of means and ends. We want things either in themselves, or as means to other objectives that are desired. Empirical knowledge, or the findings of the natural or social sciences, can serve to adjudge the appropriateness of a particular means to a given end. This provides a basis for possible 'indirect' criticism of the end as, for example, 'impracticable' in the specific set of historical circumstances, although it is logically precluded from determining whether or not the end itself should be chosen. Empirical findings can also allow us to specify the consequences which the attainment of an end might bring into being. This too has a practical bearing upon action since we can thereby indicate the likely costs, in respect of the person's other ends, that the achievement of the end in question will incur. Finally, through a process of analysis rather than empirical investigation, we can help a person to clarify the ends he holds by making clear the hierarchy in which they stand. Any claim of ends terminates in an 'ultimate value', or set of 'ultimate values', to which the actor's more specific ends are actually in some part means.

We can summarize this position by saying that, for Weber, empirical knowledge can be placed in the service of practical ends only in an instrumental fashion. The logical disjunction between facts and values, however, does not rule out the disputation of standards of value, which of course Weber accepts as a chronic phenomenon in social life. His point is not in some way to disqualify such debate, but to claim that, in so far as it rests upon conflicting ultimate values, it cannot be resolved by dint of appeal to empirical procedures. We have to 'recognize that general views of life and the universe can never be the products of increasing empirical knowledge, and that the highest ideals, which move us most forcefully, are always formed only in the struggle with other ideals which are just as sacred to others as ours are to us.'[3] Undoubtedly in Weber's writings this theme of the irreconcilable conflict of the 'warring gods', the conflict between the 'demons' that inspire men's practical activities, is directly connected with his stress upon the primacy of power, and power-struggles, in social development. The mutual hostility of the 'warring gods', of divergent systems of cultural values, cannot be resolved by demonstration of the rational superiority of one over the other, but only by the power of a group to impose its will upon those of different persuasions.[4] This is an historical rather than a logically necessary feature of

Weber's view, however: for one *could* hold that foremost among one's ultimate values should rank the principle of respect for the validity of contrasting systems of ultimate values to one's own.

In recent philosophical writings, in the English-speaking world at least, criticism of the fact/value dichotomy has been led by authors influenced by the philosophy of language of Wittgenstein and Austin, such as Anscombe, Foot, Searle and others.[5] Searle's work has provoked the most controversy, since he tries to show in some detail how an 'ought' can be derived from an 'is'. According to Searle, the descriptive statement, 'A uttered the words, "I hereby promise to pay you, B, ten pounds"', in a set of specifiable conditions, leads to the evaluative statement, 'A ought to pay B ten pounds'.[6] The conditions involved are those making the utterance of the first statement the performative of promising (rather than warning, entreating, joking, etc.). Searle's thesis has been attacked on various different grounds.[7] Two of the more important are: that the initial statement conceals an unacknowledged value premise; and that the description of a promise as a binding obligation can be eliminated by rendering it in *oratio obliqua*. in the form, 'people in society C treat utterances of type D as "promises"'.

The first sort of objection has a certain intuitive plausibility about it, since it may seem that all Searle manages to show is that there are linguistic connections between 'promises' and 'obligations': the real moral commitment, it might be supposed, is separate and additional to this. To argue in this way, however, is to miss Searle's basic point, which is concerned with the intimacy of the relation between language and the organization of social life:

> I am here challenging a certain model of describing linguistic facts. According to that model, once you have described the facts in any situation, the question of any 'evaluations' is still left absolutely open. What I am here arguing is that, in the case of certain institutional facts, the evaluations involving obligations, commitments, and responsibilities are no longer left completely open because the statement of the institutional facts involves these notions.[8]

Society and language do not exist as object and description of object; language is the medium both of the expression and the accomplishment of normative commitments and transactions.

Any literal use of concepts involved in those commitments and transactions implicates the speaker in the social web in which language and conduct are conjoined.

This leads through to the second kind of objection: the notion that we can avoid embodying evaluative connotations in descriptions of social institutions through the 'distancing' effect of *oratio obliqua*. But this presumes that the introduction of the indirect voice makes no difference to the description that is being offered. Such is not the case, as can be shown by reference to a concept that looms large in Weber's writings: that of legitimacy.[9] 'Legitimate', in ordinary usage, means something like 'being in accordance with law or right', or 'serving as justification for'. But Weber does not define legitimacy in this way, since he tries to provide a conceptualization that is neutral in respect of whatever is the content of any specific claims to legitimacy; to do otherwise would be to fail to effect the necessary severance of description and evaluation. Weber defines 'legitimacy' as 'belief in the validity of an order', stressing that 'validity' is anything defined as valid by the members of a given group.[10] If this is an 'empirical' or 'descriptive' concept of legitimacy, then we can infer that an 'evaluative' one would be something like 'justification of the validity of an order'. But 'legitimacy' in fact is closer in meaning to the second rather than to the first. Weber's definition, nominally an attempt to strip the ordinary concept of 'legitimate' of its evaluative content, is really a substantial redefinition. And it is one which, as even a casual glance at Weber's writings on authority shows, he applies only inconsistently, more often than not using the term in the usual manner.[11] It would indeed be difficult and quite unsatisfactory in terms of the sorts of analyses he seeks to develop, were he able to stick carefully to his own version of 'legitimacy'. For, as Schaar has noted, to speak of legitimacy in the usual sense implies the existence of standards external to he who claims it, whereby his claim can be scrutinized or assessed; but this is inconsistent with Weber's redefinition, which reduces the content of the concept to the (necessarily irrational) beliefs of the actors involved.[12]

Let us at this point return to Searle's discussion of promising. A further objection which might be made against Searle is that his position is inherently a conservative one, which forecloses the possibility of critique: that is to say, that it excludes the possibility of anyone holding the view that one should not honour promises.

Searle's reply to this is as follows. We must distinguish what is internal to the social practice of promising, and what is not. What is internal to the practice is that promising obligates, and this is hence involved in any description of it. But there is no logical barrier to someone morally rejecting the practice as a whole. There are two different meanings, Searle says, to the phrase 'commit oneself to [accept] the institution of promising'. One is to undertake to use 'promise' in its literal sense; it is quite a different thing to commit oneself to accept the institution where the meaning is 'endorse the institution as good'. This second type of commitment, Searle says, is 'subjective', or 'really a matter of opinion'.[13] But this is not convincing. Here we encounter, in moral philosophy, similar limitations to accounts of meaning-frames inspired by or indebted to Wittgenstein: the strongly defined tendency to take a form of life (in this case the 'institution' of promising) as a given, and to 'read off' meanings from within it, coupled to a disregard for the mediation of forms of life and for their historical development.[14] Searle's discussion is unsatisfactory on two grounds. First, the internal/external distinction upon which his analysis of the evaluative status of the practice of promising depends is not at all as clear-cut as he implies. The obligation or commitment of making a promise does not stand as a part of an isolated 'institution', but is interdependent with other beliefs and practices which influence the operation of 'bonds', 'undertakings', 'contracts', 'liabilities', etc. If there is no precise dividing-line between what is internal and what is external to promising, then Searle's distinction between two *types* of commitment in talking about promising breaks down. But it is also inadequate in the manner in which the contrast between commitments is formulated, suggesting that 'endorsing the institution externally' is 'subjective' or 'a matter of opinion' in a way in which the other type is not. This merely reintroduces the fact/value dichotomy at one step removed.

In order to attempt to meet these difficulties, it will be useful to move on to consider the second element of Weber's views mentioned above: that concerning hierarchies of values, and the existence of so-called 'ultimate values'. First of all it is important to notice a major conceptual confusion Weber makes in developing the position that the relevance of empirical knowledge to the pursuit of values can be expressed as a relation of means and ends. Weber here uses 'ends' as equivalent to 'values' ('value-ideas', 'axioms'). But ends or desires ('aims', 'objectives') are not the same as 'values', in a crucially important respect. Desires are characteristics of the individual personality; moral values or value-standards, on the other hand, are components of an institutional order. There is hardly need to point out that the conflict which can arise between personal desires and moral obligations is a classic concern of philosophy. More important is the fact that desires do not have to be rationalized, whereas value-standards do. In the course of social life, an actor may be called upon to explain why he desires what he desires, but (unless what he desires contravenes some definite value-standard) he can defend a desire merely by saying that he wants to do x because he likes doing x. This is not the case with value-standards, which are rationally defended (or attacked) in respect of the judgements that are made through and in terms of them: here just 'liking doing x' is experienced as a retreat from rational evaluation.[15] In the sphere of both ethical and aesthetic judgements, we differentiate mere personal preference from informed evaluation. The relation between empirical knowledge and values cannot be expressed as one in which the former relates only to 'means' (and the consequences of the achievement of ideals); such knowledge is definitely involved in the rationalization of evaluative statements.

This conclusion can be further supported by an analysis of what Weber calls 'ultimate values'. On examination, these turn out to be as elusive as observation statements in the positivistic philosophy of science. What defines a value as an ultimate value? Weber speaks of ultimate values as involved in both the value hierarchies of individual actors, and those of overall cultures. But we have already seen that the first only makes sense when portrayed as 'ultimate ends' or 'overriding ambitions'; value-standards are not elements of a personal hierarchy in this way. When, however, Weber refers to the 'ultimate values' of cultures, he tends to identify his 'warring gods' with empirically differing cultures. But this does not show that such cultures differ in terms of the *logical* incompatibility of their value-standards: different values are not necessarily different 'ultimate values'. How is a value shown to be an 'ultimate value'? According to Weber's view, if it is not a means to any other values – if it is not dependent upon other values. But what could such a value possibly look like? Let us suppose that 'freedom' is a candidate for an 'ultimate value'. Now the notion of 'freedom', however it be defined, is connected by a multiplicity of ties to other concepts in a language, from which it derives both evaluative and descriptive content, and upon which it is dependent. This suggests it is as misleading to represent the values, or the value-standards, of a society as a hierarchy with an easily ascertainable 'ultimate' baseline as it is to represent scientific theories as hierarchies resting upon an 'indubitable foundation' of theoretically neutral observation statements. A network conception is as appropriate in the case of the former as in that of the latter, and similarly has to be considered from an historical perspective. According to this conception, value-judgements are no more 'arbitrary' than scientific theories, and are always in principle subject to empirical appraisal, although underdetermined by it just as scientific theories are underdetermined by facts. Evaluative appraisal always involves factual elements, so that difference of moral opinion is never merely a clash of discrepant 'ultimate values'. A person may question any particular aspect, or the totality, of the practice of promising, but both involve the (potential) provision of rationalization that is in principle 'justifiable'. It is an elementary qualification to point out that an unprincipled rejection of the need or the possibility of rationalization is irrelevant here. A person *can* of course reject any knowledge-claim, by simply refusing to accept a claim of reasoning while not offering counter-arguments of his own.

(ii)   Critical theory without guarantees*

Comte and Marx, perhaps the two most prominent nineteenth-century social thinkers, shared a certain outlook in common, in spite of the wide divergencies between their views. For both, the knowledge generated by the social sciences is to rescue humanity from a past in which the most decisive events which affected social development were beyond human mastery, projecting us into a future in which we control our own destiny. In Comte's case, what matters is discovering the laws of motion of societies, this knowledge allowing the systematic prediction on the basis of which we can appropriate our own history and turn it to our purposes. *Prévoir pour pouvoir*: an understanding of social life will allow us

---

* *The Nation-State and Violence*, pp. 335–41.

to transform it in much the same way as natural science has made possible the systematic transformation of the natural world. For Marx, the era of 'history', as opposed to that of 'pre-history', will come about when the class divisions that have been the motor of social change up to the present have finally been transcended. Again, understanding our past history will allow us to shape the future and resources will become devoted to the use of the whole human community rather than being channelled to the advantage of sectional groupings.

What has gone wrong with these sorts of vision and how should we seek to reconstruct critical theory in the late twentieth century? If the early Positivist Societies are long forgotten, Marxism at least has more than lived up to the adage of its founder that interpretations of the world are ten a penny, the point being to use them to change it. Notwithstanding the enormous practical impact of Marx's writings, and the valid appraisals they contain, the twentieth-century world is very different from the future he anticipated. A viable critical theory today must be post-Marxist and must also be capable of subjecting to critique just those aspects of Marxism that lend themselves to exploitative domination. Marxism was conceived of by its originator as a critique of political economy and has certainly more than proved its worth as a source of opposition to the less salubrious influences of capitalism. But as a doctrine adopted by existing states its impact has been little short of disastrous. It can no longer be pretended, except perhaps by the most obdurate of ostriches among Marx's self-professed followers, that this is simply the outcome of distortions of Marx's ideas. Marxism has proved particularly vulnerable to becoming itself ideology and is weak in respect of providing a critique of just this vulnerability. Marxism has been proclaimed obsolescent often enough by its hostile critics, but how should those who have some sympathy with its liberative inspiration appraise its weaknesses?

If we reject evolutionism, the sort of critical theory Marx attempted to build is already attacked at its heart.[16] The transition from capitalism to a global socialist order is only comprehensible in Marxian terms if it be accepted that capitalism incorporates all the achievements of past history, ready to be actualized by the transcendence of capitalist production. If capitalism is not the high-point of an evolutionary scheme but a specific feature of the development of the European societies – and only one axis of their institutional organization at that – this standpoint collapses. The validity of much of what Marx has to say in analysing the nature of capitalist production need not be placed in doubt; indeed, a good case can be made for saying that large segments of it are correct and as relevant to the world of today as in the nineteenth century.[17] However, Marx accords undue centrality to capitalism and to class struggle as the keys to explaining inequality or exploitation, and to providing the means of their transcendence. Marxist thought is as deficient in analysing some of the major sources of exploitative domination as it is in offering plausible programmes of action for overcoming them. This judgement applies not only to the phenomena discussed . . . of surveillance and control of the means of violence . . . but also in particular to inequalities of gender and to ethnic exploitation.

Marx's interpretation of history is unified with a programme of practical action precisely because of the role which class division and class conflict play both in the structuring of capitalism and in its transcendence. Its strength, as it were, is also its weakness. Distinct from 'utopian socialism' because it addresses the real possibilities of social transformation, contained within the tendential movement of capitalism, it places the whole burden of history upon one revolutionary agency – the proletariat, acting in the context of class struggle. Critical theory today must develop substantive accounts of the origins of modernity and its global influence that do not seek to cram everything into the convenient explanatory catch-all of 'capitalism'. From which it follows that 'socialism', if understood as the negation of capitalism, is itself carrying too heavy a burden when supposed to be a generalized means for overcoming exploitation, or the sole model of the 'good society'.

In being stripped of historical guarantees, critical theory re-enters the universe of contingency and has to adopt a logic that no longer insists upon the *necessary* unity of theory and practice. How otherwise could we confront a world which, for the foreseeable future, must carry on under the shadow of possible total destruction? I do not mean by this that the Marxian theorem of the unity of theory and practice should be abandoned altogether. What we should envisage is, rather, a process of critique that does not recoil from connecting material possibilities of social reform with an utopian element. Every analysis of existing conditions of social life, because

It is 'historical', i.e. concerned with the temporality of institutions in their reproduction by human actors, generates an understanding of their potential transformation. This is a logical point, not one that specifies what a given course of action or programme can actually achieve. All social analysis, put another way, is implicitly social critique and also has transformative implications for whatever it describes. These provide the 'grounding' of critical theory, but do not in and of themselves indicate how immanent possibilities in a given set of circumstances can be actualized, or what connection that actualization might bear to more inclusive goals. The 'utopian moments' of critical theory are necessary precisely where what is immanent does not disclose a practical means of reaching those more inclusive goals; and for a critical theory without historical guarantees this situation is likely to be exceedingly common.

The diagnosis of tendential properties of social systems should remain closely connected to social critique, but is likely to relapse into dogma – as Marxism itself so frequently does – if regarded as the exclusive basis of practice. It may often be necessary to accept, even to accentuate, the gap between concrete possibilities of change and the desired outcomes of the social critic. There is, so to speak, a necessarily non-utopian element in utopianism, not just because pathways to a particular goal may be disclosed which were not previously perceived, but because the stimulus of the utopian pro-spect may itself influence the immanent possibilities of action. Such a view of critical theory should not be confused with the idea of Comte (and Marx) that the 'cognitive appropriation' of history will eventually allow human beings to control their own destiny. This kind of conception is flawed in major respects: because the under-standing of what is immanent does not guarantee its convergence with what critical theory may seek to actualize; and because any 'understanding' of a particular feature of social life or of history, in becoming part of social life, may act to fracture the very forms of control it was introduced to achieve.

A critical theory without guarantees must confront the situation that, just as history has no inherent teleology, neither are there privileged agents of the realization of processes of social reform. Just as we should resist the teleology of the Marxist interpretation of history, we should beware the associated conception that the under-privileged or exploited are the true bearers of emancipatory forms of social change. In Marxism there remains a strong residue of transmuted master – slave dialectic: 'the worker is nothing, but shall become everything.' The attractions of Marxism probably derive in some large degree just from this emphasis, which can be made to appeal simultaneously to the historicity of nationalism and to the polyarchic tendencies of the modern state. The doctrine may be morally seductive and practically consequential but it is, nonetheless, false.

If these views . . . command any credence, all four main institutional axes of modernity are 'world-historical' in their significance. It follows that a critical theory responsive to the demands of the present day should regard these as central both to the interpretation of immanent change and to the normative demands of constructing (utopian) models of the 'good society'. The most urgent issues facing us today are those to do with the expansion of the world military order, the industrialization of war and the existence of nuclear weapons. Peace movements offer the opportunity to influence the 'run-away' character of military expansion. At the same time, they supply a clear illustration of the distance between the nurturing of immanent change and the gravitational pull of utopianism. There is no option but for such movements to operate upon a tactical level, while at the same time fostering debate about 'possible worlds' in which the threat of nuclear conflict has disappeared altogether.

This has implications which those in the peace movements themselves may be reluctant to face. For discourses of utopianism can (not *must*) negatively affect tactical decisions relevant to coping with a heavily militarized world. In debates about nuclear weaponry above all we should observe Marx's directive not to judge ideas by their manifest content but by the practical consequences of their propagation. It is possible, for example, that programmes of action that seek to work 'through' official organizations, rather than merging with generalized counter-cultural protest, might be most effective in some key respects and in certain particular contexts. Walzer's point about nuclear weaponry and deterrence is an important one, showing how significant it is for peace movements to propel debates about these into the 'public sphere' in the most urgent way possible: 'Though deterrence turns American and Russian civilians (European ones too) into mere means for the prevention of war, it does so without restraining us in any way. It is in the nature of the new technology that we can be threatened without being held captive. That is why deterrence, while in principle so frightening, is so easy to live with.'[18] Sheer clamour about the 'stored-up horror' upon which deterrence depends can perhaps serve to puncture such complacency. But the enormously difficult path that must be trodden is one which somehow combines the immediate and continuing avoidance of nuclear conflict with the dissolution of the process of the industrialization of war in a radically new world order. Nowhere are the discontinuities of modern history more acute.

The inevitable primacy of these concerns over all others, of course, does not mean that the problem of the avoidance of nuclear war is entirely separable from the more traditional emphases of critical theory, or that these can be shelved while we wait to see whether the modern world will survive at all in recognizable form. The fact that the global economy is dominated by capitalistic mechanisms, and that the most influential agencies within it are capitalist states and transnational corporations, remains of fundamental importance to the nature of the world system as a whole. The highly imbalanced character of the international division of labour between core and periphery, plus the low degree of intergovernmental regulation over the world economy, are expressive of the pre-eminent influence of capitalist production world-wide. As regards the main components of capitalist production, it is surely still to Marxism that we have to look to discover the most telling critique. The contradiction between private appropriation and socialized production that Marx diagnosed as inherent in the nature of capitalist enterprise still prevails. While the division of labour nationally and internationally has become extraordinarily complex, rendering the world system increasingly integrated economically, the main propelling force motivating economic expansion remains the capitalist accumulation process. The success of labour movements in tempering some of the most noxious effects of capitalistic mechanisms within national economies has not been transferred to inequalities in the global division of labour as a whole. The divisions between First and Third Worlds, or between North and South, involve imbalances of resources of a level comparable to anything found in the differences between classes within traditional states. But it is evident that some of the most urgent problems facing the world economy are to do with industrialism rather than with the mechanisms of capitalist production as such. That is to say, they lead us to look away again from the traditional areas of concentration of Marxist theory – in its more orthodox forms at any rate – towards ecological problems.

Ecological movements and concerns are not new, in the sense that from the early impact of industrialism there were those who held that industrial production would alter – not necessarily for the better – many qualities of human life, demanding different attitudes to the natural world from those of earlier times. Although, as in so many respects, Marx's writings on this issue involve a number of overlapping strands, in general it is the case that Marx was not a critic of industrialism. Rather, for him industrialism holds out the promise of a life of abundance, through turning the forces of nature to human purposes. It is a particular mode of organizing industrial production – capitalism – that needs to be combatted, not the industrial order itself. Such a view has to be deemed essentially wanting from the perspective of the late twentieth century. Marx's paeans to industrialism might be readily understandable in the context of the nineteenth century, particularly given his dismissal of Malthus. In a world of staggering population growth, embedded in an increasingly inclusive international division of labour, the material resources required for a continuous expansion of industrial production are simply not available, and those that exist come under more and more strain.

A critical theory alert to ecological issues cannot just be limited to a concern with the exhaustion of the earth's resources – immense though may be the issues to be faced in this respect – but has to investigate the value of a range of relations to nature that tend to be quashed by industrialism. In coming to terms with these we can hope not so much to 'rescue' nature as to explore possibilities of changing human relationships themselves. An understanding of the role of urbanism is essential to such an exploration. The spread of urbanism of course separates human beings from nature in the superficial sense that they live in built environments. But modern urbanism profoundly affects the character of human day-to-day social life, expressing some of the most important intersections of capitalism and industrialism.[19]

Finally, critical theory must come to terms with those aspects of modern institutions associated with surveillance as a medium of power. Understood as the reflexive monitoring of social reproduction, surveillance has been important both to the consolidation of the world system in modern times and to the internal ordering of states. The questions raised by its role as a source of power can only increase in importance in the forseeable future. Intensified surveillance and totalitarian tendencies are intimately linked. This is not something which should lead us to despair, for administrative power and polyarchy are equally closely connected. There is not a direct relation between the expansion of the administrative power of states and political oppression. The more effectively states seek to 'govern', the more there is the likelihood of counter-balance in the form of polyarchic involvement. Given the distinctive dominance of the nation-state in the world system, however, the possibility that this might lead to the formation of a democratically ordered world government seems entirely remote. If these arguments . . . are valid, the increasing social integration of the globe does not betoken an incipient political unity.

(iii)   Utopian realism*

Yet none of this means that we should, or that we can, give up in our attempts to steer the juggernaut. The minimising of high-consequence risks transcends all values and all exclusionary divisions of power. 'History' is not on our side, has no teleology, and supplies us with no guarantees. But the heavily counterfactual nature of future-oriented thought, an essential element of the reflexivity of modernity, has positive as well as negative implications. For we can envisage alternative futures whose very propagation might help them be realised. What is needed is the creation of models of *utopian realism*.

Simply a contradiction in terms, one might think, but such is not the case, as we can see by comparing this position to that of Marx. In Marx's version of critical theory – a theory which connects interpretation and practice – history has an overall direction and converges upon a revolutionary agent, the proletariat, which is a 'universal class'. Containing within itself the accumulated residue of historical oppression, the proletariat, in making the revolution, acts in the name of the whole of humanity. But history, as noted, has no teleology, and there are no privileged agents in the process of

---

* *The Consequences of Modernity*, pp. 154–8.

transformation geared to the realisation of values. Marx retained more than an echo of the master–slave dialectic, an outlook which is attractive because it suggests that the underprivileged are the true bearers of the interests of humanity as a whole. But we should resist such a notion, in spite of its appeal for those who struggle for the emancipation of the oppressed. The interests of the oppressed are not cut of whole cloth and frequently clash, while beneficial social changes often demand the use of differential power held only by the privileged. Moreover, many beneficial changes happen in an unintended way.

We must keep to the Marxian principle that avenues for desired social change will have little practical impact if they are not connected to institutionally immanent possibilities. It was by means of this principle that Marx distanced himself so sharply from utopianism; but those immanent possibilities are themselves influenced by the counterfactual character of modernity, and therefore a rigid division between 'realistic' and utopian thought is uncalled for. We must balance utopian ideals with realism in much more stringent fashion than was needed in Marx's day. This is easily demonstrated by reference to high-consequence risks. Utopian thinking is useless, and possibly extremely dangerous, if applied, say, to the politics of deterrence. Moral conviction pursued without reference to the strategic implications of action may provide the psychological comfort which comes from the sense of worth that radical engagement can confer. But it can lead to perverse outcomes if not tempered by the realisation that, with high-consequence risks, the minimising of danger must be the overriding goal.

What should a critical theory without guarantees look like in the late twentieth century? It must be *sociologically sensitive* – alert to the immanent institutional transformations which modernity constantly opens out to the future; it must be politically, indeed, *geopolitically, tactical*, in the sense of recognising that moral commitments and 'good faith' can themselves be potentially dangerous in a world of high-consequence risks; it must create *models of the good society* which are limited neither to the sphere of the nation-state nor to only one of the institutional dimensions of modernity; and it must recognise that *emancipatory politics* needs to be linked with *life politics*, or a *politics of self-actualisation*. By emancipatory politics, I mean radical engagements concerned with the liberation from inequality or servitude. If we see once and for all that history does not obey a master–slave dialectic, or that it only does so in some contexts and circumstances, we can recognise that emancipatory politics cannot be the only side of the story. Life politics refers to radical engagements which seek to further the possibilities of a fulfilling and satisfying life for all, and in respect of which there are no 'others'. This is a version of the old distinction between 'freedom from' and 'freedom to', but 'freedom to', has to be developed in the light of a framework of utopian realism.

The relation between emancipatory and life politics forms one axis of the schema shown in Figure VI.1. The other is that of the connections between the local and the global study. Both emancipatory politics and life politics have to be tied into these connections, given the burgeoning influence of globalised relations. It is characteristic of modernity, as I have tried to show, that self-actualisation becomes fundamental to self-identity. An 'ethics of the personal' is a grounding feature of life politics, just as the more established ideas of justice and equality are of emancipatory politics. The feminist movement has pioneered attempts made to connect these concerns with one another.

Theodore Roszak is justified in criticising authors, on opposing sides of the political spectrum, who see the ethos of self-discovery merely as a desperate response to the psychologically or socially

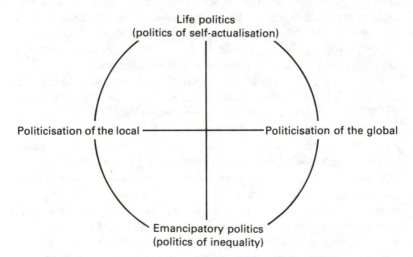

Figure VI.1 The dimensions of utopian realism

inadequate character of the larger institutions of modernity. As he says, 'we live in a time when the very private experience of having a personal identity to discover, a personal destiny to fulfil, has become a subversive political force of major proportions'. Yet he is wrong to say that 'both person and planet are threatened by the same enemy – the bigness of things'.[20] What is at issue is the interlacing of distance and proximity, of the personal and the large-scale mechanisms of globalisation. 'Bigness' is not in itself either an enemy of the person or a phenomenon to be overcome in life politics. Instead, it is the coordination of individual benefit and planetary organisation that has to be the focus of concern. Global connections of many kinds are the very condition of forms of individual self-actualisation, including those that act to minimise high-consequence risks.

This judgment must, in the nature of things, also apply to sectors of the world in which the impact of modernity still remains relatively weak. The transformations of the present time occur in a world riven with disparities between rich and poor states, in which the extension of modern institutions throws up all sorts of counter-trends and influences, such as religious fundamentalism or forms of reactive traditionalism. If I do not consider these in detail in this book, it is for purposes of economy of argument, not because I think they can be disregarded in any more concrete interpretation of likely global trends.

(iv) Emancipatory and life politics*

What is emancipatory politics?

From the relatively early development of the modern era onwards, the dynamism of modern institutions has stimulated, and to some extent has been promoted by, ideas of human *emancipation*. In the first place this was emancipation from the dogmatic imperatives of tradition and religion. Through the application of methods of rational understanding, not just to the areas of science and technology, but to human social life itself, human activity was to become free from pre-existing constraints.

---

* *Modernity and Self-Identity*, pp. 210–17.

If, with appropriate qualifications to cover over-simplification we recognise three overall approaches within modern politics – radicalism (including Marxism in this category), liberalism and conservatism – we can say that emancipatory politics has dominated all of them, although in rather differing ways. Liberal political thinkers, like radicals, have sought to free individuals and the conditions of social life more generally from the constraints of pre-existing practices and prejudices. Liberty is to be achieved through the progressive emancipation of the individual, in conjunction with the liberal state, rather than through a projected process of revolutionary upheaval. 'Conservatism', the third category, almost by definition takes a more jaundiced view of the emancipatory possibilities of modernity. But conservative thought only exists as a reaction to emancipation: conservatism has developed as a rejection of radical and liberal thought, and as a critique of the disembedding tendencies of modernity.

I define emancipatory politics as a generic outlook concerned above all with liberating individuals and groups from constraints which adversely affect their life chances. Emancipatory politics involves two main elements: the effort to shed shackles of the past, thereby permitting a transformative attitude towards the future; and the aim of overcoming the illegitimate domination of some individuals or groups by others. The first of these objectives fosters the positive dynamic impetus of modernity. The break-away from fixed practices of the past allows human beings to secure increasing social control over their life circumstances. Of course, major philosophical differences have arisen over how this aim is to be achieved. Some have supposed that the emancipatory drive is governed by causal conditions which, in social life operate in much the same way as physical causation. For others – and this is surely more valid – the relation is a reflexive one. Human beings are able reflexively to 'use history to make history'.[21]

The liberating of human beings from traditional constraints has little 'content' save for the fact that it reflects the characteristic orientation of modernity – the subjection to human control of features of the social and natural worlds that previously determined human activities. Emancipatory politics only achieves a more substantive content when it is focused on divisions between human beings. It is essentially a politics of 'others'. For Marx, of course, class was the agency of emancipation as well as the driving force of history. The general emancipation of humanity was to be achieved through the emergence of a classless order. For non-Marxist authors, emancipatory politics gives more far-reaching importance to other divisions: divisions of ethnicity and gender, divisions between ruling and subordinate groups, rich and poor nations, current and future generations. But in all cases the objective of emancipatory politics is either to release under-privileged groups from their unhappy condition, or to eliminate the relative differences between them.

Emancipatory politics works with a hierarchical notion of power: power is understood as the capability of an individual or group to exert its will over others. Several key concepts and orienting aims tend to be especially characteristic of this vision of politics. Emancipatory politics is concerned to reduce or eliminate *exploitation*, *inequality* and *oppression*. Naturally, these are defined variously by different authors, and since the main concern there is not in fact with the nature of emancipatory politics, I shall not try to chart them in a systematic way. Exploitation in general presumes that one group – say, upper as compared to working classes, whites as compared to blacks, or men as compared to women – illegitimately monopolises resources or desired goods to which the exploited group is denied access. Inequalities can refer to any variations in scarce resources, but differential access to material rewards has often been given prime importance. Unlike inequalities in genetic inheritance, for instance, differential access to material rewards forms part of the generative mechanisms of modernity, and hence can in principle (not, of course, in practice) be transformed to any desired degree. Oppression is directly a matter of differential power, applied by one group to limit the life chances of another. Like other aspects of emancipatory politics, the aim to liberate people from situations of oppression implies the adoption of moral values. 'Justifiable authority' can defend itself against the charge of oppression only where differential power can be shown to be morally legitimate.

Emancipatory politics makes primary the imperatives of *justice*, *equality* and *participation*. In a general way these correspond to the three types of power division just mentioned. All have many variant formulations and can overlap more or less substanttially.

Norms of justice define what counts as exploitation and conversely, when an exploitative relation becomes one of morally defensible authority. A limiting case here would be anarchism, in so far as this doctrine holds that a social order is feasible in which not just exploitation, but authority as such, no longer exists. The fostering of equality, in some schools of thought, is held to be a prime value in itself, and occasionally is seen the overriding aim of emancipatory politics. Most forms of radical and liberal thought, however, regard certain kinds of inequality as legitimate and even desirable – as where material inequalities are justified because they provide economic incentives which generate efficient production. Participation, the third imperative, stands opposed to oppression since it permits individuals or groups to influence decisions that would otherwise be arbitrarily imposed on them. Again ideals of democratic involvement have to specify levels of participation, as hierarchical power is not inevitably oppressive any more than all authority is inherently exploitative.

Since emancipatory politics is concerned above all with overcoming exploitative, unequal or oppressive social relations, its main orientation tends to be 'away from' rather than 'towards'. In other words, the actual nature of emancipation is given little flesh, save as the capacity of individuals or groups to develop their potentialities within limiting frameworks of communal constraint. The reluctance of most progressivist thinkers since the Enlightenment to think in utopian terms (although there are many exceptions) is one expression of this orientation. Marx's writings provide a characteristically resolute example. 'Utopian socialism' is to be avoided because it gives concrete form to the sought-after society. We cannot legislate in advance as to how people will live in such a social order: this must be left to them, when it actually comes into being.

If there is a mobilising principle of behaviour behind most versions of emancipatory politics it could be called the principle of autonomy.[22] Emancipation means that collective life is organised in such a way that the individual is capable – in some sense or another – of free and independent action in the environments of her social life. Freedom and responsibility here stand in some kind of balance. The individual is liberated from constraints placed on her behaviour as a result of exploitative, unequal or oppressive conditions; but she is not thereby rendered free in any absolute sense. Freedom presumes acting responsibly in relation to others and recognising that collective obligations are involved. Rawls' theory of justice forms a prominent example of a version of emancipatory politics.[23] The basic conditions governing autonomy of action are worked out in terms of a thematic of justice; Rawls provides a case for justice as an organising ambition of emancipation. Yet how individuals and groups in a just order will actually behave is left open.

Much the same could be said of Habermas's attempt to develop a framework for emancipatory politics in terms of a theory of communication.[24] The ideal-speech situation, held to be immanent in all language use, provides an energising vision of emancipation. The more social circumstances approximate to an ideal-speech situation, the more a social order based on the autonomous action of free and equal individuals will emerge. Individuals will be free to make informed choices about their activities; so will humanity on a collective level. Yet little or no indication is given about what those choices will actually be.

The nature of life politics

Life politics presumes (a certain level of) emancipation, in both the main senses noted above: emancipation from the fixities of tradition and from conditions of hierarchical domination. It would be too crude to say simply that life politics focuses on what happens once individuals have achieved a certain level of autonomy of action, because other factors are involved; but this provides at least an initial orientation. Life politics does not primarily concern the conditions which liberate us in order to make choices: it is a politics *of* choice. While emancipatory politics is a politics of life chances, life politics is a politics of lifestyle. Life politics is the politics of a reflexively mobilised order – the system of late modernity – which, on an individual and collective level, has radically altered the existential parameters of social activity. It is a politics of self-actualisation in a reflexively ordered environment, where that reflexivity links self and body to systems of global scope. In this arena of activity, power is generative rather than hierarchical. Life politics is lifestyle politics in the serious and rich sense ... To give a formal definition: life politics concerns political issues which flow from processes of self-actualisation in post-traditional contexts, where globalising influences intrude deeply into the reflexive project of the self, and conversely where processes of self-realisation influence global strategies.

The concerns of life politics flow directly from the principal themes of this book and I shall attempt to document them in some detail below. Although life-political issues can be traced further back, life politics only emerges as a fully distinctive set of problems and possibilities with the consolidating of high modernity. As mentioned previously, the concerns of life politics presage future changes of a far-reaching sort: essentially, the development of forms of social order 'on the other side' of modernity itself.

Emancipatory politics	*Life politics*
1 The freeing of social life from the fixities of tradition and custom.	1 Political decisions flowing from freedom of choice and generative power (power as transformative capacity).
2 The reduction or elimination of exploitation, inequality or oppression. Concerned with the divisive distribution of power/resources.	2 The creation of morally justifiable forms of life that will promote self-actualisation in the context of global interdependence.
3 Obeys imperatives suggested by the ethics of justice, equality and participation.	3 Develops ethics concerning the issue 'how should we live?' in a post-traditional order and against the backdrop of existential questions.

Life politics, to repeat, is a politics of life decisions. What are these decisions and how should we seek to conceptualise them? First and foremost, there are those affecting self-identity itself. As this study has sought to show, self-identity today is a reflexive achievement. The narrative of self-identity has to be shaped, altered and reflexively sustained in relation to rapidly changing circumstances of social life, on a local and global scale. The individual must integrate information deriving from a diversity of mediated experiences with local involvements in such a way as to connect future projects with past experiences in a reasonably coherent fashion. Only if the person is able to develop an inner authenticity – a framework of basic trust by means of which the lifespan can be understood as a unity against the backdrop of shifting social events – can this be attained. A reflexively ordered narrative of self-identity provides the means of giving coherence to the finite lifespan, given changing external circumstances. Life politics from this perspective concerns debates and contestations deriving from the reflexive project of the self.

In exploring the idea that the 'personal is political', the student movement, but more particularly the women's movement, pioneered this aspect of life politics. But they did so in an ambiguous manner. Members of the student movement, especially those associated with 'situationalism', tried to use personal gestures and 'lifestyle revolts' as a mode of throwing down a challenge to officialdom. They wanted to show not only that daily life expresses aspects of state power, but that by overturning ordinary daily patterns they could actually threaten the power of the state. Seen in this way, however, the politics of the personal only vaguely foreshadows life politics, and remains closer to the emancipatory form. For the objective is to use lifestyle patterns as a means of combating, or sublating, oppression.

Feminism can more properly be regarded as opening up the sphere of life politics – although, of course, emancipatory concerns remain fundamental to women's movements. Feminism, at least in its contemporary form, has been more or less obliged to give priority to the question of self-identity. 'Women who want more than family life', it has been aptly remarked, 'make the personal political with every step they take away from the home.'[25] In so far as women increasingly 'take the step' outside, they contribute to processes of emancipation. Yet feminists soon came to see that, for the emancipated woman, questions of identity become of pre-eminent importance. For in liberating themselves from the home, and from domesticity, women were faced with a closed-off social environment. Women's identities were defined so closely in terms of the home and the family that they 'stepped outside' into social settings in which the only available identities were those offered by male stereotypes.

When Betty Friedan first spoke of 'the problem that has no name', some quarter of a century ago, she meant that being a wife and mother failed to provide the fulfilling life for which many women, almost without knowing it, yearned.[26] Her analysis of this problem led Friedan directly to a discussion of identity and the self. The real 'question which has no name' turns out to be 'who do I want to be?'[27] Friedan specifically related the issue to her own experiences as a young woman. Having just graduated from college, she felt she had many options open to her, including that of following a professional career as a psychologist. Yet instead of taking up a fellowship she had won for a doctoral programme, she abandoned that possible career without really knowing why. She married, had children and lived as a suburban housewife – all the while suppressing her qualms about her lack of purpose in life. In the end, she broke away by acknowledging and facing up to the question of her self-identity, coming to see that she needed self-fulfilment elsewhere.

Betty Friedan's deep disquiet about personal identity, she made clear, only came about because there were now more options available for women. It is only in the light of these alternatives that women have come to see that modern culture does not 'gratify their basic need to grow and fulfil their potentialities as human beings'.[28] Her book concluded with a discussion of life-planning, the means of helping women create new self-identities in the previously unexplored public domain. Her 'new life-plan for women' anticipated many features of self-help manuals that were to come later. The new life-plan involved a commitment to personal growth, a rethinking and reconstruction of the past – by rejecting the 'feminine mystique' – and the recognition of risk.

Notes

1. Cf. Hanna Feinchel Pitkin, *Wittgenstein and Justice* (Berkeley: University of California Press, 1972) pp. 220 ff.
2. Weber, ' "Objectivity" in social science and social policy', in Weber, *The Methodology of the Social Sciences* (Glencoe: Free Press, 1949) pp. 51–2, 54.
3. Weber, ' "Objectivity" ', p. 57.
4. Cf. Anthony Giddens, *Politics and Society in the Thought of Max Weber*.
5. W.D. Hudson, *The Is/Ought Question: a collection of papers on the central problem in moral philosophy* (London: Macmillan, 1969 [New York: St Martin's Press, 1970]).
6. J.R. Searle, 'How to derive "ought" from "is" ', in Hudson, *The Is/Ought Question; Speech Acts: an essay in the philosophy of language*

(Cambridge: Cambridge University Press, 1969 [New York: Cambridge University Press, 1970]) pp. 54 ff.

7. Searle, 'Deriving "ought" from "is": objections and replies', in Hudson, *The Is/Ought Question*.

8. Searle, 'How to derive "ought" from "is" ', p, 263.

9. For various relevant discussions, see John H. Schaar, 'Reflections on authority', *New American Review*, vol. 8, 1970; Pitkin, *Wittgenstein*, pp. 280 ff; Wolfgang J. Mommsen, *Max Weber und die deutsche Politik 1890–1920* (Tübingen: Mohr-Siebeck, 1959); Jürgen Habermas, *Legitimation Crisis*, (Boston: Beacon Press, 1975) pp. 97 ff.

10. Weber, *Economy and Society* (New York: Bedminster Press, 1968) vol. I, pp. 212 ff.

11. Pitkin, Wittgenstein, pp. 280–2. The implications of this for Weber's sociology of law are traced through beautifully in M. Albrow, 'Legal positivism and bourgeois materialism: Max Weber's view of the sociology of law', *British Journal of Law and Society*, vol. 2, 1975.

12. Schaar, 'Reflections', p. 283.

13. Searle, *Speech Acts*, pp. 194–5.

14. Cf. Anthony Giddens, *New Rules of Sociological Method*, pp. 50–1.

15. Cf. Pitkin, *Wittgenstein*, p. 234; cf. also Charles Taylor, 'Neutrality in political science', in Peter Laslett and W.G. Runciman, *Philosophy, Politics and Society* (Oxford: Blackwell, 1967; New York: Barnes & Noble, 1967) pp. 48 ff. Consider in this regard the sort of statement that frequently appears in Weber's writings: 'The dignity of the "personality" *lies in the fact* that for it there exist values about which it organizes its life.' *Methodology of the Social Sciences*, p. 55 (my italics).

16. Anthony Giddens, *A Contemporary Critique of Historical Materialism*, vol. 1, Chapter 3.

17. Chapters 5, 6 and 7. Giddens, *A Contemporary Critique of Historical Materialism*, vol. 1.

18. Michael Walzer, *Just and Unjust Wars* (London: Allen Lane, 1978) p. 271.

19. Giddens, *A Contemporary Critique of Historical Materialism*, vol. 1, Chapter 6.

20. Theodore Roszak, *Person/Planet: The Creative Disintegration of Industrial Society* (London: Gollancz, 1979) pp. xxviii, 33.

21. Cf. Jürgen Habermas, *Knowledge and Human Interests* (Cambridge: Polity Press, 1987) – the classic discussion of this issue.

22. See David Held, *Models of Democracy* (Cambridge: Polity Press, 1987) concluding chapter.

23. John Rawls, *A Theory of Justice* (Oxford: Clarendon, 1972).

24. Jürgen Habermas, *Theory of Communicative Action* (Cambridge: Polity Press, 1987).

25. Barbara Sichtermann, *Femininity: The Politics of the Personal* (Cambridge: Polity Press, 1986) p. 2.

26. Betty Friedan, *The Feminine Mystique* (Harmondsworth: Pelican, 1965).

27. Friedan, *The Feminine Mystique*, p. 61.
28. Friedan, *The Feminine Mystique*, p. 68.

Select Bibliography

Works by Anthony Giddens

Capitalism and Modern Social Theory: An analysis of the writings of Marx, Durkheim and Max Weber (Cambridge: Cambridge University Press, 1971).

Politics and Sociology in the Thought of Max Weber (London: Macmillan; New York: Pall Mall, 1972).

The Class Structure of the Advanced Societies (London: Hutchinson, 1973; revised edn, New York: Harper & Row, 1981).

New Rules of Sociological Method: A Positive Critique of Interpretative Sociologies (London: Hutchinson; New York: Harper & Row, 1976).

Studies in Social and Political Theory (London: Hutchinson; New York: Basic Books, 1977).

'Introduction' to Max Weber, *The Protestant Ethic and the Spirit of Capitalism* (London: Allen & Unwin, 1977).

Durkheim (London: Fontana; New York: Penguin, 1978).

Central Problems in Social Theory: Action, Structure and Contradiction in Social Analysis (London: Macmillan; Berkeley: University of California Press, 1979).

A Contemporary Critique of Historical Materialism, vol. 1, *Power, Property and the State* (London: Macmillan; Berkeley: University of California Press, 1981).

Profiles and Critiques in Social Theory (London: Macmillan; Berkeley: University of California Press, 1982).

Sociology: A Brief but Critical Introduction (London: Macmillan; New York: Harcourt Brace, Jovanowitch, 1982).

The Constitution of Society: Outline of a Theory of Structuration (Cambridge: Polity Press; Berkeley: University of California Press, 1984).

The Nation-State and Violence, vol. 2 of *A Contemporary Critique of Historical Materialism* (Cambridge: Polity Press; Berkeley: University of California Press, 1985).

'Jürgen Habermas', in Q. Skinner (ed.) *The Return of Grand Theory in the Social Sciences* (Cambridge: Cambridge University Press, 1985).

Social Theory and Modern Sociology (Cambridge: Polity Press; Stanford: Stanford University Press, 1987).

Sociology (Cambridge, Polity Press, 1987; revised US edn, New York: Norton, 1990).

The Consequences of Modernity (Cambridge: Polity Press; Stanford: Stanford University Press, 1990).

'R.K. Merton on Structural Analysis', in J. Clark, C. Modgil and S. Modgil (eds), *Robert Merton: Consensus and Controversy* (Brighton: Falmer Press, 1990).

Modernity and Self-Identity: Self and Society in the Late Modern Age (Cambridge: Polity Press, 1991).

The Transformation of Intimacy (Cambridge: Polity Press, 1992).

A. Giddens (ed.), *The Sociology of Suicide* (London: Cass, 1971).

Emile Durkheim: Selected Writings (trans. Anthony Giddens) (Cambridge: Cambridge University Press, 1972).

Durkheim on Politics and the State (Cambridge: Polity Press; Stanford: Stanford University Press, 1986).

A. Giddens and D. Held (eds), *Classes, Power and Conflict: Classical and Contemporary Debates* (London: Macmillan; Berkeley: University of California Press, 1982).

A. Giddens and J.H. Turner (eds), *Social Theory Today* (Cambridge: Polity Press, 1987).

P.H. Stanworth and A. Giddens (eds), *Elites and Power in British Society* (Cambridge: Cambridge University Press, 1974).

A. Giddens (ed.) *Human Societies: An Introductory Reader in Sociology* (Cambridge: Polity Press, 1992).

Critical responses

The following provide a coverage of the critical responses to Giddens's writings:

C.G.A. Bryant and D. Jary (eds), *Giddens' Theory of Structuration: A Critical Appreciation* (London: Routledge, 1990).

J. Clark, C. Modgil and S. Modgil (eds), *Anthony Giddens: Consensus and Controversy* (Brighton: Falmer Press, 1990).

D. Held and J.B. Thompson (eds), *Social Theory of Modern Societies: Anthony Giddens and His Critics* (Cambridge: Cambridge University Press, 1989).

(In each of the above titles Giddens is given a chapter where he 'replies to his critics' and offers a valuable clarification of his views.)

Ira J. Cohen, *Structuration Theory: Anthony Giddens and the Constitution of Social Life* (London: Macmillan, 1989).

Ian Craib, *Anthony Giddens* (London: Routledge, 1992)

Index